THE SLOVAK-AUSTRIAN-HUNGARIAN
DANUBELAND

MÁRIA BIZUBOVÁ
DANIEL KOLLÁR
JÁN LACIKA
GABRIEL ZUBRICZKÝ

COMPILED BY: DANIEL KOLLÁR

Bolchazy Carducci Publishers, Inc.

THIS BOOK IS MADE POSSIBLE BY
the PHARE CBC Programme of the European Union
and the Slovak-American International Cultural Foundation, Inc.

2001 Reprint
Bolchazy-Carducci Publishers, Inc.
1000 Brown St., Unit 101
Wauconda, IL 60084 USA
http://www.bolchazy.com
ISBN 0-86516-528-9

and

© 2001 DAJAMA
ISBN 80-88975-20-4

The Slovak-Austrian-Hungarian Danubeland
2nd Edition, 2001

Authors: Mária Bizubová, Daniel Kollár, Ján Lacika, and Gabriel Zubriczký
Revised by: Ida Gaálová, Štefan Holčík, and Silvia Seitzová
Editors: Peter Augustini and Daniel Kollár
Responsible editor: Daniel Kollár
Author of the bike tours: Ján Hanušin
Translation: Hana Contrerasová
Language editor: Martin Styan
Photographs: Ján Lacika, Gabriel Zubriczký, and Ivan Kostroň
Plans and maps: Ján Lacika
Extracts of maps: © Vojenský kartografický ústav š. p. Harmanec
Illustrated maps: © Pegas, s. r. o., Považská Bystrica
Cover: Ján Hladík
Design and layout: Jagus DTP
Print: Kníhtlačiareň Svornosť, a. s. Bratislava

This guidebook is also available in the Slovak, German, and Magyar languages. Any, including partial, use of this work is permitted only with the written consent of GEOINFO Slovakia Foundation and DAJAMA publications.

© GEOINFO Slovakia, Ľubľanská 2, 831 02 Bratislava
© DAJAMA, Klimkovičova 1, 841 01 Bratislava

Library of Congress Cataloging-in-Publication Data
The Slovak-Austran-Hungarian Danubeland / Marie Bizubová ... et al.; compiled by Daniel Kollár.—2nd ed.
    p. cm.
  ISBN 0-86516-528-9
  1. Danube River Valley—Guidebooks. I. Title: Danubeland. II. Bizubová, Mária. III. Kollár, Daniel.

DJK76.4 .S58 2001
914.9604'56—dc21   2001035210

Contents

The Authors

RNDr. Mária Bizubová   – physical geographer at the
                                   Komensky University in Bratislava
RNDr. Daniel Kollár, CSc. – social geographer at the Institute of
                                     Geography of the Slovak Akademy
                                     of Sciences in Bratislava
RNDr. Ján Lacika, CSc.   – physical geographer at the Institute of
                                     Geography of the Slovak Akademy
                                     of Sciences in Bratislava
RNDr. Gabriel Zubriczký – regional geographer at the Komensky
                                     University in Bratislava

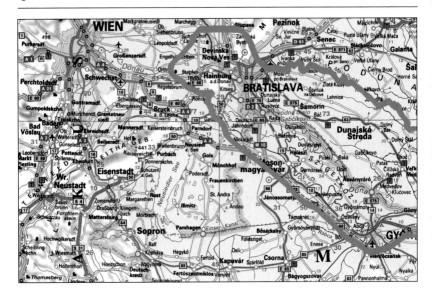

Dear readers

Since the very beginning of their existence the aim of the Foundation GEOINFO Slovakia and DAJAMA publications has been promotion of the regions of Slovakia and publication of guidebooks to its geographical and historical parts. In the series Regions Without Frontiers the guidebooks to the boundary regions and contiguous areas of Slovakia are published with the ultimate aim of propagating the idea of Euroregions as "regions without frontiers." The territories on both sides of the Slovak frontiers possess much in common in terms of history and way of life. The contemporary frontiers are not barriers any more, just the contrary. They represent links between the nations and their cultures. Those existing in the boundary areas of Slovakia offer a unique opportunity to present some remarkable details from the history and natural setting or cultural traditions of the nations living on both sides of the frontier. So far in the series of Regions Without Frontiers the book "The Slovak-Austrian Basin of the River Morava" (published in the Slovak and German languages in 1996), "The Slovak-Polish Tatras" (published in the Polish, Slovak, German, English and Hungarian languages in 1998) have appeared. Our books are always published in several relevant languages, as one of the basic aims of the publisher is to introduce Slovakia to foreign visitors.

The Danube region was prepared in the same way. The principal aim of the book **THE SLOVAK-AUSTRIAN-HUNGARIAN DANUBELAND** is to demonstrate the existence of close linkage between the three territories lying next to the Danube and present its so far unknown assets to the tourist. The territory of the Danube region essentially coincides with the historic area stretching from the former Roman camp of Carnuntum in the territory of today's Austria, along the right and left banks of the Danube up to Visegrád in today's Hungary. This territory and above all its starting and finishing points, as well as the largest town in this area symbolize several fundamental historic stages. The roman fortifications *Limes Romanus* with its most important point at Carnuntum dominated in the space almost two thousand years ago. Several centuries later in the territory of today's Bratislava two important forts sprang up and played an important role in the time of the Great Moravian Empire and later when the Hungarian Kingdom was formed. In the 14th and 15th centuries Visegrád assumed the most important position, as it was the seat of the rulers of Hungary. Bratislava and Visegrád still influence the life of the region. Visegrád symbolizes the principles of coexistence and cross-frontier co-oper-

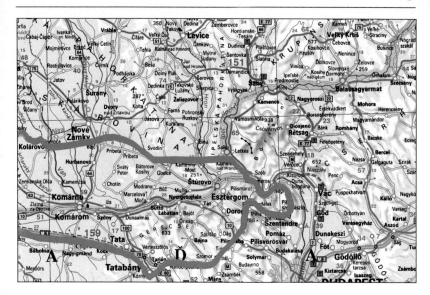

ation of the contiguous countries and Bratislava is now the dominating settlement in the area with the enormous economic, social and cultural potential of this part of the Danube region. The subtitle of this book could also be **From Carnuntum through Bratislava to Visegrád**.

Aware of the facts and linkages we arranged the book into Austrian, Slovak, and Hungarian parts of the Danube region. The division was made according to physical and administrative borders of the single areas. The introductory chapters contain the basic characteristics of the Austrian part of the territory, its nature, history, population and settlements. The following chapters are dedicated to the two parts of the Austrian region: Hainburg and Kittsee and their immediate environs. The authors offer brief descriptions of their history, cultural-historic monuments, natural landmarks, and way of life of people in this part of the Lower Austria and Burgenland. The following chapter characterizes nature, history, towns and rural settlements of the Slovak part of the Danube region from Bratislava through Šamorín, Dunajská Streda, Komárno, ending with Štúrovo. Again the chapters contain characteristics of the history, cultural-historic monuments, natural landmarks, and way of life of people residing in the Slovak part of the Danube region.

The Hungarian part of the Danube region follows the same pattern and characterizes the nature, history and territory of Mosonmagyaróvár, Győr, Komárom, and Esztergom with their immediate environs. The historical events and linkages of the individual small towns and villages, their cultural, historic and natural landmarks, and way of life of the Hungarian population in the boundary area are the subjects of these chapters. The facts concerning the towns and villages existing on both sides of the frontier are enriched by various legends, stories, myths and other interesting details, which complement the general picture of the mentality, character and cultural kinship of the different nationalities living side by side separated only by the river. In an effort to make the most attractive places of the region more accessible we also included in the book numerous photographs, maps and plans of the centres of the Danube region, which will certainly inspire you to visit it. We sincerely believe that the book will find its reader and will be a true and useful guide to everyone's strolling in this wonderful corner of Europe.

Daniel Kollár and Peter Augustini

THE AUSTRIAN DANUBELAND

Right: The Hainburger Berge Mts.

SITUATION AND DIVISION

The Austrian part of the Danube region and our area of interest lies in the eastern part of Austria next to the border with the Slovak Republic and Hungary. Two territorial units administer it: Lower Austria and Burgenland. Two villages in the district of Gänserndorf on the left bank of the Danube and six villages of the district Bruck an der Leitha described in the chapter Hainburg and environs are under the administration of Lower Austria. The chapter on Kittsee and environs describes the villages of Neusiedl am See which fall under Burgenland.

The northern and eastern borders of this territory coincide with the Austrian-Slovak frontier, in the west the area borders on the administrative territories of the villages of Engelharstetten, Eckartsau, and Petronell-Carnuntum. Its southern border forms a line, which is almost identical with the channel of the Leitha river.

NATURAL SETTING

The axis of the Austrian part of the Danube region is naturally the river Danube, which divides the area into two parts. The territory situated to the southeast of the Danube is mostly covered by the forested and in places either clear or shrub covered **Hainburger Berge** Mts. Their base rocks are combination of granite with slates and partially limestone. They consist of the individual mountains: Hundsheimer Berg, Spitzenberg, Pfaffenberg, Schloßberg and Braunsberg. Hundsheimer Berg is the tallest (480 m) of them. Hainburger Berge Mts. represent the last protuberance of the Carpathians (they are separated from the Little Carpathians in Slovakia by the Danube) and together with the mountain range of the **Leitha Gebirge** Mts. they are a kind of transition to the Eastern Alps.

On the contrary, in the east they lower into the **Haidboden** lowland between the rivers of Danube and Leitha. In the south they adjoin the **Parndorfer Platte** terrace and in the west they are

linked to the **Prellenkirchener Schotter-flur** floodplain. The gravel deposits of this part of the mountain range gradually decrease from the initial 185 m to 130 m above sea level. Both are connected by what is called **Brucker Pforte Gate** with the **Wiener Becken** basin in the west.

The river and the surface

The stream of the Danube has "struggled" for centuries with the surrounding surface. About 400 thousand years ago in the second Ice Age also called the Mindel; the Danube flowed through the Carnuntum Gate several kilometres more southerly than it does now. Finally it made use of a tectonically weaker spot and made its way into the Carpathian Basin by a route placed more northerly. As the uplifting of the Carpathian Arch was a slow process, the Danube was cutting into it. Danube flows to Slovakia nowadays through the Devín Gate, known in the past as Porta Hungarica.

Left: The Danube
Right: A view from the Braunsberg Mt.

The territory north-west of the river Danube forms a natural whole called the **Marchfeld** (the March Field). This name is very old; it originated some time in the 11th century. It was first mentioned in a document of Emperor Henry IV in 1058. The merchants or the first settlers named the lowland after the river March, which limits the Marchfeld in the east. From the geological point of view it belongs to the Vienna Basin. It is a flat graben, which fills the territory between the Alps and Carpathians. Sinking of the basin started approximately 25 million years ago. Then the sea flooded it and later a fresh-water lake followed sediments of which containing the remains of sea fauna forms the base of the basin. In spite of the fact that the Marchfeld lowland is a single natural and landscape type it can be divided into several areas. Its southern end situated in our area of interest forms part of the triangle-shaped Schloßhofer Platte plateau.

The Austrian part of the Danube Basin is the warmest part of Austria. The weather here is influenced by frontal systems proceeding from the Atlantic Ocean and its character is mild, Central European with moderate winters rich in precipitation and likewise moderate summers. The mean yearly temperature moves between 9-10 degrees of Celsius, mean July temperature reaches 19-20 degrees of Celsius and the mean January temperature moves around 0. The territory, as far as rainfall is concerned, is one of the driest in Austria with a mean precipitation total around 600 mm. The greatest amount of precipitation falls in summer in the form of short and intensive storms.

The Danube, the second longest river in Europe, drains the area. Its total length is 2,857 kilometres and the area of its basin is 817 thousand square kilometres. The mean annual discharge of the Danube in the area of interest is about 2,000 cubic metres per second. The Danube springs in the German mountain range of Schwarzwald (Black Forest) and flows into the Black Sea in Rumania. Its biggest tributary in this part of its basis is the river **March**, which flows into the Danube near Devín. The third greatest river of this part of the Danube region, the **Leitha** flows in the southern part of the territory and continues into Hungary. The Danube flooded the villages lying on its both banks for centuries. In 1810 the first plans to control its stream appeared but the works did not start before 1862. The territory has been protected against floods since 1870´s. In 1905 the construction of the protective dike was finished and on this occasion the chapel in Markthof was consecrated in the presence of Emperor Francis Joseph I as a symbol of the man's victory over nature.

The Danube and the floods

In the remote past the Danube (Dunaj in Slovak, Donau in German, Duna in Hungarian, Danubius or Ister in Latin) always won over man and influenced his life both in negative and positive ways. It modelled the territory, provided sustenance, but also took away the lives of people who lived on its banks. Floods were a constant threat, repeated every spring. They were caused by the thawing of snow in the Alps or by blocks of ice, which hindered its flow. There were numerous disastrous floods in the course of the last thousand years, but

the worst of them struck the territory of Austria in 1501 when the Danube's discharge was seven times higher than normal. Preserved flood marks in Vienna, which indicate the discharge 14 thousand cubic meters per second, prove it. It was what is called the flood of the millennium and experts assert that similar flood occurs only once in three thousand years.

Only remains of the former natural landscape with its typical vegetation survive in the Austrian part of the Danube region, because man has completely changed the environment. He also gradually made use of formerly intact swamps and forest, while cultivated steppe replaced the former meadow steppes. Antiflood control in the second half of the 19th century also meant cutting off the Danube arms, which changed these water bodies into backwaters. But some remains of the natural floodplain forests along the dike survived. In the immediate vicinity of the stream what is called the "soft" floodplain forest with willow, poplar and alder trees grows. In places, it changes into "hard" floodplain forest with oak, ash and elm

trees. Humid places boast some rare hydrophile plants while the dry ones display various species of thistle and dandelion. Soils rich in limestone in combination with low rainfall and warm climate create ideal conditions for the steppe vegetation, which occurs around Hundsheimer Berg, Schloßberg and Braunsberg. This territory is often denoted the core of the Pannonian flora.

The floodplain forests and water bodies provide unique conditions for the wild life, such as deer, squirrel and woodpecker. River otter and musk rat live next to the river. Amphibians are also abundantly represented: newt, frog, toad, tree frog, etc. The fauna of the Danube is varied and with more than 50 fish species living in its water (such as the carp, sheat fish, pike, or walley). On the tree branches on both banks of the Danube lapwin, stork, various species of heron and cormorants nest. The lowland became the home for the steppe animals after it was deforested. They are represented by rabbit, pouched marmot, hamster or

their natural enemies: fox, pole-cat and weasel. But the best know inhabitant of the lowland is the hare. Fowl is mostly represented by the birds nesting on the ground: quail and lark.

The north-western part of the Austrian territory of the Danube region is included into the **National Park of the Danube Floodplain** (in German Donauauen) which stretches from the borders of Vienna on both sides of the Danube up to the place where the river Morava flows into the Danube below Devín. On an area 93 square kilometres one of the last ecologically pure floodplain forests in Europe still exists. The National Park was declared as such in 1996 following a state agreement between Austria and the lands of Vienna and Lower Austria. It also attained international registration and the statutes of IUCN (International Union for Conservation of Nature) a year later. The diversity and attractiveness of the floodplain landscape creates ideal conditions for some precious and protected plant and animal species. The floodplain forest in this part of the territory is the natural space of flood occurrence, a reserve of high quality

Left: The Danube floodplain forest
Right: The flora at the Hundsheimer Berg Mt.

drinking water, and eventually represents the green "lungs" of the region.

The floodplains of the Danube

In not so remote past the situation in the Danube floodplains was not so bucolic as today. In 1984 the floodplain forest in this territory almost disappeared as a victim of planned water works. Thousands of conservationists supported by the wide public protested against realization of these plans and literally occupied the space between Stopfenreuth on the left bank and Hainburg on the right bank of the Danube. This folk "uprising" laid the foundations for the later creation of the National Park, which contains uncountable intimate and wild spots with abundant plant and animal species living there. Apart from several species of fish, frogs, turtles and newts, the European beaver (Castor fiber), for instance, which is able to change its environs by the dikes it constructs, returned to the old Danube arms. On the trees one can see kingfishers or spotted woodpeckers and in the forest the red deer (Cervus elaphus) lives. It is the king of the floodplain forest and one of the strongest of its kind in Austria. He can carry sixteen or twenty branched antlers weighing as much as 12 kilograms.

Apart from the Danube Floodplains National Park there are more protected areas in the Austrian part of the Danube Basin. They are situated in the northernmost part of Burgenland. **Zurndorfer Eichenwald und Hutweide Nature Reserve** (The Oak-growths and pastures of Zurndorf) with occurrence of the Pannonian oak forest and xerophile steppe vegetation stretches near the village of Zurndorf over an area of almost 150 hectares. Not far from Nickelsdorf on an area of 12 ha is the protected **Nature Reserve of Nickeldorfer "Haidel"** (the Nickeldorf Steppe), which also contains xerophile steppe vegetation.

HISTORY

The natural setting predestined the way of life of the first inhabitants of this territory. The Danube, Hainburg and the

Leitha mountains created a natural barrier, which to certain extent protected the settlers. The first inhabitants settled near the rivers and brooks, as they mostly lived on fishing and hunting. The river and the floodplain forest provided them with food. The first proofs of the settlement of this area are from the middle Stone Age (10,000 to 6,000 years BC). In the Upper Stone Age (5,000 to 3,300 years BC) and the Late Stone Age (3,300 to 2,000 years BC), the population started to look for additional sources of sustenance as manifested by tillage of soil, collection and processing of agricultural products and discovery of new work tools. The farming Neolithic culture did not avoid the Danube region. According to the typical ornamentation of the earthen vessels with linear patterns, this oldest farming culture in Central Europe is called the Linear Pottery Culture and it appeared for the first time at the beginning of the Upper Stone Age. Typical remains of such pottery were found in Kittsee, Pama and Potzneusiedl. But the density of population at that time was very low.

In the following period population substantially increased. The new settlers probably also brought a new way of decorating of ceramic pottery: painting. This became the characteristic trait of new cultural group, name of which, the Lengyel Culture derives from a site in Hungary. The Lengyel Culture also spread to the eastern Austria. The majority of finds from this period (4th millennium BC) were discovered in the basin of the Morava. In the following period the single cultures approximated each other within the framework of the Baden Culture (according to the locality of Baden in Lower Austria).

The Baden Culture was also adopted in the Austrian part of the Danube region in the second third of the third millennium.

The Stone Age was replaced by the Bronze Age at the turn of the third and second millennia BC. The Bronze Age substantially speeded up the economic development. Finds of bronze objects and pottery at Gattendorf of the culture of the Older Bronze Age provided the name of this culture. A typical sample of this culture is the jug with funnel-shaped neck from the period 1,800 to 1,600 years BC. Similar finds from the same period were discovered in Kittsee and other localities of Burgenland and the people that lived in the settlements along the rivers Danube and Leitha acquired the denomination "the people of Wieselburg Culture".

In comparison with the Bronze Age the following period (denominated by the site in Hallstatt in Austria) was scarcely represented in the districts of Bruck an der Leitha, Neusiedl am See, and Gänserndorf are. The first settlers who in-

habited this region that we know by name were Illyrians. It was an Indo-European tribe, which had its seat in Central and Southern Europe in about the 4th century BC. The Celts, the main creators of what is called the La Téne Culture (the name derives from the archaeological locality in Switzerland, La Téne) arrived from the west and the north and partially pushed out the Illyrians. The Celts improved production of iron and other crafts (pottery, production of jewels) and greatly influenced the way of life of the local population. This is the period of traces of human settlement in the environs of Hainburg connected with the Celtic fort on the Braunsberg mountain in the Younger Iron Age (400 years BC). The Celtic Boii tribe occupied the Austrian part of the Danube region and settled there side by side with the Taurici. They built fortified settlements of urban character (oppidums) and reached the apex of their development in the mid-1st century BC. But around the year 40 BC the Dacians, who arrived here from Transylvania defeated the tribe union of Boii and Taurici. Their defeat must have been indeed a disastrous one,

Left: Carnuntum

since the antique authors referred to the Boii settlements as "the Boii desert" long after and the settlement of this area was very limited afterwards. The well-known find of the Celtic treasure of coins from Deutsch-Jahrndorf is from the same time.

Arrival of the Romans meant the end of one era and the beginning of another. In the last two centuries BC the Romans occupied the provinces of Noricum (approximately the area of today's Austria) and Pannonia (today's Hungary) shifting the northern borders of their empire as far as the Danube. They gradually built a system of fortifications known as the *Limes Romanus* along the middle stretch of the Danube. Military stations and camps, as well as towns were founded along this frontier. The most important Roman town in the Austrian part of the Danube region was Carnuntum (see also the history of the villages Petronell-Carnuntum and Bad Deutsch-Altenburg).

Carnuntum

It originated on the important cross-roads of the Danube and Amber trade roads, between the modern villages of Petronell and Bad Deutsch-Altenburg. In the first years the Romans built their military camp on the site of the former Celtic settlement near which a Roman civil town was formed in the course of years. "Carnuntum" was first mentioned in the 1st century. It is a Celtic word, which means "the town on stone". Romans took over the name from the Celts and made from Carnuntum a trade metropolis and the capital of the province of Pannonia. In its best times, during the rule of the Emperor Marcus Aurelius (150-181) it had a population of about 50,000. The town to which the Romans also moved the Celts living in the Braunsberg mountain reached as far as today's Hainburg. It spread over an area of more than 10 square kilometres. Development of Carnuntum was eventually negatively affected by the Barbarian raids. It was destroyed for the first time in 166 by Quadi and Markomani. Marcus Aurelius fought against them in the years 171-173. Carnuntum was his temporary seat where he also received the German ambassadors in 171. The second destruction of Carnuntum by the Quadi in 374 was fatal. It led to disintegration of the Roman Empire on the Danube.

In the time when Carnuntum existed the surrounding settlements in today's Lower Austria and Burgenland were under its administration. This was also the time when the Roman settlements of the rural type called "villae rusticae" originated. They were donated to the Roman veterans and represented the economic hinterland of the town. Remains of the Roman settlements, and above all the coins, were found in administrative territories of almost all villages existing in the environs of the former Carnuntum and along the old Roman road which led from Carnuntum through Kittsee to the Roman frontier fort of Gerulata in today's Rusovce, urban district of Bratislava.

The Romans maintained their position on the Danube almost until the end of the 4th century, when their frontier on the Danube disintegrated. After Emperor Teodosius I died, the Roman Empire divided into the Western Roman and Eastern Roman Empires in 395 and the middle part of the Danube region fell under the Western Roman Empire. In 433 the commander Aetius handed Pannonia to the Huns and Romans lost their influence over the territory of the middle Danube region. In the following two centuries the territory of the Austrian part of the Danube region became an area of incessant war between the Goths, Huns and Avars. By the end of the 5th century the Longobards moved here and their power culminated during the rule of King Vach in the years 510-540. In 568 the members of this Western German tribe had to leave their settlements as the result of Avar pressure. The Avars stayed in Pannonia for the two following centuries. They came from Central Asia and penetrated into the Balkans in 560´s.

When Longobards retired the local population was subdued by the Avars. But the Frankish merchant Samo united an empire, which also included a part of the Austrian territory of the present Danube region in 623. This is how Avars lost their influence in this territory. But

the final liberation from Avars came only in the late 8th century. King Charles the Great of Frankish Empire defeated the Avars in the years 791-795 and started to organize the sacred and secular life in the conquered territory. The eastern part of Austria was then situated in the boundary space between the Frankish Empire and the Moravian Principality. The Moravian Prince Mojmír I annexed the Principality of Nitra to Moravia and founded the Great Moravian Empire. He also ruled over the territory north-west of the Danube. The Austrian part of the Danube region became then the stage of quarrels between the ruler of the Eastern Frankish Empire Louis II the German and Prince Mojmír I. King Louis II the German passed several times through this territory while assaulting the Great Moravian Empire. In the meantime the Magyars led by Prince Árpád settled in the lowland between the Danube and Tisa rivers and considered the territory of Lower Austria and Burgen-

land their own. At the beginning of the 10th century an administrative-territorial unit called the Eastern Mark was founded with the aim of protecting the eastern border of the Eastern Frankish Empire. After the defeat of Bavarian troops near today's Bratislava the territory of the Eastern Mark was occupied by the Magyar tribes. Only King Otto I the Great was able to break their power in this region in the battle at the Lech (a river in Bavaria) in 955. The Babenbergs, one of the most important dynasties of the contemporary Central Europe overtook the power in the Danube region after the defeat of Magyars at Lech. The dynasty was led from 976 by Leopold I who inherited the Eastern Mark from the Roman-German Emperor Otto II. In the first half of the 11th century during the reign of Henry III the eastern frontier of the Roman-German Empire was shifted to the rivers March and Leitha after conquering Hainburg and Bratislava and the victory of the united German and Czech troops over King Samuel Aba of Kingdom of Hungary. The new eastern frontier needed good protection and this was the reason why the imperial assembly in Nürnberg decided to build a stone castle on Schloßberg near Hainburg in 1050.

Hausberg

Construction of the first "hausbergs" dates to the 10th and 11th centuries. The eastern part of Lower Austria as a frontier region suffered from frequent raids and wars. The population living in this region, seeking some kind of protection, started to construct special shelters. Its basis was a hill or elevated spot, often artificially made. It was called "berg" or hill and it was surrounded by one or several banks and a moat. The second part was habitable and it was called a "haus". It was placed on top of the hill and first it was made of logs, later stones were used as building material. This is how the name of this dwelling originated: Hausberg.

The frontier between the Roman-German Empire and Kingdom of Hungary on the Leitha river stabilized. This frontier, with some exceptions, practically survived until the early 20th century. Nevertheless,

---

Left: The fort at the Braunsberg Mt.
Right: The castle of Hainburg

life in the frontier region was rather turbulent from the very beginning. The campaigns of German kings and Emperors Henry III and Henry IV against the Kingdom of Hungary provoked construction of frontier forts, which were complemented by natural barriers: the swamps and floodplain forests of the Rabnitz, Raab, and Danube, and those around Žitný ostrov (The Rye Island). Gradually a row of forts originated on the line connecting Rusovce (now in Slovakia) with Moson, Kapuvár and Sarvár lying in today's western Hungary. Westward from this defensive line up to the Leitha river was something called the border wasteland (Grenzödland or Gyepüelve) which occupied the territory of modern Burgenland. This part between the real and inner frontier of the state was scarcely populated and usually intentionally left barren. On the river Leitha and the Neusiedl lake guard settlements were founded and members of other nations (such as Pechenegs) were carrying out the role of guards. Pechenegs guarded the Gate of Bruck and Russians were in charge of the Hainburg Gate as the native population was not trustworthy. Later the defensive line shifted more to the west where numerous frontier forts were built, such as the old water castle of Kittsee.

Incessant quarrels over the throne of Hungary between the members of the House of Árpáds in Hungary were often influenced by the Babenbergs who ruled in the eastern part of the Roman-German Empire. House of Babenbergs reached its apex during the rule of King Leopold III at the turn of the 11th and 12th centuries. The battle against Magyars on July 15th 1246 at Wiener Neustadt was fatal for the

Babenbergs as the last of the family perished there. It was the beginning of the Hungarian-Czech wars for the Babenberg heritage, which also left negative traces on the territory of the Austrian part of the Danube Basin. The majority of the Austrian aristocracy finally decided to offer the country to Přemysl Otakar II who married the last female member of the family, Margaret von Babenberg in 1252. But the wars on the frontier of today's Austria and Hungary went on. In spring 1260 King Belo IV again attacked the territory , but was defeated at the battle of Groißenbrunn by Přemysl Otakar II. When Rudolf I of Habsburg was elected king of Germany it was obvious that Otakar´s power was not as great as presumed. The King of Bohemia could not accept the existing state. Decisive battle was fought on the Marchfeld in 1278 and it cost him the life. For the Habsburgs, the result of this battle meant the beginning of their 640 year rule in Austria. The Habsburgs continued the fights with the Hungarians. The situation calmed down only on August 26th 1291 when a peace treaty was signed between Albrecht I of Habsburg and Andrew

III. The territorial and administrative division of the Danube Basin also soon stabilized. The part east of the Leitha fell under the administration of the County of Moson.

The following two centuries were comparatively calm for the Danube region. Only sporadic raids by Moravian robber knights, who attacked Lower Austria and tortured the local population for almost half a century were an exception. The Austrian noble estates finished with them in 1448, when they occupied and destroyed their castles. The 15th century was also the period of the Hussite wars, which only marginally concerned the Danube region. The Hussites attacked some villages west of the Danube, plundered and burned them. Immediately after the Hussite wars finished, the war of King Matthias Corvinus of Hungary against the Emperor of the Holy Roman Empire and ruler of the Austrian lands Fridrich III for the Czech crown started. The troops of the King of Hungary led by Ján Zelený en-

tered Lower Austria and besieged Vienna in July 1477. In a month they destroyed forty villages in the Marchfeld. Fridrich III left Lower Austria and assumed the rule over it only after Matthias' death in 1490 a year after his son Maximilian cleared the Danube region of Hungarian troops.

Apart from different epidemics and floods in the Danube region the Turks also threatened the population. After the Turks defeated the Hungarian army at Mohács in 1526 they proceeded westward and in 1529 they stood on the Austrian border. Siege of Vienna in Autumn 1529 lasted more than three weeks and the price was the complete destruction of environs of the Danube. In the meantime the conflict over the Hungarian crown between Ferdinand I of Habsburg and Ján Zápoľský went on in Kingdom of Hungary. Solution emerged in 1538 and the western part of Hungary (including the today's territory of Burgenland) was adjudicated to Ferdinand. The lordship of Moson including the present-day Burgenland villages north of the Neusiedler See was very important for the Habsburgs, as it represented a buffer zone in the fight against

---

Left: The castle in Eckartsau
Right: Maria Theresa

the Turks and Ján Zápoľský. Population living on the banks of the Danube and Leitha suffered during the fifteen year war in the years 1593-1606 The Turks conquered the fort of Győr in 1594 and sacked several villages next to the Leitha. Then the troops of rebellious aristocrat Štefan Bocskay also sacked the villages in the north of Burgenland at the beginning of the 17th century.

The 17th century brought the Thirty-Year War, which, together with Rebellion of Estates led by Gabriel Bethlen, also meant hard times for the Austrian part of the Danube region. The local population was afflicted by the Swedes attacking Vienna in the years 1645-1646. Count Johann Christoph von Puchheim gathered the Imperial Army in Spring 1646 and cleared the territory of alien soldiers by the end of August. But this did not mean the end to the war events of the 17th century, since the Turkish troops again started preparations for war.

The Turks in the Danube region

In summer 1683 the Turks led by the Grand Vizier Kara Mustafa crossed the Austrian border near Hainburg and Prellenkirchen. They occupied the town and castle of Hainburg and Petronell. On July 14th the Turks, very much interested in conquering Vienna, took positions around it. Conquering Vienna meant an open way to the west for the Turks. The army of two hundred thousand besieged Vienna, but the town was resisting. Its defenders defeated eighteen Turkish attacks and almost a third of them were killed. However, the Archbishop of Esztergom Juraj Szepelcsényi revealed the plans of Turks and convinced King Jan Sobieski of Poland of the need to help Vienna. Archbishop himself put all the gold and silver from his estates in Morava and Bohemia to a total value of 170 guldens in defence of Vienna. The Polish king with his troops arrived at the Danube in August 1683. He met with the army of the imperial commander Charles of Lorraine near Tulln and together they attacked the Turks. Although the Turks outnumbered the Christian soldiers almost twice, the allied troops broke the Turkish camp and the Polish cavalry rout-

ed the Turkish army, which in great panic left the battle field and retreated to Hungary, destroying everything in their way.

The territory around the Danube experienced several following years of tranquillity but the beginning of the 18th century again brought the war. This time it was the Rebellion of Estates against the Habsburgs. The aim of this rebellion was to obtain independence for Hungary from the Austrian throne. The consequences of the fighting in the years 1704-1709 were soon manifested in the form of hunger and epidemics, which contemporary medicine was not able to cure. The situation partially stabilized by signing the Peace of Szatmár.

The 18th century was a long-awaited period of peace for the population. The Habsburgs strengthened their position and reforms of the rulers Charles VI and Maria Theresa, and eventually Joseph II, brought in progress in the economy, science and education. Crafts thrived, new guilds originated, and the business developed in favourable conditions. The people living in the villages along the Danube

family of Esterházy was one of the most important producers of sheep wool in Central Europe. The 1848 revolution, abolition of serfdom and various privileges of the aristocracy greatly helped agriculture and its production. These political measures were accompanied by scientific and technological discoveries and new kinds of energy were used. For example, the presentation of the first steam plough in Central Europe was a great historic event.

The first steam plough

The public demonstration of steam plough was organized by businessman J. Schulhoff in the administrative territory of Kittsee. It took place in June 1861 and it attracted the interest of a great number of spectators including important guests from Bratislava and Vienna. Steam engine was moving about 6 km an hour and it ploughed more than half a hectare of land in forty minutes. However, it took several decades before it was adopted and used in practice in some estates of the region.

were mostly farmers. They lived on cultivating corn and tobacco, raising cattle and sheep and fishing. Viticulture and production of good quality wine, which enjoyed a long tradition in the area, were not negligible. Viticulture was one of the main sources of sustenance for the Celts and later Romans. The favourable position of vineyards on the southern and eastern   slopes of the Hainburg Mountains and north of the Neusiedl Lake was the guarantee of a good quality wine. The Danube road was known as an important trade route for merchants in wine and the inhabitants of the frontier territories enjoyed various privileges connected with the trade in wine. Wine became an important export article and a popular beverage. The vintners had a guild of their own.

In the first third of the 19th century sheep raising was developing. Numerous estates specializing in production of sheep wool were founded. The Burgenland villages of Kittsee and Pam for instance were typical for sheep raising and the noble

The Austrian-Hungarian crises in the years 1848-1849 and the Austrian-Prussian war of 1866 slowed down the economic development of the Austrian part of the Danube Basin, but the political solution from 1867 in form of settlement between the two nations partially calmed down the situation and provided favourable conditions for further development. It was manifested in industrialization and use of new technologies in agriculture. The estates in the northern part of Burgenland were getting bigger and new settlers, mostly Hungarians, changed the nationality structure of the villages on the Leitha river. The estates were gradually changing into large agricultural and industrial complexes. But intensification of agriculture and developing factory production also influenced the gradual decay of crafts and caused emigration to the United States of America and Canada.   The agricultural crisis at the end of the 19th century also drove the population out.

The 20th century internal politics of Austro-Hungarian Empire was tense and in crisis. The state applied, imitating Germany, an increasingly centralized policy,

Left: The vine in Prellenkirchen
Right: The Leitha river

which did not take into consideration the emancipation efforts of the individual nationalities living in the monarchy. The overall unfavourable political situation climaxed by the First World War and its end also meant the end of the Monarchy. The 640 year lasting rule of the Habsburgs ended, Emperor Charles I was exiled and the Republic of Austria established. The Peace Treaties of St. Germain and Trianon changed the border between Austrian and Hungary. Hungary lost part of its territory in the west (today's Burgenland). But the newly founded Republic of Austria existed only for about 20 years before it was annexed by Nazi Germany. The Second World War with advanced arms meant great suffering for the population above all at its end, when the eastern front drew closer. The Russian troops crossed the Danube and occupied the Danube region for ten years. In May 1955 the state treaty was signed and on October 26th 1955 the last Russian occupation troops left Austria, which obtained freedom and independence. The first wave of refugees fleeing from the communist regime reached the Austrian villages and towns bordering on Hungary in 1956. The situation was repeated twelve years later on the border with Czechoslovakia. The seventies and eighties meant further deterioration of the political situation as communist Hungary and Czechoslovakia created the air-proof Iron Curtain on their borders. Only 1989 meant the fall of the hated regime in both countries. The Iron Curtain was removed and the period of build-

ing up new relations with neighbouring countries came. The boundary territory of Austria in the area of Hainburg and Kittsee is no longer the "dead corner" of Austria. On the contrary, it has become the scene of an enormous migration of people, goods and services. Cultural and economic life have developed into natural co-operation of the contiguous regions, which declare their efforts in intensive communication, and gradual creation of the future Danube Euroregion.

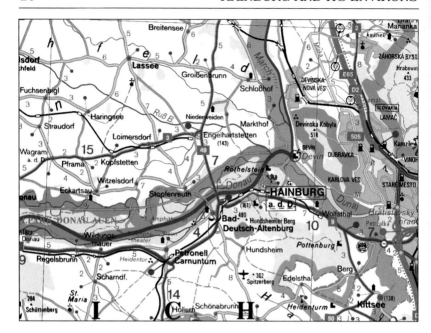

HAINBURG AND ITS ENVIRONS

HAINBURG AN DER DONAU (population 5,700) is the easternmost town in Austria situated 45 kilometres east of Vienna. It spreads between the Danube in the north and the Hainburg hills, which limit it from the north–east, and south. Its situation on the foothills of Braunsberg Mt. (346 m) and Schloßberg Mt. (291 m) makes it a town with wonderful natural setting.

The oldest traces of human settlement in environs of Hainburg date to the Younger Stone Age and Bronze Age. The most important finding places from the period before arrival of the Romans are connected with the Celtic fort on Braunsberg hill from the Younger Iron Age (400 to 9 BC). In the period of 19-9 BC, the Romans conquered the still existing castle above today's Hainburg on Braunsberg hill, as well as other territories in the Danube region. This is also the period of

the earliest evidence of German settlements in this territory. Other finds from the 5th and the 8th-10th centuries prove continuity of settlement in this area. The first written reference to Hainburg is probably linked to the year 894, when the castle of "Heimoburg" named after Heim, the butler of King Arnulf of Carinthia was mentioned. The Emperor Henry III conquered Hainburg in 1042 and pushed the eastern border of the Roman-German Empire to the rivers Morava and Leitha. Hainburg became the centre of a new mark, the task of which was to secure the eastern border. A decision of the imperial assembly in Nürnberg in 1050 to build a stone castle protecting the new border on the rivers Morava and Leitha is historically documented. A settlement developed around the castle and later became an important strategic point of the Babenberg family. In the 11th century it was a well-known market town and obtained municipal privileges in 1244. It experienced the apex of prosperity during the rule of the Babenbergs in 1252 when the last female member of this family Margaret von Babenberg married the King of

---

Right: Hainburg

Bohemia Přemysl Otakar II at Hainburg. The town became the property of the Czech king. But it did not last long, as after Rudolf I of Habsburg won the battle at Dürnkrut and Jedenspeigen, he gave the former Babenberg territory including Hainburg to his son and the area remained in the hands of the Habsburgs for the following centuries. It was still an important town. One of the events, which took place in Hainburg, was the signing of a peace treaty between King Andrew III of Hungary and the Emperor Albrecht I of Habsburg in 1291. The following two centuries were comparatively peaceful for Hainburg. The town was fulfilling its role of an advanced fort with perfect fortifications. However, the inhabitants of Hainburg experienced hard time in 1529 when the Turks destroyed the town for the first time. But the second raid of the Turks in 1683 was even worse.

The Bloody Lane

The Turks drew close to the town by the beginning of July 1683. They plundered all settlements on their way. No wonder then that all population fled away. More than eight thousand people from Hainburg and its environs sought refuge from the great carnage within the town fortifications. But the Turks conquered the town in spite of its heroic defence, burnt it down and killed the majority of its population. The reminder of this tragic event is today's Blutgaße street or the Bloody Lane next to Fischertor (Fisherman's Gate). A legend says that some people of Hainburg survived the attack hiding in the chimney of house No. 10 on Ungarstraße street. Allegedly the grandfather of the famous composer Joseph Haydn was one of them.

The town was re-colonized after Turks left by immigrants from Swabia, Silesia, Bavaria, Bohemia, Moravia, and Croatia. The people of Hainburg were mostly farmers in the past and were excellent wine and tobacco growers. Viticulture was one of the main occupations of the local population in the past. Celts who settled on Braunsberg Mt. around 400 BC started wine production in the area. The Romans brought new sorts of grapes in the 1st century, which became the fundamental ones for the future top quality wines produced in this area. The favourable situation of vineyards on southern and eastern slopes of Hainburg hills was another asset, which guaranteed quality. Rights connected with trade in wine date back to the 14th century. Tobacco growing also enjoys a long tradition. The tobacco processing plant founded in 1723 was the decisive impulse of the town's economic revival. Construction of Preßburgerbahn (Pressburg railway) in the late 19th century represented the culmination of the political connection of Vienna with Preßburg, which greatly influenced the overall atmosphere of the town. An important event in the modern history of the town was the opening of a new cigarette plant in 1962 in the old factory and a new bridge over the Danube in 1973. The eighties entered the town's history by occupation of the Danube alluvial forest in 1984 by conservationists, who protested against construction of hydroelectric power station on the Danube. But the most significant event in the modern history of Hainburg was the removal of the Iron Curtain in December 1989. Hainburg finally freed itself from its marginal situation and it even profited economically from the new situation. Opening of the frontiers

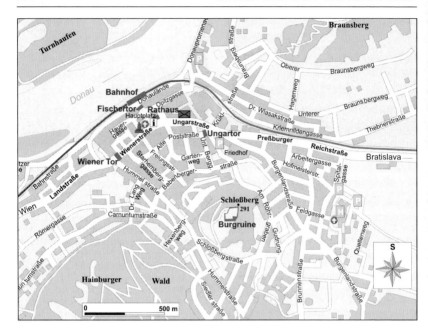

meant an accelerated development of services and the business sphere, though on the other side the incessant traffic damaged the environment and increased the influx of foreigners. The town became the link between the capitals of two neighbouring countries and a prototype of a border town of the third millennium.

Some of valuable historic monuments of the town are related to the construction of the castle and town in the 12th century in time of the last Babenbergs. More than a 2 km long belt of town walls reaching the height up to 6 m with towers and gates survived here. The most important gates in the past were the Viennese and Hungarian gates. The **Viennese Gate** (Wienertor) in the western part of the town is a bulky 20 m tall structure with an eleven meter tall roof. It is one of the most beautiful preserved town gates in Austria. The lower part of the gate was built in the 13th century, around 1240-1244. Three hundred years later the gate was rebuilt

and adapted to the defense against fire arms. Bulky outer fortifications were added to it and together with walls and drawbridge, they significantly improved the security of the gate. This remarkable structure resisted not only the Turkish attacks but also other military events in the following periods without any serious damage. It was restored in the years 1976-1977. Today it houses the **Municipal museum** (Stadtmuseum) with numerous notable archaeological finds, collections and an exhibition concerning tobacco production as Hainburg was one of the towns with the oldest tradition of tobacco growing in Austria. **Fischertor Gate** is somewhat younger. It was built at the turn of the 13th and 14th centuries. It stands on the northern side of the former town fortifications. The oldest gate **Ungartor** built around 1230 stands east of the town. It consists of two parts: a tower and the gate. The outer fortifications of this gate were built in the 16-17th centuries. A 24 m long section of them still exist.

The dominant feature of the town is the **castle in ruins** on the Schloßberg hill. It is still a favourite destination for local

---

Right: A burgher house
The Viennese Gate

trippers and visitors. The first part of the castle, the palace and the chapel were built following the already mentioned decision of the imperial assembly in 1050. Expansion of the castle started probably during the rule of Duke Leopold V in the 12th century. The castle walls were built as we see them today. The **St. Pancreas chapel**, the oldest monument within the castle, survived. It was the chapel in which the last of the Babenberg House, Margaret wedded King of Bohemia Přemysl Otakar II. The palace was built simultaneously with the chapel. The bulky structure of the palace dates to the 13th century and the 16th century gate was presumably last part of the Schloßberg to be built. In 1529 the Turks considerably damaged the north-western part of castle which fell into decay. The castle was abandoned and used only as a fort from the 17th century. It was completely ruined after the second Turkish attack in 1683. It has been under repair since the 1970's. Another **ruin** of the former castle Röthelstein is in the north-eastern part of the town next to the Danube. The castle was built at the turn of the 12th and 13th centuries and only fragments remain.

One of the secular buildings that deserve attention is the **town hall**. It probably originated in the 14th century and Gothic elements near its entrance survive from the first building. It was repeatedly rebuilt and various buildings were added to it in the course of history. The greatest building intervention was, for instance, the closure of the staircase leading from the Renaissance yard to the first floor and a change of its facade. The portraits of the past mayors of Hainburg hanging on the walls of the session hall are interesting.

Several Gothic and Renaissance **burgher houses** and the well on the square built in 1932 to commemorate the stay of composer Joseph Haydn in Hainburg are the reminders of the town's past glory. Apart from the well, a **tablet** and the composer's **bust** on Ungarn street inform about his stay in Hainburg.

Haydn and Hainburg

Haydn had a very close relation to Hainburg, the town where his ancestors lived, from his childhood. When his parents discovered the musical gift of little Joseph they sent him to his uncle Johann Mathias Franck in Hainburg. Uncle Johann took care of the general and musical education of Joseph. Little Haydn lived with his relatives at the school of Hainburg on today's Ungar street No.3, the house that also bears a tablet and contains Haydn's library. The boy met with the kapellmaster of St. Stephen's Cathedral in Vienna who admitted him to his ensemble of singers and helped him to obtain a superior musical education.

The most important sacred monument and dominant of the town is the

Roman Catholic Sts. James and Philip's Church on the Main Square. Its predecessor, the church of St. James originally stood on Market Square as early as 1236. The Gothic chancel pillars of the original church survived the mid-16th century reconstruction. St. James' church was mentioned in 1628 as a parish church. Its present Baroque appearance is from the turn of the 17th and 18th centuries. The Late Renaissance and Early Baroque elements are on its western facade. The architect Mattias Gerl rebuilt the once small Gothic tower on the eastern side of the facade of parish church as a 57 m tall Baroque tower in the years 1756-1757. A porch replaced the Baroque main portal in 1890. In the niches on both side of the portal are the statues of Apostles St. Philip and St. James. The most important Baroque work is the main altar with the painting of Ascension of Lord by Hans Michael Beckhl and the statue of the patrons Sts. Leopold and Florian.

Left: The Main Square
Right: The Pressburg railway
The church in Berg

The **Virgin Mary's pillar** was erected next to the church in 1746. It is one of the most precious and most beautiful Rococo monuments in Lower Austria. Sculptor Martin Vögerl of Bruck an der Leitha probably designed it. On top of the pillar is the statue of the Immaculate Virgin Mary. The lavishly ornamented Rococo fence with iron bars is also a master work of the Late Baroque black-smith's trade. The **synagogue** from the 15th century is a testimony to the life of the Jewish community in the town is. Hainburg's landmarks include the Romanesque **charnel** house from the 13th century placed in the yard of the local school, a **light pillar** (Lichtsäule) from the 14th century and a **parsonage** from the 18th century rebuilt after a fire in the 19th century. Next to each of the three Hainburg gates stands a **chapel**, which likewise symbolize the past and present religious life of the town.

Hainburg is a lively town all the year round. In Haydn's hall in the local tobacco factory concerts of Haydn's music are organized. The historic fair and castle theatre festival held in the area of the castle courtyard are summer attractions. Sports fans know Hainburg as the place of the spring semi-marathon on the track Bratislava-Hainburg-Bratislava. Golf lovers come to their own in the eastern part of the town, where there is **golf area** with eighteen holes situated in a wonderful natural setting. Several tennis courts, a shooting-range and a beautiful swimming pool complement the sports facilities of the town. Hainburg is also the salient point for the trips to the Danube and the **Danube Floodplains National Park**. Nature lovers, using bicycles or boats can plunge into the unique charm of floodplain forest and see lots of plant and animal species living there. The boards of an **instructive path** inform the visitors about the fauna and flora of this area. Fine views of the town and the Danube can be seen from the Braunsberg Mt. accessible by a well-maintained footpath. Those who are eager to experience the ambience of the medieval lanes and the main square certainly will not resist the numerous wine taverns, cafés and restaurants inviting them to taste typical meals of the region: the

Danube fish, game and top quality wines.

East of Hainburg, in the easternmost tip of Lower Austria is the pair of villages of **WOLFSTHAL** (population 750) and **BERG** (population 600) lying on the projecting Hainburg hills below the Königswarte Mt. south of the Danube. They were originally independent villages, joined into one called Wolfsthal-Berg in 1972, but separated again in 1996. Both villages were mentioned for the first time in 1083 in the donation document of Bishop of Passau to the monastery of Göttweig, which also mentions them as part of the parish of Hainburg. The name Wolfsthal possibly derives from the word wolf and the name Berg is the German word for hill on the foothill of which the village spreads. The first owners of the Wolfsthal estate were the family of Valchenberg. The Rohrs appear as its owners in the 15th century and the Walterskirchen family owned it in the mid-16th century. The settlements of Berg and Hundsheim also became the part of Wolfsthal estate later. The local population suffered immensely during the Turkish raids in the years 1529 and 1618, as well as during the campaign of the French in 1805. Many of the Wolfsthal people found jobs in the construction of Preßburger-bahn (the Pressburg railway) in 1911.

The Pressburg railway

An important trade road, which later served as a post road, led along the Danube as early as the Roman period. Although the plans for a railway existed in the 19th century, construction of the famous Preßburgerbahn did not start until 1911. It was finished in February 1914 when the first trip by electric tram started in Wien-
Großmarkthalle and continued through Schwechat, Fischamend, Petronell, Hainburg, Wolfsthal, Berg, and Kittsee to Slovakia. The final station was in Pressburg near what was called the Coronation Mound (today the Square of Ľ. Štúr). The ride by train was a favourite pastime in the last years of monarchy and the trips to night theatre shows to Vienna or to a good dinner in Pressburg were legendary. After five years of existence the new geopolitical situation caused the final station to be moved to Kittsee and a newly established tram No. 6 provided for the connection with Bratislava. Wolfsthal became the final station of the Preßburgerbahn in 1945.

Among the monuments of Wolfsthal worth mentioning is above all the local **castle** standing in the middle of a park still owned by the Walterskirchen family. Originally it was a water castle, fortifications of which were pulled down in 1790 and the castle was repeatedly modernized. The most important sacred monument in Wolfsthal is the Roman Catholic **St. James Church**. Its ground plan is in shape of cross and the still existing tower was added to it in 1665. Since 1710 Wolfsthal church has been an often visited place of pilgrimage. This was the reason why it was widened and two new naves were added to it. The main altar and the pulpit are from the mid-18th century. The dominant feature of the main altar is the statue of the Merciful Virgin Mary.

The Merciful Virgin Mary

A legend says that certain Hungarian nobleman was threatened by great danger on his way from Pressburg to Vienna. He asked the Virgin Mary in his prayers to get

rid of his troubles. When his prayers reached their end he fastened a statue of the Virgin Mary to a pear tree. This event took place sometime at the beginning of the 18th century and a record about an organized pilgrimage to the statue of "the Virgin Mary on a pear tree" in Wolfsthal exists from 1737. The statue was moved to the church the same year and renamed the statue of the Merciful Virgin Mary.

Now independent village of **Berg** was part of the Petronell estate in the past, which also owned the village and the parsonage. Later it belonged to the Wolfsthal estate and its people, like the people of Wolfsthal, were farmers who raised sheep and cattle. Advantageous situation of vineyards on the southern slopes of Königswarte (344 metres) was the guarantee of quality wines produced here. Viticulture was one of the main occupations of the locals. They lived through the turbulent times in the revolutionary year 1848, when the camp of Hungarian rebels

was established in its vicinity. However, Archduke Ludwig occupied it in winter of the same year. The village was annexed together with Wolfsthal to Petržalka, today's urban district of Bratislava and the Danube was the state frontier between the Slovak State and Hitler's Reich.

The most important sacred monument of the village is the Roman Catholic **St. Anna Church** from 1748. The tower was built in 1789, using building material from the original church of Sts. Peter and Paul the Apostles demolished in 1780. The church was widened in 1859. The **chapel of the Helping Virgin Mary** was also built in the same year. It contains the statues of Peter and Paul the Apostles, which used to stand on the main altar of the old church. However visitors also often go to the **Pottenburg castle ruins** between Berg and Wolfsthal. Nobleman Potho von Aspern had it built in the 10th century and its owners alternated in the course of history. In its best times it must have been an important fort as one of the documents also quotes its purchase price, which was fairly high. In 1519 it was already abandoned and it re-

---

Left: Hundsheim
Right: The Kellergasse lane

ceived the final stroke from the Turks who completely destroyed it ten years later. Lovers of good wine will certainly stop in one of the numerous **taverns** at the southern foothill of Königswarte where one can taste the local meals (for instance an excellent bacon or sausage). Taverns are the places where the cyclists stop while riding on the main bike route between Hainburg and Bratislava. The main route runs on top of the Danube flood dike and it is full of bikers in summer.

The dike of the Danube

Construction of the Danube dike between Bratislava and Wolfsthal started in 1825 as a part of control of the river channel. It was a huge project including ambitious water regulating structures realized from the beginning of the 19th century in the Austro-Hungarian Empire. Imperial commissioner Ferenc Zichy was in charge of construction of the Danube dike and there were more than 60 thousand workers involved. About 30 thousand horse driven carriages transported material and it was 3.6 m tall, 20.9 m wide and 4 kilometres long after it was finished.

HUNDSHEIM (population 550), the smallest independent village in the district of Bruck an der Leitha, had a similar history to that of Berg. It lies on the foothills of Hundsheim hill, 6 km south of Hainburg. It was first mentioned in 1123 under the name "Hundseheim". The origin of its name derives from "Hunt" (famous Hungarian noble family of Hunt-Poznans) while Hundsheim means "home possessed by the man called Hunt". Local population, mostly farmers, vintners and shepherds, were victims of the Turkish raids in 1529 and 1683. During the first of them the **chapel of St. Anna** was destroyed and its remains (gate and an arched window) are still existing in one of the Hundsheim houses. There were five defensive Gothic **towers** in Hundsheim. These structures stood in the farmyards near the entrance gates. They were equipped with loopholes and a high-situated entrance accessible only by a ladder. Today there are two of them in Hundsheim. One is in the house No. 58 another in a farmstead and they are

connected with an interesting legend from the time of Turkish raids.

The love of Hundsheim

In 1683 when the Turks completely destroyed Hundsheim three medieval fortified towers stood in the village. One villager hid himself in the tower, which still exists near house No. 58 and survived the raid. As he also had enough food he stayed in this refuge for a long time. One winter morning when he intended to take water from a well he saw fresh human footprints in the snow. He ran back into his shelter in fear that the Turks were back. But when he went out after several days and saw again the footprints in the snow. This time he noticed that the footprints belonged to a woman. He followed them up to another tower, which still stands in what is today a farmstead, and found a young girl there. She was Croatian and one of Turkish soldiers left her there. They lived together since then and the legend has that they were the parents of majority of inhabitants of Hundsheim. As a matter of fact some of them differ from the inhabitants of other villages by darker skin and hair.

The most important sacred building of the village is the Late Gothic Roman Catholic **church of the Most Holy Trinity**, probably from the beginning of the 16th century. The Turks destroyed it in 1683. Only remains of it survived in the chancel of the new Baroque church along with the tower, which was built by the end of the 17th century. As the rear part of the church and the tower fell down in 1778 the church was built again in 1779.

The environs of Hundsheim contain several landmarks. On the foothill of

Hundsheim Mt. are typical vineyards with wine taverns open the whole year round. On the southern side of the mountain is the **Günterhöhle Cave**, which was discovered behind a quarry. It is 206 m long and 21 m high and it bears the name of the court counsellor Günter Schlesinger who made the cave accessible. The cave is not open to the public at the present time. Immediately close to it is another smaller **Knochenspalte Cave**, 45 m long and 16 m high. It became famous thanks to the find of animal bones including what is called the Hundsheim rhino. The skeleton was discovered in 1900 and this 3 m long and 1.6 m tall animal lived here approximately 500,000 years ago. The skeleton is now exhibited in the Museum of Nature Science in Vienna.

The massif of Spitzenberg (302 m) separates the administrative area of Hundsheim from the neighbouring village of **PRELLENKIRCHEN** (population 1,250) to the south. Prellenkirchen includes another two villages: Deutsch-Haslau and Schönabrunn. While Prellenkirchen lies on foothill of Spitzenberg, both its parts are in the romantic setting of the floodplain forest cut by the river Leitha, in the past the border river between Austria and Hungary. Today it represents the frontier between the lands of Lower Austria and Burgenland.

The history of both villages is closely connected with Hainburg and their situation on the historic border of the two states. The local population witnessed

several military campaigns of which the Turkish raids were probably the cruellest. The villagers often found refuge in Hainburg. In time of peace they were farmers and recognized vintners. There are three **churches** (one in each of its local parts) and two **chapels** in Prellenkirchen. The famous viticultural past of the people of Prellenkirchen can be admired in the local Viticultural Museum, which presents the history of the local viticulture from the Roman period up to the present times. The typical local product is "the Blaufränkische" **red wine**, which tastes best in one of the local **wine cellars** scattered around the well-known Kellergasse lane. Kellergasse is romantic above all in autumn. In summer the visitors prefer the modern complex of swimming pools with heated water and numerous attractions. The environs of the village provide excellent hiking, biking and horse-riding opportunities. Spitzenberg Mt. not far away is also suitable for the adrenaline sports, such as paragliding or flying.

From the cultural-historic point of view the most important villages in the environs of Hainburg are the well-known spa of Bad Deutsch-Altenburg and Petronell-Carnuntum. Both of them lie on the right bank of the Danube only several kilometres west of Hainburg. **BAD DEUTSCH-AL-TENBURG** (population 1,400) lies in a depression limited by the mountains Kirchenberg and Pfaffenberg in the northeast and Greinerhügel Mt. in the southwest. Bad Deutsch-Altenburg originated in the historic area of the former Roman frontier fort of Carnuntum built in the first decades after Christ. This standing fortified camp gradually expanded to the strongest Roman fort in Austrian territory.

Left: The Hundsheimer Berg Mt.
    The swimming pool in Prellenkirchen
Right: The Carnuntinum Museum
    Bad Deutsch-Altenburg

The Carnuntinum Museum

The cultural history of the period of the Roman Empire is still very much alive in Bad Deutsch-Altenburg in the form of the archaeological museum of Carnuntinum specializing in the Roman period. After the first news about discovery of the Roman town Carnuntum at Bad Deutsch-Altenburg broke in 1875, the excavation started. Not only big structures, such as the Roman military baths and amphitheatre were discovered but also other testimonies to the Roman period were found. It was necessary to found a museum in order to concentrate the finds in one place. In 1901 construction of museum to the plans of the architect Friedrich Ohmann started. The museum building was made in style of a Roman provincial house and opened on April 27th 1904. The Emperor Franz Joseph I personally attended the opening of the Museum. Nowadays the museum with its 3,300 exhibits is the largest Roman museum in Austria. It is characterized by an intensive cultural and social life. Various concerts, lectures and wine feasts are held here the whole year round.

The village was first mentioned in 1083 under the name Altenburg. The name Deutsch–Altenburg was used only from the 14th century in order to distinguish it from the village Ungarische Altenburg (Hungarian Altenburg today Mosonmagyaróvár) situated nearby across the border in Hungary. It official name Bad Deutsch-Altenburg has been used since 1928. The name derives from that of an old castle, which used to stand north of the village. Also a church is mentioned as early as 1051 in connection with the imperial provostship founded nearby.

The most important owners of the village include the family of Dörr mentioned in the second half of the 12th century as owners of the Altenburg estate. Bad Deutsch-Altenburg was a famous market town in the 16th century.

The past of the village is closely related to its function as **spa**. Discovery of the healing capacity of the local hot springs dates to the Roman period as proved, for instance, by the stone altar from the 3rd century known as a "spa stone" exhibited in the Carnuntinum Museum. The chemical composition of the local springs classify it into the category of sulphur-chlorine springs, the same as those of Aachen in Germany or Trenčianske Teplice, Slovakia. But their content of hydrogen sulphide, the most active component of the sulphurous springs, is the highest in comparison with other above-mentioned springs. The local population, like the populations of the neighbouring villages suffered a lot from the Turkish raids. The Turks destroyed the spa and village during their first raid in 1529. Both of them were built again in 1549 and they were rented to various users for the next centuries. But the owners did not invest in the development of the spa and it fell in decay. Dr. Bastler of Vienna, who had made a new analysis of the spring in 1843 revived it. Also Dr. Kreuziger of Bratislava was active in this spa and he had the well deepened to its original depth. Dr. Kreuziger promoted the spa and attracted wealthy clients spreading its reputation and advertising the healing properties of the spa. Now it is a much sought after little spa town with more than 100 thousand overnight visits. Especially the **spa centre** Ludwigstorff (Kurzentrum Lud-

wigstorff) is known all over Austria. It consists of three hotels Kurhotel, Parkhotel and Kaiserbad Hotel) with an overall capacity of 175 rooms. It provides traditional rheumatic therapy combined with mud cures, massages, physical therapy, gymnastics and East Asian cures such as Qi Gong or Tai Chi, an efficient therapy of locomotion apparatus and rheumatism.

Secular building monuments in Bad Deutsch-Altenburg include the **Ludwigstorff Castle**. The family Dörr had it built as what is called a water castle in the 17th century on the bank of the Danube and it became their family residence. Later it was repeatedly reconstructed and its present appearance is from the early 18th century. Baron von Ludwigstorff realized reconstruction by design of the architect C. A. Carlone. Only several details out of the formerly lavish inner decoration survived the repeated fires.

Much more important than the secu-

lar monuments are the sacred buildings of Bad Deutsch-Altenburg. One of them is the Roman Catholic **church of the Virgin Mary**, probably the oldest church in Lower Austria. Its origin dates to 1000 and the legend has that its founder was St. Stephen personally, the first Christian King of Hungary. Reliable historical sources mentioned existence of the church in the 11th century. The Dörr family had the Romanesque church nave widened and the decorated western tower and Gothic chancel were built in the 14th century. The Gothic presbytery considered the most perfect work of art in the interior of the church originated in the second half of the 14th century. The parish church of the Virgin Mary in Bad Deutsch-Altenburg is nowadays the pilgrim place where every year on August 15th a great feast is held. Next to the church is the Romanesque **charnel-house** from the mid-13th century. In the cemetery not far from the church is the chapel of **St. Leonard**, which was presumably originally built as charnel-house in the first quarter of the 13th century. The chapel is built of stones bearing the marks of craft guilds, and eight pillars ending in wonderful capitals decorate its portal on the western side. The sacred buildings of Bad Deutsch-Altenburg include the **chapel of St. Elisabeth** built after the Second World War. The Countesses Maria Ludwigstorff and Anna Dyson-Ludwigstorff donated the plot for the chapel in the park in front of the castle. The building was finished in 1954 and the chapel was consecrated to St. Elisabeth of Thüringen, the patron saint of the poor and sick. A 14 metres tall belfry stands next to it.

Left: The spa centre
    The church of the Virgin Mary
Right: Archaeological park Carnuntum

PETRONELL-CARNUNTUM (population 1,150) lies on a plain south of the Danube, 7 kilometres south-east of Hainburg. In the remote past the Roman town of Carnuntum , which is today commemorated by the archaeological site bearing the same name, spread between Petronell-Carnuntum and Bad Deutsch-Altenburg. The Petronell estate was first mentioned in 1058. Its owners often changed and the best known ones were the family of Abensperg-Traun. They owned the estate from 1656. The name of the village originated in connection with the patron saint St. Petronilla and the church consecrated to her was first mentioned as early as 11th century. Thanks to its advantageous position the village was protected against the floods. It obtained its market privileges in the 14th century. The typical occupation of the local people was farming and especially viticulture has maintained its tradition since the Celtic times. Viticulture is still the typical feature of the region and good quality wines from the environs of Carnuntum can be tasted in one of the numerous taverns and restaurants in Petronell-Carnuntum. The town though, is much more visited for its abundance of Roman monuments.

The most important landmarks of Petronell are the **remains of the Roman civilian town of Carnuntum**, the largest in Central Europe. Today they are part of the **Archaeological Park of Carnuntum** founded in 1989. The **information centre** and **museum** is now located in the reconstructed **Temple of Diana**. The old town of Carnuntum lay on the site of today's museum amidst nature where the individual residences, baths, a hospital, workshops and shops can now be seen.

This part of the town provides an excellent picture of building and housing situation from the period of years 50 to 450. In the middle of the town was a 143x104 m complex, which presumably consisted of a **public bath** (*Palastruine*) complying with high technological standards. Today you can see fairly well preserved cellars, sewage, and heating complex and the remains of marble tiles or wall paintings there. South of the bath was a big yard and another group of buildings consisting of three parts. It was probably a water reservoir for the bath and the founts. The whole complex was built in 200 and later widened. One of the important parts of the Roman town was also **amphitheatre**, a 68 m long and 52 m wide oval structure for 15,000 spectators built in the first half of the 2nd century. In the middle of amphitheatre is a large hole, which served as reservoir of rainwater and the water necessary for cleaning the arena. When fighting went on in the arena, it was covered by logs. On the road from Vienna to Bratislava near the turnoff to Petronell one can see on the right side in the field the bulky **Heidentor** (Pagan

Gate). This 20 tall structure had four entrances and was built as an arc of triumph in 350. Its two massive pillars are the symbol of Petronell-Carnuntum. The gate was built of broken stone and pieces of bricks and it suggests that Petronell was beyond the peak of its prosperity in that time. It was restored in mid-19th century for the first time and again and more profoundly in 1907. Traces of the Romans were also found in the area between Petronell-Carnuntum and Bad Deutsch-Altenburg. There was a **military camp**, the most important Roman fort on the Danube in the years 35-40 AD. Remains of one of the gates (*porta principalis dextra*) and ruins of anamphitheatre, which took 8,000 visitors, were found there. Remnants of a **fort** (Auxiliarkastell), purpose of which was riding exercise, and those of the **governor's palace**, were found in the western part of the military camp. These structures are accessible as an **open-air museum**.

Apart from the finds from the Roman times Petronell-Carnuntum also boast other monuments of high cultural values. The Romanesque Roman Catholic St. Petronilla church is the most important one. It was built in celebration of the Empress Agnes who died in 1077 and is buried in **St. Petronilla's Church** of Rome. The church was built in the Romanesque style and enlarged by the Gothic lateral chapel, called Florianikapelle. In spite of repeated reconstruction the Romanesque chancel arch and a heavy cross

vault in the chancel survived. The furniture of the church is from the 17th and 18th centuries and the main altar bears the painting of St. Petronilla. The **round chapel** (Rundkapelle, sometimes called the chapel of St. John or Johanneskapelle) is also from the time when the church was built. It is one of the most valuable and the oldest Romanesque buildings in Austria. It was built in the first half of the 12th century and changed into a burial chapel of the family Abensperg-Traun in the 18th century. During the Turkish and Napoleonic wars it was very severely damaged and restored in the 1950's. The last sacred monument of the village is the **Annakapelle** (St. Anna Chapel) built in 1744.

The sacred monuments of the village are represented by the Baroque **castle** built in the years 1660-1667 to a design by the brothers Carlone on this site where stood once a water castle from the 18th century. Stones and pillars from the Roman ruins were used for its construction. The knight's hall decorated with frescoes and a wonderful courtyard of the castle are of interest. The Abensperg-Traun family now owns it. The castle has a beautiful **park** inviting for strolling and relaxation.

On the other bank of the Danube is the village of **ENGELHARSTETTEN** (population 1,750). It is situated in the southeastern part of the Marchfeld Lowland, only several kilometres away from Hainburg. The road to Engelhartstetten crosses the Danube by a **suspension** bridge.

The Danube bridge

A ford across the Danube existed precisely in the area between Bad Deutsch-

---

Left: Archaeological park Carnuntum
         A house in Petronell
Right: The Danube bridge
         The Niederweiden Castle

Altenburg and Stopfenreuth (today part of Engelhartstetten) since the time immemorial. Comfortable access to the river from both sides was well-known to our ancestors and it was no accident that the famous Amber Road connecting Rome with the Baltic lands went precisely through this area. The Roman emperors used to cross the Danube at this place while pursuing their military campaigns. Rudolf I of Habsburg also crossed the Danube on the occasion of the famous battle of the Marchfeld in 1278. Later there was a ferry and the building of the fixed bridge started only in autumn 1969. The bridge, 14 m wide, 177 m tall and more than 2 km long, was finished in three years and opened before Christmas 1972. It is one of the longest and highest suspension bridges in Austria. Simultaneously the old ferry, which served for more than 50 years closed its operation with its last trip over the Danube on December 30th 1972.

Engelhartstetten originated by joining the villages of Engelhartstetten, Groißenbrunn, Loimesdorf and Stopfenreuth in 1970. Two years later the village of Markthof-Schloßhof joined also it. Engelhartstetten, first mentioned in 1441, became the centre of the group of the villages. The name of the village probably derives from the name Engelhart, which suggests that the village is much older than the first written reference to it because the name Engelhart was scarcely used in the 15th century. The present village spreads on lands, which King Henry IV donated to the Bishopric of Passau in 1067. The most difficult period for the local population was that of the Turkish raids (above all in 1529) and during floods.

The history of Engelhartstetten is closely connected with that of **Niederweiden castle**. It stands on the site of former Grafenweiden castle, which served as a defensive point next to the ford over the Morava on the former Amber Road. In the 14th century it was owned by the Hardegg family and after 1441 it belonged to Eckartsau family. Count Ernst Rüdiger von Starhemberg obtained the castle in 1685. He had the castle of Niederweiden built on the site of the original castle Grafenweiden to the project of J. B. Fischer von Erland in 1693. This was how a hunter's castle originated on a wide plain. Its central part consists of an oval hall with a dome and two wings at the sides. When Count von Starhemberg died, his wife Maria Joshepha inherited the castle and sold it to Prince Eugene of Savoy. Then the niece of the Prince, Princess Victoria inherited the whole estate. She married Prince Joseph Friedrich von Sachsen-Hildburghausen in 1738. Prince sold the castle to Queen Maria Theresa in 1755. The present appearance of the castle is from that period. The Habsburg family owned it until 1918. It was severely damaged in the Second

World War and burnt down in 1956. By reconstruction it regained its original form, given to it by the architect N. Pacassi. The castle is two storied and its central risalite with large lateral window attracts attention at the first glance. The interior of the castle contains precious paintings by J. Pillement. The most remarkable sacred monument of Engelhartstetten is the Roman Catholic **church of St. Marco** built in the 17th century. It is a simple vaulted building with one main and two lateral altars carved in wood.

The subordinate village of **Groißenbrunn** is first mentioned in 1115 as *Chressinprunnen.* It is famous for the battle, which took place in its territory in 1260.

The battle at Groißenbrunn

The conflict started with an argument between the Kings of Hungary, the Árpáds and the House of Přemysl of Bohemia for the Duchy of Styria caused by the invasion of Magyars into what is today Austria. The army of King Belo IV of Hungary encountered King Přemysl Otakar II's army precisely at Groißenbrunn and the battle ended with the victory of the King of Bohemia. The Hungarian army allegedly fled from the battlefield across the river Morava and about fourteen thousand soldiers died in its water.

The invasions of the Turks (above all in 1683) and that of the rebellious troops in the years 1704 –1706 brought sorrow and suffering to the local population. The **church of St. Egidius**, the dominant feature of the village was built in the mid-18th century. In its interior the main altar bearing a painting of St. Egidius, as well as the lateral altars from the second half of the 18th century are interesting.

South-east of Groißenbrunn are two subordinate parts of Engelhartstetten: Schloßhof and Markthof. **Markthof** was first mentioned in the document from 1276 as Hof im Marchort. In 1906, its name was changed from Hof an der March to Markthof and in the same year it merged with **Schloßhof**. The villages acquired the common name Markthof-

Left: The Schlosshof Castle

Schloßhof and became part of Engelhart-stetten in 1972. With regard to the situation of Markthof and Schloßhof on the frontier and the river Morava the links with contiguous territory were always very important for both settlements. As early as 1771 during the reign of Maria Theresa a fixed bridge over the Morava was built between Schloßhof and the Slovak village of Devínska Nová Ves. When in 1809 the ice blocks carried it away, it was built again four years later by the noble family of Pálffy. Austrian troops in the war with Prussia blasted the bridge in 1866 and it was restored shortly after. The ice blocks finally destroyed the bridge in 1880 and it was replaced by a ferry. The remains of the former bridge are still visible. The most significant sacred monument of both parts of Engelhartstetten is the Roman Catholic **church of St. George** probably built in the later half of the 11th century. Its patron saint is St. George, the example of knighthood. In this small originally Romanesque church the coat of arms of Friedrich von Prankh from 1593 calls attention.

But the biggest tourist attraction of this part of the Austrian Danube and Morava region is the largest of **Marchfeld castles**: **Schloßhof**. Friedrich von Prankh had it built in 1620 because his original residence in Markthof became too small for him and it was also constantly threatened by floods. He built another castle on Hofberg hill. Later the owners alternated until Prince Eugene of Savoy acquired it in 1725. The Prince had the castle reconstructed to the plans of the architect L. von Hildebrandt who created of it what is called "the Little Versailles" or "Belvedere of Marchfeld" just as the Prince wished. Two wings were added to the castle, the inner halls were decorated and the park was arranged. The Schloßhof castle was supplied by water from Groißenbrunn where Prince had constructed wooden pumping equipment and water reservoirs. The water was pumped from the ponds into the tanks and supplied the pools and fountains in the castle garden. Prince Eugene enjoyed his residence only for eleven years. He died in 1736. The castle was owned for short time by his niece Princess Victoria who sold it to Empress Maria Theresa in 1755. She bought it for her husband the Emperor Francis I of Lorraine.

Maria Theresa and Schloßhof
The castle soon became the favourite of the Empress. She had the second floor added to it in 1760 and loved to stay in it. In 1765 when her husband died she mourned in Schloßhof castle. When the year long mourning was over the Empress' best loved daughter Archduchess Maria Cristina married here Prince Albert. This event commemorates the marble tablet in the chapel. The Empress often visited Schloßhof also after her husband died. She loved navigation on the Morava and Danube rivers and had four boats built in Eckartsau, which anchored at the Devín port in winter time.

The time of prosperity ended for Schloßhof when Maria Theresa died on November 29th 1780. The castle was let to the Imperial Military Academy in 1898. In the years 1920-1938 the horse riding courses and later the driving lessons for soldiers were given in the castle. Russian troops, who occupied the castle in the years 1945-46, destroyed all surviving works of art in the castle. Later it was restored and nowadays it is again open to public. It became, like the villages of Schloßhof and Markthof, a popular destination for trippers, fans of history and art. Various exhibitions, cultural and social events connected with tasting of local wines are held here regularly. The environs of the castle and the bank of the Morava is visited by those who seek relaxation amidst the almost virgin nature of floodplain forest, good fishing in the river arms or by fans of bicycle tours.

There are another two parts of Engelhartstetten: **Loimesdorf** and Stopfenreuth. Loimesdorf was first referred to in 1160. The local Roman Catholic **church of St. Magdalene** is worth to mention. Its core and tower are Gothic, they are probably from the 14th century. Nature, tourism and bicycle lovers prefer the neighbouring part of **Stopfenreuth**, one of the salient points of the trips to the **National Park of the**

Danube Floodplains. Hiking and bike routes that continue to Bad-Deutsch-Altenburg and Hainburg cross it. There is also an instructive path describing the history and nature of floodplains. Stopfenreuth is in turn visited by those, whose hobby is boating and motor boating.

On the northern edge of the National Park the Danube Floodplains lies the village of **ECKARTSAU** (population 1,100). Kopfstetten, Pframa, Wagram an der Donau, and Witzelsdorf have belonged to it since 1971. The village is documented from 1180 as *Ekkerharteshove*. Its first owners were the family of Eckartsauer who gradually obtained great fortune. The family died out when Wilhelm died in 1507. Then the owners Volestoffer and after 1661 Herberstein family followed. The Herbersteins sold the whole estate to Kinsky family and that meant a new flourishing period for the castle and the village, which possessed market rights then. In 1760 Count Joseph Maximilian von Kin-

sky inherited the estate in 1760 and sold it to Emperor Francis Joseph I of Lorraine, husband of Empress Maria Theresa. This is how the estate became property of Habsburg House.

The history of Eckartsau is mostly connected with that of the **castle**. At the beginning of the 18th century it was a four-wing water castle with a bulky tower and arcaded courtyard. This defensive structure was radically rebuilt in the years 1722-1732, when the western part of it was completely pulled down and a nice Baroque hunter's palace was built. Reconstruction included building of a new chapel; the western wing was rebuilt to the design of the Vienna court architect J. E. Fischer von Erlach. The interior of the castle is also lavishly decorated thanks to the artists L. Mattielli and D. Gran. The castle and its environs literally flourished after the Habsburgs acquired it. The Empress Maria Theresa often stayed here because hunting was her husband's passion. After her death the castle fell in decay until Archduke Francis Ferdinand discovered it in the late 19th century. He had it reconstructed and a park extending on an area 27 hectares with numerous exotic trees and shrubs, was founded to the design of the Archduke himself.

The end of the Habsburgs in Eckartsau

After the Emperor Francis Joseph I died Charles I became Emperor of Austria. The Empress Zita came to Eckartsau accompanied by her five children in summer 1918 and after the First World War finished and Charles signed his abdication, he joined his wife in Eckartsau. March 23rd 1919 was the day when he was supposed to bid farewell to Austria. At Kopfstetten railway station a mob of several hundred people gathered since they wanted to greet the Emperor for the last time. The Mayor of the town presented the alderman of Kopfstetten to the Emperor and he shook hands with both of them. Then he got into the train and left with his family for Switzerland. The ascent of the Habsburg House started on the northern edge of Marchfeld in 1278 after the victory of Rudolf I of Habsburg in battle against Přemysl Otakar II and its descent ended on the

Left: A detail of the Eckartsau Castle
Right: The Danube floodplain forest
       The port in Stopfenreuth

southern edge of Marchfeld on March 23rd 1919 when this important Royal House stepped out of Austrian history.

Now the state owned the castle and it became the seat of the Federal Forest Administration (Bundesforstverwaltung). It is one in the chain of Marchfeld castles, which attract visitors with their history, cultural events and wonderful parks. The Roman Catholic **church of St. Leonard** is one of the sacred buildings that deserve attention. The original church probably existed at the time of the first written reference to Eckartsau. The documents from 1300 also contain the reference to a parsonage existing in this place. These presumptions were confirmed in 1977 during restoration of the church when a bulky chancel arch from Romanesque times was discovered. The church was later rebuilt in Gothic taste and today's church in Renaissance-Baroque style is from the second half of the 17th century when it was restored after invasion of Swedes. The church finished in 1658 did not have three naves any more; it was a chamber church with casette ceiling. In its interior the main altar with a painting of St. Leonard is of interest. A cemetery with fine tombstones from the 18th century spreads around the church. An onion-

shaped tower of the church preserved its form, but today a copper sheet-metal roof has replaced the original wooden shingles.

The Eckartsau castle is an ideal salient point for trips to the Danube alluvial forest and the National Park of the Danube floodplains. Roaming in the environs of the castle and along the banks of the Danube can be refreshed by the visit to the lesser villages of the district. **Witzelsdorf** is a village lying between Eckartsau and Stopfenreuth. It was first mentioned in 1212. Its dominant feature is the Roman Catholic **St. Martin's Church** from the 13th century. North of Witzelsdorf is the trio of settlements of **Kopfstetten, Pframa and Wagram an der Donau** which were settled by Croatian immigrants who fled from the Turkish threat in the later half of the 16th century. Wagram an der Donau bore the name Croatian Wagram until 1890. The oldest of the three villages is probably Kopfstetten (first mentioned in 1233) which entered history on the occasion when Emperor Charles I left the monarchy in 1919. **St. Bartholomew's Church** is the sacred monument worth to see. It is a former pilgrimage church built on the site of a medieval *hausberg*. The church of Holy Trinity from the second half of the 18th century is also interesting.

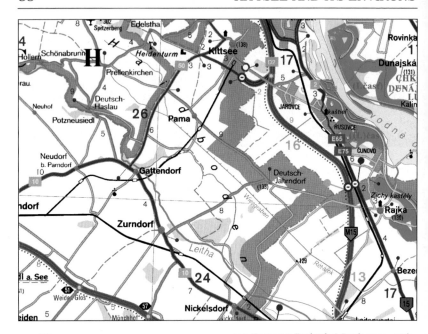

KITTSEE AND ITS ENVIRONS

KITTSEE (population 2,000) lies right on the frontier with Slovakia, not far from Bratislava. Finds from the remote past (Younger Stone Age) demonstrate early settlement of the administrative territory of this village. Vessels of people of the Linear Pottery Culture and the people of the Wieselburg Culture document continuity of settlement of this area. Importance of the settlement in the first centuries is emphasized by the fact that it was situated on an important Roman road, which led from Carnuntum to the frontier Roman fort of Gerulata.

Situation of the village was also strategic in the period when the Kingdom of Hungary was formed. Then the ruling House of Arpad invited the tribe of Pechenegs to protect the western border of the Kingdom. The local population lived through a turbulent period in the 12th century when King Gejza II of Hungary invaded Austria and above all in 1189, when the troops of the third crusade led by Ger-

man Emperor Fridrich I Barbarosa gathered and camped in the territory of the village. A positive event though, was the meeting of the King of Hungary Belo IV' son with his future wife Kunhuta of Brandenburg, niece of King Přemysl Otakar II of Bohemia on the Kittsee field. At that time the frontier fort, an old water castle, which Přemysl Otakar II conquered eight years later, already existed here. Another written reference to the fort called "Castrum Kuchhe" is from 1363, when there was also a toll station in Kittsee. The settlement then called *villa Koeche* was administered by the County of Moson and owned by the family Scharfenecker until the 15th century, when it was mentioned as *oppidum Kwkche*. Later it became royal property and afterwards the owners alternated. The best known of them were Counts of Sv. Jur and Pezinok. Turkish invaders brought great misfortune and suffering to the locals in 1529. Many houses along with the church were burnt and the village plundered. When the Turks left Croatians re-colonized the village and represented half of the population until 1659. But the bad time returned

Right: The Kittsee Castle

in 1679 with plague and in 1683 Turkish raids drove out the people who fled to Hainburg where most of them perished. Several Jewish families settled in Kittsee after they were forced to leave Pressburg in 1700. The village was then owned by the Esterházy family, which held the estate until the late 19th century. French troops occupied the village in 1809. The local people were mostly farmers. Sheep raising became a wide spread occupation in the 19th century as the Esterházys, important wool producers in the region, promoted it. Kittsee fell under the Austrian Republic after the First World War. The end of the Second World War was hard for the Kittsee people as the village was in the middle of military operations. After the war Kittsee found itself on a "dead" frontier and consequently its further development was hindered. This situation dramatically changed after the fall of the Iron Curtain in 1989, when opening of the borders meant increase of the cultural and economic significance of Kittsee as a point of intensive co-operation of the Austrian-Slovakian-Hungarian frontier area.

The dominant feature of the village is the Baroque **"New Castle"** built by Johann Listy of Transylvania in 1668. In the years 1730-1740, Prince Pál Esterházy had it rebuilt and later the family Batthyány-Strattman owned it. In the 19th century it still had a moat and a defensive bastion. In 1969 the village of Kittsee acquired it and had it thoroughly repaired. The interior of the castle contains artistic works of the blacksmith's trade, which adorn the luxurious staircase. Since 1973 the castle has housed the **Ethnographic Museum** with outstanding collections of folk culture and arts not only from Austria but also from the countries of Central and Eastern Europe. A wonderful **park** founded by Prince Ladislav Batthyány-Strattman following the example of English parks surrounds the castle. In the past there existed a road framed by rows of trees heading to the north, connecting the castle with Bratislava Castle. Looking out from the upper floor of the castle the traces of this road are still visible. The main gate with iron bars which used to adorn the Austrian-French pavilion at the Paris World Exhibition in 1900 is also of interest.

Another interesting and valuable historic monument of Kittsee is the old **water castle** from the 12th century, later repeatedly rebuilt. This originally three-storied and four-wing building was a frontier fort protecting the Austrian-Hungarian border in the time of the Árpáds. Only some of the original elements such as the staircase bearing the coats of arms of important families and the tower survived following repeated reconstruction. Behind the castle is a well-maintained **Jewish cemetery**. Interesting buildings include the remains of the **tower** from the original church of St. Michael, which was one of the few buildings to survive the Turkish raid of 1529.

Kittsee was an important parish already in the Middle Ages. A Romanesque church existed there as early as before 1250. The old church was destroyed during the Turkish wars, restored in 1548 but burnt in the late 18th century. In 1808 the local people built a new church, which did not survive because it was destroyed in the Second World War.

The existing Roman Catholic **church of Ascension of Cross** was erected on the ruins of the original church in the years 1948-1952. This tall three-nave structure with in-built tower bears features of the style used for construction of basilicas. In its interior the tall altar with a Baroque group of statues of the Crucifixion from the 18th century is of interest. The sacred monuments of the village also include **three pillars** from the 18th century: the pillar of the Immaculate Conception of the Virgin Mary, the Holy Trinity pillar, and what is called the Blue Cross with coat of arms of the Batthyányi family in its lower part.

Apart from its history, today's Kittsee is an important centre of railway transport and a point of multicultural and cross-frontier co-operation. The space between Vienna, Bratislava and Győr in Hungary is increasingly attractive from the economic and cultural points of view. Numerous exhibitions, concerts, educa-

tional, cultural and social events held all the year round in the local castle prove it. **KUKUK** (Verein zur Förderung von Kunst, Kultur und Kommunikation) or Association for promotion of arts, culture and communication is one organization, which very actively prepares such events along with the local music association and the Pannonian Forum Kittsee.

The school and KUKUK

*A symbol and example of a perfect cross-frontier co-operation is the local school and KUKUK Association. The school celebrated the 50th anniversary of its existence in 1999. It boasts a UNESCO prize obtained in 1995 for inter-cultural exchange, under which dozens of children from Bratislava participate daily. Not only the school in Kittsee but also the mentioned KUKUK Association organizes intercultural life. KUKUK was founded in 1998 with the aim of creating at Kittsee Castle a meeting place for artists, researchers and experts in the educational field for both, Austrians and Slovaks. In the framework of the inter Areas (Interregional Centre for **ART, RESEARCH**, and **EDUCATION** Aus-*

Left: The Kittsee Castle
Right: Vineyards near Edelstal
        The fireman's feast

tria-Slovakia) project the castle now houses the centre for the mentioned fields in the Slovak-Austrian boundary area.

While Kittsee is a famed producer of apricots, the neighbouring **EDELSTAL** (population 600) is known for its viticulture and the local mineral springs. It became part of Kittsee in 1970, but became independent again after 1992. The remote past of the settlement is proved by the finds of the Roman period and more than 250 graves from the Migration Period with abundant ritual and burial accessories which are now exhibited in the museum of the Hungarian town of Mosonmagyaróvár. In the Middle Ages the village was part of the Passau estate like the neighbouring villages of Hundsheim and Prellenkirchen. Among its other owners the families of Hung and Scharfeneck are the best known. The first written reference to the village then called *Etlastal* is from 1529. After the Turkish raid in the same year it was referred to as wasteland and also in 1675 it was mentioned as "Udolsthal, the abandoned village". It was re-colonized after the local population fled from the Turks to Hainburg in 1683. The owner of the estate Nicolas Esterházy had the village revived after the Turkish raid and re-settled it with the Protestants from Bavaria and Saxony. But the following period was not too kind to the settlers as they suffered during the Estate Rebellion, when it was sacked by the troops of Ferenc II Rákoczi and had to take refuge in Hainburg in 1704. Then the Napoleonic wars followed. It was no accident then that the people of Edelstal emigrated abroad. Both World Wars took their toll as well. Their victims have a **monument** here erected in 1963. The most important building of the village is the Roman Catholic **church of St. Stephen** from 1740, and consecrated to the first king of Hungary. It was restored in the second half of the 18th century and its nave made longer. In the interior the main Baroque side altar from the Augustinian monastery in Eisenstadt and the lateral Baroque altar moved here from the St. Clara monastery of Bratislava are worth seeing. The sacred monuments include several crosses and pillars, as well as the **chapel of St. Urban** in Kellerviertel (cellar quarter).

However, the symbols of Edelstal are wine and the mineral spring called **Römerquelle** (the Roman spring with radioactive medicinal water). The spring was already well-known in the 19th century and people from a large area came here to cure their maladies. A swimming pool was opened here in 1932 and the water was also bottled. The share-holding company Römerquelle offered jobs to the locals and has made the village famous all over Austria. Many tourists and bikers though, prefer to visit the popular Kellerviertel with more than eighty small taverns and cellars. One can also visit it by coach rented along with a guide. Romantic ambience of **Kellerviertel** is best experienced tasting the excellent wine of local production accompanied by local bacon or sausage.

Several kilometres south of Kittsee, between the Danube and Leitha rivers is **PAMA** (population 1,000). Archaeological finds confirm settlement of its territory already in the Stone Age. The Roman period also left its testimony here in the form of finds of Roman graves. The first written reference to the village called *Kurhuel* is

from 1208, the name *Paam* appeared in 1368. The village lying in boundary area bore various names in the past. The Hungarian name Körvélyes (The Pear Tree Garden) partially copied the German name Baumern (Next to the Trees). After it was re-colonized by a Croatian population in the 16th century the name *Bijelo Selo* (The White Village) derived from the Latin name *Albavilla* was used. In the 13th century it was property of the Poth, later of the Scharfenecker families and from the 15th century the Kittsee estate owned it. It was plundered in the 1529 Turkish raid and repopulated by Croatians in 1559 and 1564. Croatian population also prevailed in the 18th and 19th centuries, and even in 1923 it represented one third of the total population in the village. Croatian traditions, songs above all, are still alive and maintained by the **local ensemble Radost** (Joy) which often performs at various events held in the village or in the wider neighbourhood.

Left: Kellerviertel
         Pama
Right: Church in Deutsch Jahrndorf

The dominant building of the village is the Roman Catholic **church of All Saints**. This was originally a Romanesque structure with Gothic tower. It was renewed in 1860. Further adaptations were made in the 1980´s and 1990's. The altar painting of All Saints from 1805 restored in 1963 is the interesting item of its interior. The **cemetery** next to the church is remarkable for its Baroque portal. Other sacred monuments are the **chapel of St. Hubert** from 1850, the **chapel of the Virgin Mary of Seven Sorrows** from 1911 and several **pillars** and **crosses** scattered in the territory administered by the village.

East of Pama, at the junction of frontiers of three states: Austria, Slovakia, and Hungary lies another small villages of northern Burgenland and the easternmost one of Austria, **DEUTSCH JAHRNDORF** (population 600). The territory of this village has also been settled since the remote past. Finds of silver and golden Celtic coins, remains from the Roman and Celtic time prove continuity of the settlement. The village was first mentioned as *Ceud* in 1208. The name Jarendorf appeared in the 15th century. Life of the villagers was hard in the 16th century when the Turks plundered it in 1529 and when the Silesian horsemen sacked it in 1594. This was also the century of the Reformation. A wave of Protestantism arrived there in the years 1620 and 1630 brought by the Evangelical population from Swabia. But the Catholics occupied the Evangelical church in 1671, and the local Evangelicals had to commute to their church as far as Pressburg. The frontier position of the village proved to be fatal also in the 17th century during the Rebellion of Estates and the second Turkish in-

vasion in 1683. Likewise, the troops of rebellious nobles at the beginning of the 18th century and the Napoleonic wars caused a lot of misery to the local people. The situation stabilized only in the 19th century but then the people emigrated abroad in pursue of jobs. The village is also today what is called in German a "Pendlergemeinde" since the majority of its people commute to more or less distant Austrian towns and villages.

The sacred structures of the village include the Roman Catholic **church of St. Bartholomew**. The medieval church was rebuilt in the Baroque style and enlarged in 1738. After a fire in 1975 it got a new roof. In the interior of the church is a remarkable main altar with figures of St. Bartolomeo and Rochus carved in wood from the 18th century and a painting of the Martyrdom of St. Bartholomew. The most valuable work of art the church boasted until the early 20th century was a wonderful Gothic monstrance 95 cm tall (from around 1515), which is now in Győr Cathedral. The local Evangelicals built a church of their own in 1838 with an interesting pulpit adorned by fine iron bars from the 18th century. Then there is the **chapel of Holy Cross** in Zeiselhof (part of the village), the **plague pillar** from 1857 and a **cross** from the 18th century.

The tourist attraction of Deutsch Jahrndorf is **Dreiländerecke** or the "the three-country corner", (i.e. of Austria, Slovakia, and Hungary) where domestic and foreign artists created remarkable sculptures symbolizing the fall of the Iron Curtain when the frontiers were opened in the nineties. A hiking path leads to this place, part of the Burgenland long-distance tourist path starting precisely in Deutsch Jahrndorf next to the Evangelical church and running along the Austrian-Hungarian border. The Day of Tourism is held in the village every year on August 15. The environs of the village also provide an ideal space for biking and horse-riding. South of the village in the basin of the Leitha are the remains of the original floodplain forest and a **nature reserve** which protects bustards.

The hiking path leading from Deutsch Jahrndorf southward along the Austrian-

Hungarian border crosses after several kilometres an important road communication connecting Burgenland with Mosonmagyaróvár in the village of **NICKELSDORF** (population 1,600). East of the village is also the road border crossing Nickelsdorf-Hegyeshalom to Hungary. The territory of Nickelsdorf like those of the neighbouring villages was settled in the remote past. Finds in the cemetery from the Bronze Age, remains of settlement and graves from the Roman and Avar periods prove it. In the 11th century, Pechenegs who were in charge of border protection lived here. The first written mention of the village then called *Turdemech* is from 1276 and the name *Niclasdorf* appeared in the mid-15th century, when the Altenburg (today Mosonmagyaróvár) estate owned it. The village was repeatedly sacked and destroyed in the past. In 1594 it was plundered by Habsburg mercenaries, in the 1609 groups of rebels of Stephen Bocskay sacked it and perhaps the greatest damage was caused by the retreating Turkish troops in 1683. But the village also suffered in 1703 to 1709 when Napoleon's army camped near the village.

Precious visits

The legend has that in 1809 Napoleon Bonaparte personally visited the village. He stayed overnight and continued on his way to Ráb (today Győr) the next morning. Although Napoleon's visit is not documented, Nickelsdorf as an important settlement on the route from Győr to Vienna indeed hosted precious guests in the revolutionary year 1848. Croatian Ban, Josip Jelačič, an ally of Austria against the Kingdom of Hungary, crossed the village and also the leader of Hungarian revolution, Lajos Kossuth stayed there on the occasion of important discussions with the generals of the Hungarian army.

Years of uncertainty for the locals followed the end of the First World War and only November 1921 brought peace and development in the new state. The Second World War meant not only air raids but also an influx of refugees to Nickelsdorf. The village also helped thousands of refugees during the Hungarian revolution

Left: The monument in Nickelsdorf
Right: Church in Zurndorf

in 1956. As a frontier settlement lying on the important communication B 10 Nickelsdorf lived through dramatic changes above all after the fall of the Iron Curtain. Empty houses were changed into shops and tourism rapidly increased. Foundations of new co-operation with the neighbouring Hungarian villages intensified the culture and social life. The symbols of such co-operation and co-existence included erection of a memorial to Lajos Kossuth.

Both village churches are interesting sacred monuments. The original 16th century church stood at the local cemetery. Local Evangelicals built their own **church** in 1787 to which a tower was added in 1826. The Roman Catholic **church of St. Nicolas** was built in 1904 and in its interior the Neo-Gothic altars and woodcarving works from the early 20th century are worth attention.

Nickelsdorf is now a village with busy international tourism. Apart from standard amenities it offers the beautiful natural environment of the surrounding alluvial forest where silence and wonderful setting enhance the impression of seeing rare xerophile flora in **Nature Reserve Nickelsdorfer Haidel** (The Steppe of Nickelsdorf). Fans of horse riding find ideal conditions for their hobby in the form of a riding school with a hall. Sightseeing trips by coaches are also attractive.

The neighbouring **ZURNDORF** (population 2,000) is somewhat larger. Continuous settlement of its territory in the Bronze and Roman Ages, as well as in the Middle Ages points to its significance in the past. It was first mentioned as *Zaran* in 1209. The name probably referred to its founder of Slav origin or a border guard from the Pecheneg tribe. By the end of the 14th century the village obtained the market and municipal privileges and from the mid-15th century it is referred to as *Czurondorf*. Like Nickelsdorf it was part of the Altenburg estate. The village was sacked in the early 17th century by Bocskay's and later Bethlen's troops and the Turkish invasion in 1683 almost meant its end. Immediately after it was restored, in the years 1703-1706, it was assaulted by the troops of the rebellious estates and seven years later many of its inhabitants lost their lives in a terrible wave of plague epidemic. It was approximately in the same time that Empress Maria Theresa, who liked to visit the local hunting castle, stayed in its environs. Nothing remains of that castle. In 1809 many Napoleon's soldiers stayed in the village during their march towards the east. Thousands of Hungarian soldiers passed through Zurndorf during the 1849 revolution and after their defeat at Fischamend near Vienna they were pursued by Prince Alfred von Windischgrätz up to the territory of the village. Repeated military manoeuvres were organized in the surroundings of the village in 1850's and they winded up by an outbreak of fire in 1857 in the village. The fire destroyed many houses and the tower of the parish church. Only the interwar period and especially the period after the Second World War finally brought the peace necessary for reconstruction. Zurndorf now is one of the most beautiful villages of the Burgenland region. The village actively participated in numerous crossfrontier projects and programmes, among them the one of alternative energy resources with emphasis on the use of wind energy.

The Communal Forum

Zurndorf led by its mayor Rudolf Suchý is one of the villages that are involved in cross-frontier co-operation. The origin itself of such co-operation was the initiative of the village when it founded The Communal Forum, an association of the frontier villages of Austria, Slovakia and Hungary with the only aim of exchanging experience, preparing the common cross-frontier projects and promotion of the area. The main aims of the association consist of common steps with the aim of conservation, and creation of the environment, construction of bike and hiking paths and organization of social and cultural events.

The spiritual life of the local population is manifested by several sacred monuments. The most important one is the Roman Catholic **church of Sts. Peter and Paul** built in 1270 with surviving elements of the Romanesque and Gothic ar-

chitecture. The church tower was built again after the 1857 fire. The interior of the church contains the valuable altar painting "The Farewell of the Apostles Peter and Paul" from the years 1770-1780 by F. A. Maulpertsch. The local Evangelical congregation built their single-nave church in 1787. In the interior of this **church** the altar picture and pulpit from the 18th century are of interest. There is also the **chapel of St. Michael** from the first half of the 18th century and in front of it the **pillar of the Immaculate Conception**.

The environs of the village offer excellent opportunities for hikers, cycling or horse riding, as the village also has a riding school. Nature fans will not miss the opportunity to visit the **Nature Reserve Zurndorfer Eichenwald und Hutweide** (The Oak Wood and Pasture of Zurndorf) displaying the remains of the Pannonian oak woods and xerophylous flora. **Instructive path** informs the visitor about the past and the present of this precious biotope and how it is being conserved. The pond serves for bathing in summer and skating in winter.

The adjacent village of **GATTENDORF** (population 1,100) also boasts a rich history. It is an important archaeological locality of the northern Burgenland. The Wieselburg Culture of the people of the Older Bronze Age, which even acquired the name the Gattendorf Culture for the abundance of the finds, is the one most abundantly represented here. The symbol of culture of that period is a jug with funnel-shaped throat from the years 1,800 to 1,600 BC.

The medieval Gattendorf was an important strategic point and defensive fort of the Hungarian State; the role carried out by the tribe of Pechenegs invited here from the steppes of the Volga. The village entered the medieval history by the battle between the King of Hungary Gejza II and the Bavarian Prince Henry, which took place in its administrative territory. The first written reference to the village as *Kata* is from 1209. In the 14th century the old mill, which stood on the northern

bank of the Leitha, then the frontier between Austria and Hungary, was also mentioned. An old trade road went around the mill where there was also a toll station and connected the contemporary Pressburg with Ödenburg (today Sopron in Hungary). In the 15th century the family of Rauscher owned the village and they also re-colonized it with Croatian immigrants. The 17th century brought a sequence of unfortunate events for the locals. The old mill, the bridge over the Leitha, and the toll station were destroyed during Bocskay' s rebellion. Five years later the bridge was built again and the Habsburgs granted the village the toll privilege. The Turks led by the Grand Vizier Kara Mustafa crossed the Austrian frontiers and broke their camp near Gattendorf. When they were defeated and gone, they left behind only ruins. The village was rebuilt in 1704 and sacked again in 1709 by the imperial and rebellious troops. After the Rebellion of Estates was over the Esterházy family moved into the old castle (first mentioned in the 17th century) and brought with them prosperity. This was the time when the existence of a Jewish community in the village was also mentioned.

The Jews in Gattendorf

The first written mention of the Jewish community in Gattendorf is from 1739. The Jews built their synagogue approximately at that time. The prevailing occupation of the local Jews was trade in meat and cattle. In the second half of the 19th century the Jewish community gradually diminished and many of them moved to towns. The synagogue, which comparatively successfully survived the 19th and 20th centuries, was demolished in 1996. The old cemetery on the edge of the village now commemorates the past of the Jewish community.

Gattendorf belonged to the Esterházy family until the mid-19th century. During that period the famous composer and virtuoso Franz Liszt visited the village and stayed with his relatives. In the 1850's the Batthyányi family acquired the village and later sold it to businessman Karl Ritter

---

Left: Riding a horse in Burgenland
Right: Rural houses in Gattendorf

von Offermann. Some parts of the estate were also owned by the Pálffy and Czello family, the later of them still owns the local castle. Three formerly independent villages of Gattendorf, Neudorf and Potzneusiedl joined into one and separated again in the 1990's.

Visitors find some remarkable monuments in Gattendorf. The oldest secular building of the village is the **Old Castle**. It was built in the 17th century as a yeoman's yard and reconstructed to a residence in the years 1715-1720. Esterházys used it as their residence and the seat of the family firm. It fell in decay in the 20th century. The architect C. Pruscha acquired it in the seventies and saved it from demolition. The **New Castle** is also one of the secular monuments of Gattendorf. Its oldest parts are from the 17th century. It was finished in the 18th century and its appearance substantially changed. The castle is now in private ownership and a wonderful **English park** surrounds it.

The sacred dominant of the village is the Roman Catholic **church of the Most Holy Trinity**. It has medieval foundations and was rebuilt in the 17th century in the Baroque style. It was several times restored and rebuilt. During reconstruction fragments of Romanesque architecture from the 12th century were discovered in its lateral chapel. In its interior the main altar from the second half of the 18th century with a painting of the Most Holy Trinity is of interest. South of the village is the **chapel of St. Anna** built in 1712 by the Esterházys. Masses in the German, Croatian and Hungarian languages are still held occasionally in this chapel.

The environs of Gattendorf provide ideal conditions for relaxation and recre-

ation amidst a beautiful setting. Alluvial forest along the Leitha river invites the fans of horse or bike riding and the hikers. Farmsteads can be visited and local gastronomy tested. But tourists often prefer to visit the castle in the neighbouring village of **POTZNEUSIEDL** (population 500). The territory of this village has been settled since the remote past. Numerous archaeological finds from the Younger Stone Age, Bronze Age and Roman period testify to it. Graves and remains of Roman settlement above all abundantly represent the latter. The East Frankish King Louis II the German donated the territory of the village then called *Lithaha* to the Bishopric of Passau back in 833. The name *Pozkneuselde* similar to the one used now appeared only in the second half of the 13th century. We have almost no information on the village from the 14th and 15th century. The 1529 Turkish raid caused a lot of damage and it had to be re-colonized in the second half of the 16th century by Croatians. The village was in the ownership of the Harrach estate seated in Bruck an der Leitha. Its later owners were the family Bender and Bátthyány, who in-

cluded the village in their Kittsee estate in the 19th century. It was also the time, when the Baroque castle and tobacco factory were built in Potzneusiedl. Although the local infrastructure improved in the course of the 20th century, its industrial traditions did not develop further. Potzneusiedl joined Gattendorf for some time but now it is an independent village again.

The dominant feature of the village is the Classicist **castle** built in 1808 by the Batthyányi family. It is a three-wing building with a charming park surrounding it. At the present time the castle houses the first Austrian **museum of icons**. Lovers of antiquities and history frequent the castle the whole year round. Many of them visit it while participating in one of the numerous cultural events held here every season. The most important sacred monument of the village is the Roman Catholic **church of St. Marco** built on medieval foundations and mentioned for the first time in the 13th century. In its interior can one admire the main altars with the painting of St. Marco, statues of Sts. Peter and Paul and the Rococo side altar of St. Sebastian. The village also has a pillar of St. John Nepomuk, a pillar of the **Most Holy Trinity** and a pillory from the 18th century. The local curiosity is the oldest tree in Burgenland, an enormous ash.

Left: The Potzneusiedl Castle

THE SLOVAK
DANUBELAND

SITUATION AND DIVISION

The Danube region, with its special landscape is situated in the south of Slovakia. The south-western and southern limits of the region follow the Slovak-Hungarian frontier running along the stream of the Danube. The western limit of this territory borders on the city of Bratislava; the northern limit coincides first with the Malý Dunaj river then with the northern border of the town of Komárno. The northeastern and eastern borders are the Parížsky kanál channel and the lower reach of the river Ipeľ, which flows into the Danube near Štúrovo. The territory of the Slovak part of the Danube region is administratively part of the provinces of Trnava and Nitra, and it consists of the districts of Dunajská Streda, Komárno, and Nové Zámky.

Left: The Danube
Right: Landscape park next to the Malý Dunaj in Bratislava

NATURAL SETTING

The prevailing part of the territory lies in the **Danube lowland** and its units are the Danube Plain and the Danube Hill Land. Its geological development was determined by tectonic dissection of the Inner Carpathians in the Upper Tertiary period. In the sinking parts on its edge the sea and later lake sediments consisting of gravel, sand, clay, conglomerates and limestone of considerable thickness were deposited and today they represent the base rock of the Danube lowland. The southern part of the lowland is the **Danube Plain**, which occupies the majority of our territory of the Slovak part of the Danube region. It consists of river sediments in places covered by deposits of blown sands. The youngest parts of the plain are the floodplains of the individual streams. Above the flat surface of the floodplains with the remains of dead arms moderate heights rise, they are aggradation ramparts consisting of gravel and sand-gravel, mostly covered by clay river sediments or locally by blown sands and loess. The most extensive heights run along the middle of Žitný ostrov (The Rye Island) and represent its morphologically oldest and driest part. Slightly elevated hill land spreads around the whole of Žitný ostrov and along the streams of the Danube and Malý Dunaj. The river network broken into little arms on top of the elevation supported deposition of material. The space between the elevated ramparts and edges of its depressions was waterlogged. Some parts of it were swamps that became lakes in times of high water levels. The elevated part of the plain consists of river terraces located about 30 metres above the Danube.

The eastern part of our territory is the **Danube hills**. The rivers Nitra, Žitava, Hron, and Ipeľ cut through an old planated surface, which originated by the end of the Tertiary period in the hill lands of the Nitrianska, Žitavská, Hronská and Ipeľská pahorkatina. Their elevation difference is 30-100 m. Plain terrain occupied considerable areas along the rivers. The geological base consists of the Lower Tertiary lake clay, sand, and gravel sediments covered by blown loess. River sediments cover the floodplains of the streams and the depressions are mostly moors and peat bogs. Along the streams terraces also survive, which are in fact the old beds of the Quaternary rivers. The hill relief is characterized by alternation of broad depressions of different depths separated by flat ridges or plateaux with distinguishable traces of wind and water erosion. The only mountain range in the Slovak part of the Danubeland is the volcanic **Burda**. It represents an uplifted block of the earth's crust, which is separated by the valley of the Danube and Ipeľ from the neighbouring Pilis and Börzsöny mountain ranges in Hungary. The mountain range consists of rocks, which originated during volcanic activity some 15 million years ago. The prevailing rocks are volcanic erupted rock; mostly firm lava or tuffs in places alternating with andesite sometimes covered by loess.

The river **Danube** was always the primary cause of all that had happened in the region of the Danube region over the history. This second greatest river of Europe, 2,857 km long, flows to the territory of Slovakia from Austria, is joined by the Morava under Devín Castle and ends its short route in the territory of Slovakia by the confluence with Ipeľ near the village of Chľaba. The Slovak part of the Danube is 172 km long and out of this 142 km coincides with the frontier with Hungary. As the river enters the Devín Gate near Bratislava its stream changes and its gradient becomes more moderate. The sudden change of gradient caused by tectonic sinking of the Danube lowland causes deposition of material, origin of fords and an extensive system of river arms, which created here the inland delta of the Danube.

The Danube and its deadly embrace

The main channel of the Danube and its branches lived their own life until man started to control its flow. The river normally crept through its fertile floodplain, but an occasional and sudden rise of water spread horror. The water carried away every potential barrier: fences, trees, whole houses. It also carried away gravel, sand, earth or

fertile soil and deposited in other places. Great floods occurred in the years 1012, 1210, 1501, 1572, 1789, 1850, 1954 and 1965. The disastrous flood in 1965 when the dike near Čičov and Patince broke destroyed some 4 thousand houses and damaged another 6 thousand. The greatest flood, which had ever stricken Žitný ostrov occurred in 1501 when the discharge of the river was 14,000 cubic metres a second.

The longest and the greatest left arm of the Danube, which deviates from the main stream, is below Bratislava, the **Malý Dunaj** or the Little Danube. It flows in a man-made channel up to the village of Most pri Bratislave and continues in its original meandering bed 30-50 metres wide with the typical floodplain forests surrounding it. The more than 150 km long river flows around Žitný ostrov (Csallóköz in Hungarian). The origin of the Hungarian name of Žitný ostrov, Csallóköz is related to the name of the Danube arm Csalló. The island's name (Žitný ostrov) derives from the one of the northern branches of the Danube, now called Malý Dunaj. Its Slovak name originated by

adaptation and translation of the German name Schüttinsel. This largest river island in Europe is 84 km long and 15 to 30 km wide and it lies between the main stream of the Danube and the Malý Dunaj. It spreads over an area of more than 1,600 square kilometres between Bratislava and Komárno (i.e. its part lying in the territory of the Slovak Republic). Its surface is flat, not exceeding altitudes above see level of 105 to 129 metres.

The Danube gravel and sand contain 39 minerals. Gold is one of them. It was not long before people realized it and tried to extract gold from the river. The content of gold in the Danube's gravel and sand is 12 to 125 mg per ton. But the Danube brings much more valuable riches than gold. Žitný ostrov has abundant reserves of high quality ground water and part of the territory is a protected area, which accumulates water in natural way. The discharge of the Danube oscillates between 570 to 10,254 cubic metres per second. After the Gabčíkovo Dam was constructed

the discharge of the original channel of the Danube near Čunovo is from 200 to 7,680 cubic meters per second. The reservoir of Hrušov, which is outside our interest area spreads up to Dobrohošť, where part of the Danube water flows into the feeding channel. The original channel of the Danube continues from Sap, where the canal rejoins it. The main stream was made into a channel for navigation and the individual arms of the river were gradually liquidated. They were preserved only in the inundation areas.

Near Komárno the river Váh flows into the Danube. The river Hron joins the Danube near Štúrovo and the river Ipeľ flows into our greatest river in the easternmost part of the territory. All the tributaries of the Danube more or less flow in the north-south direction following the fault lines of the terrain. The river Váh is also navigable from Sereď through Šaľa to Komárno where its discharge is more than 150 cubic metres a second. Dlhý kanál or the Long Channel flows parallel to Váh and flows into the river **Nitra**. The Nitra flows into the Váh north of Komárno. The river Nitra along with its tributaries, the

Left: The Malý Dunaj
Right: The Gabčíkovo Dam

greatest of them being the **Žitava**, is regulated. The Hron flows into the territory of the Danube Lowland through the Slovenská brána Gate. The easternmost river of the Slovak part of the Danube Basin is the **Ipeľ** and as far as flood-control measures are concerned, its stream is also adapted. However, the **Gabčíkovo Dam** is undoubtedly the biggest attraction of the Danube basin at present.

The sea in the Danube region

The main reasons speaking in favour of construction of this dam were protection against floods and improvement of navigation between Bratislava and Budapest. After thorough investigations and plans were made, an inter-state agreement was signed between the former Czechoslovakia and Hungary about the joint construction of the System of Dams of Gabčíkovo-Nagymaros in 1977. The building works started in March and finished in 1989 when the Hungarian party stopped construction of its part of the dam, which was the Dunakiliti floodgate and eventually completely stopped its participation in the project. After a series of unsuccessful negotiations Slovakia put into operation the structures on the left side of the Danube. Construction renewed in 1991 culminated in October 1992 by damming the Danube near Čunovo. The dam consists of several structures. The reservoir in Hrušov has a 25 km long right-bank dike, which starts in Bratislava and a left-bank dike, which also starts in Bratislava and ends next to the floodgate at Čunovo. The ooze channels on the outer sides of the dike are also part of the dam. The feeding channel is 17 km long, and 267-737 metres wide. Its depth oscillates between 7.3-14.3 m. The Gabčíkovo dam has two navigation locks 275 m long and 34 m wide, by means of which the ships overcome the elevation difference of 23.3 m. There is also a water power station with 8 turbines and installed performance of 720 MW. At present it produces more than 2 billion kWh a year. The waste water channel is 8.2 km long and 16 m deep.

Construction of the dam between the old bed of the Danube and the feeding channel created an artificial island with

the villages of Dobrohošť, Vojka nad Dunajom and Bodíky, which is sometimes denominated **Malý Žitný Ostrov** (Small Žitný ostrov). The dam positively influenced the groundwater level and the vegetation existing in the system of river arms is not only surviving, but also thriving. A great number of waterfowl live on the extensive water table of Hrušov and the feeding channel. Swans and black cormorants have returned to their nesting localities. The vast water areas offer recreation for people as well. Bathing but above all various water sports such as yachting, windsurfing and rowing are possible here. A recreation area with rowing tracks, boatyards and swimming pools is now under construction. The traditional beauty of the Danube is enhanced by occurrence of several thermal springs in this region. Open-air swimming pools can be used the whole year round. The first thermal springs were discovered in 1880's and the best-known and most popular thermal springs are in Štúrovo, Komárno, Veľký Meder, Patince.

As far as the climate is concerned, the prevailing part of the Danube region lies

in the warm climatic zone, while the Burda mountain range is in the moderately warm zone. The surroundings of Štúrovo with the mean yearly temperature +10,4 °C is the warmest area in Slovakia. The highest mean annual temperature 11.7 °C was taken here in 1951 and the highest mean monthly temperature 23.5 °C was also taken in Štúrovo in July 1952. The highest immediate temperature 39.8 °C was taken in Komárno on July 5th 1950. The Danube lowland also boasts the highest number of sun radiation hours (2,165 hours in Hurbanovo), but it also has the least amount of rainfall. The mean January temperature in the flat part of the territory is -1 to -2 °C while the mean July temperature is more than 20 °C and the mean annual rainfall total is 550-600 mm. In the hills the mean January temperature is -1 to -4 °C, the mean July temperature moves between 18 and 20 °C and the mean annual rainfall total is 600-700 mm.

Left: Kováčovské kopce hills
Right: The Devínska Kobyla

Man has modified the local landscape over history by deforesting and draining the extensive areas changing them into arable land. Original vegetation survives in the inundation zone of the rivers, in enclaves of alluvial forests and on old aggradation ramparts and dunes, where one can find, though considerably altered, natural oak forests. One finds what is called the "soft" floodplain forest consisting of woods on humid or waterlogged places in the immediate vicinity of streams, while on the dry gravel elevations the "hard" floodplain forest consisting of oaks, elms and ashes is typical. The dunes are covered by vegetation thriving on sand, swamp associations live in waterlogged areas and the moors are populated by salt vegetation. Only remains of the original oak-hornbeam forests with dominating locust trees survived in the Danube hill land. In the area of the Danube lowland about 20% of wild animals, which do not occur in any other place in Slovakia live. Associations of floodplain forest and cultural steppe are typical. The typical representatives of wild life of cultural steppe are the hare, pheasant, quail or poached marmot. The most precious area not only of the Danube region, but also of the whole of Slovakia is the mountain range of Burda, with its **Nature Reserve of the Kováčovské kopce – juh**. It contains the richest choice of rare species of thermophile plants in Slovakia. The mountain range is covered by oak and oak-hornbeam forests. Some plants grow only here. The rare species of wild life which live only here are the numerous species of steppe bugs and butterflies. The unique assets of the Danube region were the reason several small protected areas of various categories exist there, including the **protected landscape region of Dunajské luhy** established in 1998.

The protected landscape area of Dunajské luhy (The Danube floodplain)

The Slovak-Hungarian reach of the Danube with the extensive system of river arms represents a unique natural setting in the Central European region. From the viewpoint of nature conservation, the 80 km long section between Bratislava and Zlatná na Ostrove is the most valuable one. Forest, water, swamp, and meadow plant associations occur in a comparatively small territory. The protected area consists of five independent parts. The first two of them are near Bratislava, on both banks of the Danube and include dry and water ecosystems. The third, forested part is the system of the left-bank arms of the Danube, between the villages of Dobrohošť and Sap. The section between the villages of Sap and Čičov is similar. Its rarity lies in the deep stationary blind arms of the Danube near Čičov and Kľúčovec. Its last part is the forest landscape of Veľkolélsky ostrov near Zlatná pri Ostrove. The protected area of Dunajské luhy is included in the list of waterlogged areas of international significance.

The **Malé Karpaty Mts.** (Little Carpathians) spread in the west of the Slovak part of the Danube region. This mountain range between the Podunajská and Záhorská nížina lowlands is the south-western edge of the massive Carpathian Arc, which returns back to the Danube after running 2,000 kilometres across Slovakia, western Ukraine and Romania. The eastern and central parts of the mountain range consist of extensive granite massifs. On the western side of the Little Carpathians there is a narrow belt of folded sediments with sandstone, dolomite and shale rocks. For instance, the rock of Devín is mostly sandstone with small karstic formations.

The southern part of the Little Carpathians is called the **Devínske Karpaty**. The tallest mountain here is **Devínska Kobyla**, which with its 514 metres above sea level is also the highest point in Bratislava. In the south this bulky hill drops into **Devínska brána**, the gate between the mountains, which the river Danube uses to cross the Carpathians. In the east the relief of the Devínske Karpaty passes to the **Bratislavské predhorie**. In the north the Devínske Karpaty Mountains are limited by another lowering, the Lamačská brána Gate. The **Lamačská brána** Gate is especially windy as it acts as a sort of funnel for the winds blowing from the Záhorská nížina lowland.

North of the Lamačská brána Gate is the southern part of the **Pezinské Karpaty** Mts. running to the north-east far beyond the northern border of Bratislava.

The Little Carpathians are mostly covered by broad leafed forests and are the most compact and most extensive forested territory of Bratislava. Oaks and hornbeams prevail in lower positions, while beeches are typical of the higher parts. However, vineyards replaced the forests on the eastern side of the Little Carpathians and those of Devínske Karpaty had to make the way to construction of residential quarters. The **Protected Landscape Area of the Malé Karpaty** statute has protected the preserved Little Carpathian forests since 1976. The administration of the protected area is located in Modra. The Little Carpathians are the most important recreation zone for the citizens of Bratislava who can enjoy it for the whole year round. The hills become especially attractive on hot summer days when it is more pleasant to pass the day in the forest than in the street. In winter they offer the possibility of winter sports. Often

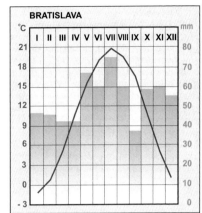

landscape. The landscape conserved its unique natural value only due to the fact that it was strictly guarded as the frontier territory shared with Austria. It is also in the **protected landscape area** called **Záhorie** since 1988.

when there is not a trace of snow down in the city, the Carpathians boast a typical white winter. In spite of the fact that the forests are frequently visited, there is comparatively abundant wild life there including deer, fox, hare, squirrel, and numerous species of fowl. An occasional encounter with boar is not impossible either. In the part of the Little Carpathians around Bratislava there are nine small protected areas. The oldest one, established in 1964, is the **National Nature Reserve Devínska Kobyla**. It protects the thermophile flora and fauna. An instructive path through the area provides information about its specific features.

The southernmost tip of the **Záhorská nížina** lowland reaches as far as the territory of the city. There is the shallow Bystrická depression west of the village of Záhorská Bystrica and a flat river terrace north of the village of Devínska Nová Ves, where the Volkswagen car factory stands. The alluvial forest along the **river Morava** is a special and well-preserved natural

The centre of tectonic sinking in the **Podunajská nížina** (Danube lowland) moved to the area of Žitný ostrov that became the core of today's **Danube plain** in the Quaternary. The **river Danube** formed this plain landscape. The second largest European river with its sediments gradually over millennia filled the vast natural hole between Bratislava and Komárno. In the course of two million years it created a big inland delta here. The thickness of the Quaternary sediments rapidly increases from the west to the east from 10-15 metres in the Old Town of Bratislava to 60-70 metres near Čunovo. In the centre of this depression, that is Dunajská Streda, it reaches as much as 500 m. Under the Žitný ostrov island an enormous amount of ground water of the best quality has accumulated. It represents the largest reservoir of drinking water in Central Europe.

The part of Bratislava stretching onto the Danube lowland is the **warmest and driest climatic area of Slovakia**. The mean annual temperature here is 10.3 °C, the annual rainfall total is 642 mm and the sun shines here an average of 2,100 hours a year. The warmest month of the year is July with a mean monthly temperature over 20°C.

Left: The Morava river
        Mean monthly temperatures and rainfall

HISTORY

The history of settlement of the Danube country is very old. It began at least in the last inter-glacial period. This early dawn of human history is documented by finds of a fist wedge and flint spikes and the remains of prehistoric aurochs and mammoths, now displayed in Žitnoostrovské Museum in Dunajská Streda and in Podunajské Museum in Komárno. Remains of all cultures, which alternated in the course of three thousand years BC in the area of the middle Danube, were found in this territory. The river Danube with its fish, waterfowl and wild life attracted the old family and later tribal associations. Advanced Neolithic structures developed in this territory in the Upper Neolithic period. Farmers and shepherds replaced the wandering hunters and food gatherers. The natural landscape changed into an agricultural landscape. The new settlers cleared and burnt the woods and changed them into fields and pastures. The oldest farmers built their settlements on terraces near the rivers and on sand or loess elevations. The inhabitants of the middle Danube were the people of the Linear Pottery Culture, the Želiezovce group pottery and people of the Lengyel Culture.

The oldest farmers

On an elevation south of the spa Veľký Meder archaeologists discovered a Neolithic settlement with oval hollows and a system of troughs, the purpose of which is still unknown. In four inhumation graves individuals buried in crouching position typical for this period were found. Inhabitants of the Upper Neolithic left there numerous objects of everyday use: stone axes, earthen vessels, some of them filled with corn, farm tools and pieces of pottery.

In the Aenolithic period the area of the Danube basin was settled by farmers of what is called the of Furrowed Pottery people. Settlements of the Kosihy-Čaka group are preserved in Žitný ostrov. One of the outstanding finds is an earthen mould used for casting copper axes with a single blade, one of the oldest finds in our territory, which testifies to the beginnings of metallurgy in Europe. A new method of tillage was introduced at that time as well, and our ancestors were starting to breed farm animals. They buried their dead in barrows or by cremation. At the turn of the older and middle Bronze Age the farming culture called Magyar developed and spread in the Danube Basin. Fortified settlements and the above-mentioned bi-ritual way of burial characterized it. Tilling farming and cattle raising were fully developed. Settlement of the territory by warriors of the Middle Danube Barrow Culture in the Middle Bronze Age was a short episode in about the second half of the 2nd millennium BC. In one place remnants of a big bin used for storing corn and a bronze hair pin were found. The bin also contained a part of its carbonated contents. The North Pannonian Culture spread to the basins of the Nitra, Hron, and Ipeľ. Opulent barrows of dead princes were found in the administrative territory of Janíky. By the end of the 8th century BC and the beginning of the Iron Age in this area various tribes (the Skythians or Tracians) known from the writings of ancient historians appeared. Some finding places, for instance those in the area of Šamorín and Gabčíkovo date to the Iron Age. Expansion of **Celts** also concerned the Danube area. The Celts proceeded across the Danube fords up the stream of the river Hron by the end of the 5th century BC. They contributed advanced processing of iron, production of pottery, weapons, jewels and glass. Celtic influence was manifested only later in the first half of the 1st century BC. The Danube Basin became the crossroads of various significant trade routes. The oldest of them, called the Polish road was used in the pre-Roman period and it connected the Danube region with the Baltic area and led along the river Nitra. These roads were used by trade caravans in all directions and also by migrating tribes, the carriers of cultural exchange. The river Danube was a water route mentioned already by the ancient Greek sources and it also represented the boundary between different races and cultures. It was an important dividing line between the civilized classi-

itary camps built by the end of the first century were found near the bridgehead of the large Roman fort of Brigetio. Important Danube trade route from Galia to the Black Sea passed precisely by this place, near Brigetio and not far from today's Komárno. Another trade route called Czech headed to the west passing through the area of today's towns of Nové Zámky and Trnava. There was also the Váh trade road, which separated from the one connecting the Danube with the valley of the Nitra. Traces of Roman buildings and finds of Roman coins from the 1st to the 4th centuries AD were found in several localities of the Danube Basin.

The Romans at Iža

Remains of the Roman military camp of "Castellum Romanum" in locality of Kelemantia, today Dievčí hrad are in the administrative territory of the village of Iža near the bank of the Danube. The camp was built in time of the Emperor Domitian and it was next to one of the principal fords over the Danube. It occupied an area of more than three hectares on a square ground plan with rounded corner and dimensions of 172x172 m. The wall was 2 m thick and 4-5 m tall. Its wall had 20 towers. The buildings inside the fort were arranged in a street pattern -- there were barracks, stores, workshops, stalls, baths, wells and baking stoves. The building material such as travertine, limestone and sandstone were brought here over the Danube. The fort was one of the numerous buildings of the frontier fortification system and the bridgehead of the important town of Brigetio. The original fortifications built in time of Emperor Marcus Aurelius in the 170's were made of earth and timber. Only after the Markoman wars finished, Romans built here a military camp made of stone. The archaeological finds include numerous coins, pottery, parts of weapons and military equipment, jewels, toilet utensils, work tools, and other objects of daily use.

cal world and the "Barbarian" world, which was a collective name for those who were not Roman citizens. The defensive system of the frontier along the Danube was called **Limes Romanus**. In time of Emperor Augustus, the founder of the Roman Empire the Romans started to expand to the north and subdued the individual tribes in the Alps. They stopped on the middle reach of the Danube inhabited then by the Celts around the year 12 BC. Three years later the **Quadi**, who advanced further east as far as the valleys of the lower section of the Hron in the first century, replaced the Celtic population. The fight between Rome and the new Germanic population for the middle Danube meant arrival of the Roman legions in this area. The territory of Žitný ostrov was swampy and criss-crossed by numerous arms of the Danube. The Romans made use of fords, for instance, the ones in Medveďov and Komárno to be able to advance further north. Remains of their mil-

The stage reached by the Romans when they subdued the Quadi after 97 lasted until the mid-second century. Roman civilian towns were founded in the neighbourhood of the military forts

Left: The Roman tombstone
Right: Kelemantia - Iža

equipped, as usual for southern cultures, by all sorts of amenities, for example, baths and open-air theatres. The area of Žitný ostrov and adjacent plains of the lower parts of the Váh, Nitra, and Hron rivers were presumably controlled the by Germanic Quadi. German cemeteries from the 2nd – 3rd centuries found in Dunajská Streda and the settlement found in Veľký Meder prove it. At the beginning of the Roman Emperor **Marcus Aurelius' reign** (161-180) part of the military garrisons was moved to the east of the Empire. This was the moment the Germanic tribes made use of the opportunity to cross the frontier of Empire for the first time in history. The Emperor used all his forces to push them beyond the Danube again. The writing on the wall below the castle of Trenčín carved by the Roman soldiers in 179 testifies to how far into territory of the Quadi the Romans got. Until recently this inscription was considered the oldest continuous text found north of the Danube. Skirmishes between the Romans and various German tribes culminated during the reign of Marcus Aurelius. The Emperor spent more of his time in the province of Pannonia and the territory of today's Slovakia than in Rome, that is "in the Quad country over the Granua (the river Hron)" where he started his philosophical book Meditations. He died unexpectedly in Vindobona (Vienna) in spring 180.

The Successor of Marcus Aurelius, the Emperor Comodus preferred to give up the conquered Transdanubian territory in exchange for peace and the Emperor Septimus Severus even paid the Quadi for peace. The Romans undertook the last efforts to fortify the Danube frontier suffer-

ing from the continuous Quadi raids in the second half of the 4th century, but they finally left the area of the Danube by the beginning of the 5th century. After the fall of The Empire and departure of the Romans, the Danube area was flooded by waves of migration, which erased all remains of the Roman way of life along with all assets of its civilization. The German Quadi retreated to the west at the beginning of the 5th century and their place was taken over by the Huns coming from the east. The Longobards left under the pressure of **Avars** in 568. In the Migration Period several nations and tribes alternated in this territory in the course of the 5th and 6th centuries. The Avars became the decisive ethnic group in the Carpathian Basin. They formed a strong military state formation called the Vetvar Caganate, which also included Žitný ostrov.

Two different cultures met in the Transdanubian area: the Slavs and Avars. The Slavs, who first co-existed with the Avars in a comparatively balanced way, eventually rebelled against them and led by the Frankish merchant Samo created an empire of their own (623-659). It in-

cluded the Danubian region. In the course of the 8th century the Great Moravian Empire was founded by joining the Slav tribes of Pribina's and Mojmír's Principalities. The whole territory was comparatively densely populated then. A firm system of settlement was created from the original forts, castles and settlements existing next to them. Production was based on agriculture with especially developed cultivation of corn, cattle raising, but also viticulture and horticulture. The Danube still represented an important trade road. Monasteries and the Bishopric of Nitra also played an important part in the Slovak area. The oldest monastery was the Benedictine monastery in Zobor, the eastern part of the territory was under the influence of the monastery existing in Sv. Beňadik. The monasteries owned many settlements in the Danube Basin. But the Frankish raids and the pressure of the Old Magyars coming from the east in the late 9th century finally contributed to the disintegration of Great Moravia with its

Left: Pottery from Dunajská Lužná
Right: A Romanesque window from Šamot

remarkably developed culture, arts and linkages to the western community. In the first half of the 10th century the Old Magyar horsemen occupied the strategic points in the southernmost parts of the Slav territory. Bigger and well-formed groups of Magyar population immediately followed them. The first tribes to settle in this area were the **Nyék** (led by Árpád) and **Megyer** giving the name to the nation, which later developed in this area. The Slav settlement survived even in spite of adverse conditions. Dispersed groups of Slavs, remnants of the Avars and Old Magyar tribes populated the area of the Danube Basin then. Since then a mixture of ethnicities, above all the Slovaks and Hungarians have inhabited this territory. The presence of different nations and ethnicities is testified to by the place names and cultural monuments.

Place Names

The place names in the area of the Danube Basin originated at different times and different nations created them. The names of rivers are considered the oldest. The majority of the names of rivers in Žitný ostrov are of Hungarian origin. Nevertheless, the oldest names of the settlements and their administrative areas are from the late 9th and early 10th centuries i.e. the period before arrival of Magyars. There are also names deriving from market days, for example Dunajská Streda (Streda = Wednesday) or Štvrtok na Ostrove (Štvrtok = Thursday). Some names derive from the names of animals or insects, such as Medveďov and Komárno (medveď = bear and komár = mosquito) or from activities. Kľúčovec (kľúč means key) or Trhové Mýto (in English Market Toll).

The Magyars and their rulers of the Árpád dynasty, including for instance Michal, Belo, Gejza or Ladislav controlled the development of settlement in the area of the Danube lowland. The territory was included in the Kingdom of Hungary in the time of King **Stephen I** (1000-1038). The basic administrative units were counties – castle estates, for example, that of Komárno. New elements of the settlement structure were the towns and market places. After his coronation Stephen I also issued a document concerning construction of churches, which ordered that every ten settlements were obliged to finance the building of a church and provide land and a sufficient number or serfs to cultivate it. The king contributed equipment and the task of the bishop was to provide for the priest and books. The first churches were built in the area of the Danube basin and above all in Žitný ostrov most probably at this time.

Protection of frontiers and fords was provided for by other nationalities, for instance the **Pechenegs**. Their presence is mentioned in historic documents related to the village of Padáň. The arrival of Pechenegs was accompanied by that of groups of Moslems who were involved with money exchange and toll collection. They had a village of their own near a ford over the Čiliz brook. Apart from royal properties, aristocracy also had property in the 11th and 12th centuries. Members of castle retinues and other feudal landlords who bought land or obtained it represented another kind of property. The later became the gem of the yeoman estate, which developed, in the late 12th century and in the 13th century. The richest of the Church institutions was the Archbishopric of Esztergom and its chapter. Belo IV, rightly denominated the second founder of the Kingdom of Hungary, tried to foster the royal power and to stop the aristocratic families expanding their landed property at the expense of the royal property. The Tartar invasion interrupted this process. The troops of Hungary suffered a fatal defeat near the river of Slaná in 1241 and the whole country, including the Danube Basin was at the mercy of the Tartar hordes. As a great part of the population of the area fled or perished during the invasion, it was necessary to repopulate the vast territory, by what is called yeoman colonzation. In the northern part of Žitný ostrov partly German and partly Croatian immigrants settled down. German colonization continued in the 13th and 14th centuries. When the Árpád dynasty died out, **Charles Robert** (1308-1342), the founder of the House of Anjou obtained the Hungarian crown. The Angevin dynasty ruled

over Slovakia for almost the whole of the 14th century and owned the land around the Danube.

Agriculture and production developed in favourable conditions during the rule of the Angevin House. Culture was prevailingly of a religious nature. Its main centres were the orders, new monasteries were founded and municipal schools opened. Gothic architecture of many still surviving buildings reached quite a high level. New settlements were founded by division of the aristocracy's property. The decree of King Sigismund of Luxembourg from 1405 allowed for the origin of towns. Two types of town were founded. First of all there were free royal boroughs and then there were little serf towns called **oppidums** or rural settlements lacking municipal privileges. This type of town included, for instance, Dunajská Streda, Štvrtok na Ostrove and Veľký Meder. The political and economic situation changed in the first half of the 15th century, when the Hussite movement arrived in Slovakia. Its effect was observable also in the territory of the Danube Basin, which became the place of important political and mili-

characterized by further development of the settlement system, but it was later interrupted by Turkish invasion. In the consequence of war many settlements disappeared. Towns were the main protagonists in the defence of the country and the existing castle fortifications, such as the castle of Komárno, were constantly renewed and improved. The fight against Turkish expansion was complicated by the internal political situation and struggle for power. Power and the political administration of the country was in hands of the ruler and aristocracy.

Important noble families

After Ferdinand I of Habsburg was elected king he was obliged to confirm all rights and freedoms to the Hungarian aristocracy. He and his successors created new aristocrats and provided them access to the property of old noble families such as the Counts of Jur and Pezinok, the Újlakys, Báthorys, Amadeos and other. The Thurzos, Illésházys, Révays from petty aristocratic or burgher families were given the opportunity to gain power through military and political functions and this was also the case of the Báttyhányi, Pálffy, Balogh, Esterházy, Zichy and other families who owned estates in the Danube region.

tary events in the Kingdom of Hungary. King Vladislav Jagiłło of Poland was given the throne after the death of Albrecht of Habsburg and it was generally expected that he would be able to face and defeat the Turks. Albrecht's widow gave birth to Ladislav V the Posthumous in Komárno in February 1440 and he was also declared the King of Hungary. He was replaced later by **Matthias Corvinus**, one of the most important personalities of Slovak history. All larger towns existing on the royal land became free royal boroughs, the number of yeoman towns increased so did the number of feudal estates during his reign. It was precisely Matthias Corvinus who granted municipal right to many villages in the Danube Basin, including Holice and Veľký Meder. The town of Komárno experienced its most intensive development in Corvinus' time. Corvinus built several houses in this town and expanded the castle at the confluence of the Danube and Váh rivers. The period of the 15th century and the early 16th century is

In the mid-17th century, when the territory of the Danube *region* hardly assimilated the preceding Turkish occupation, it was stricken by other dramatic events connected with the series of anti-Habsburg rebellions. The biggest rebellion in the area of the Danube region was undoubtedly the one of 1604 led by István Bocskay, when his troops besieged the castle of Nové Zámky. The Emperor Rudolf II's brother Matthias, later King Matthias II, representing the Emperor, concluded a very disadvantageous peace treaty with the Turks in 1606 for the following 20 years. He committed himself to pay the Turks 200 thousand guldens and gave up the occupied territory. History recorded the event under the name "the Žitava peace with Turks". After the new and open outbreak of the Hungarian-Turkish wars in 1663, the Turks succeeded in breaking the domestic defence, oc-

Left: The portal of church in Báč
Right: The fort in Komárno

cupying practically the whole territory of the Danube region and conquering such an important fort as Nové Zámky.

The Danube Basin was very exhausted by the long-lasting Turkish occupation and the Estate Rebellions at the beginning of the 18th century. Plague and hunger killed several thousand people. The situation started to settle down only after signing of the **Peace of Szatmár** in 1711. New guilds were founded and the number of craftsmen organized in guilds was increased. Hatters, coopers, shoemakers, carpenters, smiths, tailors, button-makers, and goldsmiths were the most typical guilds of the region. Markets and fairs contributed to the revival of trade. The majority of the population lived on farming and cattle or sheep raising. Tobacco was introduced at the beginning of the 19th century. The oldest non-agricultural occupations were fishing and milling. But the economic development was hindered by frequent earthquakes, floods, plague, cholera, and fires in the course of the 18th and 19th centuries. The territory of the Danube Basin was administratively divided into several counties: those of Bratis-

lava, Komárno, Esztergom, and Hont, while the villages of Kľúčovec, Čiližská Radvaň, Medveďov, Baloň, Ňárad, and Sap were in the County Ráb (Győr).

The revolutionary years 1948-1949 were very dramatic and agitated also in the Danube Basin. When the Hungarian revolution was defeated in 1849, the administrative division of the country changed. The counties survived until January 1st 1923, when they were replaced by larger counties and district offices. Disintegration of the Austro-Hungarian Empire and the origin of the Czechoslovak Republic meant the end of national oppression in 1918. The region was divided into two great counties: the County of Nitra and County of Bratislava in the years 1923-1928. Division into lands after 1928 meant that there were districts of Šamorín, Dunajská Streda, Komárno, Parkan (today's Štúrovo), and Stará Ďala (Hurbanovo). However, the size of land administered by these districts differed from the present ones. The nationality structure varied. For instance, there were very strong **Jewish communities** both in Dunajská Streda and Šamorín.

The little Jerusalem

More than 2,000 people (35 percent of the population) adhered to the Jewish religion in Dunajská Streda in 1930. The town was nicknamed the Little Jerusalem or the Little Palestine. The Jewish community of Dunajská Streda along with that of Šamorín was the centre of Jewish learning not only in Slovakia but in the whole of Central Europe. The Holocaust and postwar years was a tragic period for the Jews and very few material and historical monuments survived it. The Great Synagogue of Dunajská Streda was bombed and pulled down after the Second World War. Today the monument commemorating the victims of Holocaust stands there.

After the Vienna Arbitrage of 1938 the Slovak part of the Danube region belonged to Hungary until 1945. The Second World War caused great damage to the region. Many structures were destroyed, the life was deeply altered by the war. Social-

ism brought collectivization of agriculture, nationalization of industry, trade, crafts, elimination of small and medium businesses. Co-operative farms were founded in the majority of villages. Several plants of the civil engineering, electro-mechanical, metallurgical and food processing industries were built in the territory. The shipping industry was developing and today's shipbuilding company Slovenské lodenice Komárno is more than hundred years old. Number of people living in towns has substantially increased. The villages of the region became part of the provinces of Nitra and Bratislava after 1949. The region gained new dimensions after the origin of the independent Slovak Republic in 1993.

The historical development and favourable natural conditions of the area were the factors, which contributed to the fact that the Danube region is the most densely populated area of Slovakia. The territory was settled since the oldest times and it became the scene of migration of various tribes and ethnicities. From the point of view of nationality structure, the Hungarian nationality predominates at

Left: Shipyards in Komárno
Right: The swimming pool in V. Meder

present. The highest number of Hungarians in terms of districts of Slovakia lives in the districts of Dunajská Streda (more than 80%) and Komárno (70%). The ratio of the Slovak and Hungarian nationalities is more balanced in other parts of the region. The population concentrates in towns. The biggest town of the region is **Komárno** (population 31,000) followed by **Dunajská Streda** (24,100), and **Štúrovo** (13,300). The remaining towns are smaller, their population ranging from 7,000 to 12,000 and they rank among small towns of Slovakia.

Tourism is the industry, which is markedly developing in the Danube region at present. It concentrates around the **Gabčíkovo Dam**, and the environs of towns with thermal springs and thermal swimming pool opened the whole year round. They are: Dunajská Streda, Veľký Meder, Štúrovo, Komárno, and Patince. The Burda mountain range is also attractive for hikers. The Danube, in turn, invites navigation on boats and to fishing. There are several fresh-water fish species living in the Danube and its arms. The dike of the Danube has a marked bike-route from Bratislava to Komárno and it is the part of the International Danube bike route starting at Passau in Germany and leading to Budapest in Hungary. Various wine bars and taverns so typical for the villages of the region are another attraction. Lovers of water sports (canoe, kayak-paddling or rowing) visit Čilistov.

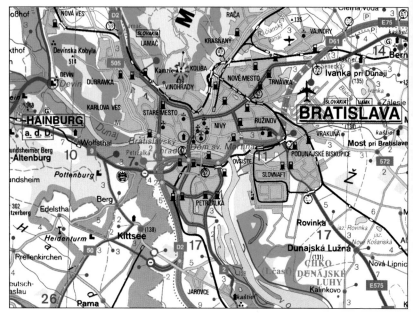

BRATISLAVA

The geographical position of Bratislava is very similar to that of the neighbouring Vienna or Budapest. These three Central European metropolises lie on the banks of the river Danube in places, where the great river leaves behind mountain ranges. Bratislava is only 65 kilometres from Vienna and only 50 from the Vienna's international airport of Schwechat. The distance between Bratislava and Budapest is 180 km, and that between Bratislava and Prague is 330 km.

The territory of Bratislava is crossed by the 17th meridian of the Eastern Hemisphere. It runs across the municipal part of Devín and the 48th geographical parallel almost touches the southern border of the city near the municipal part of Čunovo. The geographical co-ordinates of Bratislava are 17° 7' east for longitude and 48° 9' north for latitude.

The position of Bratislava is eccentric with regard to the territory of the Slovak Republic. It is situated at its extreme south-western corner. A comparatively long section of the city border coincides with the frontier, a rare phenomenon in comparison to other European capitals. It is a long way to Bratislava from any point of the country. In spite of this, Bratislava is relatively near the economically and culturally advanced western part of the Old Continent. The city is part of Euroregion constituted by the triangle between Bratislava, Vienna and the Hungarian town of Győr, estimated by an international expert group as the one with the best outlooks within Europe.

Bratislava and Pressburg

Bratislava and Pressburg are two names of the same city used in different historical periods. The older name of Pressburg *was used for more than a thousand years. Besides the German name* Pressburg *and Slovak name* Prešpork, *the Latin name* Posonium *or its Hungarian form* Poszony *was also long used. The modern name* Bratislava *has been the official name of the city since the end of the First World War. The author of its primitive form*

Right: The Roman pottery from Gerulata

Břetislav is the Slovak scientist Pavol Jozef Šafárik who published it in 1837. Later Štúr's followers modified it to Bratislav.

Bratislava is one of the youngest European capitals. It was capital during the short existence of the Slovak State in the years 1939-1945. Later in 1993 it again became the capital of the independent Slovak Republic. The territory also referred to as Greater Bratislava has an area of 367.5 square kilometres with population 451,400 (to December 31st 1998) equalling to about eight per cent of Slovakia's total population. Pursuing the new administrative arrangement of 1996 Bratislava became the part of province Bratislava and out of the eight districts of the smallest Slovak province five are inner administrative units of the capital. They are the districts of Bratislava I, Bratislava II, Bratislava III, Bratislava IV, and Bratislava V.

The smallest district not only of Bratislava, but also of the whole Slovak Republic with an area of 9.6 square kilometres is the district of Bratislava I. Greater Bratislava consists of 17 municipal parts and 266 town wards. The body of local self-government is the municipal council chaired by the Mayor. The municipal parts have their mayors and local representations.

HISTORY

The history of creative presence of man in the territory of today's Bratislava goes back several thousand years. To know the first inhabitants of the town, we should go back as far as the **Older Stone Age**. Finds of at least four localities in the inner medieval town, in Mlynská dolina, Lamačská brána and Devín date back to the **Younger Stone Age**. In the **Late Stone Age** probably the oldest fortified settlements originated on the castle hills of Bratislava and Devín. The advantageous position of both settlements offered their population good control over the movement on the ancient trade routes heading to fords over the Danube. The people of furrow decorated pottery living in these settlements more than four thousand years ago mastered some crafts and traded their products.

The first copper objects announcing the arrival of the **Bronze Age** found in the soil of Bratislava, are some of the oldest in Central Europe.

The Iron Age in the history is one of the most important periods for Bratislava. The older time often denoted as Hallstatt period is documented by the traces of the people of **Calenderberg culture**. Several lowland settlements, for instance in Devínska Nová Ves, Trnávka, and Ivánka pri Dunaji (next to Bratislava airport) were found. In addition there are two high-situated settlements on the castle hills of Bratislava and Devín.

The Celts brought a revolutionary change in the history of Bratislava. They were the first inhabitants whom we do not have to identify by means of pottery or the way they buried their dead as they left us written texts (so far only on coins) and who lived in the first predecessor of Bratislava, which can be regarded as a town. The Celtic tribes, which subdued a substantial part of the northern half of Europe, also settled in the territory of modern Bratislava. They maintained contacts with more civilized southern half of the

Old Continent. They were often inspired by progressive elements of Classical times, imitating especially the Romans. The towns were one of them. They built up a large settlement which the experts call the **Oppidum of Bratislava**, the nature of which was undoubtedly urban as the Celtic finds testify. It means that Bratislava with its two thousand years old municipal tradition is one of the oldest towns in Central Europe. Traces of Celtic settlement were found in the territory extending over sixty hectares, which was larger than an average medieval town. The majority of Celtic artefacts are concentrated in the space of the historical centre, which constituted the core of the oppidum. For the time being it is not sure whether the localities situated out of the centre (for instance the square of Námestie slobody), were its part. It is also possible that this was an agglomeration of settlements. Another imported item from the Classical world was money, heartily welcomed by the Celts. As the Central European Celts

possessed admirable skills for work with metals, they were able to produce coins of high quality comparable with those of the Romans or Greeks. The Celtic coins bear the oldest writing used in the territory of Slovakia, including the territory of Bratislava. The texts on these coins are easy to read as the writing is practically identical with ours taken over from the Romans. The inscription BIATEC frequently appears on the reverse of the coins and this is why the coins are called **biatecs**.

After a short Dacian episode, which took place short before the arrival of new era, another important period of Bratislava's history started, which can be called after the prevailing ethnicities the **German-Roman period**. As the Romans were not able to push the frontiers of the Empire up to the crests of the Carpathians, the territory of Bratislava became part of the turbulent contact zone separating often hostile Romans living south of the Danube and Germans ruling over the areas north of this great European river. For approximately four centuries the area immediately neighbouring the Danube found itself on the border between two dif-

Left: The Bratislava Castle
Right: Remains of church in Castle

ferent worlds, which meant permanent political and economic instability. The part of modern Bratislava lying south of the Danube belonged to the Roman province of Pannonia administered the Roman legions settled nearby in **Carnuntum** (today Bad Deutsch-Altenburg in Austria). There were (within the territory administered now by the village of Rusovce) a Roman fort called **Gerulata** with a settlement bigger than usual and a market place.

The fall of the Roman Empire was followed by a cultural, economic and political vacuum. Several waves of migration passed over the territory of Bratislava during the **migration period** of the 4th to 6th centuries. Avar tribes invaded Central Europe and influenced the history of the region for at least three centuries. The Avars gradually settled down and mixed with the original, prevailingly Slav population. In the seventh century the development reached the point when a joint Avar-**Slav state** was created and **ruled by the Frankish merchant Samo**.

Agitated Europe politically calmed down in the 8th and 9th centuries. The fact that the eastern frontier of the Frankish realm united by Charles the Great stabilized amidst the territory inhabited mostly by the Slavs was especially important for Bratislava. Now it was in a boundary position. Charles´ descendants fighting between them for the crown of the successor state of the Western Roman Empire tried to conquer this territory. But they met with resistance from the Slav princes Mojmír and Pribina, who were not on particularly good terms with each other either. When the Moravian prince defeated his rival Pribina from Nitra and drove him out of the country, he built the stable foundations of the powerful though not long existing **Empire of Great Moravia**. A large portion of the populations of this new state formation, which reached its apex in the second half of the 9th century, inhabited forts, and two of them were constructed in the territory of Bratislava. One was situated below the Devín castle rock, and the second occupied the castle hill of Bratislava.

Arpád's direct descendant **Stephen I** elected as the first King of Hungary in

1000 was even seated at the Bratislava castle for some time. While dividing Hungary into **royal** *comitats* or counties, King Stephen also remembered the castle of Pressburg when he chose it as the seat of a *comes*, the royal official, who administered these medieval administrative units. The fact that the Slav element preserved itself also after the fall of the Great Moravian Empire is proved by the Slav names such as Lavka, Ivanka or Jaroslav on the list of the counts, who lived at the Pressburg Castle. They were probably the representatives of the domestic Slav nobility.

The date of **December 2nd 1291** is not the date of birth of Pressburg. One should take it rather as the date of its school leaving certificate, which confirms the aptness of its inhabitants to become the free citizens of a royal borough. The last king of the Arpad dynasty **Andrew II** granted the town several **privileges** usual for the Hungarian towns directly ruled by the king. Royal clerks ran Pressburg in the same way as other Hungarian towns. Some groups of population, above all the **German** "guests", enjoyed special personal privileges even before 1291. The domestic inhabitants were

unprivileged subjects. All burghers got their privileges from King Andrew. The town had its own administration and judicial system. They elected their **mayor** and twelve counsellors every year on April 24th (St. George's day). They were entitled to administer the municipal matters, to judge the accused and solve arguments with foreigners. Only the mayor could judge the citizens of the town. The royal privileges also regulated the relation of nobility to the town, only the Church preserved its autonomy and the provost decided all its matters. Another important group of privileges provided for the economic development of the town. It concerned **trade and the crafts**. The citizens were entitled to free use of the port and ford on the Malý Dunaj river near Vrakuňa, the ford over the Morava river, etc. Sale of wine was facilitated by exemption from the fees for vineyards, both existing and ones, which would be created in future. Another municipal privilege worth mentioning concerned the defence of the town.

Left: Baštová ulica street
Right: St. Martin's Minster

The town walls of Pressburg restricted a comparatively small medieval town. Between the 14th and 16th centuries inside the fortifications a **Gothic town** had developed, from which much more had survived than from its Romanesque predecessor.

A special and above-standard relation originated between Pressburg and the **King Sigismund of Luxembourg** who ascended to the throne in 1387 and reigned for fifty years, longer than any other Hungarian ruler. In 1430 Pressburg received another privilege, the **right to strike coins** in its own mint. The prestige of the town grew with the granting of a coat of arms in 1436.

When the King Sigismund of Luxembourg died the Hungarian nobility favoured Albrecht of Hapsburg in the argument over the empty throne. Abrecht, like his predecessor, dedicated attention to historic Bratislava. He had a bridge over the Danube constructed (it lasted until 1445) and the town was granted the **privilege of toll for the goods transported over the river**.

Ladislav's successor was Hunyady's son **Matthias Corvinus**. Traditional sympathy of the Hungarian sovereigns to Pressburg also continued during his thirty-year reign. Ceremonious confirmation of the privileged position of the town by **The Golden bull of King Matthias** in 1464 and the addition of a new **privilege**, that of **the sword**, in 1468 manifested it. The name of King Matthias is connected with the penetration of humanistic ideas into Central Europe. The king's second wife Beatrix of Naples was an enthusiastic fan of humanism and the Renaissance. The arrival of this Neapolitan princess in Buda was accompanied by that of numerous scholars who later inspired the king on numerous occasions. The result of one such inspiration was the opening of university, which followed the example of the oldest university at Bologna. Pressburg was chosen for the seat of this university and its name was **Universitas Istropolitana** (often and incorrectly referred to as Academia Istropolitana). In spite of its short duration, Pressburg became known in the cultural Europe of that time.

The defeat of combined Hungarian forces at the **battle of Mohács** in 1526 was disastrous for the country. The army of the Ottoman Sultan Süleyman II first deprived the country of its king and then of its freedom. But Pressburg paradoxically benefited from the situation.

The fall of Székesfehérvar meant that Hungary lost its traditional coronation town. This is how Pressburg won another **privilege, the one of coronation of the Hungarian kings** and their spouses. It was another, though temporary function to be kept until 1830 and used nineteen times. The first king crowned in St. Martin's Minster in Pressburg was Ferdinand's son Maximilián II on September 8th, 1563.

The years of precarious armistice signed with the Turkish Sultan by Emperor Maximilian II terminated in a fifteen year war during the reign of Rudolf I. Fortunately, it did not directly affect Pressburg. However, peace did not last and in 1605 fighting burst out again in the town. This time it was not the Turks in front of the gates but the rebels led by the Transylvanian prince **István Bocskay**, the leading opponent of the Habsburgs. His soldiers plundered the environs of Pressburg, destroyed the suburbs but did not enter the town. The rebellion was definitely terminated by the signing of what is called the Vienna Peace on June 23th 1606. Among other things it fostered religious freedom and the members of Protestant churches were now allowed to practice in public. Especially the Hungarian estates adhering to the Reformation improved their position. Another anti-Habsburg rebel, **Gabriel Bethlen** was one of them. He conquered the town in 1619, while the castle was still held by the Imperial troops.

At the beginning the persecution related to Counter-Reformation in Pressburg was not as ruthless as, for instance, in Bohemia after the Biela hora event. The municipal council was long tolerant to the domestic and newly arrived Protestants and did not recourse to any harsh measures. The Protestants of Pressburg were even granted the permission to build two churches, and the larger one of them was

constructed right next to the Town Hall. In spite of adverse times a Evangelical gymnasium or grammar school was also established in 1607. The Archbishop **Peter Pázmanyi**, who also invited Jesuits to the town to help him with the task, brought the first comparatively intense re-Catholicizing efforts to historical Bratislava.

Wesselényi's unsuccessful rebellion in 1667 had a sad conclusion in Pressburg. Emperor Leopold I responded to another rebellion of the Hungarian estates by depriving Hungary of many of its rights.

The last act of the **Turkish wars** that took place in the area of historic Bratislava started in 1683. One could say that this was also the most dangerous one of all. The town prepared itself for the attack although it was expected that the Turkish Sultan Mehmet IV would be more interested in neighbouring Vienna. **Imrich Thököly** and his Anti-Habsburg revolt aggravated the complicated situation. Twenty thousand men soon occupied almost the whole of territory of Slovakia, and so instead of the expected Turkish troops the suburbs of Pressburg were full of Thökö-

ly's soldiers. At first Pressburg refused to follow the example of other towns, which surrendered to the rebels without fight. However, after they started to bombard the town from what is today Krížna street, the citizens preferred to open the town gates to the invading army. The castle with its garrison loyal to the Emperor did not surrender and resisted the siege. The last episode of the series of Anti-Habsburg rebellions of estates was the revolt of the Hungarian Catholic nobleman **Ferenc II Rákóczi**.

It opened the calmer 18th century though it did not bring any changes on the throne. The rebels got as far as the gates of Pressburg but did not try to conquer the town. They were contented with 1,500 guldens of contribution. The period of wars and rebellions was terminated by the Szatmár peace treaty signed on April 30th 1711.

The 18th century can undoubtedly be describe as the best period in the long history of Pressburg, although it did not look so at the beginning. A terrible **plague**

Left: Pressburg in the 16th century

swept the town in the years 1710-1713 and caused the death of about one tenth of its population. During the reign of Charles VI the **Hungarian Governmental Council** started to function.

The period of greatest prosperity and expansion is connected with the forty-year rule of **Maria Theresa** on the Hungarian throne. Her indeed unusually positive relation to Pressburg may have originated on the day of her pompous coronation on June 25th 1741. After this she used every occasion to visit the beloved town. Thanks to the queen's favour the life of the town became more varied and refreshed by various attractive events and feasts. Every ambitious nobleman in Hungary was longing to get as close to his queen and her court as possible. They visited her in Pressburg during her frequent stays in this town. For the sake of comfort, many aristocrats decided to own residences or fashionable **palaces in Pressburg**.

The queen also wanted to make her stays in Pressburg more pleasant and decided to **reconstruct the castle**. The Renaissance palace of Pálffy was adjusted and the style adapted to the most recent trends of fashion. New buildings in castle area and a big Baroque garden of French type were added to it. The castle almost entirely lost its defensive function and its residential and prestige functions were emphasised. In 1766 a Rococo palace called the **Theresianum** next to the eastern wing of the castle was constructed for the governor. This important office was given to **Prince Albert**, the queen's son-in-law, and spouse of her daughter Christina.

Maria Theresa's wars with Prussia luckily did not affect Pressburg at all. A long period of peace similar to that in the 14th century was repeated. All areas of human activity throve in such a favourable: Trade, crafts, learning, education, arts, and spiritual life. The spirit of **enlightenment and tolerance** entered Pressburg. Number of its population increased more than three-fold. The town sheltered 33 thousand inhabitants and it meant that Pressburg was the largest city in Hungary. Pressburg was larger than Buda, Pest or Debrecen. The town was expanding and new suburbs were originating outside the inner walls. The municipal fortifications again became the principal obstacle to the further urbanistic development of Pressburg. It was obvious that the town had to be liberated from its **restraining ring of the town walls**. Maria Theresa had the inner walls pulled down.

Son of Maria Theresa, Emperor **Joseph II** was much less interested in Pressburg than his mother. The political position of Pressburg weakened during the reign of Joseph II although the city still had good conditions for economic growth.

The economic growth of Pressburg was slowed down by the **Napoleonic Wars** at the beginning of the 19th century. French troops came close to Pressburg twice. The first time was in 1805, when they easily took the town. A squad of thirty cavalrymen occupied the shuttle bridge over the Danube and opened the way to three hundred cavalrymen and 9,000 infantry soldiers. Shortly after the Battle of Austerlitz (today Slavkov) took place. The peace treaty that entered history as the Peace of Pressburg confirmed Napoleon's famous victory. The documents were signed on December 26th 1805 in the Hall of Mirrors of the Primatial Palace. The treaty brought about great losses of territory for the defeated kingdom.

The **1848-1849 Revolution** was very dramatic in Pressburg. In its first phase the city was the venue of passionate debates in the Hungarian Parliament. Kossuth's radical Liberal Party provoked an open conflict with the Austrian Chancellor Metternich. There were Imperial troops gathering around the city as they expected the attack of rebelling peasants led by the Hungarian poet Sándor Petőfi. In its session of March 18th 1848 in Pressburg, the Parliament adopted a series of social acts that are remembered as the **March Laws**. Emperor Ferdinand V confirmed them with his signature on April 11th again in Pressburg. Immediately after the Emperor dissolved the Parliament. The following revolutionary actions moved to Budapest. In summer the **Slovak voluntary corps** joined the revolution in defence of the Emperor and the citizens of Pressburg responded by founding an association which sent the municipal guard to intervene against the Slovak volunteers. The chief commander of the Hungarian revolutionary troops Artur Görgey, who placed his headquarters in Pressburg, occupied the city as was to become the main salient point of the attack against Vienna. However, Hungarian troops were defeated at Schwechat in Austria and the Imperial army occupied Pressburg in December and Budapest in January. The repression that followed also affected Pressburg. After the definite suppression of the revolt its followers were imprisoned in the Vodné kasárne of Pressburg and Primatial Palace was the building, where the military court of justice pronounced the sentences against the rebels. Thirteen of them were executed. By the end of May the allied army of the Tsar's Russia with its chief commander General Paskievič settled in the city and its environs. This was how Pressburg changed into a gigantic barrack for 94 thousand soldiers and 20 thousand horses in October 1849. A month later the Slovak revolt officially ended with a ceremo-

nious military parade: 1,200 Slovak volunteers marched in front of the Austrian generals. The day after handing in the arms, the chief commander Lewartovski dissolved the corps at Pressburg Castle.

The second half of the 19th century is characterized by the onset of the **industrial revolution**. The Austrian gas company founded the first gas plant in Hungary in 1856 in historical Bratislava. The number of industrial plants working in the city jumped up to forty-one in the sixties. In 1869 there were 2,392 firms employing 5,293 workers. And before the end of the 19th century another 19 factories giving jobs to additional 1,700 people were founded. The biggest factories of Pressburg originated in the years 1873 to 1911. Dynamit-Nobel (1873), Stein Brewery (1873) Apollo Refinery (1895), Cvernovka (textile factory) (1900) and Gumonka (rubber factory) (1911) are worth mentioning. The first power plant in Pressburg was put into operation in 1895.

Left: The station of the first steam railway
Right: The Bratislava Castle

The development of industry was accompanied by that of modern transport. The introduction of **steam engine in river navigation** in 1818 meant a revolutionary progress in the industry. Travelling to the right bank of the Danube by the **Pressburg "propeller"** was a favourite pastime of the citizens. The following year they even could walk to the Petržalka park via the first fixed bridge over the Danube, later called after the Emperor Franz Joseph. In 1840 the **first train on the horse railway** left Pressburg for Svätý Jur. Pressburg did not lag too much behind the rest of the world in the sphere of steam engines. **The first steam locomotive** entered its railway station on August 30th 1848. The railway track of the trains going to Marcheg was later extended to Vienna, and this track is linked with the oldest railway bridge and tunnel in the former territory of Hungary. When in 1895 the **first tram** set out on a journey across the city, it meant the beginnings of the modern municipal transport. **Trolley buses** were introduced in 1911.

Pressburg entered into the second half of the 19th century with a population of about 42 thousand, which rose to 78,000 by the First World War. This almost double population was due to in-migration intensified by the decree abolishing serfdom issued in 1848. The new inhabitants were mostly settling in the expanding suburbs of Pressburg. New quarters were springing along with new factories, which too, were constructed outside the town's core and prevailingly on the north-eastern edge of the city.

Pressburg was spared the direct impact of the **First World War**. The population suffered from the war only indirectly. Nevertheless, the war lasted longer for the citizens of Pressburg. When the arms stopped firing on all the fronts, the battle for Pressburg only began. When the Czechoslovak Republic was declared on the ruins of the Monarchy on October 28th 1918 and two days later was confirmed in Martin by the Slovak National Council, the destiny of Pressburg was unclear. The Czechoslovak units consisting of experienced legionaries started to march to Pressburg on December 30th.

They occupied the main railway station on New Year's Eve and the next morning they controlled the whole town. The 1st of January 1919 became the day of annexation of Bratislava to the Czechoslovak Republic. The victorious powers supporting the origin of the new states in Central Europe approved the step.

On February 2nd 1919 the Slovak Government led by Vavro Šrobár moved from Žilina to Pressburg, which became the capital of Slovakia. Pressburg lasted only for another month, because on March 6th 1919 its **name was changed to Bratislava**. The first years of Bratislava in interwar Czechoslovakia were the ones of establishment of numerous national institutions, such as the Slovak National Theatre, Comenius University, etc. The population increased from 83,000 in 1919 to 124,000 in 1938. Bratislava remained a city of three nationalities also after the disintegration of Monarchy, only in different ratios. The share of Slovaks (and Czechs) increased from 33% in 1919 to 59% in 1938 (Czechs were represented by 17%). The share of Germans dropped in the same period from 36 to 22%, and in case of Hungarians it was from 29 to 13%. The Jewish community in the city amounted to 14,454 in 1938.

When on March 14th 1939 the independent Slovak State was declared, **Bratislava became its capital**. President Jozef Tiso had his seat in Grassalkowich's Palace. The state created under the pressure of the Nazi Germany did not last long. It practically disappeared in April 1945 with the entry of the Red Army accompanied by the Romanian troops. Post war Bratislava experienced development to an extent unparalleled in its history. In four

decades the population of the city quadrupled. **The extreme population increase** was attributed to in-migration from the whole of Slovakia. People were coming in search of jobs and possibility to obtain flats. The post-war city was experiencing an unusual boom. But it has to be said that the development was extensive. Mass construction of housing estates started. Flats were built but the basic amenities lagged behind. In pursuit of space additional villages around Bratislava were agglomerated: Devínska Nová Ves, Záhorská Bystrica, Vrakuňa, Podunajské Biskupice, Rusovce, Jarovce, and Čunovo in 1972. This was how Greater Bratislava was created with an area of 367.5 square kilometres. In 1978 construction of flads continued on the right bank of the Danube, in Petržalka. Petržalka with its 120,000 inhabitants became in ten years the biggest housing estate in Czechoslovakia. This extensive growth stopped after the November 1989 revolution and the population stabilized for the whole following decade at about 450,000. **Bratislava became again the capital of the independent Slovak Republic** after the division of the Czech and Slovak Federal Republic on January 1st 1993.

URBAN DISTRICTS

The Staré Mesto

The centre of Bratislava is also referred to as the Staré Mesto or Old Town (134 m above sea level, population 46,550). It became the district of Bratislava I in 1996 and its area 9.6 square kilometres makes it the smallest one of Slovakia. It is simultaneously the most densely populated district (4,790 inhabitants per square km). The Old Town includes the historic core of the city and adjacent quarters, originally medieval suburbs. The eastern part of the Old Town is flat and covered by dense urban fabric. The western part lies on the hills with greater part of urban greenery compared to the rest of the city. The southern limit of the Old Town coincides with the channel of the Danube.

Michalská and Ventúrska streets

You should start at Hviezdoslavovo námestie square with a wonderful view of the slender silhouette of Michalská veža tower with its typical onion-shaped roof. The view of this traditional landmark is framed on the left by the modern building of the **Dom obuvi** (House of Shoes) colloquially called by the natives Veľký Baťa. The building of the first large-capacity shoe shop was built in 1930 following the design of the architect V. Krafik. It was soon found that the planned building would cover the original view of the historic parts around Michalská tower so the plan was changed and the right part of the building lowered. Opposite the shoe shop there is a functionalist building of the **Café Regina** from the 1930's. There use to be café house in the building before but the art gallery **Galéria Cypriána Majerníka** replaced it. The café was opened again in the building after many years, but only in its ground floor.

The beginning of Michalská street runs along the old stone **bridge of St. Michael** over the former water moat. It was built in the first half of the 18th century and replaced the original wooden

Left: The Old Town Hall

drawbridge. On the left side of the bridge the passers-by get a nice view of the rest of the former **town moat**. Left from the Michalská veža tower the parts of the double **town walls** have been preserved. The preserved and visible part of the walls consists of higher and lower parts. The lower part was added to the original higher part in the time of Turkish wars, approximately in the mid-16th century. It stands on the foundations of older medieval fortifications. If you bend a little over the railing of the bridge at the extreme left, the half-circle of the **Prašná bašta bastion** appears. It was preserved in the back part of house No. 11 standing at the bend of Zámočnícka ulica street. It was first referred to in 1520. The upper section of Michalská ulica passes through the preserved remains of **barbican**, which protected the entry into the inner town from 15th century. The curve of the street was intentional as it prevented the direct artillery attacks on the actual Michalská brána gate.The Baroque house built into

Left: Michalská ulica street
Right: Ventúrska ulica street

the barbican in the second half of the 18th century shelters the **At the Red Crab pharmacy** which contains the original furnishing of one of the oldest pharmacies in Bratislava and also the Museum of Pharmacy. Before passing under the Michalská brána gate do not forget to look at the narrow house on its right side. It is **house** with the narrowest facade in the city (1.6 m), which documents the skills of Bratislava's medieval builders when they had to come on terms with the limited space inside the town walls. The width of this extremely narrow house corresponds to that of the moat and its peripheral walls coincide with those of the fortifications.

The **Michalská veža** tower constitutes one of the symbols of the city. It is the only one preserved out of four providing for the entry into the fortified medieval town. It provided for the passage into the town from the north, coming from the Záhorie or Moravian regions. In the night it was closed. Its name derives from the village that existed in early Middle Ages beyond the gate and around the long before demolished church of St. Michael. The tower has seven floors now. One can identify several architectural styles from Gothic to Baroque. The lowest part is the passage with a brick cross vault and five floors of a massive four-sided tower. The part from the second floor down to the ground is the oldest. It originated as a Gothic fortified gate sometime in the first half of the 14th century. The rest of the prism with another three floors was added in the first third of the 16th century when Turkish attacks were expected and the city was more thoroughly fortified. Under the tower is the **zero kilometre**, from which the distances of the individual Slovak settlements are calculated.

On the right of the tower is **Baštová ulica street.** Its name derives from the bastions, which used to be part of the defensive system north of the street. The headsman used to live in this street and that is why the name of the street before 1879 was Katova or Headsman's street. People rather avoided the street whenever possible. They feared the headsman's sword hanging on the wall opposite the door. When somebody entered the house and the sword moved without any obvious reason, it was an omen suggesting that the person would die on the scaffold. The bad fate could not be avoided even by moving out or fleeing to the forests.

Standing at Michalská tower one gets a view of the whole of **Michalská ulica street,** which is one of the oldest in the city. Its lower part existed as early as the Romanesque period of Pressburg. Later it was widened by the addition of more houses along the road used by merchants on their way from the north to Bratislava's ford over the Danube. The builders of the inner town walls set its present length sometime in the 14th century. The modern urban fabric of Michalská street is varied in styles with preserved or restored Renaissance houses prevailing.

Let us stop first at **Segner's curia** (house No. 7) in the western row of houses, which attracts attention with its two two-storied oriels. It is also the house where his grand-grandson **Johann Andreas Segner** (1704-1777), a scientist of European rank was born.

Jeszenák Palace (house No. 3), built in 1730 as a city palace, is the second oldest of Bratislava. Only Esterházy's palace in Kapitulská street is older. The royal counsellor Pavol Jeszenák built it in the 17th century. It is similar to Hillebrandt's palace of Daun-Kinsky in Vienna. A comparatively modest building with simple Neo Classical facade standing on the eastern side of Michalská street hides one a pleasant surprise: the wonderful Gothic interior of the **Chapel of St. Catharine.** The charm of the remote past breathes from the white walls with tender arches. The chapel is one of the oldest surviving buildings of Bratislava. The Cistercian Francis de Columba, the chaplain of the Pope's ambassador Cardinal Gentile, built it. The chapel was consecrated in 1325.

The most magnificent building of Michalská street is at its lower end. It is **Palác Uhorskej kráľovskej dvorskej komory** (the palace of the Hungarian Royal Court Chamber), today the University Library. In its central hall the lower council of the Hungarian Parliament formed by the county deputies, free royal borough,

and chapters, had its sessions in the years 1802-1848. This is the place, where the manifests of the followers of the radical wing of the Hungarian nobility against the obsolete social system in the country were read and where the passionate speeches of Juraj Palkovič and Ľudovít Štúr concerning national and social rights were heard. This body adopted social laws, including the one on abolition of serfdom in 1848. The building was adapted to the needs of the **University Library**, its present purpose, in the years 1951-1953.

Ventúrska ulica street, continuing Michalská, bears the name of the family Ventura from Italy. Their original name was Bonaventura de Salto and the first members of this family appeared in Pressburg in the 13th century.

Ventúrska street is connected with Michalská by a short tapered section caused by close proximity of the facing houses. One of the buildings forming this bottle neck is the **Palace of Leopold de Pauli** (house No. 13). It was built in the years 1777-1776 for the main administrator of the royal property on the former

royal plot. Gothic houses probably occupied the site before this. The chamber architect F. K. Römisch, who probably followed the design of Hillebrandt, built it. De Pauli's city palace is a nice sample of the new trend in the architecture of Pressburg's city palaces applied in the last quarter of the 18th century. The fashionable Neo Classical architecture is obvious in various elements of its facade including the portal. Rococo bars adorn the courtyard with galleries. The interior of the palace was rather insensitively adapted to the University Library, which expanded here from the neighbouring building. This palace has got all that is absent in other palaces. In its interior there is a garden with a graceful Rococo **music pavilion**. Some sources assert that in 1820 **Franz Liszt** gave a concert there.

The corner of Ventúrska and Prepoštská streets is occupied by **Zichy Palace** (house No. 11) with its smart and strictly Neo Classical facade. Its builder was F. Feline. It was built on the site of three older medieval houses as a four-wing building with inner gallery-rimmed courtyard. Count Franz Zichy had it build in 1775. The palace was restored for the purpose of ceremonies and feasts in the 1980's. **Pálffy Palace** (house No. 10) which was reconstructed in 1747 stands on corner of Ventúrska and Zelená streets. The tablet on the facade of Pálffy's palace facing Ventúrska street announces that it was presumably the venue of the concert of the then six year old child known by the whole world as **Wolfgang Amadeus Mozart** (1756-1791).

In two venerable looking **houses** opposite Pálffy's palace the history of university education in Pressburg started more than 500 years ago. It includes the thirty-year lasting activity of the first humanistic university in Hungary known as the Academia Istropolitana. Today historians point to the incorrect reference to this institution as the founding act says **Universitas Istropolitana** and not Academia Istropolitana. Universitas Istropolitana was ceremoniously opened on July 20th 1467. Lectures started in autumn of the same year. The new university with four

Left: Michalská ulica street

faculties chose its teachers well, as several personalities came to lecture here. At the Faculty of Free Arts there was Martin Bylica from Poland, the Faculty of Theology such personalities as the widely recognized expert on the Old Testament, Vavrinec Koch of Krompachy or the librarian Nikolaus Schricker of Hüttendorf.

Ventúrska street slightly widens in its lower part. The narrow triangle is very probably the remnant of an old market place from the beginnings of the medieval settlement below the castle. Its western part is occupied by **Erdődy's palace** (house No. 1) The former private seat of the state judge Count György Erdödy is the last palace built in Pressburg from the second generation of the city palaces. The local architect Matej Walch finished it in 1770. It is in the Rococo style but fully enriched by Hillebrandt's Neo Classical interpretation of architecture. It has a Rococo portal with a balcony, which looks too small in the wide facade. Originally there were two floors and in the first half of the 20th century a third floor was built on top of them.

St. Martin's Minster and Kapitulská street

The pride of every Christian city is its parish church. This is undoubtedly the case with **St. Martin's Minster**, Bratislava's biggest, oldest and most spectacular church. First the Pope's approval was needed to move the provost's church dedicated to the Most Holy Saviour from the castle into the settlement below the castle Pope Innocent III approved the request of the King Emerich of Hungary.

Reconstruction, which was carried out since the 14th century under the patronage of the ruler and the town council, was in the Gothic taste. As usual in all big European churches, construction of **St. Martin's Minster** also took several decades. After 1401 two western chapels were added to the church. In the northern part of the tower is the **chapel of canons**. It has preserved its original ribbed vault with a protruding boss. On the opposite side is a two-storied chapel of Sofia of Bavaria, which was later consecrated to

St. Joseph. The third **chapel** is the one of **St. Anna**, which was added to the Minster in the latter half of the 15th century, and it has the similar net vault like the hall of the church.

The recognized artist Georg Rafael Donner was entrusted with more works in the interior of the church. The new bulky Baroque altar with Donner's monumental **group of statues of St. Martin** replaced the removed Gothic one. This wonderful sculpture made in 1744 from lead represents a Roman soldier from Transdanubian Pannonia, who cuts his cape in two in a mighty movement of sabre to give half of it to a beggar suffering from cold.

The Baroque **tower** was destroyed by fire caused by lightning in 1833. It was only three years after the last coronation was held in the Minster. Reconstruction was entrusted to an important Pressburg Classicist architect Ignác Feigler senior. He chose the fashionable **romanticizing style**. The tower was given the Neo Gothic face, which has survived until today. The tower of the Minster is 85 metres tall. At its top is a gilded 2x2 m cushion bearing the **copy of the Hungarian royal crown**. The imitation is one metre tall and weighs 300 kilograms.

The visitors of Bratislava Minster's monumental interior of 70x23 metres can admire there many remarkable works of art, and others are deposited in the parts of the church closed to the public. There is a valuable one metre tall **Late Gothic monstrance** from 1517. The **chalices** made in the 15th and 16th centuries are also of high artistic value. The **chalice-shaped Gothic font** made in 1402 of bronze is worthy of attention. In the lateral Neo-Gothic altar is the **Renaissance relief of Pieta** from 1642. The most valuable **grave monument** is that **of Georg Schomberg** made of sandstone. The vice-chancellor of Universitas Istropolitana had it made before he died in 1470 and it bears his portrait. On the wall of presbytery there is the **epitaph of Miklós Pálffy** from 1601 made of red marble. The modern tombstone of the author of the first Slovak novel and the canon of Pressburg chapter **Jozef Ignác Bajza** is placed in the chapel of St. Anna. His body is deposited in the crypt of the

Minster. The marble board bearing the portray of the writer was made by Jozef Pospíšil in 1933.

South of the St. Martin's Minster is the rectangular **Rudnayovo námestie** square. Its position in the neighbourhood of the Minster predestined the older names of this square: *Domplatz* in German or Dómske námestie in Slovak. There was a cemetery with numerous chapels on the site of today's Rudnayovo námestie square until the 18th century. The name of the square used since 1939 commemorates **Alexander Rudnay** (1760-1831), the first Slovak who achieved the title of Cardinal.

The street leading northward from presbytery of the Minster is called **Kapitulská**. Its length was determined by the town fortifications at its northern end. This is one of the oldest streets of the town and the Church dignitaries, who were moved from the castle to the settlement below the castle by the beginning of the 13th century, created it. The houses of

---

Left: Rudnayovo námestie square
Right: Kapitulská ulica street
     The Jesuit College

provost, canons and priests formed the street. It used to be the main street of the Romanesque Pressburg. It ran further to Zámocká ulica and the castle. Expansion of the town in the 14th century pushed the street to the western edge of the town.

In the right corner, at the end of the eastern row of houses of Kapitulská ulica street stands a big building with a comparatively large forecourt. It originated in 1632 by reconstruction of an older house as ordered by the then provost Juraj Draškovič. The provost used it and this is the reason why it is called **Prepoštský palác** or the Provost's Palace. The present Provost's Palace though, is a two-storied Renaissance building with short lateral wings, which close the mentioned forecourt or rather a garden. The **Late Renaissance portal** in the wall of the courtyard of honour of the Palace from 1632 is quite different from the simple facade. It is a unique architectural element in Slovakia. The **statue of St. Elisabeth of Hungary** by sculptor Alojz Rigele from 1907 standing in the courtyard represents the Saint allegedly born in Pressburg Castle in 1207. The Provost's Palace is today the seminary for priests.

The **Jesuit College** built opposite the Provost's Palace continued this educational tradition. It was erected on a plot with three older houses, which the Archbishop of Esztergom and Cardinal Peter Pázmány donated to Jesuits in 1626. The medieval school was in one of these houses. After abolition of the Jesuit order by King Joseph II in 1782 first the town school and later the censor's office got the building of the Jesuit college. Finally it was restored for the Imperial and Royal Law Academy. One of its famous students was the Slovak writer, dramatist, and journalist **Svetozár Hurban Vajanský** (1847-1916). The Law Academy became part of the newly founded **Hungarian Royal University of St. Elisabeth**. After the First World War two faculties of **Comenius University** seated in the building – the Faculty of Philosophy moved there in 1918 and Faculty of Medicine in 1919. In 1926 a modern **aula** (great hall) with a statue of Roman orator and philosopher Cicero on the facade was added next to the right flank of the building. It was given back to the Church after the Second World War and the still existing **Faculty of Roman Catholic Theology** was established in it.

The next building in the western row of houses in Kapitulská street is **Collegium Emericanum**. The Italian architect Jakub and Giovanni Rava erected this building in the years 1641-1642. Archbishop Emerich Lósy, who decided to establish a seminary for secular priests of the Esztergom Archdiocese, funded it. The name of this school institution derives from the Latin name of the Christian name of its founder.

The **Esterházy Palace** (house Nos. 6-10) is the only secular building on Kapitulská street. It is one of the oldest palaces in the city, as it was built almost a century before the city was seized by building frenzy in time of Maria Theresa, which gave origin to plenty of wonderful Baroque, Rococo, and Neo Classical palaces. It was built in the mid-17th century and restored in the Baroque style in the following century. The Liszt family owned the original house. Later Count Esterházy bought it. The governor Albert, son-in-law of Queen Maria Theresa also lived in the house for some time.

The venerable looking **Gothic house No. 4** in the northern part of Kapitulská street called **Malý prepoštský dom** or the Small Provost's House will certainly attract the visitor's attention. As a matter of fact, it consists of two Gothic houses from the 15th century, as the gap in the middle of the plot, now bridged by the arch of the gate, suggests. Some of the inner spaces have barrel vaults. Behind the eastern row of the houses of Kapitulská ulica are the **western town fortifications**, which

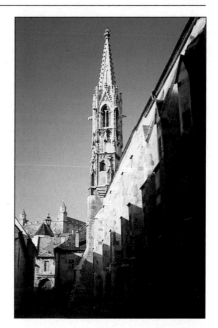

were subject to extensive reconstruction, when the New Bridge over the Danube was constructed in the early 1970's. The massive **Vtáčia bašta** (Bird's Bastion), which was the defensive counterpart of the Luginsland bastion at the opposite slope of the castle hill, stands outside of the fortifications.

Prepoštská ulica connects Kapitulská and Ventúrska. It has always been the connecting lane between the inner town and the walls of the western part of fortifications. The oldest reference to this street is from 1420 and it is mentioned as an access road to St. Martin's Minster.

A bit further to the north is the short **Farská ulica street** parallel to Prepoštská. Farská connects Kapitulská and Klariská streets and also Michalská street through the passage in the building of the University Library.

Klariská ulica street is longer and richer in monuments than Farská. Both streets have the same origin. This street also originated with the construction of the Cistercian monastery. The street ran from the monastery to the town walls on the northern side of the fortifications.

Right opposite the passage to Michalská ulica is the **house** called **U dežmára**. Originally it was a Gothic house with passage, rebuilt in Renaissance style in the latter half of the 16th century. It attracts the passers-by with its original facade ornamented by graffito. Careful restoration brought additional discoveries of original Gothic windows and a preserved remnant of the Gothic plaster. The name of the house and restaurant on its ground floor is connected with the person who collected the taxes – the tenths.

The dominating building of Klariská street is the **St. Clara church** and monastery. Monastic building have stood here since the 13th century. They were originally Cistercian nuns, who along with Franciscan monks, were the first to come to Pressburg. By the end of the 13th century the **Gothic nave of the church** was started and it was finished in 1375. The vault of the church had to be restored again after fire in 1515. **Presbytery** was added to the nave and both are vaulted

with ribbed cross vaults. In the early 15th century a five-sided **Gothic tower** lavishly adorned by pinnacles, gargoyles and little statues in what is called the Beautiful Style was added on the side of Farská ulica street. Today there are true copies of four statues on the tower. The original statues are kept inside the church. This Bratislava's landmark is impressive not only for its beauty, but also for its bold architectural solution. The builder decided for an unconventional approach when he did not build the tower on the foundations buried in earth. He rather built it on the lateral wall of the church nave.

The original Gothic **monastery of St. Clara** became dilapidated, when the nuns left Pressburg fleeing from the Turks in 1526. The order moved to Trnava. Later they came back only to face ownership problems with the city and the consequences of another fire. Finally it was Archbishop Peter Pázmány who decided for a deep change of architecture of the monastery. He supported all Catholic institutions within the framework of the Re-Catholicizing program of the Church and also helped to the nuns of St. Clara's order.

Left: The western town walls
Right: Keglevich Palace

The **new monastery** was built on the foundations of the old. The former monastery was reconstructed in the years 1957-1961 and it became the seat of the Slovak Pedagogic Library. The monastery now shelters the **Office of the European Council**.

Panská and Laurinská streets

Panská and Laurinská form together the longest street line in the historical centre of Bratislava with total length of 700 m. In the past they bore the common name of Dlhá or Long street. The more easterly-situated Laurinská is busier with more shops and less luxurious houses. Panská (or Lordly) street is what its name suggests, as there are many city palaces, which used to belong to the nobility and rich burgers. There are also numerous embassies and travel agencies. Panská and Laurinská are the oldest of Bratislava streets. They have seen the oldest times of the city including that of the primeval settlement below the castle. They originated in the same way as Michalská and Ventúrska along the old trade route called the Danube road, which headed to the Bratislava ford, bringing the merchants from the east: from Nitra and Trnava.

Panská ulica street is the one more westerly situated of the inseparable twin street. It starts at the former Vydrická brána gate and ends at the crossroads with Rybná brána. If you want to gain an idea of the development of building styles used in Bratislava in the 18th century you only have to walk down Panská ulica from Csáky's palace to Esterházy's palace.

The corner of Panská street and Rybné námestie square is occupied by the house No. 41 which is known under its common name **Bibiana** as it is the venue of Biennial of illustration of children books. The immediate vicinity of the Bibiana totally changed when the New Bridge was built. The rather awkward situation of the bridge reduced the former Rybné námestie square to two small areas. The upper one originated on the site of the disappeared main synagogue of Bratislava built in a typical historicizing style. Unfortunately, the pair of its nice towers reminiscent of

Oriental architecture can now be seen only on photographs or in the drawing on the **Wall of Memories,** which closes the square from the side of the New Bridge. **The Holocaust Memorial** stands on the very site of the disappeared synagogue, in the middle of the small square in front of the Bibiana. It is a four metre tall bronze sculpture on a marble plinth bearing an inscription in Hebrew: REMEMBER!.

At the southern end of the house built in the former moat parts of old stone architecture can be seen. It is a small part of the former **Vydrická brána gate** in the town walls. A part of wall with disclosed face of ashlaring can be seen.

The Neo Classical **Csáky Palace** stands at the point, where Panská ulica street opens to the rectangular area of Rudnay's square. The domestic builder Mattias Walch built it for Count György Csáky in 1775.

The Keglevich Palace stands on the corner of Panská and Strakova street. Side by side the proud Erdödy Palace it looks like a country mansion of some yeoman from the north of Slovakia. The short facade of the single floor house compen-

sated by the tall red roof typical of old village mansions causes this rustic impression. The Baroque palace originated by rebuilding an older burgher house.

The **Pálffy Palace** at Panská Nos. 19-21 revealed some pleasant surprises to the historians and archaeologists in recent years. The oldest written documents relating to this palace on today's Panská street are from 1415 to 1516. The Pálffy family bought the house in 1715. Count Pálffy was later nominated palatine and state judge. He paid thirty thousand guldens for the house. In the first half of the 19th century the Pálffys unified the original building in the Neo Classical style with the facade preserved up to now. In 1885 the rear parts of the palace were pulled down and a new palace was built facing the Promenade (Hviezdoslavovo námestie square).

Extensive reconstruction of the interior of the palace carried out in the 1980's adjusted the palace for the purpose **of Art Gallery of the city of Bratislava**.

Left: The British Embassy
Right: Divadlo P. O. Hviezdoslava theatre

A defensive tower occupied the site of **house No. 17**, now used by the *British Council*, in the 13th century. The Gothic house from the 15th century belonged to palatine Rozgoň, the protagonist of the civil war between the castle and the town. The owners of the house alternated until the Pauline monks from Marianka bought it. The Paulines wore typical white gowns and that is why the house was called **The House of the White Monks.** In the second half of the 17th century the Paulines changed the back part of the house into a **chapel of the Most Holy Trinity**. The later owners of the house pulled down the chapel of which only the Early Baroque portal with the year 1671 carved in it has survived.

Let us go back to the southern part of Panská. In its middle there are two palaces. It is good they are standing side by side because we can compare the heavy, majestic Baroque building with the light and graceful Rococo house. **Esterházy Palace** (No. 13) on the left was built in 1746 for Count Ján Esterházy, a member of one of the richest noble families in Hungary. The palace was one of the most luxurious in the city, though its exterior does not confirm it. The Rococo **Balassa Palace** standing on the right (No. 15) is quite different from its neighbour. The three-storied house is lower, less massive and the ornamentation of the facade is considerably finer and more elaborate. The Rococo sculptured ornamentation of the facade is full of symbols and allegories of the Classical deities.

The crossroads of Rybárska brána, Panská and Laurinská street is certainly the liveliest spot of the city. People like to stop here to listen to the street musicians and the tourists love to have a snap made with **Čumil** in background.

Rybárska brána street is a short street in the historic centre of Bratislava and part of the already mentioned *Corso*. It is a pedestrian zone between Hlavné námestie and Hviezdoslavovo námestie squares.

Next to house No 1 stands a life-size statue with a top hat in his hand and a welcoming gesture. In contrast to the statue of Čumil this one painted in gleaming silver paint represents a real person, a native of Bratislava nicknamed **Schöner Nazi** (Fair Naatsi). His real name was Ignác Lamar, and he was born on August 12th, 1897 into the family of a shoemaker in Petržalka. He was lucky to escape the post-war displacement of the Germans living in Bratislava to Germany. Schöner Naatsi frequented Bratislava's pubs and coffee houses and became an inseparable part of the city's folklore.

Laurinská ulica street is the prolongation of Panská. It starts at Rybárska brána and ends in Štúrová. It has lost most of its historical buildings. Modern buildings, more or less happily included in this inner town environment, have replaced them. Shops, restaurants or coffee-houses compensate for the absenting history in Laurinská. It is also a bit more animated than other streets of Bratislava.

The first (No. 1) in the northern row of houses on Laurinská is a four-storied house with a Neo Classical facade. It was built after design of Ignác Feigler Senior in 1846. First of all it was the seat of the **Prvá prešporská sporiteľna** or the First Pressburg Saving Bank founded in 1842 as the oldest bank institution in the city. Opposite the First Pressburg Savings Bank is a modern corner building, **Dom slovenských spisovateľov** (House of the Slovak Writer**s)**. There is a bookshop in its ground floor. On the corner of Laurinská and Radničná the Neo Classical **house of Baron Walterskirchen** (No. 3) was built in the 19th century.

Motešicky's house (No.10) belongs to the generation of houses built on Laurinská street in the second half of the 19th century. It was built on foundations of an older house, which used to be the inn of *The Wild Man*. The inn was considered a better one, where the deputies were accommodated in the time when the Hungarian Parliament had its sessions in Pressburg. Nowadays two restaurants occupy the ground floors of the front wing of Motešický's house.

House No. 9 standing in the northern row of the street originally consisted of two Renaissance buildings. They were attached to each other by adjustment of their facades into one. The facade is Neo

Classical from the first half of the 19th century.

At the eastern end of Laurinská street stands the **theatre building of Divadlo P.O. Hviezdoslava**. **A copy of bars** hangs across the street and above the heads of passers by just to remind us that it is the place where **Laurinská brána gate** used to stand. The first reference to the gate is from 1412, and it even quotes the salary of the gatekeeper. Contemporary drawings show that the two towers, Michalská and Laurinská were very similar. Both were protected by barbicans, and the curve of the upper part of the streets was the same. The tower of the gate had a shingle roof ending in a ball with a banner. For some time it was used as a jail. Laurinská brána was pulled down in 1778.

The Hlavné námestie or
The Main Square

Out of the three central areas in the historic centre of Bratislava the Main Square with its squarish ground plan is the most impressive one. Through the his-

Left: The Hlavné námestie square

tory it was the stage and witness to practically every important event, which took place in the town. It used to be the main market place, stage for the Passion plays, gatherings, and the place, where the rulers were greeted and welcomed, but also where executions or public punishments were carried out. The splendid coronation trail headed by a new King of Hungary always attracted the crowds to Hlavné námestie. The affection of Bratislava's citizens toward their square survived. They still like to go to traditional Christmas fair, performances of musical bands, tower concerts of trumpeters and other events or simply to relax next to the Renaissance fountain or under the sunshades of cafés.

People often meet next to **Maximilian's fountain** in the western part of the square perhaps the same as Londoners meet at Piccadilly Circus under Cupid's statue. The square lacked a public water source until the second half of the 16th century. Only in 1572 the financial contribution of King Maximilian II made it

possible to finish the fountain, which now bears his name and portrait.

Every building at Hlavné námestie deserves attention. The most important of them is the **Stará radnica** or the Old Town Hall. Its appearance is owed to a complicated architectural development marked by numerous changes of style and reconstruction. The history of this wonderful building started in the remote past, when the city was founded. If we leave out the Celtic, Roman or Slav settlement of this locality, we can say that the oldest predecessor of the Old Town Hall was **Mayor Jacob's fortified house** built on the north-eastern side of the new central square.

Pressburg was the first town in the Upper Hungary to acquire the building of Town Hall of its own. The municipal council had its sessions in Jacob's house even before the town bought it. The rebuilt Pressburg Town Hall on Hlavné námestie was fully used only after 1434. A new **passage** opening the entry into the Town Hall from the square was made before 1442. This remarkable architectural element has been preserved in its full beauty up till now. The original segmental quadripartite vault has five bosses with figural-heraldic ornamentation.

The Town Hall of Pressburg entered the 16th century in a new Late Gothic shell and became the dominant building of the square and an important part of the city's silhouette. In the second half of the 16th century the tower of the Town Hall was slightly adjusted to the principles of the Renaissance style. Three earthquakes, which struck the city in the last decade of the 16th century, required more interventions. Six identical **Renaissance windows** were put into the facade facing the square; Unger's house had another two from 1581. **Renaissance arcades** on pillars, preserved up to now, and made by the stonemason Bartolomej from Wolfs-thal were added in 1581. But the most beautiful thing that happened to the Town Hall came at the end of the 17th century when Bastiano Corati Orsati made the lavish stucco ornamentation of the rooms: rims of the vaults and frames in which the painter Johann Jonas Drentwett from Augsburg placed beautiful **wall paintings**. He followed in style the Italian and Flemish patterns of the 17th century. The painting placed in the middle of the vault represents the theme of the Last Judgement.

Description of Pressburg from the first half of the 18th century written by Matej Bel contains information about the Baroque reconstruction of the Town Hall. Bel mentions the archives on the first floor, the hall with portraits of Kings Leopold I and Charles VI with flattering inscriptions, court room and office room (today's Pompeii hall). He also mentions the Renaissance jails in the wing turned to Obilné (today's Primatial) Square.

In the 19th century the Town Hall became too small and the municipal authorities of Pressburg were compelled to solve the problem of space for the ever-expanding office. They bought the neighbouring Apponyi Palace.

When it became obvious that not even the Aponyi Palace would satisfy the needs of the Pressburg municipal authorities, the councillors proposed the purchase of the Primatial Palace. It was eventually

bought in 1903. The project was completed in 1912 and it involved construction of the eastern and southern wings of the Town Hall. All later interventions were mere repairs and reconstruction of some hidden valuable architectural details. While restoring the facade the **cannon ball** stuck in the facade, which commemorates the attacks of Napoleon's army in 1809 was also preserved. There is also a **board with a line** marking the water level of the Danube at the time of the disastrous floods on February 5th 1850.

The Apponyi Palace next to Unger's house is out of the Hlavné námestie square in a short **Radničná ulica street**. It was build in the years 1761-1762 for count Juraj Apponyi, a member of a rich Hungarian noble family from Oponice near Topoľčany. At present the Apponyi Palace shelters the **Viticultural Museum** and regional library. The collections displayed on the ground floor and basement of the palace document the rich history of wine growing in the traditional viticultural region of the Little Carpathians. An original press used in wine production is placed in the courtyard.

The house (No. 2) standing opposite the Apponyi Palace with its main entrance from the Hlavné námestie square is one of the oldest in the city. Due to remarkable discoveries of very old architectural elements from the last third of the 13th century the citizens of Pressburg know it as a **house with a tower**. Extensive renovation of the building in the 1980's century led to discovery of the remains of an original burgher house with tower which was, like the predecessor of the Old Town Hall, made for living. The last of the trio of houses at the southern part of Hlavné námestie is the **Jeszenák Palace**. The Baroque building on the corner of Hlavné námestie and Rybárska brána was built in the 18th century at the site of an older house. The stone cartouche on corner bears the coat of arms of the original owner of the palace, Baron Ján Jeszenák. Recently the stylish and in the past very popular **café and sweet shop Café Mayer** returned to the ground floor of the palace.

The western row of houses at Hlavné námestie is the youngest one. **House**

No. 5 is especially interesting. It was built in 1906 on the site of an older medieval house of the Auer family from the 15th century. Queen Mary, the widow of King Louis II lived in it for some time. Today it is the seat of bank, but it has also the **café U Rolanda** on its ground floor. The interior of the café was refreshed by a true imitation of Kempelen's chess automate. The **Palugyay Palace** (No. 6) standing on the corner of Hlavné námestie and Zelená ulica street acquired its Neo Baroque appearance in 1880. The style is based on the traditions of the French Baroque. It was built for an important businessman trading in wine, František Palugyay.

The opposite corner of **Zelená street** is occupied by the **Zelený dom** or the Green House (Sedlárska street No. 12). The name derives from the green painted facade and in its ground floor was a popular tavern and restaurant.

The front wing of the Zelený dom overlooks the **Sedlárska ulica street**. This

Left: Maximilian's fountaine
Right: Interior of Mirbach Palace
        Gate of Mirbach Palace

medieval street, along with Rybárska brána, connects Michalská and Laurinská streets. Its name (The Saddler's street) suggests that in the past it was inhabited above all by saddlers. Today this street is the favourite route of walks of the citizens and a most lively part of what is called the **Bratislava Corso**. In the sixties the avant-garde theatre of *Divadlo na korze* (now the building of the Hungarian embassy) attracted the young audience, while today it is rather the Irish pub **The Dubliner** that has won popularity among both the younger and older generations.

Let us go back to the Hlavné námestie square along the western wing of the **Kutscherfeld Palace** turned to Sedlárska street. The windows of the palace (No. 7) overlook Maximilian's fountain. The corner two-storied palace is one of the most beautiful Rococo buildings in the city. It was built in 1762 on the site of several medieval plots. Today the Kutscherfeld Palace houses the **French embassy** and the **French Institute**. The presence of the French on Hlavné námestie square is suggested also by a recently installed bronze **statue of an Frenchman** of a man in uniform wearing a typical three-horn Napoleon hat. The soldier looking like Napoleon himself leans on a bench, a favourite spot of the tourists making snapshots.

When in 1723 **Palác miestodržiteľskej rady** (the Palace of royal governing council) was established, Pressburg was chosen as its seat. It was placed in the house in the north-eastern corner of Hlavné námestie. The city obtained this top office which represented the ruler in Hungary seated in Vienna. It was not entitled to take final decisions as it had to have them approved by the ruler represented by the Hungarian Office in Vienna. In 1762 the office also bought the neighbouring house. The two buildings were connected and rebuilt as the palace of the royal governing council. The eastern facade of the palace faces Františkánske námestie square and its southern side overlooks the Hlavné námestie square. The two-storied building with interior courtyard was reconstructed in Rococo style. The carriages entered the yard from the Hlavné námestie square and left it by the exit to Františkánske námestie square or vice versa. There is again a top governmental body seated in the palace: the **Office of the Government of the Slovak Republic.**

The Františkánske námestie square

Františkánske námestie square is a kind of counterpart to busy Hlavné námestie or the Main square. It offers a much quieter, almost chamber ambience amidst antique historic houses. Františkánske námestie originated some time in the 13th century, hence it is one of the oldest in the town. Its present name is linked to the presence of the church and monastery of the Franciscan order.

Biela ulica or White Street is a short connecting street between Františkánske námestie square and Michalská ulica street. It originated in the 15th century. Its name derives from the fact that the facades of houses were painted in white to make the narrow and dark lane look lighter.

The northern row of houses of Biela ulica street continues with a block of medieval buildings, which taper along the upper part of Františkánske námestie square. Part of this block is what is called **Vinohradnícky dom** (the Vintner's house) (No. 10), the best preserved burgher house in the city with original medieval inner division. Some fragments such as the main segmented portal, the original truss of the roof and medieval basements have been preserved from the Late Gothic form of the house. In the upper floor of the house a valuable Late Gothic painting from late 15th century was discovered. In

the 16th century Evangelical school used the house. This is also the period of arcades in the courtyard. The name Viticultural house suggests that it was the seat of the vintners association. The tradition is maintained by the popular **tavern Veľkí františkáni** in the basement stretching as far as the neighbouring Mirbach Palace.

The **Mirbach Palace** is the architectural gem of the upper part of Františkánske námestie square. It is rightly admired along with the Primatial Palace as one of the most beautiful sights offered by Bratislava. This Rococo building was built by Matej Hörlligl in years 1768-1770 on the site of the former Weitenhof house (Wide Yard House). It was a city property bought from the Franciscans.

The Mirbach Palace was presumably built for a rich brewer of Pressburg, M. Speech. However, he sold it immediately after it was finished to Imrich Csáky. The owners of the palace alternated until Count Emil Mirbach bought it and eventually donated to the city in his last will, with the conditions that it would become an art gallery. The city fulfilled the princi-

pal condition of the testament. The **Art Gallery of Bratislava** is located in the palace and offers valuable occasional fine art expositions along with standing collections of the Baroque artists whose work or life was connected with Bratislava. There are, for instance the famous heads by František Xaver Messerschmidt and canvasses by František Xaver Palko.

Opposite to the Mirbach Palace is the Franciscan church. Let us stop first at the neighbouring building of the monastery, the history of which is closely connected with this church. It used to belong to the monks, who were among the first to come to Pressburg. Inside the monastic complex the original **arcade stations of cross-corridor** built around the squarish cloister has survived. The present **facade** of the main monastic building facing Františkánske námestie dates from the latter half of the 19th century.

The **Franciscan church** consecrated to the **Annunciation of the Virgin Mary**

is very old. It is the oldest preserved sacral building in Bratislava. Unconfirmed sources have that it was built by the King of Hungary Ladislav IV in honour of the victory over the King Přemysl Otakar II of Bohemia in the famous battle on the Marchfeld in 1278. It was built in Gothic taste as a simple single-naved church. The earthquake of 1590 caused the fall of the Gothic cross vault. It was replaced by a new **Renaissance vault**. The original Gothic **presbytery** and the **lateral walls** of the nave were preserved and today are the oldest part of the church. The **main altar** is from the mid-18th century and bears the painting of glass of the Assumption of the Virgin Mary from the end of the 19th century made according to the original painting from the 18th century. The **side altars** are also in the Baroque style, all of them are from the mid-18th century. The pulpit from 1756 is in the Rococo style and it is adorned with several notable reliefs. One of traditional ceremonies of the Pressburg coronations took place in the Franciscan church. It was the promotion of selected aristocrats to the **Knights of the Golden Spur**.

Left: Promotion to the Knight
    of the Golden Spur
Right: The pulpit of the Jesuit church

There are three chapels around the Franciscan church. Two of them are next to the northern side of the nave and the third is near the sacristy. The oldest Gothic church from the end of the 13th century had its chapel which was consecrated a year before the church was. It was probably pulled down on the orders of the mayor Jakub II, who wanted to build a new one: the still existing **chapel of St. John the Evangelist**. The Gothic building is a very pure and balanced example of a two storied burial chapel. The famous Sainte Chapelle of Paris inspired its creators. They were indeed successful. Pressburg acquired one of its most beautiful Gothic buildings.

The **chapel of St. Rozália** originated afterwards. It was built in the 15th century and consecrated to St. Sebastián. It was placed on the opposite side of the church and it can be seen from the open plot in front of the Ursuline church in Uršulínska ulica street. The third chapel is the youngest and adjoins the first chapel. It dates from 1708. Like additions to some other churches, its interior tries to imitate the legendary dwelling of the Virgin Mary in Loretto. For this reason it is called the **Loretánska kaplnka** that is the Loretto Chapel.

The best view of the couple of very different chapels next to the northern wall of the Franciscan church is from the short Franciscan street. It was originally a lane inside the wall of the northern fortifications of the medieval town. It was first mentioned in 1457. Besides the abovementioned chapels there is another interesting building on Františkánska street. The House of Hussites or **Husitský dom** at No. 3 stands right in front of them.

The **Jesuit Church** in the lower part of the square was not always owned by the Jesuits. The German Evangelicals of Pressburg built the church following the royal consent in 1636. The re-Catholicizing pressure became stronger during the reign of King Leopold I and Archbishop Szelepcsényi took away the temple of the Evangelicals. The German church was given to the **Jesuits** who dedicated it to **the Most Holy Saviour**. The new administrators of the church started its recon-

struction. The facade remained almost intact, except for the original Renaissance **portal**. Jesuits installed a lavishly ornamented and **multi-coloured symbol of their order** on it. **The main altar** from the 19th century bears the picture of Christ on the Mountain of Tábor by S. Majsch.

Sightseeing of the square ends under the **pillar of the Virgin Mary the Victorious** which the oldest of the kind in the Kingdom of Hungary. It belongs to the group of pillars built by the Habsburg's all over the country in honour of their military successes. The one of Františkánske námestie stands here since 1675.

The Primaciálne námestie square

Today's appearance of the Primatial square is the result of recent reconstruction finished in 1976. The new pavement is cherished especially by young roller skaters. Archaeologists used the occasion and at the time of reconstruction discovered an **old well**, which has been included in the renovated area of the square.

The **Primatial Palace**, which with his bulky building occupies the whole south-

ern side of the Primatial square, is considered the most beautiful in Bratislava. It was built in the years 1778-1781 on the site of an older Archbishop's palace. The front wing overlooking the Primatial square is strictly Neo Classical.

One enters the Primatial palace through a three-axial vestibule where a wide flight of stairs leads to the main halls on the first floor or Piano nobile. It overlooks the square and is directly connected with the main representative hall of the palace in its eastern wing. The huge hall looks even bigger because of the numerous mirrors on its walls. It is called the **Zrkadlová sieň** or the Hall of Mirrors. The role of the mirrors was to make the hall look bigger but above all to improve the lighting. The buildings surrounding the Primatial palace shade it and reduce its lighting. The 1805 Christmas season was a time celebrated by the French as one of their historic moments. After the battle at Austerlitz representatives of the countries which took part in it met in the Primatial

Left: The Primacial square
Right: The ceiling of St. Ladislav chapel

palace. The victorious Napoleon Bonaparte was represented by his Minister of Foreign Affairs Maurice Talleyrand and Prince John of Liechtenstein represented the defeated Emperor Francis I. The treaty, later called the **Peace of Pressburg** was signed on December 26th 1805 in the Hall of Mirrors. Austria lost the territories of Tyrol, Istria, Dalmatia, and Venice and her access to the sea. France gained self-assurance and greed. The memory of the Peace of Pressburg was expressed by giving the name of the city to one of the Paris streets: *Rue de Presbourg* still existing near the Arc de Triomphe. The city bought the palace in 1903 with the intention to expand the Town Hall. During reconstruction of the palace some folded pieces of cloth were found. When they were spread on the floor of the corridor, the astounded custodian of the Municipal Museum August Heimar found out that it was a series of precious tapestries now known as the **Bratislava tapestries**. The Archbishop as owner of the palace gave up the precious find in favour of the city with the particular that they would be displayed in public. But first they had to be restored in the artistic workshops of Belmonte in Hungarian town of Gödölő. The German expert and connoisseur of tapestries W. Zisch from Berlin estimated that the tapestries of Bratislava were made at the royal weaving workshop at Mortlake near London. The trade mark woven into the edge used by this particular workshop in the years 1616-1688 is the proof. The series of tapestries was made after the cartoons painted by Francis Cleyn from Rozstock. Tapestries were woven on wool and silk and the style of this true work of art is called mannerism.

The story of Hero and Leandros

The sad story of the couple of immortal lovers has been the subject of many artistic works of different genres. It originated in the fifth century before Christ in verses of a mythological poet, an alleged pupil of the divine Orpheus. Four centuries later it was refreshed by the great Ovidius, who brought the lyrical love poetry to the very peak of perfection. The Mortlake weavers used this story and transformed it into the woven beauty in six big tapestries creating one complete series. The story took place on the coast of the antique Helespont strait (today's Dardanelles). The Greek Leandros fell in love with beautiful Hero, who lived on the opposite shore of the strait. The first of the series of Bratislava tapestries called The Meeting of Hero with Leandros *depicts the first encounter of the lovers at a ceremony, where they fell in love with each other. Since then Leandros undertook every night the troublesome and exhausting journey of swimming across the strait to see his beloved Hero (*Leandros swimming to Hero*). The light of the lamp at the window of Hero's house showed him the way. The third tapestry called* Janthe announces Leandros' arrival to Hero *represents the moment when the tired, though happy Leandro overcomes the last stretch of the journey. The fourth tapestry is called* Hermiona tries to discourage Leandros from the passage over the strait. *The overall mood of the scene depicted on the tapestry is distressing, Leandros did not obey the warning of his sister and entered the turbulent waters of Helespont. When the wind put out the flame in Hero's lamp, Leandros lost his way in the dark and got drowned in the sea. Eventually a wave threw his dead body out on the shore, where the desperate Hero found it. The tragic end of the story is depicted on the fifth tapestry called* Hero mourns dead Leandros. *Hero responded in the same way as Juliet from* Romeo and Juliet' *story: She jumped from a steep cliff into the waves of the Helespont to meet her beloved on the way to immortality. The last tapestry* The mourning Eros *is the epilogue to the story. The little god of love is contemplating the water of Helespont and thinking about the unfortunate lovers Leandros and Hero.*

In the vestibule there is also a passage to the inner square courtyard. In its centre is the **fountain of St. George**. The group of statues made of sandstone represents the legendary knight fighting against a dragon.

In the back and on the right there is the **chapel of St. Ladislav**. Its interior with oval ground plan contains a couple of fairly precious artistic works. The dome of

the chapel is adorned by remarkable **illusionist fresco** called *The Miracle of St. Ladislav*. The presumed artist is A. F. Maulbertsch. The wall painting represents a scene from the life of St. Ladislav, King of Hungarian from the Arpad dynasty who, as a legend says, opened a rock cliff by a single stroke of his lance and the rock released a spring of water for his thirsty soldiers.

Opposite the Primatial palace is **Nová radnica** (the New Town Hall). This modern building replaced the 17th century Jesuit monastery demolished in 1948.

The eastern side of today's Primatial palace is closed by the buildings, which have their entrances from Uršulínska and Klobúčnícka streets. **Klobúčnícka ulica street** as we see it now, is a comparatively young street. It was built in the 18th century, though there must have been some street before, in the Middle Ages. Perhaps the one called today Nedbalova. When the town walls were pulled down in 1775, the eastern part of the inner town was rearranged. New buildings covered the narrow and winding lanes of the medieval quarter of merchants and crafts-

men. The dominating building of Klobučnícka street is the Neo Baroque tenement house No. 2 from 1910. In the yard of the smart four-storied house with attic roof is what is called **Hummel's house**. It is a small and picturesque Renaissance house often denoted as the native house of **Johann Nepomuk Hummel** (1778-1837). This world famous composer and pianist though, was born in the house, which existed there before. Hummel's house contains now part of the **musical exhibition** of the Municipal Museum, which documents the life and work of the composer, and the musical history of Bratislava.

Around today's **Nedbalova ulica street**, perpendicular to Klobučnícka, was the **Jewish ghetto** with a synagogue.

Nedbalova ulica, as we know it now, originated as the street skirting the town walls of the medieval town. It followed the eastern section of the fortifications. Opposite the school standing near the crossroads with Klobučnícka street there is a preserved **section of the town wall** from

the 15th century. The inner part of the stone wall reaching the height of the neighbouring two-storied house is visible here.

Uršulínska ulica street connects Laurinská street with Primatial square and the square of the SNP. The **Ursuline church** and **monastery** at its western corner unifies the eastern row of the Ursuline Street. Before the nuns came, the Evangelicals occupied the western edge of Bratislava's former Jewish ghetto. The Evangelicals built the church in 1640 for their Slovak and Hungarian believers. The Ursulines consecrated the church to the **Virgin Mary of Loretto**. The outer appearance was not changed at the beginning and the simplicity of style was preserved until 1745 when a wooden church tower with onion shaped roof was built next to it. Extensive adjustments were made in the interior of the church. Shortly after the arrival of children, the Ursulines built a new **main altar** with a **statue of the Black Madonna**, a copy of the Virgin Mary of Loretto. The painting of St. Augustín and St. Anna on the lateral altars were painted by M. Speer. The Ursu-

Left: The Bratislava Castle

line monastery was started on the site of the former Jewish ghetto in 1676 and its construction took ten years. Due to the support of Archbishop Emerich Esterházy the monastery was enlarged in 1731.

The Bratislava Castle

The monumental building of **Bratislava Castle** that cannot be confused with any other building in the city is visible from a great distance. Certainly every visitor of Bratislava notices the pronounced silhouette similar to an overturned table. The majestic impression is enhanced by the hill it stands on some eighty-five metres above the water level of the Danube.

The inhabitants of the height settlement left the oldest traces here from the end of the **Younger Stone Age**. They were the people using what the experts call volute pottery. The castle hill above the Danube was not deserted in the Iron Age either. People who left us heaps of objects evidencing their skills in crafts and cultural progress settled it. Pottery, jewellery and Celtic coins made several decades BC were found on the castle hill as well as down in the city. Immediately after the Celts left, the Germanic tribes and Romans came. The castle hill had a special function within the system of **Great Moravian fortified settlements**. It was an important fortified settlement in the last third of the 9th century as it is mentioned in the Salzburg annals in relation to a bloody battle between the Bavarians and early Magyars. On the western side of the hill where a medieval castle was later built there was a seat of some noble. The Church with a three-nave **stone basilica** and a cemetery occupied the eastern part of the hill top. The whole settlement was skirted by a defensive wall made of thick oak logs connected into chambers filled with earth and stones. Fortification enclosed an area equalling in size to six football grounds.

Building activity documented by archaeology took place on the castle hill of Bratislava as early as the 10th century. But another three centuries were needed before at the site of the old settlement a Romanesque castle was built, attributed to the period of the Arpád dynasty. Its re-

sulting form, which it acquired in the 13th century, was preceded by a comparatively complicated development. First there was a pre-Romanesque **stone palace** in the 11th and 12th centuries. The fortification of the castle hill made use of the defensive system of the previous fortified settlement. In the second half of the 13th century the castle progressively gained the shape of the Romanesque **Arpád period castle,** which it kept until the Gothic reconstruction carried out in time of King Sigismund in the first half of the 15th century. Solid stone castle walls with a high prismatoid tower were built around it. The plan of the Arpád period castle can be seen on the pavement of the courtyard of the existing castle palace. They are discernible by different colour of the paving stones. The tower is the only building element of the Romanesque castle that was preserved until now. After numerous building adjustments it became the core of the biggest of the castle towers later called **Korunná veža** (Crown Tower). It is the only one, which does not stand on the castle wall, but it has its foundation in the ground and stands outside the ground plan. Generous reconstruction of the castle started in 1423 during the rule of Sigismund of Luxembourg, but it was not finished in time of his death in 1437. The result of this reconstruction was a Gothic castle referred to in literature as a **Sigismund's castle**. Two semicircular cannon **bastions** reinforced the castle walls. The northern bastion was called **Luginsland**. Even today it is the dominant architectural element of Bratislava's castle well visible from the Hodžovo or Župné squares. A new entrance to the castle via **Žigmundova brána** (Sigismund's Gate) was built on the steep slope of the castle hill above the Danube.

Only the **tower** at the south-western corner was left while the older architecture was pulled down. An impressive four-wing palace with a square courtyard was added to the tower. The western wing fulfilled another important role, that of defence because it was on the most vulnerable side of the castle hill. This was the reason why the thickness of its wall was doubled. The seven meter thick walls were in-

Left: Fire in 1811
Right: Exposition of the Jewish culture

deed unique in Europe. Only the arrival of Emperor Fedinand of Habsburg brought about a positive change in the history of Pressburg Castle. The castle became an important strategic point in country's defence after the Mohács tragedy and fall of Buda in 1526.

When the Emperor's intention to modernize the Pressburg Castle was approved by the Diet in 1552, the **Renaissance restoration of the castle area** could start. The result of the 1552-1562 reconstruction was a well-fortified and simultaneously luxurious Renaissance seat of one of the most powerful rulers in Europe at that time.

Reconstruction of the castle generally referred to as **Pálffy's** was carried out in the period of the fading Renaissance style. Pálffy's luxurious castle palace was a part of ambitious plan for reconstruction of the whole castle hill, with the settlement below it included in a massive fort with a complicated system of bastions and ramparts arranged in an irregular seven-

pointed star. Out of this extensive project led by the Italian builder Jozef Priami only a tiny part was made reality. Only two cannon bastions were added to the castle. A long tunnel was drilled under the southwestern one. The tunnel was used as an entrance gate and its name was **Leopoldova brána** (Leopold's Gate). However, it proved to be an error as it was not conveniently situated and moreover it was rather unattractive from the architectural point of view. A new and more pompous entrance gate was started. Since it was situated on the western edge of the castle hill and as it was on the road from Vienna it acquired the name **Viedenská brána** (Vienna gate). This gate similar to Antique triumphal arches was ceremoniously opened on the occasion of Charles III's coronation in 1712. It has remained the main entrance to the area of Bratislava Castle until today.

The last stage of big building adjustments of the Pressburg Castle was accomplished under the orders of Queen Maria Theresa. The ruler tried to rid the castle of any outdated functions of the former military fort as the political climate of the 18th century was that of relative peace. She had all fortifying elements removed and simultaneously improved or widened its residential function complying with the criteria of what was considered the utmost luxury. The works pursuing the project of reconstruction as presented by the imperial architects Jean Nicolas Jadot, Giovanni Batista Martinelli and Nicolas Pacassi started in 1755. The castle now called **Theresian** was prepared to serve the royal court in 1765. The obvious and intentional disproportion between the dreary exterior and impressive interior was again applied. Money not spent on the outer appearance was invested in the interior of the castle. The simplicity of the outer facades complied with the canons of Classicising Baroque. In front of the southern facade a couple of Baroque guard houses were built and on the southern terrace a kind of **čestné nádvorie** (courtyard of honour) was created. The most interesting building though was that of the **Theresianum** built next to the eastern side of the palace in 1768. This lovely Rococo palace was the seat of the Governor, Prince Albert, who acquired the office after he married Archduchess Maria Christina, daughter of Queen Maria Theresa. But the palace burned down in 1811.

The rococo taste was also applied in the decoration of the state rooms of the old palace. The prettiest sample of the style was the **stairway** that originated by partial demolition of the massive peripheral wall of the western wing of the palace from the times of King Sigismund. Its beauty was enhanced by the most recent restoration.

The departure of the Governor Albert in 1780 meant the end of the good times for Pressburg Castle. It lost its noble lord and artistic collections, and the crown jewels were moved to Vienna. Joseph II' intentions for the abandoned castle were quite different. He had it adapted for a newly established **General Seminary**. The castle was in hands of the Church until 1802 when it was passed over to the army. But the army did not stay long. In May 1811, a devastating fire burst out in the castle and soon spread to the Podhradie or the settlement below the castle.

For the next hundred and fifty years the people had to tolerate the sad picture of the destroyed castle on top of the hill, a vanishing symbol of the city's past glory. The most important phase of the castle's reconstruction was finished in 1968. The palace was prepared for ceremonious opening on October 28th and signature of the Act on the Czech-Slovak Federation. **Three lime trees** planted next to the Great Moravian basilica at the southern corner of the eastern terrace commemorate the event. Renovation of the Bratisla-

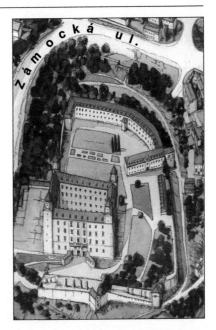

va castle though has not finished. Several historical buildings including the above mentioned Theresianum palace should be reconstructed in the future.

Some parts of the castle are open to the public. They contain permanent exhibitions of the **Slovak National Museum**. There is an exhibition of **historical furniture** in the main palace and a remarkable collection of exhibits called the **Jewels of Slovakia's Remote Past**. Exhibits documenting the **history of musical instruments** are displayed in Luginsland bastion.

The Western part of the Staré Mesto

The western part of the Old Town is quite different from the other parts. It spreads over the foothills of the Little Carpathians and its urban fabric consists predominantly of family houses. On a flat hill at its south-eastern edge is the **Bratislava Castle** and on its eastern and southern slopes is Podhradie, the historic settlement below the castle.

Several buildings in Beblavá, Židovská, Mikulášska streets and at the stairway called Zámocké schody deserve attention. Let us look at them and start with the house at the lower end of **Židovská ulica street**, which is rightly, considered one of the most beautiful in Bratislava. It is the impressive **Dom u dobrého pastiera** (House of the Good Shepherd, Židovská ulica street No. 1) and its conspicuously slender construction makes it the best specimen of small-scale Rococo architecture in Bratislava. Its name derives from a tiny statue of Christ – Good Shepherd – standing on its corner. It was built in 1760. Since 1975 the House of the Good Shepherd has sheltered the **exposition of historic clocks** of the Municipal Museum. Also the collection of portable sun dials from the 16th- 18th centuries is interesting. **Zsigray's curia** standing at the opposite end of Židovská street (No 7) offers the opportunity to see the exhibits of the **Museum of Jewish Culture in Slovakia** explaining

the history of the Jewish community of Bratislava and Slovakia. On the slope of the castle hill above **Mikulášska ulica street** there stands the **St. Nicholas'** (Sv. Mikuláš) **church**. Originally there was rotunda later replaced by Gothic church from the 14th century. The church standing there now is a Baroque building from 1661. Count Pálffy's widow had it built. The church has belonged to the followers of the Eastern Orthodox Church since 1950. The most frequently used access road to the castle since the Early Middle Ages was **Zámocká ulica street**. The Jews inhabited it from the 17th century. The orthodox part of the Jewish community built a synagogue there in 1863. On the outer side of the street was the big Pálffy's garden. In the lower part of the street, the **pension and restaurant Chez David** provides excellent Jewish cuisine.

Beblavého ulica street climbs the castle hill from the corner of the House of the Good Shepherd. It was the shortest possible connection between the castle and St. Martin's Minster. As the famous Hungarian poet Sándor Petöfi lived in its upper part the street bore his name for

Left: The Bratislavské vŕšky hills
Right: The house of the Good Shepherd

some time. Today it offers an opportunity to sit and chat in pleasant stylish little cafés and restaurants in venerable houses from the 18th century. At the lower end of Beblavého street stands the Late Baroque **house No. 1** from the late 18th century. It contains the **Museum of crafts** exhibiting works of artisans made of glass, porcelain, various types of jewels, toys and liturgical objects. In the upper part of **Zámocké schody stairs** are two Renaissance houses from the beginning of the 17th century. The house on the corner of Beblavého was once the **Town Hall of Podhradie**. After Podhradie obtained municipal privileges in 1713 the magistrate consisting of six aldermen and a notary used to have sessions in the house. The former Town Hall is now the **Arkadia restaurant**, a smart place, the name of which derives from its main architectural feature – an open pillar arcade passing through two of its wings.

The round hills of Bratislava spreading from Štefánikova ulica street up to Dolná Mlynská dolina valley were for centuries a viticultural landscape with scattered little huts. This attractive locality acquired a new function only in the first half of the 20th century. The footpaths between the plots changed to streets built up with elegant villas; the property of the Bratislava's privileged class and social elite. The locality is the most expensive and most luxurious quarter of the city. It main street is **Mudroňova ulica street**, originally called *Kaiserweg* or the Emperor's Road. Next to the castle on the Vodný vrch hill is the modern **building of the National Council of the Slovak Republic**. It was opened in May 1994 and the Slovak Parliament moved here from its old seat in Župné námestie. The new buildings of Parliament also include the popular **Parlamentka restaurant** with a terrace above the Danube offering a wide view of the city.

At the upper end of Mudroňova in the north-east is **Murmannova výšina** hill with the **House of Ekoiuventa** built in 1952, colloquially called "Michurin" (surname of Soviet scientist known for bold experimentation with plants). The building is a perfect sample of what is called

Stalinist architecture. It is still serving its original purpose – it provides space for children's leisure activities. Stará vinárska ulica street starting nearby leads to the neighbouring height (252 m) with the **monument Slavín** and military cemetery where 6,845 Soviet soldiers who died while liberating Bratislava by the end of April of 1945 are buried. When the war was over all soldiers who died in the are of western Slovakia were concentrated to this cemetery. Architect J. Svetlík designed the project of the monument and it was finished in 1960. It stands in a park boasting various wood species brought here from different areas of the former Soviet Union. The eastern terrace of the hill provides a panoramic view of the city.

The Northern part of the Staré Mesto

The quarters in the north of the historic centre of Bratislava are full of contrasts. There are busy wide streets and romantic narrow alleys. One can walk in wide squares and pleasant parks. Vener-

Left: Interior of the Trinitarian church

able buildings breathing with history stand side by side with modern buildings. In the northern part of the centre are the buildings of the government, ministries, the Presidential Palace and the seats of many other central administrative bodies and institutions. The main railway station in the northern centre is the place of the first contact with the city for visitors to Bratislava.

Several squares originated around the disappeared town walls. One of them is **Župné námestie square** connected with the contiguous Hurbanovo square in the east. In the Middle Ages it was the site of the settlement of St. Michael, which later developed into a suburb. In time of Turkish wars the aldermen themselves decided to demolish the suburbs for the sake of better control over the immediate space beyond the town walls. Such was the destiny of the St. Michael suburb including its Gothic church bearing the name of the same patron saint. It was pulled down in 1529. The **Trinitarian order** later built one of the most beautiful Baroque

churches in the town on its ruins.

When the Trinitarians left, the building was given to the county administration. But it was not suitable for the offices. It was pulled down and in its place a new **Župný dom** (County House) for the Pressburg county administration office was built in 1844. In the years 1939-1994 the Slovak legislative bodies held their sessions in the Župný dom and after 1945 it became the seat of the Slovak National Council (in 1992 renamed to the National Council of the Slovak Republic). Since 1994 the sessions of the Slovak Parliament are held in a new building on the Vodný vrch hill.

The shortest western side of the triangular Župné námestie coincides with the facade of the **Capuchin church** consecrated to **St. Stephen of Hungary**. The Capuchin church was consecrated by Bishop L. A. Erdödy of Nitra in 1717. Part of the church was pulled down and rebuilt in 1735. The space in front of the Capuchin church is adorned by the **Morový stĺp** (Plaque pillar).

The environs of **Panenská ulica street** belonged to the Pressburg Evangelicals or Lutherans since the late 17th century. They lost their two churches in the town centre in 1672 and a special imperial commission prohibited the Evangelical service in the inner town. They were ordered out to the northern suburb, a scarcely built area between the Suché mýto and Kozia gates. Construction of the **Large Evangelical Church** on Panenská ulica took place in years 1774-1777. The architect M. Walch tried to imitate the original German Evangelical Church, which used to stand near the Old Town Hall. It is built in the Neo-Classical style. The building is divided into three naves by prismoid pillars. The interior has got excellent acoustics, an asset appreciated by music lovers, who attend concerts held in this church. The **altar** from 1776 forms a whole with the **pulpit**. The artist who created the altar is P. Brandenthal. A. F. Oeser, a Pressburg native, painted the **painting of the altar**: *Christ in Emaus*. A year after opening of the Large Evangelical Church the Slovak and Hungarian Evangelicals also built theirs. The **small**

Evangelical Church on Panenská stands on the site of the former wooden articled church from 1682. It is again Walch's design and it is equally simple. The interior of the church on an irregular ground plan was modernized in the 1970's. The original furniture from the 18th century with the exception of the altar and pulpit was not preserved.

Konventná ulica street is closely associated with Evangelical schooling in Pressburg, the beginnings of which date to 1606. The Evangelical community of Pressburg was one of the largest in Hungary in the early 18th century. It associated about seven thousand believers of the three nationalities. The community invited to its Lycée in Pressburg **Matej Bell** (1684-1749), the former student of this institution in 1714, immediately after the retreat of the plague epidemic. It soon became obvious that it was a good move. Matej Bel was not only a scientist of world importance, but also a good teacher and educator. He wrote and published text books, adapted the Latin grammar and initiated the publishing of the newspaper *Nova Posoniensia* (Pressburg Newspaper) in Latin. He became the first priest of the German Evangelical Church and the chancellor of the Lycée. For his scientific achievements he was referred to as *Magnum Decus Hungariae* (The Great Ornament of Hungary).

In 1783 the still existing building of what is called the **old Evangelical Lycée** (No. 15) on Konventná street was built. Although the Pressburg Lycée was a German school above all with tuition in Latin, numerous students of Slav nationalities attended it. Slovaks, Czechs, Serbs and Croatians were among them. This is why the Lycée gradually became a place where the idea of Pan-Slavic solidarity spread.

The Evangelical community of Pressburg started to plan construction of a new building for the Lycée after the revolutionary years 1848 and 1849 were over. This was realized in the years 1854-1855 in the neighbourhood of the old building. The **new building of the Evangelical Lycée** (No. 13) is the work of the architect Gottfried Bendl who built it in the Neo Classical style.

Suché mýto square appeared in the historic documents in 1375 under the name *Dauermauth*. It was the medieval toll entrance into the inner suburbs through the gate and bridge over the moat. The modern Suché mýto is completely different in comparison with the past. Demolition of old houses and reconstruction of the transport system connected Suché mýto with what is now **Hodžovo námestie square** into one big open space framed by modern buildings. One of them is the **Forum Hotel** on the south-eastern side of the square. The hotel built according to design of the architect J. Hauskrecht has a capacity of 450 beds and was opened in 1988.

The dominant building of Hodžovo námestie square is the **Presidential Palace** built after 1760 as the **garden palace of Anton Grassalkovich**. The building of this wonderful Rococo palace was outside the town and it was placed between the garden of the summer Archbishop's Palace and the town. The Chairman of the Hungarian Royal Court Chamber, the guard of the crown, comes of the Novohrad County, Anton Grassalkovich

had it built. The central architectural element of the palace is the **pavilion** in its middle from which **two palace wings** spread. In front of the palace is a **courtyard** skirted by an impressive fence with a pair of gilded metal gates.

Grassalkovich's garden originated simultaneously with the palace. Originally there were vases and baskets with flowers, cypresses and oleanders. It was partially opened to the public in the late 19th century. It was repeatedly modified. The last modification was made in 1999. The Grassalkovich Palace became the seat of the President in 1939. In the years of the Second World War it served the President of the Slovak State, Jozef Tiso. The top representative of the state returned to the palace when the Slovak Republic achieved its independence in 1993. It was adapted as the presidential residence of President Michal Kováč. The Palace, in contrast to the garden, is not accessible to the public except for occasional "open door days ". The space in front of the palace got the

Left: Grassalkovich's garden
Right: Obchodná ulica street

fountain called **the Earth, Planet of Peace** made by Tibor Bártfay in 1982.

The buildings on Štefánikova ulica and the contiguous streets are mainly smart residential houses, which document the wide range of architectural styles, used in the city.

The **letný arcibiskupský palác** (summer Archbishop's Palace) on the upper part of Námestie slobody square lived through the good and bad times together with the garden. Today it is the seat of the **Office of the Government of the Slovak Republic**.

The Eastern part of the Staré Mesto

This part of the centre attracts the shoppers and visitors of Bratislava, because it has the majority of shops, shopping centres, and department stores. The busiest spot is the **Námestie Slovenského národného povstania** (SNP) or Square of the Slovak National Uprising. Its current name SNP has been used since 1962. It commemorates one of the biggest national anti-Nazi uprisings in Europe which burst out in Central Slovakia at the end of August 1944. **The monument to the SNP** with a trio of big bronze statues by Ján Kulich is associated with this significant event of the modern Slovak history.

In the upper part of the square is the spacious building of the **Old** or **Main Post Office** (houses Nos. 34-36).

A bit lower, on the corner of Uršulinska street, is the building of the **Tatrabanka** (No. 33) built in the years 1922-1925. Milan Michal Harminc was its designer. When it was under construction the workers found at the site a unique treasure of 399 Celtic coins. The building was used by the Slovak Television and now it is the seat of the Ministry of Culture. Left form Tatrabanka is the **Dom odievania** (House of Clothing, No. 31) built in the years 1978-1985 following the design of the architects Peter Minarovič and Ján Bahna. The left neighbour of this building is an interesting construction **Obchodný dom Dunaj** (No. 30). It is one of the oldest of Bratislava's department stores, dating from 1936 and originally called Brouk a Babka after its owners. The last building of the SNP square on the lower end of the side bordering with historical part of the city is the building known under the name **Manderla** (No. 23). This eleven-storied house is the first of Bratislava's "skyscrapers", and for long the tallest building in the city. It was built in 1935 for the rich businessman trading in meat Rudolf Manderla.

The dominating building of the north-western side of the triangle-shaped SNP square is the Neo Romanesque **Calvinist church** with a tall tower. It was designed

by the architect F. Wimmer and built in 1913. The biggest building of the square though is the **church and monastery of the Merciful Brothers** (Milosrdných bratov) in the north-east.

Obchodná ulica street starts at Hurbanovo námestie square and runs in north-eastern direction. It is one of the oldest streets that existed outside the medieval fortifications.

If you continue from Obchodná to Radlinská ulica street you enter the area where there was the **Blumentál suburb** in the past. It developed from a medieval settlement. Its original German name *Blumenthal* (Flower Valley) appears in the historic sources from the 17th century. On the farther side of the suburb the outer earthen dikes were built. The striking feature of this quarter of the eastern city centre is the Roman Catholic **church** of the **Ascension of the Virgin Mary**, better known by the public as **blumentálsky kostol** (the Blumentál church). It is the parish church of the quarter Nové Mesto established in 1770 for the believers in the suburbs. The existing parish church was built in the years 1885-1888.

The **Špitálska ulica street** starts in the SNP square and heads to the northeast. Its name is linked to the fact it has been the site of several hospitals since the Middle Ages. As early as 1307 the municipal council agreed with the Antonite Order about administration of the hospital built on plots east of the town. The municipal **hospital of St. Anton** stood opposite today's St. Ladislav's church. The hospital was demolished along with the Špitálska brána gate standing near in fear from the Turkish attacks in 1529. It was restored at the order of Ferdinand I in 1543 when the Turkish raids finished. Next to the **hospital of St. Ladislav** was a cemetery with a chapel. The central architecture of the complex is **St. Ladislav's church**.

Some metres away from St. Ladislav's church are the **Elisabethan church and monastery**.

Dunajská ulica street starts in the lower part of the SNP square and heads eastward. It originated from what used to

Left: The Blue Church
Right: The Danube embankment

be the Danube trade road running from Pressburg over the ford near Prievoz outside the town. In the 15th century Dunajská brána gate was built near where Rajská ulica street starts. This gate was the easternmost passage through the palisade fortifications. The first reference to the gate is from 1493 and it was pulled down in 1825.

The quarter south of Dunajská ulica street originated only at the beginning of the 20th century. The citizens of Pressburg called this area of alluvial forests, wet meadows and gardens *Grössling*, the name perhaps derived from the German word for the Danube fish *kressling*. Before the later half of the 19th century only several bold fellows built houses in this land flooded only too often. The track of a horse railway crossed the area in 1845 approximately coinciding with today's Dostojevský rad street. Only after the Danube arms were filled and the main river channel regulated, did the lands become more attractive for builders. By the end of the 19th and beginning of the 20th centuries modern blocks of flats were built here creating a rectangular street network.

The new quarter lying next to Starý most bridge also got a new church in 1913 thanks to Countess G. M. Szapáry. It was a beautiful one, still to be seen on **Bezručova ulica street**, and known by the natives as **Modrý kostolík** or the Blue Church. It is a wonderful example of the Art Noveau style in sacred architecture.

Šafárikovo námestie square originated after 1891, when the first fixed bridge was built over the Danube.

Varied buildings frame Šafárikovo námestie square. One of the most recent is the **Comenius University** (house No. 5). Architect F. Krupka built it in 1930 for the stock exchange following the winning design. Today it is the seat of the vice chancellor's office, Faculty of Law and part of Faculty of Philosophy of Comenius University.

Let us go via **Štúrova ulica street** back to Námestie SNP square where we start our trip around the eastern centre. Today's Štúrova ulica was only a narrow alley heading across Grössling to the main bed of the Danube until the latter half of the 19th century. One of few big buildings,

which used to stand here, was Landerer's palace. When in 1891 the **bridge of Francis Joseph** (the existing Old Bridge) was opened, the narrow street gained importance and it changed to one of the most beautiful and elegant Pressburg streets. Tenement houses in the Art Noveau style that provided luxurious housing for the better-off social classes built it up.

Bratislava's embankment

Today the area around the embankment of the city between the historic centre and the left bank of the Danube are the favourite routes of walks, occasional visits to a museum or gallery or meetings in one of the boat hotel restaurants on the river. The route starting at the Old Town and heading up stream toward the Botanical Garden is perhaps the most popular one for a Sunday afternoon walk.

The first part of the route runs along **Fajnorovo nábrežie embankment** bearing the name of the Evangelical bishop and writer **Dušan Fajnor** (1876-1933). Even before the origin of embankment the

oldest of the existing four Bratislava bridges over the Danube, now called the **Starý most** (Old Bridge), was built. The bridge opened a day before the New Year's Eve of 1890 and remained the only over the Danube in Bratislava for another 83 years. In the space between Fajnorovo and Vajanského nábrežie embankments is the **building of the Slovak National Museum** built in the years 1924-1928 for the branch of the Czech *Zemědělské museum* or Museum of Agriculture. Now the Museum contains exhibitions of natural history. The monument to the Czech and Slovak statehood adorns the space in front of the Museum. It was ceremoniously introduced to the public on October 28th of 1988. A bronze **statue of lion** leaning on the state symbol of the former Czechoslovakia stands on almost fifteen metres tall pylon.

The passenger port Danubius is at the eastern end of Fajnorovo embankment. It operated sightseeing navigation on the Danube.

Vajanského nábrežie embankment bears the name of the Slovak politician, journalist, and writer, **Svetozár Hurban**

Vajanský (1847-1916). The most interesting building on Vajanského embankment from the architectural point of view is **Jurenák Palace** (house No. 4). In this Neo Classical house of burgher K. Jurenák, composer **Johannes Brahms** (1833-1897) stayed during his visit to Pressburg. Next to the building of the Slovak Philharmonic Orchestra the embankment opens onto **Námestie Ľudovíta Štúra square** skirted by elegant buildings. Until 1938 it bore the name *Coronation square* as it used to be the setting of the final ceremony of coronations. Now there is the **monument of Ľudovít Štúr**, made by T. Bartfay and J. Salay and erected in 1972.

On the eastern side of the square is **Lanfranconi Palace** (No. 1). It was built in the later half of the 19th century on the site of the former salt office. Successful Pressburg businessman E. Lanfranconi ordered construction of the Neo Renaissance house designed by Ignác Feigler junior. What is interesting about the building is its roof construction, which was moved here from the Viennese World Exhibition. The building now belongs to the Ministry of the Environment of the Slovak Republic. Opposite is the **Dessewffy Palace** (No. 2). It was built in the latter half of the 19th century and the name derives from its owner Count Dessewffy. It used to be one of the most elegant and luxurious palaces in the city. Original ornamentation and antique furnishing from the 17th and 18th centuries in its interior partially survived.

The short **Mostová** (The Bridge) **ulica street** connects Námestie Ľudovíta Štúra with Hviezdoslavovo námestie squares.

Left: The Slovak National Theatre
Right: The Water Tower

Now the principal landmark of this street is the **Reduta** building. It was built in 1911-1915 as designed by the Budapest architects M. Komor and D. Jakab. The monumental silhouette of this elegant building tries to copy the basic shape of the older building of the **provincial granary** which was built here in the years 1773-1774. The Reduta is now the seat of the **Slovak Philharmonic Orchestra**. Occasionally it hosts the top domestic and foreign musical ensembles and outstanding soloists of classic music. The concert season culminates in the **Bratislava Music Festival** organized in Autumn every year.

Hviezdoslavovo námestie square is a wonderful and lively place. The most impressive building on Hviezdoslavovo námestie square is the **Slovak National Theatr**. The elegant eclectic theatre building has adorned the city since 1886. The SND put on dramas and operas until 1955 when the drama ensemble moved to a separate new building on Laurinská street leaving the stage of the SND to ballet and opera only. The SND hosted some important figures of world opera and ballet. It was also here where several opera stars of Slovak origin started their careers: Peter Dvorský, Edita Grúberová, and Lucia Poppová.

The space in front of the SND building is adorned by **Ganymedes' fountain**. The fountain is the present of the First Pressburg Savings Bank. Ganymedes' fountain is not the only artistic work on the rectangular area of Hviezdoslavovo námestie square. There is also the **monument to the poet P. O. Hviezdoslav with its fountain** standing here since 1937.

The south-eastern part of Hviezdoslavovo námestie square widens into a small squarish area with a park. This was the plot originally reserved for the **church of the St. Augustin of Notre Dame female order**. Only the chancel with a little porch added in the 19th century was built. The park with the adjacent area of Hviezdoslavovo námestie square was the place where the "**candle demonstration**" took place on March 25th 1988. The security units using water cannons cruelly attacked the calmly protesting and praying believers with lit candles.

Rázusovo nábrežie embankment running from Námestie Ľudovíta Štúra to the New Bridge was created in the 18th century in the place where there was a fishermen's village before. Building in this space started in the mid-19th century and the embankment was called Dunajské. Now it bears the mane of the Slovak poet, writer and politician **Martin Rázus** (1888-1937).

The oldest building on Rázusovo embankment is the compound of former barracks called **Vodné kasárne**. The building was adapted in the years 1949-1951 for the **Slovak National Gallery** (SNG). The collections of the SNG include the most important works of the Slovak fine arts since the 13th century until the present time and examples of European arts from the 15th to 18th centuries. Beside the permanent collections, interesting temporary exhibitions are sometimes held. West of the SNG complex is the **Devín Hotel** (entrance is from Riečna ulica street). It originated in 1954 according to the plans of an outstanding Slovak architect E. Belluš.

The western part of the Rázusovo embankment has undergone dramatic changes since the end of the 1960's. In 1973 the second bridge over the Danube was built in this place. A great part of old Bratislava was pulled down. The bridge's original name *Most SNP* (The Bridge of the Slovak National Uprising) was recently changed to **Nový most** or The New Bridge. The bridge is 432 metres long and its steel constructions weighs 7,537 metric tons. The structure of the bridge is hung on two massive pylons by thick steel cables. Inside the pylon on the left hand side is the lift to sightseeing **café Bystrica**.

Close to the New Bridge is the area of the historic settlement below the castle or **Podhradie**, which existed for several centuries as an independent settlement. As a matter of fact, there were two of them on what is now the embankment: Vydrica and Zuckermandel. By the end of the 1960's Vydrica was completely demolished. When everything was pulled down, the remains of **Vodná veža** or the Water Tower were found.

Vydrica was separated from medieval Pressburg by **Rybné námestie square**. It originated in the second half of the 18th

century on the vacant space in front of Vydrická brána gate. The dominant feature of today's Rybné námestie square is **trojičný stĺp** (the Holy Trinity pillar) erected in 1713 immediately after the plague swept the town.

The busy traffic in the western part of Bratislava embankment can be avoided in two ways. The first option is to walk on the pathway leading along the left bank of the Danube.

The second route avoiding busy embankment communications leads from Vodná veža on **Žižkova ulica street**. In contrast to Vydrica several most valuable cultural and historical monuments of the former settlement **Zuckermandel** have survived here. The group of the surviving buildings includes only the church, two Renaissance curias and one Rococo house.

Karlova Ves

Closest to the centre is the urban district **Karlova Ves** (32,950 inhabitants). The north-western limit of Karlova Ves is Devínska Kobyla Mountain and its southern limit is the Danube.

The Roman Catholic church of **St. Michael Archangel** in Karlova Ves was built in the 1940's. It incorporates an originally Baroque chapel from the last third of the 18th century. It is a single-nave building with its front wall decorated by the **ceramic relief of St. Michael Archangel** by I. Bizmayer. The adjacent cemetery with a small **chapel** was founded in Karlova Ves in the 1920's.

The most visited places of Karlova Ves are the Botanical garden and the Zoo. The **Botanical garden** on Botanická ulica street is owned and administered by the Faculty of Nature History of Comenius University. It lies close to the Danube, west from the Lafranconi bridge. It was founded in the years 1942-1943 on an area 50.7 hectares. When the green house was constructed the garden acquired many tropical plant species. The pride of the green house is a little lake with precious water plants and numerous collections of cactuses. Today there are about 5,000 foreign plant species including 650 wood species. The botanical garden is interesting in every season, but it is most beautiful in the spring when the flowers are in full bloom.

Dúbravka

North of Karlova Ves is the village of **Dúbravka** (38,400 inhabitants). Its western part enters into the area of the Devínska Kobyla massif. The old part of the village lies on the eastern foot of the Dúbravská Hlavica hill (360 m a.s.l.) and

the new housing estate was built on the plateau of the edge of Lamačská brána.

The Baroque Roman Catholic **Church of St. Cosma and Damian** built in 1723 on the foundations of an older building is Dúbravka's most important cultural and historic monument. The Late Baroque altar of this church is from the last third of the 18th century. The lateral altar of the Virgin Mary made in the work shop of G. R. Donner was moved to its original place, the summer Archbishop's Palace now the Office of the Government of the SR. The Early Renaissance **chapel** from the late 16th century in the local cemetery was built on the Gothic foundations. The last of the sacred buildings of Dúbravka is the Baroque **chapel** near the parish office from the latter half of the 18th century.

The glass factory **Slovenské závody technického skla** has stood in the northwest of Dúbravka since the 1960's. Behind the factory and in the middle of a field are the foundations of a **Roman building** of the *villa rustica* type. The villa rustica of Dúbravka was a well equipped farming and craft homestead building with living and servicing rooms, a bath and maybe a sanctuary. The dimensions of the known ground plan are 11.20x13.20 m. Outside the basic, almost square ground plan were four apsides.

Lamač

In the east Dúbravka borders on the urban district **Lamač** (7,050 inhabitants). In the east it reaches the plateaux of the Little Carpathians, where it borders on the urban districts lying on the other side of the mountains. In the north it borders on urban district Záhorská Bystrica. Lamač

Left: Church of St. Cosma and Damian
Villa rustica
Right: St. Rosalia church

entered history in July 1866 with the last battle of the **Prussian-Austrian war**. The sacred buildings of Lamač are its main historic monuments. The Roman Catholic **St. Rosalia Church** is the oldest of them. It was built in the years 1568-1569 outside the village and on a hill presumably on the foundations of an older church. Great part of it fell down and the building had to be reconstructed. It was accomplished in the years 1667-1673 when the new tower was built and the church got a Baroque vault. The much younger Roman Catholic **Church of St. Margaret** was built in the years 1947-1949 following the design of M. M. Harminc.

Záhorská Bystrica

Záhorská Bystrica (1,900 inhabitants) is the northernmost urban district of Bratislava. It spreads on a comparatively large area, a great part of which lies in the Little Carpathian woods. The village spreads on the western foothills of the mountains, only two kilometres from the famous pilgrim locality of Marianka.

The Baroque-Neo Classical Roman Catholic **church of Sts. Peter and Paul the Apostles** is the historic monument, which survived in Záhorská Bystrica. It was built in the years 1830-1834 on older foundations. The Baroque **chapel** next to the road leading to the villages is from the late 18th century. Its facade was changed in the 20th century. The Roman Catholic **parsonage**, a one-storeyed Baroque building from 1737 is another sacred monument. The **Carpatia** co-operative founded in Záhorská Bystrica in 1967 deals with the breeding and training of horses and in the south-western end of the village is the modern complex of buildings of the private **TV station Markíza**.

Devínska Nová Ves

The urban district **Devínska Nová Ves** (16,850 inhabitants) lies on the north-western edge of Bratislava. Its western border coincides with the state frontier with Austria that in fact is in the middle of the river Morava.

The originally Renaissance Roman Catholic **Church of the Holy Spirit** built in the early 16th century and later adapted, is the cultural monument, which deserves attention. The Neo Classical structure of the **customs station** from the 18th century was recently adapted to the town hall. The building of the **steam engine-operated brickyard** founded in 1891 is historically interesting.

The **National Nature Reserve of Devíska Kobyla** is a unique locality of special fauna and flora is. It lies in part of the Devínske Karpaty Mountains on an area 101 hectares between Devínska Nová Ves, Dúbravka and Devín; 234 species of mushrooms, 110 species of lichens, 100 species of mosses, and 1,100 plant species confirm the originality of this place. Xerophytes and thermophiles with precious and protected plant species and animals live on the southern and south-western slopes of Devínska Kobyla. The forests on the south-western slopes are the remains of the original thermopile oak growths. An **instructive path** leading through the reserve provides visitors with information about the occurrence of special vegetation

and wild life. It has got seven stops with information panels. The most interesting locality of the National Nature Reserve Devínska Kobyla is the sand profile on the **Sandberg** mountain. There are rock remains of the Tertiary sea with horizontal layers, the age of which is estimated at 14 to 16 million years. Another **instructive route** was prepared in 1996 over the flood plain of the Morava which runs along the river Morava from Devin to Devínska Nová Ves and ends in Vysoká pri Morave (outside Bratislava). The 23 km long route has 16 information boards.

Devín

The urban district **Devín** (750 inhabitants) lies below the Devín Castle at the confluence of the Danube and Morava. Devín is ten kilometres away from Bratislava. The village with castle lies on the spot where the Danube enters the Devínska brána (Devín Gate).

Devín Castle standing on a massive rock hill above the confluence of the Danube and Morava is an unusually impressive landmark. Its ground plan is very irregular and adapted to the shape of the rock it stands on. On the western side a steep rock face overtowers the confluence of rivers and behind it is a lower hill with mildly inclined slopes. The whole castle area consisting of a foreground, lower, middle, and upper castle is enclosed by continuous walls with three gates. The northern side which was considerably

more vulnerable than the southern one is protected by a long **northern rampart**. I was made already in the time of the Emperor Valentinian I in the 4th century. Timber palisades reinforced the fort in the 10th century and in the 15th century the rampart was opened to provide a shortcut between Devin Castle and the serf town through the northern **Devínska brána gate**. Today we enter the castle through the western **Moravian Gate**. The southern gate protected by a pair of semicircular bastions was built in the 15th century on an older Great Moravian rampart. Close behind the gate and on the right side of the path is a precious archaeological monument from the Roman period of Devín's history. The ground plan of the **remains of a bulky stone building** from the 4th century suggests a Classical tomb. Fragments of wall with preserved plasters up to 85 cm tall and the original floor were found there. Especially the **iron cross** is interesting. If it is the Christian symbol then it is the oldest sacred monument found in the territory of Slovakia. Left from the path and near the Moravská brána gate Old Slavic graves from the 10th and 11th centuries were found. The path divides into two on the ridge of the castle hill. The left branch leads to the place where stood a **Great Moravian church** in the 9th century. One can see its rectangular ground plan with an apsid and a small model on a plinth shows what the church might have looked like. The archaeologists also found **remains of a hut** from the period of migration of people under the north-western corner of the **church foundations**. South of this church another smaller sacred building from the 11th and 12th century and **cemetery** with

---

Left: Devínska Nová Ves
    A model of the church in Devin Castle
Right: Devin Castle seen from Sandberg
    Devín Castle

graves from the 10th to 13th centuries were found. East of the Great Moravian church is the eastern **Pressburg gate** in the Renaissance style. The first branch of the path leads to the conserved ruins of the middle and upper part of the **medieval castle**, which was smaller than the Great Moravian fort. In the first half of the 15th century the Gothic **Garay palace** with two stories was built and the Renaissance palace and fortifications were added in the 16th century. Some vaulted spaces of this palace are today used for exhibitions. The origin of the 55 metres deep **castle well**, which is on the courtyard of the middle castle, is linked to the period when Garray was the owner of the castle. Archaeologists found **remains of Roman architecture** under debris near the well. The structure built of quarry stone had about 4 or 5 rooms. Near the well is also a terrace with view of the abandoned **amphitheatre**, the Danube and the mountain of Braunsberg in Austria. In the wonderful setting above the bicolour confluence of the Danube and Morava an elegant tower with battlements stands out. It is the **Virgin tower**.

A bridge over a moat and stairs lead to the top platform with remnants of a guard tower from the 13th century rebuilt in the 15th century with panoramic view of the surroundings.

The most valuable historic monument is the Roman Catholic **church of the Virgin Mary**. Originally it was built in the Gothic style in the first half of the 14th century. It was restored in the Baroque and Neo Classical taste in the years 1677-1772. There are **two manor houses** in Devin. The first in the Late Renaissance style was built in the first half of the 17th

century and the second was built in the second half of the 17th century in the Early Baroque style.

Nové Mesto

The north-eastern part of Greater Bratislava consists of three urban districts, the outer edges of which reach as far as the forests of the Little Carpathians. Rača is in the north, Vajnory in the east and the suburb of Nové Mesto the closest to the city centre. The northern suburbs include plains and the slopes of the mountain range. Older rural settlements or their remains alternate here with residential quarters or industrial areas.

The urban district of **Nové Mesto** (32,500 inhabitants) or the New Town links Rača and Vajnory with the city centre. It originated by building on agricultural land. It also encompasses extensive forested territory of the Little Carpathians including the Horná Mlynská dolina valley. A special part of this territory consists of the quarters of Kramáre and Koliba. The axis of the central part of Nové Mesto is the Račianska ulica street starting in

the centre of Bratislava and running to the quarters of Rača in the north. Similar axis in the east is Vajnorská ulica street connecting the centre with Vajnory in the north-east. In the north of the area between these two key streets lies the industrial zone of Istrochem. The south-eastern limits of the urban district Nové Mesto are represented by Trnavská cesta road and Rožňavská ulica street separating it from the urban district Ružinov. In the south Nové Mesto borders on Staré Mesto or the Old Town.

No compact settlement existed in the territory of today's Nové Mesto. For centuries there were only isolated houses or farms amidst meadows and fields. Two roads crossed the area. One of them, Račianska ran from Pressburg through Rača to Modra, and Vajnorská road connected Pressburg with Vajnory. On the edge of the Nové Mesto and along the now disappeared Mlynské rameno arm of the

Danube there ran another road, Trnavská, heading to Trnava and Nitra. The brickyards in the open agricultural landscape and quarries on the edge of the Little Carpathians were sources of economic activity.

Urbanization of today's Nové Mesto started on the site of two toll stations, where the mentioned medieval roads crossed the outer defensive ramparts of Pressburg. Two squares that originated around them still bear the word "mýto" (toll) in their names: Račianske mýto and Trnavské mýto. **Trnavské mýto** is today a busy crossroads of four Bratislava's principal streets. It developed around the toll station standing on the crossroads of Vajnorská and Trnavská. There was a cross and statue of St. John Nepomuk in 1783. In the first half of the 19th century the space around the toll station and the local inn changed into a cattle market. The importance of Trnavská toll station increased when a **horse railway station** on the track from Pressburg to Svätý Jur and Trnava was also built next to it in 1840. Fortunately, the railway station building, very modern for that time, escaped demolition in the 1980's. This building with a typical tower on the corner of Krížna and Legionárska streets is depicted on the coat of arms of the urban district of Nové Mesto.

The wide meadows and fields with isolated farms between Vajnorská and Trnavská cesta roads were built up only recently, in the course of the 20th century. Only the name of one of those farms called Jurajov dvor survived. In the area of *Ziegelfeld*, the German for Brick Field in the neighbouring Pasienky were brickyards. However, Bratislava lost Petržalka during the Second World War and the city

---

Left: Trnavské Mýto square
    Kramáre and Kamzík Mountain
Right: The horse railway station
    The Winter Stadium of Ondrej Nepela

was deprived of almost all of its sport grounds and football stadiums. Consequently, in the years 1939-1940 new sport area in **Tehelné pole** and later also in **Pasienky** was started. The **swimming pool** called **Tehelné pole** on ulica Odbojárov street was the first to be finished. But the **football stadium of ŠK Slovan Bratislava** is the biggest sport structure there. It was built in the years 1939-1944. Another combined athletics and football stadium was built in neighbouring Pasienky, belonging to the first league football team of **Inter Bratislava**. The stadium of "black and yellow" team with the first artificial tartan track in Slovakia hosts also the world top athletes participating every summer in the popular light athletic meeting called **Grand Prix Bratislava**. The **Winter Stadium of Ondrej Nepela** stretches between Odbojárska and Trnavská streets. It was built in 1938 and twenty years later also roofed. The second ice-rink sharing the roof with the Winter Stadium was built in 1973 on the occasion of the world championship in figure-skating.

Račianske mýto is a complicated crossroads where as many as seven streets meet. A toll station stood there as early as 1767. Urbanization of the western side of Račianska neighbours with a belt of vineyards, which cover the south-eastern slopes of the Little Carpathians. On the slope of Briežky Mt. one can admire a valuable **technical monument Rösslerov lom** or Rössler's quarry. Historic documents refer to the quarry as early as 1405 and it was used until the 20th century. By the end of the 19th century the terrestrial funicular was used for the first time in Slovakia for the work in this quarry.

More than a half of the area of the urban district of Nové mesto is occupied by the landscape park called **Bratislavský lesný park**. This indeed large (17 square kilometres) recreation area on the territory of Bratislava is the forested territory of the southern part of the Little Carpathians. It is divided by Lamačská brána Gate into two independent parts. The one in the south consists of the massive mountain Devínska Kobyla. The northern part is bigger and borders on the Nové Mesto. This part consists mostly of meadows and broad-leaved forest, which offer possibilities of relaxing in a pleasant setting. The area has numerous marked hiking footpaths and tourist amenities. The citizens of Bratislava have used the area since the first half of the 19th century, and the most popular spot was **Železná studnička** (The Iron Well). In 1826 construction of spa started at Železná studnička. The spa, which was given the name of Emperor Ferdinand V and was later bought by the rich Pressburg businessman Palugyay, exploited two local springs of ferrous water. But the importance of the spa diminished and the place became more popular as a recreational area.

The road starting at Železná Studnička heads to the north-west and runs along the Bystrička brook to the former game-keeper's house **Kačín**. It is a favourite picnic place and the destination of family trips. Near Kačín one can see what is called the **Written Stone**. It commemorates an event in 1600. The town of Pressburg was in dispute with Palatine Miklós Pálffy.

A road and hiking path run along the Horná Mlynská dolina valley. Close to the demolished eighth mill called **Klepáč** is a baroque **pillar**. Below Klepáč is the lower pair of **lakes**, which animate the natural setting of the valley. Below them the valley opens into the wide **Partizánska lúka meadow**, the place full of Bratislavians during weekends.

The massive mountain of **Kamzík** (439 m) in the southern part of the Little Carpathians is a place frequently visited by Bratislava trippers. It is easily accessible by an asphalt road from Koliba. The name of the mountain originated from

German *Gemsenberg*. At the crossroads next to its top is a **pillar** from 1683, which recalls the last stay of Turkish troops and their collaborators in the environs of the town immediately before the famous defeat at Vienna. Another **monument** standing below Kamzík in turn commemorates the last battle of the Prussian-Austrian war in 1866, which took place in the forests on the slopes of Kamzík. However, the main tourist attraction of Kamzík is the 200 metres tall **TV tower** built in 1974 on its top. The revolving restaurant on top of the tower offers panoramic view of the environs reaching, in fair weather as far as the Neusiedel lake and the Alps in Austria. On the eastern side of Kamzík is the meadow called **Cvičná lúka** or the Exercise Meadow. Standing near the stalls with refreshments one gets a fine view of the wide plains of the Danube lowland. Cvičná lúka with its ski track is an ideal slope for the beginner skiers and sledders. The summer sled bob track attracts the trippers in summer.

Rača

North of Nové Mesto is the urban district **Rača** (21,000 inhabitants). It is about 8 kilometre away from the city centre. The administrative territory of Rača stretches over an area of 23.9 km. In the west it includes part of the forested massive of the Little Carpathians and in the east it borders on Vajnory.

The history of Rača is closely linked to its **viticultural traditions**. The local vineyards are referred to in the oldest historic document from 1237. The medieval prosperity of viticulture can be attributed to favourable climatic conditions. Warmer climate supported expansion of vineyards even to elevated positions in the Little Carpathians. There are still heaps of stones removed from vineyards called "hroble" to be seen high above the existing lower limit of the forest.

Medicinal wine
Rača wine was always one of the best quality wines produced in the region of the Little Carpathians. It was also always

Left: Altánok na Kamziku
Right: Etiketa račianskeho vína

somewhat more expensive than the rest of them. The vintners of the surrounding villages used to buy Rača wine to mix it with their own in order to improve its taste. Račišdorf (now Rača) wines were often sold as dessert wines. They were successfully exported as far as Silesia. They would certainly have found clients in Austria, if not for various customs and import restricting measures. Pressburg did not support the trade in the excellent Rača wine because then nobody would buy Pressburg wine, which was not as good. The famous connoisseur of Hungarian viticulture Matej Bel estimated Rača wine high above that of Pressburg. He especially appreciated its taste, aroma and medicinal effects. The good reputation of the wine of the local vineyards was also propagated by the Pálffy family, who owned the village for a long time. Count Miklós Pálffy was a great fan of Rača wine. Thanks to his contact it was also sold in foreign market. It arrived at the Imperial court in Vienna as well. Legend has it that Maria Theresa liked Rača wine. Once, when Her Majesty fell ill while staying in the Austrian Alps, she was sent an efficient medicine. It was a consignment of Red Frankovka from the Rača priest and worked. The Queen liked the wine a lot and as a token of gratitude Maria Theresa pardoned the people of Rača the due tax from the harvest and promoted the priest to noble estate in 1776. Frankovka was never missing on the tables of the Imperial court from that time.

ročník 1998

SLOVENSKÉ AKOSTNÉ VÍNO
Bratislavský vinohradnícky rajón

RAČIANSKA FRANKOVKA

ZNAČKOVÉ VÍNO SUCHÉ

VÍNOPRODUKT

RAČA

A visit to Rača is an excellent opportunity to see a typical Little Carpathian viticultural village in its almost intact form. The oldest core of the village extends from Námestie hrdinov square to Evangelical church. Right in the square and on Alstrova ulica street are several **yeoman curias**. Historically the most valuable building in Rača is the **Roman Catholic parish church of St. Philip and St. James** with a massive rectangular tower ending in a tall prismoid roof. The church was built before 1390 in the Gothic style. It was given Renaissance form in 1629 and Baroque reconstruction was carried out in 1732. The **Evangelical church** is much younger. Pressburg builder B. Pandl built it in the years 1834-1835. The tower was built only in 1905. At the opposite end of the village only **St. Anna's chapel** survived from several old buildings. There are also typical **rural houses** in Rača. They are mostly concentrated on Alstrova street. When the street row of houses was full, the new houses were built behind with entrances from long yards. In some yards one can see five or six houses built in a row. The peasant houses of Rača were adapted to their main occupation – wine production. They had to have enough room for pressing and storage of wine. Some vintners emptied the front room of the house to use it as a tavern. Rača is rich in various folk traditions. It is rare to meet people wearing folk costumes, but they do put them on at the time of the traditional vintage.

Vajnory

The urban district **Vajnory** (3,450 inhabitants) is on the north-western edge of Bratislava, about 10 km away from the city centre. In the north-west a narrow

protuberance of its area enters the south-eastern slopes of the Little Carpathians. In the south it reaches the road to Senec. The north-eastern and eastern borders of the administrative area of Vajnory coincides with that of Greater Bratislava.

Although Vajnory became part of the city, it preserved its traditional rural character. The oldest peasant houses of Vajnory are from the early 19th century. The Roman Catholic **church of St. Ladislav** was built in the 14th century in the Gothic style. A new nave was added to it in 1771. The main altar dedicated to the patron saint of the village is from the late 19th century. Roľnícka ulica street is the main street of the village and narrow houses with long yards skirt it. One of the Vajnory houses on Roľnícka ulica street was adapted as an ethnographic exhibition in 1966. The **Vajnorský ľudový dom** (The Folk House of Vajnory) (No. 185) is not only a representative example of a traditional dwelling of a vintner of Vajnory, it

Left: St. Philip and St. James church
     The taverns in Vajnory
Right: Csáky's manor house in Prievoz

also offers wonderful products of folk painters in its interior. One can see there various folk paintings with varied patterns of ornament. Especially the kitchens were decorated. The paintings are the works of the natives. One of the last living artists was Katarína Bruderová, who painted houses of Vajnory in the first half of the 20th century. Pottery and embroidery supplement the interior of the typical house. The colourful local folk costume is also the pride of Vajnory. In spite of its close proximity to the metropolis, the village still preserves many folk customs. Vajnory also has **Vajnorák**, the oldest **brass band** in Slovakia founded in 1866.

East of Bratislava centre are three urban districts. Ružinov is nearer to centre, while Vrakuňa and Podunajské Biskupice are on its eastern edge. The eastern suburbs extend on a flat landscape where mosaics of former villages, large housing estates, industrial zones, but also gardens, fields and floodplain woods alternate.

Ružinov

Ružinov (73,000 inhabitants) is the second largest urban district as far as the area and population are concerned. The name of this part is comparatively young and in its German form *Rosenheim* it appeared only in the early 20th century. Prievoz is also an appropriate name as it denoted the oldest settlement in the territory of Ružinov, but it is only a part of Ružinov.

The cultural monument of Prievoz is the **Csáky's manor house** built around

1900. Part of it is a later built **oratory of The Sacred Heart of Jesus** administered by the female congregation of St. Francis of Assisi and today it is the parish church. At present the manor house is the hospital and Franciscan female monastery. There is also **Evangelical church** in Prievoz built in the 1930's. Prievoz was the only village now included in Bratislava, which had a **town hall** of its own standing on the Radničné námestie square.

The territory of today's Ružinov has experienced great changes recently. When the Danube was finally controlled and the danger of flooding of the orchards and gardens was averted in the twentieth century, the area became interesting for architects and builders. The first worker's colonies originated here in inter-war period. West of Prievoz were the Hubertova and Klingerova colonies. Next to the textile factory on the northern end of Miletičova street another colony was built and the *Dornkappeln* colony has existed on the territory of present **Trnávka** since the twenties. The colony provided living to the working class in small houses with a piece of garden. The Masarykova colony was added in the thirties. The Salesian order decided to construct a church in the area and the oratory with the **Don Bosco's Church** were started in 1937 in Trnávka. Gabriel Schreiber prepared the designs. As the Salesians went short of money they built only a part of the three-nave church with presbytery before 1938. The church was rebuilt in 1968 and widened. The Salesians of Bratislava also built the Salesian monastery in Miletičova street in the time of the First Republic. It was confiscated in the fifties and after the Velvet Revolution, the **Salesians** restored their **monastery** standing on the corner of a busy crossroads and added to it a modern church.

The biggest urbanistic project realized in the territory of the urban district **Ružinov** was the series of Greater Bratislava housing estates: Štrkovec, Ostredky, Trávniky and Pošeň which took in about fifty thousand inhabitants. They were built between the years 1962 and 1970. The fifth quarter, Starý Ružinov, was built

as the last one in the eastern part of Záhradnícka ulica in the eighties. Ružinov progressively acquired several modern service structures such as the **Bratislava Hotel** (1974), The **Winter Stadium of Vlado Dzurilla** (1979), and the **Junior Hotel** (1982), the **department store of Ružinov** (1984), **House of Culture of Ružinov** (1985), a **hospital with policlinic** (1985), several shopping centres and administrative buildings.

In the southern part of **Ružinovská ulica street** a **park** was founded, and designed by Ferdinand Milučký. The the park originally bore the name of the Slovak politician Karol Šmidke, but its present name is the **Park of Andrej Hlinka** (1864-1938). Recreational activities of the quarter concentrate around **Štrkovecké jazero pond**, known for its swans. In June every year the race of unconventional vessels is organized on the pond.

Vrakuňa

The urban district **Vrakuňa** (18,500 inhabitants) spreads on the eastern edge

of Greater Bratislava. The urban fabric connected Vrakuňa with the contiguous urban district of Podunajské Biskupice. This common settlement is in the uppermost part of Žitný ostrov. In the west it borders on the urban district Ružinov.

Vrakuňa did not have a church of its own until recently. It had only a **chapel** of **the Holy Name of the Virgin Mary** standing by the road and built in 1879. The single-nave rectangular building has a Prussian vault. It also has a little rectangular tower and on the main altar is the oil painting of the Immaculate Conception from 1879 by Károly Jakobey. The modern **church of the Holy Name of the Virgin Mary** next to the chapel was built in 1994. Besides the family houses in the territory of Vrakuňa there are also modern housing estates. The axis of the new part of Vrakuňa is **Rajecká ulica street** with pedestrian zone and shops. On the

Left: Trojičné námestie square
Right: The garden arbour in the Sad Janka Kráľa park
Sad Janka Kráľa park

western edge of Vrakuňa's territory is **Ružinov cemetery**, the largest in Bratislava. It was opened in 1982 and the entrance is from Popradská ulica street. On the left **bank of the Malý Dunaj** or the Little Danube is the quarter called Nová Vrakuňa consisting mostly of family houses, which originated on the land formerly belonging to the Pálffys. In the south of Vrakuňa is the **landscape park of Vrakunský les**.

Podunajské Biskupice

The urban district **Podunajské Biskupice** (20,500 inhabitants) lies south of Vrakuňa and east of Ružinov. In the south, the administrative territory of Podunajské Biskupice reaches as far as the Gabčíkovo dam. Biskupice borders on the area of Slovnaft in the south and on the villages of Žitný ostrov in the east.

The most important cultural and historic monument of the village is the Roman Catholic **parish church of St. Nicholas**. It was built before 1250. It was originally a Gothic church, but was several times rebuilt. It was severely destroyed during the Turkish wars and had to be almost entirely reconstructed. In 1750 its interior was adapted in the Baroque taste, and shortly after an Archbishop's oratory was added to it. Re-Gothisizing interventions were made in 1901 and the reconstruction of 1937-1938 meant the addition of two lateral structures. The original Gothic details of the St. Nicholas church partially survived in the tower and the sacristy, where there are two reliefs depicting the Lamb of God and Christ's Head. The presbytery contains the copy of the Baroque sculpture of the sitting Madonna. Inside one of the church walls a stone with Roman inscription from Carnuntum was found. On Krajinská street is a Neo-Classic **manor house** with a **chapel** from the 18th century. In the 19th century it was rebuilt as a **hospital**, which exists there also today. The remains of another **manor house** are in the locality **Lieskovec** south of the Slovnaft area. Originally it stood amidst the disappeared **Archbishop's park**.

Petržalka

The urban district **Petržalka** (125,300 inhabitants) if it was independent settlement, would represent the third largest city in Slovakia. The result of enormous building activity on the right bank of the Danube can be best appreciated from the southern terrace of Bratislava Castle. This "concrete jungle" is home of every fourth Bratislavian.

Petržalka became the green hinterland of Pressburg and a very popular one in the course of history. The citizens of Pressburg imitated the lordly pastimes seen in Paris, London or Vienna. Especially the ceremonious opening of the Bridge of Francis Joseph (today the Old Bridge) on New Year's Eve of 1890 is memorable. The Emperor himself opened the traffic on the first fixed bridge across the river. From 1914 the local electric railway connecting Pressburg with Vienna was using this bridge as well. The Vienna tram, as it was nicknamed by the Bratislavians, crossed Petržalka, Hainburg and Petronell to end its journey in Vienna. Its home depot was in Kittsee in Austria. The Vienna tram was stopped in 1938 and after the Second World War only the city trams crossed the Old Bridge to Petržalka. Later trains used the bridge, but today the railway track is not used.

The park of Petržalka, today called **Sad Janka Kráľa**, possesses a kind of primacy. Few of the European metropols can say that they have the oldest public park. The citizens of Pressburg had the revolutionary idea of founding a garden for all, accessible to the general public, not only to the privileged classes, in the 1770's.

They chose for the purpose the alluvial forest on the right bank of the Danube lying right opposite the historic city centre. A public collection gathered the means necessary for felling trees. The trees were felled in a way, which created the pattern of an eight-tip star along which later rows of trees were planted. The park was called *Sternallee* (A Star Tree Row).

Sad Janka Kráľa park was profoundly reconstructed in the 1960's. All undesired vegetation was removed and the result was more space that enhanced the beauty of the big old trees. The park now has several sculptures. One of them is the **statue of Janko Kráľ** (by F. Gibala). The **statue** of the Hungarian revolutionary **Sándor Petőfi** was moved here from the former Promenade (today Hviezdoslavovo námestie square). The unique garden arbour, originally the **tower of the Franciscan church** is also impressive. The wonderful Gothic tower used to be one of the most beautiful in the Kingdom of Hungary. But it suffered from an earthquake so that it was dismantled and reerected on the place where it stands now.

Old Petržalka as remembered by the medium and old generation of Bratislavians has practically disappeared in the process of urbanization. One of the few buildings left is the Roman Catholic **church of the Exaltation of the Holy Cross**. It stands to the north-west of the Panónska cesta road. It was built in 1932 to plans by V. Karfík. Two years later it became the seat of the newly created parish of Petržalka. This church was built because an older church from 1672 was pulled down when Viedenská cesta road had to be widened. The businessman Tomáš Baťa contributed to the construction of the new church, which was built in incredible six months. The existing interior contains the original pews and the organ made in Rigler's workshop. The Pressburg sculptor Aloiz Rigele made the **statue of Christ Crucified**. The most precious monuments are in the park in front of the church. One of them is the **statue of**

the **Virgin Mary** standing on a stone Baroque pillar from the 18th century moved here from the Viedenská cesta road. The **statue of St. John of Nepomuk** moved here from the park near the Danube is another. The first houses of the gigantic **housing estate Petržalka** were started in 1976. Since then every year about 6,000 new flats were added to the vast area on the right bank of the Danube. About 10,000 workers were employed in its construction. Gradually 120,000 inhabitants moved onto the right bank of the Danube. There is probably no housing estate of comparable size in the whole of Europe.

Rusovce

Rusovce (1,700 inhabitants) is the biggest of the three urban districts of the other bank of the Danube lying south of Petržalka. Rusovce is a very old community. Though its territory was settled already in the Older Bronze Age it became most notable in the first four centuries when the northern frontiers of the Roman Empire moved to the middle section of the Danube. The territory of today's Rusovce found itself in the Roman province of Pannonia administered from Carnuntum. Romans built there the military camp of **Gerulata** as a part of the *Limes Romanus* defensive system, securing the northern limit of the Empire against the raids of German tribes. Romans left numerous traces of their stay in Rusovce. Archaeologist gradually disclosed various remains of architecture, such as the ruins of the Roman forum, a well, remains of furnaces, tombstones and altar stones, but also individual bricks and shingles with

Left: The building of Technopol
      Petržalka
Right: Gerulata
      St. Vít and Modesta church in Rusovce

symbols of the XIVth Roman legion. Four cemeteries, a great amount of coins, fragments of pottery, utensils of everyday use made of bronze and iron were found here. Especially precious was the find of a deformed helmet of the Roman officer who was probably killed in the war with Markomani. The antique history of Rusovce is documented in the exhibition of the **Municipal Museum Múzeum antiky – Gerulata** (open only in summer).

The ground plan of Rusovce has a typical spindle-shaped form, which was enlarged by modern urbanization. The older generation of houses is from the 19th and early 20th centuries. The architectural feature of Rusovce is the Neo-Classical **manor house** built in 1840 on the site of an older manor house from 1521. The manor house acquired its attractive facade by application of the Romanticizing style of what is called the Windsor type imitating English Gothic. It has towers, battlements and a central risalite with terrace. In front of the manor house is the **statue of a lion** standing on a pillar. The manor house has got a big **park**, composition of its wood species is not especially varied but the trees are tall with big crowns. Oaks and plane trees prevail. The manor house serves the **folk ensemble SĽUK**, which moved here in 1951. The village of Rusovce has got two churches. The **St. Vít and Modesta church** is older and stands on the edge of the park. It was built in 1613 in the Renaissance style using the remains of an older Romanesque church from 1208. The church was rebuilt in the historicizing Neo Romanesque taste in the second half of the 19th century. The second, Roman Catholic parish **church of St. Maria Magdalene in Rusovce** is from

1662 and it is built in then fashionable Early Baroque style. The main altar of Maria Magdalene made of wood is from the mid-17th century. The Late Renaissance sculptures of St. Stephen, St. Ladislav and the kings of the Old Testament, David and Salamon adorn it.

Jarovce

The village of **Jarovce** (1,100 inhabitants) stretches along the south-west of the right bank of the Danube and is one of the oldest, judging from the existing historic documents, in this area. The oldest documents referring to the village in connection with arrival of the Croatian immigrants are from the 16th century. The presence of Croatians in the village is obvious also from the older names *Horvátfal* (1522) and *Kroatisch-Jahrendorf* used since the 18th century.

The Roman Catholic **church of St. Nicolas** was built in 1764-1765 in the Late Baroque style. The sponsor of the building was Count Esterházy. The monumental tower of the church was built in 1884. German troops blew it up on April

folk houses of Jarovce are clay structures. The walls are built from burned or un burned clay.

Čunovo

Čunovo (800 inhabitants) was in the past an independent village and now it is the remotest part of Bratislava on the right bank of the Danube. The settlement of the territory of this village is archaeo- logically documented from the Roman and Old Slavonic periods. Inhumation graves from the 2nd to the 4th centuries and sever- al centuries younger Slav-Avar burial place were found here. The first written reference to Čunovo is from the first half of the 13th century.

The most valuable historical monu- ments of the village is the Neo-Classical **curia** from the end of the 18th century and the Roman Catholic **Church of St. Michael** built in 1783 in the Late Baroque taste. In its interior are the Late Baroque altar, Neo-Classical pulpit and an organ from the 18th century. The Gothic **chalice** from the second half of the 15th century is also valuable. On the main altar is the statue of the patron saint of the church and parish of St. Michael the Archangel.

North of the villages is the **Nature Re- serve Ostrovné lúčky**. The locality is no- table for occurrence of precious plant species, especially the orchids. Part of Os- trovné lúčky is a multicultural growth of Canadian poplar planted here in 1958. Attraction of the environs of Čunovo is the **Gabčíkovo dam** and a **modern water sport area**. **Mini-Slovakia** is a recently founded gallery containing miniature copies of the most important cultural and historical monuments existing in Slovakia.

3rd 1945. The existing tower was built in the years 1969-1970. The single-nave church with a semicircular presbytery contains the original furniture from the 18th century. The wooden Late Gothic sculpture of the Madonna is older, as it dates from the late 15th century. The main altar of St. Nicolas and the two lateral al- tars are from the early 20th century. The wooden Baroque sculpture *Ecce homo* is from the late 17th century.

Folk architecture from the 19th and the beginning of the 20th century survived on Mandľová ulica street. Years 1850, 1865, 1885, and 1895 are carved on the facades of the oldest houses. The typical

Left: St. Nicolas church in Jarovce
Right: Under the Michalská brána gate

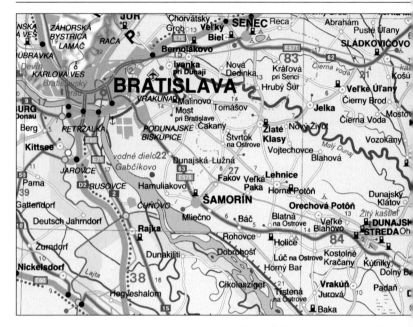

ŠAMORÍN AND ITS ENVIRONS

The region of Šamorín lies in the Danube lowland and its partial unit called the Danube plain. It is situated in the western part of Žitný ostrov near the capital of Slovakia, Bratislava. The plain landscape in between the villages of Most pri Bratislave and Nový Život, is refreshed in the north by the meandering stream of the Malý Dunaj. Its southern part is near the Gabčíkovo dam. The territory also includes Malý Žitný ostrov between Dobrohošť and Bodíky. The districts of Senec and Dunajská Streda administer this region.

The town of **ŠAMORÍN** (Somorja in Hungarian, population 12,300) is the centre of the western part of Žitný ostrov (The Rye Island). It is only 24 km away from Bratislava, near the Danube, the access to which was cut off by the canal of the Gabčíkovo Dam. It is 25 km away from the district town of Dunajská Streda and

Right: The square in Šamorín

it also includes several surrounding settlements: Bučuháza, Čilistovo, Kraľovianky, and Mliečno. The origin of the town is not quite clear. Historic documents with references to its oldest history are missing. But Matej Bel, the recognised historian and geographer, asserts that the name of the town derives from the patron saint of the local church, which was built in honour of the Virgin Mary. A settlement was founded around a church and its people were granted the rights of free citizens by King Stephen I. The present name originated by a progressive change of the original one in the following order: *eclessia Sancta Marie − villa Sacta Marie − Zenth marya − Zenthmariaria − Samaria − Somorjaa − Šamorín.* The village was first referred to in 1238 in connection with construction of the church and as a village in 1285 and 1287 when it belonged to the Bratislava Castle estate. The town obtained its privilege of a Danube port with ford from Queen Elisabeth in 1328. It became a trading centre of Žitný ostrov and a place visited by rulers (Sigismund of Luxembourg in the years 1411 and 1425 or Matthias I in 1466).

Apart for the right to annual fair obtained from King Sigismund of Luxembourg, Šamorín was also a market town with weekly markets. Various craftsmen such as wool-cloth makers, boot-makers, silk traders or farmers from all over Žitný ostrov offered their commodities in the market place of Šamorín. The first guild founded in the town was that of fur-makers, later followed by guilds of tailors, boot-makers, millers, wheelwrights, belt-makers, wood-carvers, weavers, soap-makers, cutlers, and cattle-traders. Šamorín was a port town until the 15th century because the main stream of the Danube was in fact the arm of the river flowing trough the town. But this period is better known for inquisition trials with women accused of witchcraft. The Danube was used for "the water test", when the suspects were thrown into the river. The ones who survived, were burnt as the water test proved their alliance with the devil.

In 1580 the town became property of the Pálffy family, who included it in their Bratislava Castle estate. Nine years later Šamorín lost the privilege of a free royal borough. István Bocskay had his headquarters in the town in time of anti-Habsburg rebellion in 1605. The town suffered a lot from Turkish raids. It became the seat of one of the districts of the Bratislava estate in the 17th century and its importance diminished to a market and economic centre of this part of Žitný ostrov, though it won back the privilege of annual fairs in 1712.

The town suffered from great poverty during the Second World War. There was a camp for prisoners of war nearby with Russian and Italian prisoners. Šamorín was annexed to Hungary in the years 1938-1945. After the war finished a food-processing plant, new housing estates, and cultural centres were built in Šamorín, which was a district town until 1960.

Visitors who are interested in cultural monuments should start with the unique Reformed **church** which is one of the beautiful Gothic churches in Žitný ostrov. Emperor Joseph II's resolution abolished the religious orders and this also con-

cerned Franciscan monastery in Šamorín. The parish church lost its owner. After lengthy negotiations it was eventually bought in 1789 for 2,000 guldens by the Calvinist Church, which established its centre for Žitný ostrov there. The originally Late Romanesque church from the end of the 13th century was rebuilt in the 14th and 15th centuries in Gothic taste and it represents the oldest sacred Gothic monument of the town. Fire destroyed the roof of the church and damaged the tower in 1826. The porch and sacristy were added to the church and other adjustments were made in the 19th and 20th century, the most recent ones are from 1991-1995. The chancel contains unique and thoroughly restored Gothic wall paintings from the 13th century depicting various events from Bible. The Romanesque windows contain symbolic paintings representing the Creation. Above the Gothic stone font is the painting of an angel bringing the Lord's Message.

The second **church**, which is Evangelical or Lutheran, is from 1784-1785. It is Neo-Classical, but its interior bears traits of the Baroque style. The builder J.

G. Altenburger designed it, and 814 inhabitants from 136 Evangelical families helped with its construction. The dominating elements of the church are the altar and pulpit with the painting of Christ's Resurrection and guards of the grave from 1785 by the Austrian painter F. Oelenhainz. The Roman Catholic church of **the Virgin Mary's Ascension** built in the Late Baroque style is also one of the gems of the local sacred architecture. The main altar with painted pillar architecture and the statue of Madonna, the Baroque wall paintings depicting the life of St. Francis of Paula by F. Sigirst are the main attractions of its lavishly decorated interior. The pulpit with the relief of the Mount of Olives and the font are from the time when the church was built. The stained glass windows are also notable. The church forms a complex with the Pauline monastery and is connected with it by a corridor and sacristy.

The Pauline monks in Šamorín

St. Francis of Paula founded this order and Pope Sixtus IV confirmed it in 1474. Its members, apart from other vows, were not allowed to eat meat and dishes cooked on fat or butter. The order spread to the Kingdom of Hungary after the death of its founder. After the recommendation Archbishop of Esztergom, J. Széchényi it settled in Šamorín in 1660. The Paulines built the church and monastery here in 1778. The monastery consisting of only four teachers, two priests, one male nurse and one warden did not stay for long. Emperor Joseph II abolished the order in 1786.

Left: The town hall in Šamorín

The Baroque monastery, like the church, is probably the work of the builder J. G. Altenburger. It was adapted in the 19th and 20th centuries. It represents the type of monastery built around a courtyard with a cloister. The Church owns today part of the building and another part belongs to the town. The frescos and protected parts of the interior have been under restoration since 1992. A unique type of sacred architecture can be seen at the **church of St. Margita**, which is to be found outside the town in a little settlement called **Šamot**. Originally it was built in the Romanesque style in 1260. It is a single-nave church with flat ceiling. A sacristy was added to its northern wall. On the right side of the entrance is a Romanesque basin made of roughly worked stone which has probably served as a font for many centuries. The church was not much used or visited in the 19th century. It belonged to the Roman Catholic parish of Šamorín. In the years of forced atheism (1950-1980) the church was used as a corn store, then it was partially conserved. The Museum of Žitný ostrov passed the building to the Church. The archaeologists confirmed existence of a medieval settlement and a cemetery in the environs of the church of Šamot.

The Jewish community living in Šamorín built their **synagogue** in 1912 in the romanticizing and historicizing style. The women's gallery divided its space into two floors. In the time of Holocaust almost all the Jewish families were deported and one of the most beautiful synagogues existing in Žitný ostrov lost its believers. The synagogue was also used a corn store for several decades. Its interior is used as a fine art gallery, concert and theatre hall since 1996. Four Tibetan monks created a unique sacred symbol made of sand called mandala.

Secular monuments include the interesting municipal poorhouse. This building with Baroque windows and arches served later as hospital, today it houses the old people's home. There is also a Neo-Romanesque **chapel** from 1873. The former **town hall**, now the municipal office, was originally a Renaissance structure, which was repeatedly adapted. The

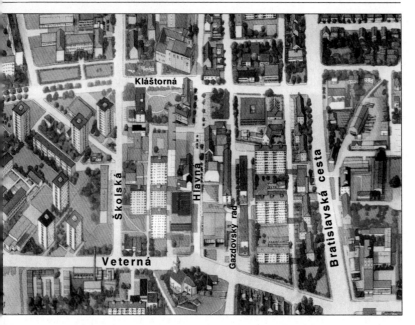

well-conserved **burgher houses** are also notable.

The families living in Slovak towns of Myjava, Senica and Brezová used to send their children to Šamorín to learn Hungarian and German in the late 19th century. The ten years old **Milan Rastislav Štefánik** was also one of the students of the local Evangelical gymnasium in 1889/1890. The monument with his relief on a plinth is standing in front of the Evangelical parsonage. The relief is by L. Majerský and it was moved to its present place from the wall of parsonage in 1900. There are also other figures connected with Šamorín: ornithologists Károly Kuns and Lajos Csiba, composer Štefan Németh-Šamorínsky, painter István Tallós-Prochádzka, the ladywriter Dömötör, and ethnographer Antal Khin, the founder of the Museum of Žitný ostrov (Žitnoostrovné múzeum).

A permanent exhibition of the town's history can be seen in the **Mestský vlastivedný dom** (The Municipal House of Homeland Studies). There are some objects connected with the history of **gold washing** activity in Žitný ostrov. Every year the event called the **Days of old**

Samária becomes the summer attraction of the town. If you are a fan of fine arts then you should visit the private art **gallery called AT HOME**. The **House of Arts** or Dom umenia of Šamorín originated by joining the restored old Jewish school with a big garden existing not far from the synagogue. It is the place of short-term stays of domestic and foreign artists, organizing workshops and youth camps for young people coming from the countries of Central Europe. It is also a venue for concerts, various conferences, symposia, open-air theatre shows and other cultural events. Horse riding is another activity, in which Šamorín has got some history. There are three race courses and a horse breeding station. Full-blooded and half-blood racehorses and breeding studs are raised in Šamorín. The International races **Dunajský pohár** (The Danube Cup) and run races **Jarná cena Šamorína** (the Spring Prize of Šamorín) are activities connected with horse riding. Šamorín has got an **open-air swimming pool** which, as it lacks a source of thermal water is opened only in summer.

The village of **Čilistov** was annexed to Šamorín in 1960. It is first referred to in the documents from 1238. Its name derives from that to the Čiliz brook. It was an arm of the Danube and it meandered through the whole of Žitný ostrov to join the main stream near the village of Čičov. The village was owned by various aristocrats in the past. Its people lived on farming and haulage. Čilistov is now better known for its recreation area with thermal **swimming pool called Lagúna** near the Hrušov dam. Another, originally independent village, now part of Šamorín is **Mliečno**. Mliečno was referred to as *Tejfalu* for the first time in 1298. Later it was mentioned as *villa Timothei* or *villa Laktis*. The name *Milchdorf* (German for Milk Village) proves the German origin of its inhabitants. In 1940 the communities Bučuháza and Kraľovianky (Királyfia in Hungarian) were annexed to Mliečno. The Jewish prayer room built in the 19th century was used as a store during the Sec-

ond World War. It was pulled down in the mid-20th century. The chapel called Boží dom from the 19th century stands in a nice little park in the middle of Mliečno. It is a simple building on rectangular ground plan with an adapted tower, which has a large entrance hall.

BÁČ (Bacsfa in Hungarian, population 600) is mentioned for the first time in historic documents from the 13th century as *Boch*, which was probably only a transcription of its present name. The Hungarian name also bore the suffix *falva* or village and its shortening gave origin to the name Bacsfa. It used to belong to the yeomen of Vojka nad Dunajom. The village was stricken by plague and cholera epidemics, fires and floods. The surviving population expressed their gratitude by building a **chapel** in 1725. Destructive fire burnt down the whole village in 1866. Báč is in fact a compound of three villages Svätý Jur and Svätý Anton. The three villages adopted the name Bacsfa in 1781. Archbishop of Esztergom J. Lippay had a **church with monastery** built near the homestead of Svätý Jur. It was started in 1660 but the works were interrupted after the Archbishop's death. J. Szelepcsényi, the new Archbishop continued with the construction of the church. The Roman Catholic church with monastery were built simultaneously in the Early Baroque taste in 1674. It was the time, when the Archbishop of Esztergom invited the St. Francis of Assisi male order to settle in the monastery. The single-nave church with barrel vaulting was adapted in the 18th century. Original wall paintings in Art Nouveau style from about 1900 represent the valuable part of the church, but the main altar from 1782 with the painting of the Virgin Mary from the late 18th century and one of Anton of Padua from 1801, the former patron saint of the church, are also precious. Historic monuments are concentrated in the park, which is a **protected area**. After abolition of the Franciscan order the monastery was used as a granary and the church served as a hayloft. The Franciscans were allowed to come back by the Pressburg administration only in 1811. The Neo Gothic Calvary from 1867 and a round chapel of St. An-

Left: The reservoir in Hrušov
Right: The church in Báč

thony of Padua also enrich the spiritual life of the village. **Pilgrimages to Our Weeping Lady** are held in June and September. The Neo-Classical manor house from the early 19th century built on older foundations is the building reminiscent of the Apponyi aristocratic family.

Báč is not far from the little village of **TRNÁVKA** (Csallóköztárnok in Hungarian, population 400). It was mentioned for the first time in a document form 1275 as *Tarnuk*, when ancestors of the Olgay family owned it. From the 16th century it was a serf village of the Veľký Máger estate, a property of the Pressburg (old name for Bratislava) of the Clarist convent. When the convent was abolished in the 19th century, the village passed to the ownership of the Esterházy and then Zichy and other noble families. The Neo Classicist **chapel** of the Virgin Mary built in 1849 got a new tower by the beginning of the 20th century. **MACOV** (Macháza in Hungarian, population 100), now an independent village, was annexed to Trnávka in the years 1976-1990. This village was first referred to in 1367 as *Machhaza*. It was a royal property and later belonged to the Pálffy family. The Slovak name has been used since 1927. After 1920 Czech, Moravian and Slovak families settled the confiscated Pálffy lands and the descendants of the settlers still live there.

In the western part of Žitný ostrov, 5.5 km north-east of Šamorín is the village of **VEĽKÁ PAKA** (Nagypaka in Hungarian, population 700). It is known as an archaeological locality with finds of graves of the Magyar Culture from the Older Bronze Age. It originated by joining of the villages of Veľká, Malá, and Čukárska Paka, which existed on the lands administered by the original settlement called Paka. The first reference to the village is from 1222. Veľká Paka was a serf village of the Bratislava Castle estate. Malá Paka was owned by several aristocratic families and became part of the Eberhard estate of Malinovo in the 18th century. Čukárska Paka was part of the lands owned by the Csukárd yeoman family and later its owners changed frequently. The most important sacred monument of the village is the Baroque Roman Catholic **church of St.**

Ladislav built in 1678. The chancel of the original church was adapted to a lateral chapel in 1937. The new nave built in transversal position towards the original building has a panelled ceiling. The altar of the old chancel is Neo-Classical with painting of St. Ladislav from the second half of the 18th century. The **Chapel of the Holy Cross** from the second half of the 19th century built on older foundations is important for the spiritual life of inhabitants of **Malá Paka**.

West of Šamorín is the village of **HAMULIAKOVO** (Gutor in Hungarian, population 800). Although it is situated on an aggradation rampart of the Danube it is the lowest situated settlement of the Senec district (129 m above sea level). The first reference to this village is from 1222 as *Gutt*. After 1284 it is referred to as *Gutor* and also the church dedicated to the St. Cross is mentioned. In 1287 and alternative name of *Gvttur* appeared. The village is the birth place of Guthori family, who also owned other property within the County of Bratislava. The yeoman Ladislav Nagy, the Comes of Bratislava County, later Vice Palatine was and im-

portant lord of the village around 1450. The family Sidó owned the village from the late 15th to early 20th centuries. The village suffered a lot from floods, for instance those of 1679, 1809, 1862, 1928, and 1929. The villagers lived on farming, fishing and milling. There were 22 mills working on the Danube by the early 20th century. Fishing disappeared only in the 1950's. Fishing thrived not only in the Danube but also in the lateral and dead arms of the river. The best known fishing family was the Lengyels. Several 19th century **farming houses** made of unburned bricks and reed roofs, the traditional building technology used in the area, have survived in Hamuliakovo, while Nos. 72 and 82 are the most picturesque ones. The Slovak name of the village Hamuliakovo has been used use since 1948.

The most important sacred monument is the local Roman Catholic **church of the Holy Cross** from the 13th century. It stands in the centre of the village on the

bank of a former lateral arm of the Danube. It is one of the most important brick Romanesque sacred buildings in Slovakia. Its present appearance is the result of repeated reconstruction in the period of Baroque and in the 19th and 20th centuries. The main altar with two Neo-Classic statues from the early 19th century, Baroque statues of St. Barbara and St. John Nepomuk from the late 18th century are the attractions of the interior of this church. The fresco decoration from the second half of the 14th century is unique. It consists of Gothic wall paintings inspired in old Church symbols.

Hamuliakovo, as a typical yeoman village used to have numerous curias and manor houses. Only two **curias** survive. The village is adorned by several monuments and smaller sacred buildings. As far as natural landmarks are concerned, near the Hrušov reservoir are the remains of the oak forest, which used to be the pride of the village and a hunting ground. It was cut when the dam was built. Only a row of lime trees survived at the road edge, which once led to the gate of the Neo-Classical manor house. In front of disappeared Szmrtnik curia an elm tree used to stand called "the Rákóczi fa" under which the anti-Habsburg rebel Ferenc Rákóczi II was allegedly buried. The tree was cut in the 1960's. The landscape park of the manor house was founded in 1860. Its later owner, Baron Juraj Leonhardhi changed it to an Arboretum with countless exotic wood and shrub species at the turn of the 19th and 20th centuries. This park also disappeared in the 1960's. The administrative territory of Hamuliakovo included floodplain forest with protected tree species, on the Cormorant Island, which lay between the main stream and the Danube arm.

Situation of the village on the shore of the Hrušov reservoir is a very advantageous one, as it has all attributes of a tourist locality.

KALINKOVO (Szemet in Hungarian, population 900) is 3 km away from Hamuliakovo. Its existence was confirmed for the first time in 1288 when it belonged to Bratislava Castle. It is known under various historic names, for example: *Scemet*,

Left: The church in Hamuliakovo
Right: Nové Košariská
        Pottery from Dunajská Lužná

Zemeth, Zemety and the present name Kalinkovo, used since 1948. In the 15th century it was property of the Counts of Sv. Jur and Pezinok, later it was included in the Eberhard estate. It was often flooded. The villagers lived on farming and gardening. Brick houses with gables and saddle roofs survive here from the late 19th century. The ruins of the Romanesque church, which disappeared in the 1930's, are from 1260. The Roman Catholic **church of St. Francis Seraphin** represents sacred architecture from 1910. It is a historicizing building with Neo-Romanesque elements.

DUNAJSKÁ LUŽNÁ (population 2,900) originated after January 1st 1974 by joining originally independent villages of Nové Košariská, Jánošíková, and Nová Lipnica. The population of the three villages was involved in farming, cattle raising, weaving and haulage in the past.

History of the local nomenclature

Nové Košariská (New Košariská) gained its name in 1945 as immigrants from the area of Košariská in the Myjava region settled it. Its original Hungarian name was Misérd (in German Mischdorf). The village of Jánošíková also acquired its name because of the origin of its new settlers. They came from Terchová, the birth place of the Slovak national hero, Jánošík. Before that it was called Dénesd in Hungarian (Schildern in German). The history of the name of Nová (New) Lipnica is the same. Its immigrants came from Lipnica in the Orava region (Lipnica was annexed to Poland). The original name of Nová Lipnica was Torcs in Hungarian and Tartschendorf in German.

Jánošíková was mentioned for the first time in a document from 1206 when it was property of Bratislava Castle. In 1258 the Benedictine monastery of Panonhalma in Hungary owned it. The geographical and historical lexicon by Ján Matej Korabinský from 1786 mentions this village as a place where good quality bags for millers and soap-makers were woven. The most important monument of the village is the Roman Catholic **church of the Exaltation of the Holy Cross**. Abbot Somogyi had it built on the site of a Romanesque church from the 13th century in the years 1786-1797. The church was also a pilgrim place until 1945. The main altar contains a very old statue of the Blessed Virgin Mary with the Child Jesus. The statue is carved from a pear tree wood and it is from the 13th century. It is subject of various legends and unexplained stories, usually connected with the miraculous cure of the sick. People called it "the Helping God's Mother". Along with a similar statue in Mariánka it is probably the oldest preserved medieval sculpture in Slovakia. Its official name is

the Statue of the Madonna on a Throne and it is a **cultural monument**.

Nová Lipnica was first mentioned in 1230 as *Torch*. It was royal property administered by Bratislava Castle. In the 17th century the lords of Sv. Jur owned part of this village, later it belonged to the Eberhard estate. There are still **houses made of earth** from the late 19th and early 20th centuries. Visitors to this part of Dunajská Lužná will perhaps be interested in the Neo-Gothic **belfry** built in 1864, the bell of which used in the past as an alarm in case of emergency. The oldest settlement and part of today's village existed in the administrative territory of **Nové Košariská**, which is an important archaeological locality.

The Hallstatt barrows

The group of 3 m tall and 40 m in diameter barrows is one of the most important finding places of the East Hallstatt Circle of the Older Iron Age. Inside the cremation graves unique vessels were found..

Left: The church in Jánošiková
Right: The statue of the Virgin Mary

One of the graves contained as much as 80 vessels of unusual artistic value and pottery decorated by animal patterns. The buried people were members of the Calenderberg Culture in the years 700-550 BC.

The Quadi later occupied the territory, and Avars arrived in the 6th to 8th century. There are also traces of Slav settlement in Nové Košariská. The village was first mentioned in 1212 as *Mysser*. It was owned then by Bratislava Castle and later it was part of the Eberhard estate. The originally Gothic Roman Catholic church of St. Martin of Nové Košariská was rebuilt in Baroque taste in the 18th century. In 1852 the whole village including the church burnt down. Only the polygonal chancel of the church survived. It is today the **chapel** of St. Martin. Its main altar contains the Baroque sculptures of the Virgin Mary and St. John Evangelist from the 18th century and a more recent statue of St. Martin. The Neo-Classical Evangelical **church** was built in 1814. The spiritual life of the villagers is also symbolized by small chapels, crosses and a Lourdes Cave from 1928. The channel of the Danube is 3 to 4 km away from Dunajská Lužná. The protective dike runs along the south-western edge of the village. When a new dike was built for the Gabčíkovo dam, the old one was preserved as a **technical monument**. In the administrative territory of the village are numerous artificial water bodies such as Malá voda and Piesková jama, which originated as gravel pits. Now they are used for fishing and recreation. The natural landmarks of the village include the 200 hundred year old protected **plane tree of Nová Lipnica** and the **300 year old oak tree** in the yard of the municipal office. The International Bike route Passau-Budapest crosses this village.

MILOSLAVOV (population 800) lies next to Dunajská Lužná, 8 km south-east of Bratislava and 10 km from Šamorín. The core of the village was two country estates: Alžbetin majer and Anna majer. **Alžbetin majer** is the older of the two, it originated in the 13th century around the Romanesque church of St. Elisabeth. The settlement called *Szent Erzsébet* (St. Elisabeth) and its church is first mentioned in 1339. The village became from later property of the Benedictine Abbey of St. Martin at Pannonhalma in Hungary, which sold it to the Pauline monastery in Mariánka in 1521. The plague, which swept over a great part of Žitný ostrov region also caused depopulation of this village in the 16th century. Sv. Alžbeta estate was mentioned as a deserted one containing bare ruins in 1634. The Archbishop of Esztergom, György Szelepcsényi, sponsor of arts and saviour of abandoned homesteads influenced the later development of the village. He renewed the village in the years 1666 to 1679 by inviting colonists from Croatia. Croatians in fact inherited the village from Germans, Hungarians and Slovaks. The settlement became part of the Eberhard estate owned by the Apponyis from 1810. The Knight Wiener-Welten of Vienna bought the village and added it to his estate of Hubice in 1882. He expanded the estate, which then consisted of eleven buildings including a granary, stables, store buildings, inn, an old parsonage, houses for workers, wheelright's workshop, an inn and furnace for the lords and a church. Not far from Alžbetin majer another country estate called **Anna majer** sprung up in the early 19th century. It bore the name of Anna Apponyi, who bought the Eberhard estate. Anna majer is represented on old maps under the Hungarian name Új major (The New Country Estate). It consisted of four farm buildings and later passed to the hands of Wiener-Welten. The life of both estates changed a lot after the disintegration of the Austro-Hungarian Empire.

Alžbetin majer estate was later renamed Alžbetin dvor and it was also parcelled. Later it was added to Miloslava and both settlements now form the village of Miloslavov.

The oldest sacred monument of the two settlements is the former Roman Catholic church of St. Elisabeth of Hungary built in the 13th century in the Romanesque style. The church ant its environs was a much sought after pilgrim destination. It lost this function by the end of the 18th century and the Apponyi family gradually changed the church into a gra-

nary. The Roman Catholic Church owns it again nowadays, although only its outer walls survive. Reconstruction into its Early Baroque appearance with presentation of the preserved Romanesque architectural elements is now considered. The church is one of the items in the list of cultural monuments. A new Roman Catholic **church of the Holy Mercy** was started in 1997 and finished according to the plans of the architect K. Trizuliak in 1998. It stands on the square of the former Alžbetin dvor not far from the old church. It calls attention with its ground plan shaped as a ship, as it symbolizes the ship of St. Peter. Relief of Jesus Christ according to the vision the beatified sister Faustina, work of from the sculptor Vincent Hložník is the interesting item of its interior. Fourteen windows symbolize the fourteen stations of the Cross. The **prayer room** of the Brotherly Unity of Baptists from 1926 is another sacred monument of the village. This single-nave building with flat ceiling immediately adjoins the parsonage and congregation room. The village has got two **belfries**. The one in Alžbetin dvor is from 1947 and the belfry in

Miloslavov was built in 1935. Several surviving houses are reminders of the period when the colony was founded. The oldest colonial house from 1921 is the building No. 200. Juraj Stanko, the bricklayer, who came here from Hungary, owns it.

The village of **ROVINKA** (Csölle in Hungarian, population 1,200) is 2.5 km away from Dunajská Lužná. The first reference to this settlement is from 1287. This village was divided into two in about the second half of the 14th century to form Dolná and Horná Čela. Horná Čela and a half of Dolná Čela were owned by the Archbishopric of Esztergom until 1375. Its inhabitants were farmers. There are **earthen houses** in the village surviving from the end of the 19th century. The Roman Catholic **church of the Most Holy Trinity** was built in 1789. Its main altar is from the 20th century. Secular monuments are represented by the Neo-Classical **manor house**. The ground floor rooms of this two storied building are vaulted. The village is now part of the suburban recreation zone of Bratislava with its **lake Rovinka** which originated after extraction of gravel.

An interesting tourist route is that from Šamorín to in the direction to the north-east. The first village in this direction is **KVETOSLAVOV** (Úszor in Hungarian, population 800), territory of which was inhabited as early as in Roman times. Later it was depopulated. The first reference to the village is from 1282 under historic name *Vuzor* or *Uzor*. Its present name has been used since 1948. The village used to belong to several noble families. Germans settled here in 1787 and called the village *Austern*. The population lived on farming. The only sacred monument there is the **chapel** of the Assumption of the Virgin Mary from 1883. It is a romaticizing building with Neo-Gothic elements, its interior contains Baroque painting of the Virgin Mary of Rosary from the late 18th century.

The contiguous village of **HVIEZDOSLAVOV** (Vörösmajor in Hungarian, population 300) is one of the youngest of the district Dunajská Streda. It originated by joining the settlements of Nemčok and Červený majer. The Apponyi family founded Červený majer or Vörösmajor although the Pálffys later bought it. Nemčok or Németsok in Hungarian containing service buildings of the Apponyis was later acquired by the Wiener-Weltens. Expropriation of enormous properties of the aristocracy started after the disintegration of the Austro-Hungarian Empire and it also affected the Pálffy and Wiener-Welten estates. People who came here from Ústie na Orave in the north of Slovakia then colonized Červený majer. The name of the village was changed after their recommendation to Hviezdoslavov, after a poet from of the Orava region. This was the village with the first school in Žitný ostrov region where the tuition was given in the Slovak language in 1922. The lime tree planted on the ceremonious occasion is still there. The people were mostly farmers. The village was annexed to Hungary for a short time while Alžbetin dvor, which was only one kilometre away remained on Slovak territory. The Slovak settlers of Hviezdoslavov had to flee, when Hungarian soldiers came and carried away everything they could, for instance, the bell, farm tools, etc. The village lost its independence as it was annexed to Štvrtok na Ostrove. The houses were sacked, fields abandoned and the village was decaying. Some of its original inhabitants returned to their houses after the Second World War and the vacant and abandoned ones were again settled by people from the villages of Orava, which disappeared when the Orava dam was constructed. Hviezdoslavov became again an independent village only in 1951. The most notable buildings of the village are undoubtedly those of the former Pálffy estate in the western corner of the village square. The first Slovak school in Žitný ostrov is now empty. In the middle of the park stands the **statue of P. O. Hviezdoslav** from 1971 by the sculptor T. Baník and the architect R. Janák. Several houses of the first colonist survived in the village, and in Nemčok is the building of the former stable of the Wiener-Welten's estate from the 19th century.

Right: A sun flower in Kvetoslavov

Archaeological finds in the village of **MIEROVO** (Béke in Hungarian, population 400) document settlement in Classical times and Migration Period. The village was first mentioned in a document from 1252 as *Beke*. It used to belong to the St. Jur estate and then from the 17th century to the Eberhard estate. The oldest sacred monument is the Roman Catholic **church of St. Michael the Archangel** built as a brick Romanesque church in the 13th century. It was adapted in the Baroque style in the 18th century and rebuilt in the 20th century. Its single-nave building with chancel has a flat ceiling, the interior furniture is Baroque from the second half of the 18th century. The Late-Baroque **manor house** from the second half of the 18th century, which was adapted in the 19th century is the witness to the life of yeomen.

Two kilometres from Mierovo is the village of **OĽDZA** (Olgya in Hungarian, population 300) mentioned in several historic documents. In 1239 it was referred to as *Olgia* and in 1251 as *Ouga*. It belonged to Bratislava Castle and later to various noble families, especially the Olgyays. There is a Neo-Classical curia in the village built on older foundations from the first half of the 19th century. The ceilings of the rooms of this ground floor building facing the street are flat.

The village of **NOVÝ ŽIVOT** (Illesháza in Hungarian, population 2.000) lies further north on the road from Zlaté Klasy to Sládkovičovo. It acquired its present form by joining the villages Eliášovce, Tonkovce and Vojtechovce in 1960.

The subordinate village called **Eliášovce** (Illésháza) was first mentioned in 1238. It was the property of Illésházy family and the seat of the estate. The village was sacked during the Rebellion of Estates. In the 19th century it was property of Batthyányi and Pálffy families. A ford on the Malý Dunaj river where gold was once washed belonged to the territory of the village. Solitary houses and homesteads dispersed around the village were also its part. The most important was that of Szerhásháza, which merged with Eliášovce in the 18th century. Another settlement was Svätý Peter (Szentpéterfölde).

People of Eliášovce were farmers. An important sacred monument of the village is originally Gothic Roman Catholic **church of St. Peter and Paul** from the second half of the 15th century, adapted in Neo-Classical taste in the 18th century. Its interior is notable as it contains the main altar of St. Peter and Paul the Apostles from around 1800 with a Gothic sculpture of the Madonna from 1458. In the wall of the Gothic sanctuary is the epitaph of Provost Matthew Illésházy made from red marble and adorned by his life-size relief. Not far from it is the tombstone of the Illésházy family, who is buried in the church grave, covered during the Baroque reconstruction. The family of Count Illésházy died out in 1838 by death of Stephen, who is buried in the new church and commemorated by a monument in the local church. There is also a Neo-Classical **chapel** from the 19th century at the crossroads and next to the church is the Late-Baroque **Calvary** with sculptures of the saints from the 18th century.

The subordinate village of **Vojtechovce** (Bélvata) was mentioned for the first time in the 1239 document as *Vo-*

jtha. It was property of Bratislava Castle. One on its landmarks is the belfry with a prismoid roof and bell from 1924. **Tonkovce** originated by joining the villages of Tonkháza and Malý Máter into one village called in Hungarian Tonkháza. The first of the two above-mentioned villages is documented from 1308 as *Tonkvatha* and the other was mentioned in 1298 as a property of Bratislava Castle. In the 17th century the greater part of Tonkáza was owned by Illésházys, part of Malý Máger was the property of the Clarist convent in Bratislava. One of the interesting monuments of the village is the single-floor **curia** and the originally Baroque **manor house** from the early 18th century. Another **manor house** was built in the second half of the 18th century and rebuilt by the end of the 19th century in a romaticizing historicist style. Now it houses the House of International School Relations. This extensive building with two lateral wings stands in the local park.

Left: The manor house in Tonkovce
Right: Flora from the area of the Malý Dunaj

BELLOVA VES (Vitény in Hungarian, population 160) is a village, which originated by separation from Tonkovce in 1955. The original village of Vitény was mentioned only in the mid-19th century. In the years 1976-1990 it existed jointly with the village Blahová. **BLAHOVÁ** (Sárrét in Hungarian, population 400) originated in 1951 by separation from the village of Lehnice. The majority of its population were colonists of the 1920´s, who were forced to leave when both villages of Lehnice and Blahová were annexed to Hungary. The Gothic Roman Catholic **church**, the only sacred monument of the village, is from the second half of the 14th century. Next to the village and in a pleasant setting of the Malý Dunaj river is a popular recreation place **Madarász** with a swimming pool, mini-golf course and tennis courts.

Cultural monument enthusiasts should turn off the main road between Šamorin and Zlaté Klasy and visit the village of **ŠTVRTOK na Ostrove** (Csallóközcsütörtök in Hungarian, population 1,700). This settlement was mentioned for the first time in the document from 1206 as *Stwrtok* and in 1240 in the German form *Leupsdorf*. Then it was mentioned as *Lopesdorf* in 1254 and as *villa Leopoldi* in 1311. King Andrew II of Hungary donated the village to the lords of Pezinok and Sv. Jur in 1206. It developed into a town with market and fair rights in the 14th century. It was owned by the Serédyi, Amade, and later in the 16th century by the Pálffy and Wiener-Welten families. The people lived on farming and trade in agricultural crops. The unique Roman Catholic **church of St. James** is a Romanesque building with Gothic bell from the 13th century with two towers, which was adapted in the 16th century in the Renaissance style. The most valuable part of the building is the Romanesque portal of the western group of three towers and the Renaissance epitaphs from 1572. There are fragments of Gothic wall paintings in the interior of the church. The church was adapted again in the 19th century. The settlement formerly included the solitary homesteads of Červený majer, Nemčok, Anna majer and Alžbetin dvor, which were parcelled in the 1920's and became the homes of Moravian, Czech and Slovak colonists.

North of the village is **ČAKANY** (Csákány in Hungarian, population 500) first mentioned in 1254 as *Chakan*. Originally it was a serf village of the Cistercian Abbey at Zirck. The Abbey settled the village with the Moravians in the 13th century. The colonists soon mixed with the original Hungarian and German population. The villagers were mostly farmers, they raised cattle and sheep after the 18th century. The Baroque Roman Catholic **church of St. Michael the Archangel** from the late 17th century, later adapted in the Neo-Classical taste is one of important sacred monuments of the Danubeland It intrigues with its main altar bearing a painting of the patron saint and the wall paintings from the second half of the 18th century, which were repainted in the late 19th and early 20th centuries. The village has a well-preserved Baroque **manor house** from the end of the 17th century, adapted in 1712 and rebuilt in 1824. Archbishop Juraj Szelepcsényi had it built. The manor house is now a home for

abandoned children. The former French park around the manor house is a **protected area**.

The village of **HUBICE** (Gomba in Hungarian, population 300) is situated 12 km north-east of Šamorín. It was mentioned in historic documents for the first time in 1293 as *Gumba*. The name Gomba appeared as early as in the years 1298 and 1301. It was owned by the Gombay and other aristocratic families from the 15th century. Plague epidemics repeatedly struck the village in the 16th and 17th centuries. Archbishop György Szelepcsényi became the landlord of the village at the end of the 17th century. The Knight Rudolf Wiener Welten bought it in the 19th century, settled there with his family and founded a breeding station for full-blooded horses. The present name has been used since 1948. The most important sacred monument of the village is the Romanesque Roman Catholic **church of the Visitation of the Virgin Mary** from the 13th century. It was rebuilt in the Gothic style in the 15th century and adapted in the Baroque taste in the 17th century. The main altar made of wood with pillar architecture and a central painting of the Visitation of the Virgin Mary is the most interesting part of its interior. The altar was reconstructed in 1998. The stay of the aristocrats and Archbishops of Esztergom is testified to by numerous important secular monuments.

The manor houses of Hubice

The older and bigger manor house was built in 1830 probably on older foundations. In the 17th century the Archbishop of Esztergom György Szelepcsényi founded here a factory of Dutch type for production of wool cloth in the original building and in-

troduced sheep raising. He also founded ponds and a game enclosure. The manor house is now private property. Better conserved and kept is the younger and "smaller" manor house from the first third of the 19th century built in the Neo-Classical style with two ground floor lateral wings. It originated by reconstruction of a horse stable. The park and the manor house were inhabited by the Knight Rudolf Wiener-Welten until 1948 when he moved to Vienna. This manor house is also now private property.

The **park** around the manor house, the area of which is 40 hectares originated in the 1880's. In its centre was a pond with swans and an island. The banks of the pond were framed by yew trees and beyond them was a water reservoir in the Neo-Gothic style with musical clock. Another interesting place in the park was the "Alps", a coniferous wood in the upper end of the park consisting of firs, spruces and pines. The man-made cave hidden in the shadow of the trees contained an artificial spring with a several meter long stream that fed the pond. The channel was crossed by several bridges made of wood overgrown with roses or stone bridges overgrown with ivy. The park also had a Tyrolean pavilion. Not far from the manor house and near to the entrance to the rose garden with 2-3 thousand varieties of roses stood the bust of the composer F. Schubert. The park contained many notable buildings. The burial **chapel** of the Wiener-Welten family from the end of the 19th century is worth to mention. A cave called "the bear cave" was built of stone and its interior was lined with boards and tree bark. The lords of the manor house used the cave in time of hot weather as an ice store. One can see remains of a stone bridge next to the cave and at the end of the park stands the gate called Čakanská which led to the road to Čakany lined with rows of trees.

The **curia** of the Kempelen family is also an interesting building. Jan Kempelen rebuilt the original Baroque one storey floor curia from 1722 as a Neo-Classical

---

Left: The church in Štvrtok n. O.
Right: The church in Hubice
         The manor house in Hubice

summer residence. The inventor Wolfgang Kempelen lived in this curia in his older age. Hubice became world famous for its horse breeding station introduced here by the noble family of Wiener-Welten. English thoroughbred and half full-blooded horses as well as various horse breeds of draught were bred here. Behind the curia is still a surviving stable for young stately horses bearing the traces of Neo-Classical architecture. In the former area of stud three circular stables for young horses existed and one of them was preserved in its original state, the other is in ruins and the third was pulled down. The stud farm was moved to Šamorín in 1958.

ZLATÉ KLASY (Nagymagyar in Hungarian, population 3,300) were founded in 1960 by joining the villages of Čenkovce, Maslovce, and Rastice. The subordinate village of **Maslovce** (Vajasvata) are referred to in historic documents from 1239 as *Watha*. The settlement was royal property of Bratislava Castle. After some time two villages Bél and Vajas-Vata originated nearby as serf villages of the Clarist convent in Bratislava. The Esterházy family owned them from the 19th century. In the subordinate village **Rastice** (Nagymagyar) an inhumation cemetery was found. The village was first mentioned in 1237 as *Mager*, the royal property. Afterwards they belonged to the Clarist convent and later to other owners. The village populated by mixed German and Hungarian population had the right to one fair a year in the 17th century. Its inhabitants lived on crafts and trade. Sheep raising was quite common as well. In the early 19th century the village had its brewery and an inn for travellers. The name Rastice has been used from 1948, it derives from the name of the

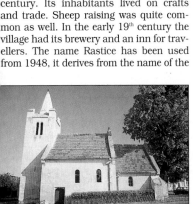

Great Moravian Prince Rastislav. The most important sacred monument in the village is the Roman Catholic **church of Exaltation of the Holy Cross**. It was built in 1889 in the then fashionable romantic historicist style on the site of an old Late Gothic church. The Neo-Classical **chapel** from the mid-19th century complements the sacred monuments of the village. The Baroque and Neo-Classical tombstones represent the remains of the Jewish cemetery from the 18th and 19th centuries. The secular monument of the village is the Neo-Classical curia from the first half of the 19th century.

ČENKOVCE (Csenke in Hungarian, population 900) is now an independent village. It is situated south-east of Zlaté Klasy. It originated at the turn of the 11th and 12th centuries and its task was to protect the frontiers of the Kingdom of Hungary. It appears in historic documents for the first time in 1211 under the name *Chenkez*. Another document from 1240 by which King Belo IV donated it to the family of Csenkey quotes the name *Chekenel*. Several noble families, among them the Esterházys and Zichys owned this village

in the 18ᵗʰ and 19ᵗʰ centuries. The village acquired its Slovak name in 1948.

Archaeological finds of barrows from the Lower Bronze Age and Older Iron Age made **JANÍKY** (Jányok, population 800) famous. It is situated 3 km north-west of Zlaté Klasy and originated by joining the settlements of Dolné Janíky, Horné Janíky and Bustelek in 1940. The first written reference to the village appeared in 1278 under the name *Janok*. Fourteenth century documents record three villages Horné, Dolné and Malé Janíky, the two last mentioned bore the name Bústelek in the 18ᵗʰ and 19ᵗʰ centuries. Horné and Dolné Janíky were serf villages of the Clarist convent in Bratislava and various yeoman families owned Bústelek. The local people lived on farming. The most important sacred monument is the Roman Catholic **church** from 1914 built on the site of an original chapel in romantic style. Stone statues of St. Michael and St. Vendelín from 1921 stand in front of the church.

TOMÁŠOV (Fél in Hungarian, population 2,000) is 1.5 km away from Janíkov. This village originated by joining the villages of Fél, Hideghét and Madarász in one under the name *Fél*. The village changed its name to Tomášov after 1946. The former Hideghét was annexed to the village of Most pri Bratislave after 1955. Fél is first mentioned in 1240 as a property of Bratislava Castle. In the 13ᵗʰ century different yeoman families owned it. Madarász is first referred to in 1333 as a property of Hody family. It belonged to the town of Trnava in 1553. Both settlements were owned by the Eberhard estate and the Counts of Sv. Jur and Pezinok in the 16ᵗʰ century. Today they also include small settlements of Malý Madaras and Doma.

The Baroque Roman Catholic **church of St. Nicolas the Bishop** was built in the years 1750-1755 on older foundations. Its facade was adapted in the romantic spirit in the 19ᵗʰ century. In its interior the main altar from the second half of the 19ᵗʰ century, the font and pulpit from the second half of the 18ᵗʰ century are of interest. In the cemetery is the Neo-Gothic **chapel** of the Holy Cross from the end of the 19ᵗʰ

Left: The manor house in Tomášov
Right: The Malý Dunaj near Vlky

century. The wooden sculptures of St. John Nepomuk, St. Krištof and St. Dominik in its interior are from the second half of the 18th century. Secular monuments in the village include the originally Baroque **manor house** from 1736. It was adapted in the last quarter of the 18th century in the Baroque-Neo-Classical style and again in 1953 adapted in historicizing style. This extensive U-shaped two-storied building is situated amidst an English park. Now it shelters the children's centre.

A small village of **VLKY** (Vök in Hungarian, population 400) is located in the north-western part of Žitný ostrov not far from the Malý Dunaj river. It was first mentioned in 1260, when it was owned by the Bratislava Provost and Chapter. The Church obtained this property from King Belo IV and King Ladislav IV confirmed the donation. The name of the village changed in the course of history. The local tradition says that the name derives from its founder or its first inhabitant called Welk. In 1553 when it was owned by the Pálffys, its name is quoted as *Weok*. Two mills were working on the Malý Dunaj then. But the water was also the cause of great suffering to the people. Frequent floods caused a change in position of the village. The present village is on top of the aggradation rampart of the Malý Dunaj river. The properties of the Bratislava Chapter were bought out by the late 19th and early 20th century by the local farmers. The villagers were mostly occupied in farming and fishing.

A wonderful sacred monument of this village is the area of the **Lourdes cave**. The structure was built in 1933 by Baltazár Hideghéty. The cave is a small stone building with a relief of Christ made by the stonemason Eugen Jakóczy from around 1950. The statue of the Virgin Mary of Lourdes is from Rome and the walls of the cave are covered by tablets expressing gratitude for healing. A row of chestnut trees rims the road to the cave surrounded by a garden. The most important secular monument of the village is the Hideghéty **curia** built in 1920. It is a one storey building with an L-shaped ground plan. The life of the rich villagers is testified to by several **houses**. The vil-

lage has preserved its typical appearance from the late 19th and early 20th centuries.

MALINOVO (Eberhard, population 1,300) is 3 km away from Tomášov. The village is situated on the aggradation rampart of the Malý Dunaj. Existence of this village is documented from 1209 as *Ybreharth* in relation to the local water castle. It was owned by the Counts of St. Jur and Pezinok in the 13th century. After the 17th century it became the property of the feudal estate of Eberhard, later its owners alternated. In the 1920's a colony, now an independent village, originated on the territory of Eberhard when the parcelled fields were colonized. It is called **Zálesie**. The originally Renaissance **manor house** built on the foundation of a disappeared water castle is from the last third of the 17th century. The Neo-Gothic Roman Catholic **church of St. George the Martyr** was originally the burial chapel of the Apponyi family from 1872. This brick building without plaster has a big pointed window above portal. In its interior the main altar from time when the church was built with a sculpture of St. George from the middle of the 18th century is of

interest. In the eastern wing of the church is the Renaissance **chapel** built around 1677. Other church monuments also prove the religiousness of the local population. They are the Neo-Classical belfry from 1862 and the Baroque road statue of St. John from 1793. The village boasts the oldest school of gardeners in Slovakia. The school building has a wonderful garden with imported wood species. The village was annexed to Hungary in years 1938-1945 and the present Slovak name has been used since 1948.

MOST pri Bratislave (population 1,500) as it is now, originated in 1955, when a part of Tomášov called Hideghét was annexed to Most na Ostrove. Historic documents mentioned the village for the first time in 1283 as *Pruk*, later it was denoted as *Hidas*. It used to belong to the Eberhard estate and partly also to other yeoman families. Hideghét is quoted as *Heet* in 1294. It was owned by yeoman families, by the Archbishop of Esztergom

in the 14th century, and various noble families in the 17th century. It was colonized by colonists from Carinthia in Austria in the mid-18th century. The population were prevailingly farmers. The important sacral monument of this village is the Roman Catholic **church of the Most Sacred Heart of Jesus**. An originally Gothic church from the first quarter of the 14th century was adapted in the 16th and 19th centuries and widened in the Neo-Romanesque style in 1910. In the original part of the church a stone font and wall painting from the 14th century have been preserved. There are also several Baroque statues placed on more recent altars, a Rococo confessional and several interesting paintings of the saints.

The south-eastern direction of the route around Šamorín also offers some interesting natural and cultural landmarks. Not far from Báč is the notable village of **ROHOVCE** (Nagyszarva in Hungarian, population 1,000). It was first mentioned in 1250 as *Zerva*, later as *Zarwa* or *Nagyzarwa* (Great Sarva).

The estate of Great Sarva

Great Sarva was on of the most important estates of Žitný ostrov. The centre of the estate was the manor house of the Illésházys. It originated in the second half of the 16th century by reconstruction of a small manor house with moat, then owned by the Sárkányi family. King Louis II with his wife spent several days in this manor house as a guest of the Sárkányis. The estate was also owned by the Bátthányis in the 19th century and Pongráczs who owned the property until 1945.

Part of the village called Malá Sarva was an independent village until the 18th century. Then it was joined to Veľká Sarva, The Slovak name of the village has been used since 1948. The most important sacred monument is the originally Romanesque Roman Catholic **church of St. Andrew the Apostle** from the 13th century, adapted in the Gothic taste in the 15th century and rebuilt in the Baroque style in the 18th century. The main altar bearing a painting of St. Andrew the Apostle is from the second half of the 19th cen-

Left: The ferry in Kyselica
Right: The church in Vojka n. D

tury. Originally Renaissance **manor house** from 1570 is now cultural monument. It acquired its present appearance after the Baroque reconstruction in 1730. It is surrounded by the local **park**, a protected area.

The village of **KYSELICA** (Keszölcés in Hungarian, population 100) is the smallest one of this part of the region. But it is one of the oldest settlements as it was mentioned in a historic document from 1205. The name *Keseulces* known from 1323 might have been derived from the acid spring (kyslý in Slovak means acid) or the acid grass growing around the village. The greatest wealth of the settlement in the past were the Danube islands with meadows and pastures, abundance of timber and game. The banks of the Danube were framed by mills. The Neo-Classical Roman Catholic **church of St. Rozália** built in 1889 is the sacred monument of the village. Kyselica was annexed to Vojka in 1940 and again separated 1981 when the feeding channel of the Danube was constructed. It has been an independent village since 1991. The two separated villages of Vojka and Kyselica are now connected by a **ferry**.

VOJKA nad Dunajom (Vajka in Hungarian, population 400) is 9 km southeast of Šamorín, in the western part of the island limited by the old channel of the Danube and the new feeding channel. Finds from the Migration Period were discovered in the environs of the village. It was first referred to as *Vayka* in documents form 1186. It was property of Bratislava Castle and Chapter. King Belo IV later donated it to the Archbishop of Esztergom The name of the village is related to the name of the first King of Hungary Stephen I, whose name before he was Christianized was Vajk.

The legends about Vajk

One legend says that Vajk was hunting in the woods of the surrounding islands. Once he shot a deer, which fell into water. While pulling it out, Vajk also fell in the water, but two local fishermen saved him. As a reward, Vajk donated them land on which their huts stood including the Danube islands. Fishermen called the set-

tlement Vajka. Another legend says that Vajk also lived there and allegedly it was the place from which he started his campaign for the conversion of Hungary to Christianity.

Vojka nad Dunajom was the centre of a special unit called the **Liberty of Vojka** subject to the Archbishopric of Esztergom. This liberty was a kind of state within the state. It had its proper court of justice, an administrator, mayor and notary independent from the County of Bratislava. Apart from Vojka it included Kyselica, Pinkove Kračany, Moravské Kračany, Dobrohošť, Báč, Dolný Bar as several other, now disappeared villages. The task of the inhabitants of this church unit was to organize an equestrian squad, to participate in military campaigns led by Archbishop and to protect his property. The administration of this special church liberty had four sessions a year and they solved all kind of problems. This separate group of petty nobles was abolished by the patent of 1853.

Vojka was often inundated by the Danube and it was stricken by fire in

1858. The villagers lived on fishing, gold washing and farming. The village enjoyed municipal privileges until the later half of the 19th century. Vojka lost part of its administrative territory after 1918, when it was annexed to Hungary.

The old village architecture of **earthen houses** with saddle reed roofs and original furniture is now represented by the **Vlastivedný dom house**. The Neo-Classical Roman Catholic **church of St. Michael** the Archangel is the most significant sacred monument in the village. It was built in the early 18th century on the site of an older church from the 13th century. In its interior the altar painting of St. Michael the Archangel, Neo-Classical pulpit with sculpture of St. Peter, font made of red marble from the beginning of the 19th century, 14 stations of Cross, and the reproduction of Luigi Morgan's paintings are of interest. The Lourdes cave was built in 1994.

One can also see a part of the **system of arms of the Danube** with surrounding

floodplain woods in the village. Especially the fans of water sports, fishermen and lovers of cycling will find the natural setting ideal for their hobbies. There are numerous artificial lakes, former gravel pits around Vojka. The new channel of the Danube also offers numerous opportunities for recreation in and on water. The ferry connecting Vojka with Kyselica operated free of charge by the company running the basin of the Danube is also one of the attractions for tourists.

One of the oldest settlements of Žitný ostrov is **DOBROHOŠŤ** (Doborgaz in Hungarian, population 400). The still not precisely defined "pagan" barrows in the environs of the village document very old settlement of this place. It was first mentioned under the name *Dobrogoz* in the document from 1237 when it was owned by Bratislava Castle. The village formed part of organized protection of frontiers as early as the 13th century. Archbishop of Esztergom promoted many of Dobrohošť serfs to nobles, members of the Liberty. The village and a part of its administrative territory was owned by Jakub Svätojurský from the end of the 13th cen-

---

Left: The arm of the Danube near Bodíky
Right: A nook near the Danube

ury. Old documents mentioned a church in the village, but it did not exist anymore in the 19th century. Poor villagers tried to live on gold washing in the past. The milling trade survived for a comparatively long time. But only two of many mills that used to exist on the main stream of the Danube survived until the mid-20th century. Basket-making is the craft with long tradition in this village. Basket-makers mostly sold their products which included brooms, baskets used for carrying hay, corn, poultry and even for keeping bees and transport of fish, at the markets of Šamorín.

The Danube fishermen

Fishing was one of the occupations of the population living on the banks of the Danube. The right of fishing was granted to some fishermen's families. They were the families of Khín, in Dobrohošť and Šamorín, or Herbergers in Bodíky, who carried out this occupation from their immigration in the mid-19th century until the mid-20th century. Both families were living on the river, they employed fishermen and organized their work. They caught fish mostly on the Danube arms using boats and large nets. They sold fish as a profitable article to the local Jewish fishmongers.

Dobrohošť was repeatedly flooded by the Danube. The landless villagers also pastured their cattle on the Danube islands and eventually founded there a new settlement, which was called Doborgaz Sziget (sziget is Hungarian for island). When the channel of the Danube was changed in 1896 this new settlement found itself on the other side of the river. But its people still frequented Dobrohošť using boats as transport means, buried their dead and married in Dobrohošť. The village was eventually annexed to Hungary in 1920 and after it was joined to a pair of other villages it exists under the name Dunasziget.

On the right bank of the feeding channel as if cut-off the rest of the world lies the village of **BODÍKY** (Nagybodak in

Hungarian, population 300). It was first mentioned in 1245 as *Bodak*. The later name *Wamosbodak* points at the fact that there used to be a ford with toll station next to the village. It was a serf village of Bratislava Castle and later it belonged to the Pálffy family until the end of the Monarchy. The villagers lived on pasturing cattle, fishing and milling. Cabbage and fruit cultivated in its environs won a wide reputation. There were fourteen mills on the main river stream next to Bodíky in 1881. They all disappeared destroyed by the floating blocks of ice in the extremely cold winter of 1926. Then the farmers used the steam and power driven mills in Baka and Šamorín.

The local architecture from the 19th century of this village was famous for its uniqueness. There were earthen houses painted in white with brick gables and saddle roofs. In front of the houses usually stood bread furnaces and near the stream of the Danube were picturesque prismoid fishermen's huts made of reed. The great flood in 1965 damaged these structures and many of them were completely destroyed and carried away. The only sacred monument in the village is a new **church** built in 1996. The village acquired its Slovak name in 1948. Not far from Bodíky is the **natural landmark of Kráľovská lúka** with the protected remains of the Danube's dead arm with water, swamp and meadow plant associations. **The National Nature Reserve of Ostrov orliaka morského** spreads on the islands with alluvial woods among the branches of the Danube.

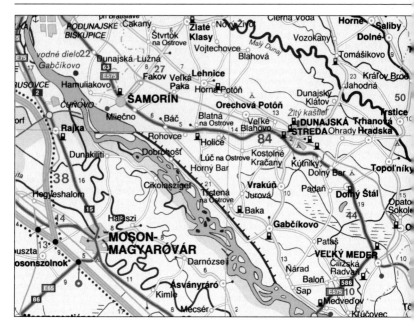

DUNAJSKÁ STREDA
AND ITS ENVIRONS

The territory of this district occupies the prevailing part of Žitný ostrov, which is geographically part of the Danube plain. The flat landscape limited in the north by the Malý Dunaj river and in the south by the main stream of the Danube is covered by far-reaching fertile fields, in places separated by groups of trees and small woods, which as ones comes closer to the Danube change into thick flood-plain woods. Žitný ostrov is criss-crossed by a system of channels, the original purpose of which was to drain the swampy terrain.

The cultural and economic centre of Žitný ostrov is the district town of **DUNAJSKÁ STREDA** (Dunaszerdahely in Hungarian, population 24,000) situated 49 km from the capital Bratislava. The oldest settlement of the territory dates to the

Right: Shops in Dunajská Streda
The Bonbón Hotel

Bronze Age, evidence of the Roman and of Migration periods was found as well. The finds include a stone axe, bronze bracelet lance tips, copper earrings, an earthen bowl and two Roman clips found in the gravel pits in the environs of the town. The old settlement situated at the cross-roads of trade roads was a busy place. Such could have been also the Roman set-tlement in the territory of the present town, which lay by the frequented road leading from Carnuntum in Austria to the settlement of Audation not far from today's Kolárovo, which continued further to Brigetio in Hungary. There are no writ-ten documents confirming the early me-dieval history of the town. We know only that in the first half of the 9th century during the rule of Charles the Great, the territory of Žitný ostrov was part of the Avar province of Vetvar. Some sources as-sert that the oldest written reference to the settlement is from 1162. It was prob-ably King Belo III who founded a market place there, which became the core of the later town of Szerdahely (*szerda* means Wednesday and *hely* means place). The document of the Palatine and the comes

Lorand from 1250 quotes the name of the settlement *Zerda* in other document names *Svridahel, Zerdahel, Zredahel, Serdahel* appear. It was owned by the Archbishopric of Esztergom in the 13th century, later it belonged to Bratislava Castle. The Pálffy family owned it from 1600 to 1848. An important period of development of the settlement was the 15th century. The decree of King Sigismund promoted it to a yeoman town in 1405. In the 16th century it was a town with market and fair privileges. The population, apart from farming, lived by production of clothes and hats of woollen cloth, traded in corn and cattle. Other crafts such as hat-makers, shoemakers and coopers associated in guilds in the 17th century. The period of the Turkish wars in the 16th and 17th centuries also affected Dunajská Streda. Many houses were destroyed and the Turks took away all cattle. Annexation of the settlements Újfal, Nemesszeg and Elötejed to Szerdahely in 1874 gave origin to a town, which became the centre of trade and crafts in Žitný ostrov.

The old settlements
The individual small settlements that used to exist in the territory of today's town were separated from each other only by streets. For example, the frontier between Újfal and Szerdahely was the Main Street running from east to west. In Újfal the most beautiful yeoman houses were built, including the disappeared White Manor House of the Bacsák family, the Yellow Manor house, and curias of noble families. The part called Nemesszeg, south of Dunajská Streda was the centre of craftsmen mostly containing houses of craftsmen and service buildings of the yeoman families. There were often 10 to 15 families living in a common yard and small huts. Elötejed was a typical farming settlement. Many houses had reed roof until the mid-20th century.

The first cultural establishment of the town and its environs was the District Casino. It was founded in 1860 in a much-frequented inn called Zelený veniec or The Green Ring. It was the venue for theatre shows and other cultural events. The Casino Library contained 1,500 volumes and it remained the only cultural institution of the town for many decades. The Casino was closed in 1919, the library fell in decay and many books were lost. Its activity was renewed in 1939 though it never regained its past level and it was finally closed in 1944.

The first municipal printing house was founded in 1888 by Leopold Goldstein followed by another two opened by Izák Rimstein and David Weinberger. By the end of the 19th century the railway track between Bratislava and Dunajská Streda and Komárno was finished and the town became more accessible. Great

and font with a small sculpture of Christ's christening are from the time of the last Baroque adaptation of the church in the 18th century. The remaining inner furniture is from the end of the 19th century. Late Baroque sculptures of St. Nicolas, the Most Holy Trinity from the 18th century and that of the Virgin Mary from the late 19th century also belong to the church. The church is an example of Late Gothic sacred architecture. Around the church a market place formed in the Middle Ages and it remained there until the present time. The **Evangelical church** built in the Neo-Gothic style in 1883 is also worthy of attention. The building with great hall and semicircular space, roofed by a semi-dome, has in its interior a Neo-Classical altar from 1933, font from 1883 and an organ from 1903. The Late Baroque statue of St. Nicholas from the 18th century placed near the church also documents intensive spiritual life of the inhabitants. The greatest Jewish temple in Žitný ostrov used to be the **synagogue** from 1870, but it was demolished a bomb struck it in 1945. The town also had a Jewish basic school in the 18th century, but it was abolished in 1944.

The **Žitnoostrovné museum** with a permanent ethnographic and archaeological exhibition is now in what is called the **Žltý kaštieľ** or Yellow Manor house. Bishop Mikuláš Kondé had this originally Baroque building built in the first half of the 18th century. It was adapted in the Neo-Classical style in the early 19th century. The Museum was placed in this structure in the years 1970-1972. It continued in the tradition of the museum, which was founded by Antal Khin in Šamorín in 1927. An exhibition hall was opened beside the manor house in 1986. The Museum seated from 1964 in what was called **Biely kaštieľ** or White Manor House, which was built in romantic Neo-Classical taste in the late 19th century. This two-storied building was demolished after the Museum was moved. The Slovak National gallery has exhibitions in the **Vermes Villa** built at the turn of the 19th and 20th centuries. The villa with park consists of two structures. The original building is from the late 19th century and the rectan-

unemployment after 1918 in Dunajská Streda resulted that the town became the centre of revolutionary movement of agricultural hands. The Slovak name of the town Dunajská Streda has been used since 1920. It has been the district town since 1923. It was annexed to Hungary in the years 1938-1945. Dunajská Streda is now a modern town, which became the natural centre of the food-processing industry.

Sightseeing of the town can start at the rare sacred monument of the Roman Catholic church of **Assumption of the Virgin Mary**. This was originally a Gothic church from the 14th century dedicated to St. George. It was repeatedly adopted. Its chancel contains the painting of St. Nicolas the Bishop and on the southern facade is the painting of Calvary from the late 14th century restored in 1955.The main altar with pillar architecture and central painting of Assumption of the Virgin Mary, side altars of Piety and St. Stephen the King, Baroque-Neo-Classical pulpit

---

Left: Žitnoostrovné museum

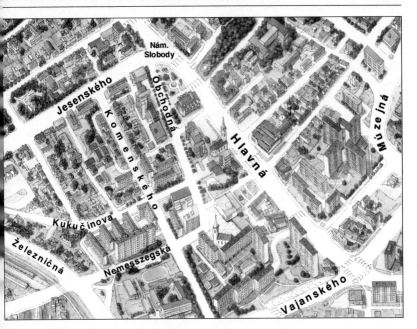

gular structure by its side was added to it in the 1950´s. The main entrance to the building protected by a wooden arbour is from the yard.

Many natives from Dunajská Streda became important figures.

Famous natives of Dunajská Streda

One of the best known natives of Dunajská Streda is Ármin Vámbéry (1832-1913), an important orientalist, traveller and member of a number of academies of science. He was one of the greatest orientalists of his time and a recognized expert for the Near East and Central Asia. He could speak various languages and dialects. He was involved in research of the origin of the Hungarian language and its relationship to the Turkish and Tartar languages. He published several books, such as My Wanders and Experience of Persia. Another important native of the town was Mikuláš Kondé, who had built the Yellow Manor House. He was born in the village of Újfalu as the descendant of one of the oldest families of Žitný ostrov. He became bishop of Varadín in 1800. The third important personality born in Dunajská Streda was Benedek Csaplár (1821-1906), a priest, professor and member of the Royal Academy of Kingdom of Hungary where he was director of the Historical Society. He specialised in literature and ethnography.

The town boasts busy social life to which the Žitnoostrovné Museum, local library and cultural centre contribute. The centre has been accessible to public since 1977. It has a theatre stage, a panoramic cinema, and various clubs. Fine arts exhibitions are usually organized in the exhibition pavilion of Žitnoostrovné Museum, in the Gallery of the Contemporary Hungarian Artists and in the private Gallery ART-MA. **Dunajskostredské hudobné dni** or The Music Days of Dunajská Streda is certainly one of the most important cultural events of the town. They are usually held in April while the competition of children's ensembles called **Podunajská jar** (Spring in the Danubeland) takes place in May every year. October is reserved for the fans of folklore dancing. September attraction is the **fair of Žitný ostrov.**

By the beginning of the 1970's the town became popular as a summer tourist centre. It was the time when the area of thermal swimming pools was opened. The area offers seven swimming pools with medicinal thermal water with proved effects on the loco-motion apparatus. There is a swimming pool with temperatures from 20 to 25 degrees Celsius operating seasonally, Italian swimming pool with temperature 28 °C, another sitting-bath pool with temperature 36 °C, children's pool with temperature of 30 °C and two additional children's pools with whole year operation and temperatures of 28 °C and 36 °C. The pools are fed by geothermal water from a well 1,600 m deep and the water has the temperature ranging between 54-56 °C. The yield of the spring is 30 litres per second. The area also contains a natural lake suitable for boating. There is a car-camping site available nearby. Thermal water is also used for heating of green houses and the surrounding service buildings. The town also boasts a **horse-riding area.**

Four important roads start in Dunajská Streda. The first villages in the direction of Galanta are **MALÉ DVORNÍKY** (Kisudvarnok in Hungarian, population 800) and **VEĽKÉ DVORNÍKY** (Nagyudvarnok, population 700). Archaeologists discovered finds from the Older Bronze Age and Migration Period, as well as a Great Moravian burial site there. Today's Malé Dvorníky was first mentioned in 1250. The document from 1356 refers to it as a yeoman village. Veľké Dvorníky was first mentioned in 1341. Both villages

Left: Thermal swimming pool in D. Streda
Right: Dunajský Klátov

were part of the property of Bratislava Castle and royal servants inhabited them.

An earthen castle
Near Dvorníky an earthen castle called Szolgagyör, mentioned in the document from 1399 as Zogagyeur used to exist before the Tartar invasion. It was an independent administrative unit and centre of the lower Žitný ostrov. It offered shelter to travellers halfway between the Bratislava and Komárno estates. The original fortifications by walls made of palisades and earth were destroyed and its remains were probably used for reconstruction of the villages damaged by the Tartars.

Veľké Dvorníky was a serf village of several noble families from the 16th century. Reminder of this period is the originally Later Renaissance **manor house** from the 17th century in **Veľké Dvorníky**, which was adapted in the early 19th century. The religious life of the local population is illustrated by the Roman Catholic **church** from 1955 with an altar of the Virgin Mary from 1859, the **chapel** of the Most Holy Trinity from the end of the 19th century and a **stone cross** from 1877.

DUNAJSKÝ KLÁTOV (Dunatökés in Hungarian, population 500) is the village next to the Malý Dunaj river, which was first mentioned as *Theukes*. In the wetland around the confluence of the brooks no traces of the old settlements were preserved. The owners of the village were the families Zomor and Kondé. The administrative territory of Dunajský Klátov also included an area called Malý les (Small Forest) and a mill at the beginning of the 20th century. The attribute Dunajský or Duna in Hungarian (Danubian) was added to the name of the village in 1910 and the Slovak name has been used since 1948. Dunajský Klátov became an independent village in 1990, after a period of thirty years when it formed one settlement with Jahodná. The 25 km long Klátovské rameno arm flows through the village and it is one of the natural landmarks of the Danube region. It is fed by underground water from the parallel stream of the Malý Dunaj and its width along with the growths on its banks is 25 to 70 metres.

Along its stream stretches the **National Nature Reserve of Klátovské rameno**, which represents an oasis of conserved nature with typical floodplain forest, abundant water and swamp flora and protected water wild life amidst the agricultural landscape. Oak and poplar trees are the most frequent wood species growing there. Sixty eight species of water fowl nest here. The locality is one of the most sought after by the fans of water sports and fishermen who can also pursue their hobby on the Malý Dunaj and on three peat lakes.

A remarkable **technical monument** stands of the bank of the Klátovské rameno arm. It is **Klátovský mlyn** or the Mill of Klátov. It is a brick building of, as experts say, the Anglo-American type. The original water mill was reconstructed in 1920 and was operating until 1941. Today it contains a permanent **exhibition** the and it is part of the Žitnoostrovské Museum. It is a favourite stop of tourists.

The places on this route include **JAHODNÁ** (Eperjes in Hungarian, population 1,400). It is situated on the bank of the Malý Dunaj river, 9.5 km north-east of Dunajská Streda. The settlement was mentioned in documents from 1522 and 1553. As a serf village is was owned by the Thurzo family in the 17th century and later by the Esterházy family. The villagers live by farming, haulage and milling. Cattle and sheep raising were also a common occupation. In addition they hauled salt from the salt store in Trstice. The most important sacred monument of the village is the Roman Catholic, originally Baroque-Neo Classical **Church of Sts. Peter and Paul** from the 18th century, which was adapted after the Second World War. The interesting interior of the church contains the altar of Piety with a folk sculpture, Neo-Classical pulpit, the statue of St. John Nepomuk from the second half of the 18th century and a marble font from the late 19th century.

The past glory of milling on the Malý Dunaj river is recalled by one of the conserved water **mills**. The natural setting of the water mill with reed growing on the river banks is a protected area and simultaneously a tourist attraction. The water wheel, which was used for driving a water saw, is now under reconstruction. The vil-

century the Pálffy family owned it. The local population lived on farming and cattle raising. There were several mills on the Malý Dunaj. **Earthen houses** from the 19th century with saddle roofs covered by reed still exist in Horné Mýto. The most important sacred building of the village is the Roman Catholic **church of St. John Nepomuk** from 1775 rebuilt in the Neo-Classical style in the early 19th century.

One of the largest settlements of Žitný ostrov with an area 2,476 hectares is **TRHOVÁ HRADSKÁ** (Vásárút in Hungarian, population 2,100) situated 10 km from Dunajská Streda. The name (The Trade Route) derives precisely from what it suggests: the trade road, which ran through it. The oldest reference to the village is in a document from 1235 as *Vasarut*. It was a then property of the Bratislava Chapter. The Counts of Sv. Jur and Pezinok tried to acquire it in the 16th century. The dispute about ownership with the chapter culminated in a complaint presented to King Vladislav II. No information survived on how it was resolved. The village was promoted to a yeoman town in the Middle Ages. The most common occupation of the local people was farming and cattle raising. The village was widely known for its cattle market visited by the farmers from wide environs. In the mid-19th century a good quality tobacco was grown here and sold mostly in Bratislava. The Chapter of Bratislava still had some properties in the village at the beginning of the 20th century. Part of it was leased to Emil Popper who ran a brewery and distillery in the village. The Slovak name of the village has been used from 1927. After it joined to the settlement of Horné Mýto in 1960 both villages bore the name Trhové Mýto until 1990, when they became independent again.

The centre of the village is the Roman Catholic church of **St. Anthony** built by Count Batthyányi supported by the Bratislava Chapter in 1906 in the Art Nouveau style with Neo-Romanesque traits. It originated on the site of two older churches. Their chancel and remains of side walls of the nave have been preserved. In the interior of church surrounded by a park, the Baroque chalice made from gild-

lage also has an interesting **park** with rare wood species. The bank vegetation containing poplar and willow trees along the Klátovské rameno arm with occurrence of numerous protected plant and animal species are to be seen in the **protected area of Rencsésov rybník pond**. The Malý Dunaj river near Jahodná is a popular spot for practising water sports. Bathing, boating and fishing are also possible. The administrative territory of the village contains a hunting ground for pheasants.

Between the meandering stream of the Malý Dunaj and its Klátovské rameno arm runs the road from Jahodná to the village of **HORNÉ MÝTO** (Felsővámos in Hungarian, population 900). It was first mentioned in a document from 1268. Its older name used until 1913 was *Vámosfalu*. The owners of this village alternated in the Middle Ages. It was divided in the 17th century, part of it was owned by the Sv. Jur estate and another part belonged to the Eberhard estate. From the mid-18th

Left: A water mill in D. Klátov
Right: A port at the Malý Dunaj

ed silver from 1749 is of interest. The Catholic parsonage is a Late Baroque building from 1774. Sacred monuments worth mentioning include two stone road crosses, the Trinity pillar on the square from 1846, and the statue of St. Florián from the 19th century. the Malý Dunaj river flows trough the territory of the village and in the past sturgeon was caught in its water.

Next to the confluence of the Malý Dunaj and its Klátovské rameno arm in the eastern part of Žitný ostrov is the village of **TOPOĽNÍKY** (Nyárasd in Hungarian, population 3,000). It is documented as *Horný Ňáražd* from the 13th century donated by King Belo IV to the Chapter of Bratislava and family of Ágh. In the 13th century another small settlement in its vicinity called Dolný Ňáražd was mentioned. The village had several owners. It used to be the centre of the estate of Dolný Ňáražd from the beginning of the 18th century. In 1787 Pálffy family, who had a curia there containing abundant works of art and furniture of tremendous value, owned it in 1787. A notable brewery and cattle market existed here in the

19th century. The village with a renowned inn, the building of which still exists, was an important stop on the way from Pest to Pressburg (historic name of Bratislava). Famous figures, such as Lajos Kossuth and Ferenc Deák who attended the sessions of the Diet in Bratislava visited the inn. This also was a place where sturgeon was caught and the village supplied almost as much of this fish as Buda or Komárno. Salted sturgeon was exported to Kiev, Warsaw, Vienna and Paris. Dolný Ňáražd and Horný Ňáražd merged in 1940 and adopted the name Nyárasd which is the Hungarian version of Ňáražd. Today's name of the village has been used since 1948.

The local Roman Catholic **church of the Birth of the Virgin Mary** is perhaps the most important monument of the village. This originally Gothic building was adapted in Neo-Classical taste in 1852. Its main altar with the painting of the Birth of the Virgin Mary and the pulpit are pseudo-Romanesque. The remaining interior dates from the 20th century. The road statues of St. John Nepomuk from the 18th century and St. Joseph from the 19th cen-

tury are of interest. The monument in the local park symbolizes the status of the town with the right of sword granted to it in 1796. The cylindrical pillory from 1796 bears the symbol of the right of sword owned by the local yeoman. The monument called Orol standing at the end of the village and the obelisk dedicated to the war heroes buried in the local cemetery commemorate two battles which took place in the village in the revolutionary years 1848-1849 between the Imperial troops and Hungarian rebels for the ford over the Malý Dunaj. Thanks to the local hot springs and three **thermal swimming pools** with water temperature of 36 degrees Celsius Topoľníky became one of the most visited places of Žitný ostrov. The area is near an arm of the Malý Dunaj river. The quality of this medicinal water is comparable to that of Piešťany. The area also contains a car-camping site. Geothermal water is used for heating the local sports hall and green houses. Topoľníky organizes summer camp for artists in July.

In the eastern part of Žitný ostrov, 11.5 km of Topoľníky is the village of **OKOČ** (Ekecs in Hungarian, population 3,700). The first reference to the village under the name *Ekech* is from 1268. Komárno Castle, the Archbishopric of Esztergom and other owners, for example the Zichy family owned it. The ancestors of the villagers were mostly fishermen who fished in the Azsód pond for the lords of Komárno Castle and the Church. Later they turned to cattle and sheep raising. The medieval village had a toll station.

The village acquired several rights and privileges and they had no other duties apart from fishing. This was the cause of frequent disputes between the population and their lords and finally the people preferred to leave the village to avoid problems. The Zichys re-colonized the village by inviting Slovak colonists who were assimilated in the 19th century. Two churches represent the sacred monuments of the village, the **chapel** of St. Vendelín with a stone statue of the saint and a stone statue of the Immaculate Conception from the 19th century. The Roman Catholic **church of St. Vendelín** in the Baroque and Neo-Classical taste was built in 1790. The built-in tower and the main altar with a painting of St. Vendelín from the end of the 18th century are the interesting parts of this church. The facade of the Neo-Classical Reformed church built in 1882 was changed in the early 20th century.

Originally an independent village, today part of Okoč, **Opatovský Sokolec** (Apácaszkállas in Hungarian) was first mentioned in 1221. The Clarist convent in Bratislava owned it from the 16th century and after the convent was dissolved, it belonged to the Esterházy family. The villagers were mostly farmers. This small village possesses some remarkable cultural monuments. Sacred architecture is represented by the Roman Catholic **church**, one of the oldest in Žitný ostrov, and the Neo-Classical Reformed church from the last third of the 18th century. The two-storied building of the Neo-Classical **manor house** from the 19th century is situated in the **park**, which is a protected area.

Another tourist route in the environs of Dunajská Streda leads to Veľký Meder. One of the villages of interest is **KÚTNIKY** (Hegyéte in Hungarian, population 900). It lies on the south-eastern edge of Dunajská Streda. It originated in 1940 by joining the villages of Hegybenéte and Töböréte and the new village Hegyéte was renamed Kútniky in 1946. Today's Kútniky includes the villages of Blažov and Kolónia. The first reference to the original settlement of *Ethey* is in a document from 1250. Blažov is mentioned in the document from 1380. They were owned by yeoman families. **Earthen houses** with saddle reed roofs

Left: The environs of Okoč
Right: A detail of rural house

survive in the village and they are fenced with typical wooden fences. **POVODA** (Pótajed in Hungarian, population 800) situated nearby originated by joining the settlements of Csenkeszfa, Lidér-Tejed, and Pódafa into one. The Slovak name of this village, Povoda, has been used since 1948. **Pódafa** was mentioned in historic documents from 1332 as *Poda Ety*. From about 1455 until the end of the 18th century it was owned by the yeoman family Poda. At the beginning of the 19th century, a steam mill was built here. It operated until the early 20th century. Čekensfa (Csekenszfa) is documented from 1300. It was property of the Pócs family, later it was owned by various yeoman families. The village of **Lidér-Tejed** is known from 1231 when the settlement Teyed owned by Bratislava Castle existed here.

Not far from Dunajská Streda is the village of **OHRADY** (Csallóközkürt in Hungarian, population 1,100). Its name was derived from that of the Magyar tribe Kürt. It was mentioned for the first time as *Kurth* in the document from 1252 when King Belo donated it to the Bratislava Provostship. It belonged to the Pezinok-Sv. Jur estate from the beginning of the 17th century and later in the 18th century it belonged to the Dolný Ňáražd estate. Its population lived by cattle raising and farming. The only sacred monument of the village is the originally Gothic Roman Catholic church of **St. Stephen the Martyr** from the 15th century mentioned as early as 1138. It still contains a bell from 1482. It fell into decay in 1634, was restored at the beginning of the 18th century and later it was rebuilt. Only a part of the lower walls survived from the original Gothic building.

The village of **DOLNÝ BAR** (Albár in Hungarian, population 500) was mentioned for the first time in documents from 1245 and 1296 as Baar. It must have originated earlier, probably between the 10th and 12th century when it served as a supply base for the frontier defensive zone. Three settlements were mentioned in the documents from the 14th century. The yeoman families of Illéshazy and Amade owned it. At the beginning of the 20th century this settlement situated on

the railway track Komárno-Dunajská Streda was a little town with its own notary, post office and telegraph. Its citizens were mostly farmers. The village of Malý Bar was annexed to it after 1888 and in the years 1960-1990 it also included the settlement of Mad. The Slovak name has been used since 1927. **Earthen houses** with one window, asymmetrically situated on the facade and saddle reed roofs still exist here. The Neo-Classical **manor house** built in the second half of the 19th century deserves attention. Church architecture is represented by the Neo-Classical Roman **Catholic church of St. Anna** built in 1790 and later adapted. Its interior contains a Late Baroque Main altar with a painting of St. Anna from the end of the 18th century. In front of the church stands the St. Mary pillar and a stone Classical cross from the 19th century.

The neighbouring village **MAD** (Mad in Hungarian, population 500) is only 2,5 km away from Dolný Bar. The first reference to the village is from 1256 and its function was to supply the settlements guarding the border.

King Matthias in Mad

The village used to belong to the royal court and King Matthias I Corvinus liked to visit it. He allegedly had a little hunting cottage in the wood. King Matthias was very angry when the people of Mad cut down a beautiful lime tree next to his cottage, as he liked to rest under its wide crown. Some say that the people of Mad did it on purpose in order not to have to look after the royal visitor. The King's anger meant that none of them could obtain a higher office and the people from surrounding villages mocked the people of Mad.

Several noble families owned the village in the 17th century. The people cultivated rye, cabbage, maize and potatoes. **Houses made of clay** with saddle roofs covered with reed still stand in the village. Spliced fences enclose large yards. The Reformed church represents the sacred monuments. This Neo-Classical Toleration building from 1788 was reconstruct-

Left: The Boheľovský rybník pond
Right: Thermal swimming pool in V. Meder

ed in the early 20th century. The interior furniture is from the time of its building. The village also has the Roman Catholic **church of St. John Nepomuk** built in 1869 in Neo-Classical style.

The route of trip leads through **DOLNÝ ŠTÁL** (Alistál in Hungarian, population 2,000). This village originated by joining the villages of Dolný Štál, Horný Štál, and Tôňa in 1940. Its predecessor Staul was first mentioned in 1254. The name probably derives from the French word *staul* (stable in English) because horse breeders lived here and looked after the royal horses in the settlement of Opatovský Sokolec. The name Alistal appeared in 1260. Various yeoman families, among them Alistál, Molnár, Biroó and Nagy owned the village. **Horný Štál** was mentioned under the name *Feliztar* in 1291 as a property of Comes Kozma of Pezinok. **Tôňa** was first mentioned in a document from 1256 as *villa Tunna*. In 1553 it belonged to nuns from Margaret's Island in Budapest, later the Clarist Convent in Bratislava when the nuns of this order moved there in fear from the Turks, and finally the Amade and Bátthyányi families bought it. The local people were farmers and concentrated on cultivation of potatoes. The examples of folk architecture consist of adapted **earthen houses.** Two churches represent the sacred monuments of the village. The Gothic Roman Catholic **church of St. Martin the Bishop** from the 15th century was rebuilt in 1746. The Neo-Classical main altar with a painting of the saint and four candelabras are the most precious items of its interior. The Reformed **church** is from 1786 and in its interior the valuable tin and silver church utensils from the end of the 18th century are of interest.

Two and a half kilometres from Dolný Štál is the village of **BOHEĽOV** (Bögellö in Hungarian, population 300). It probably originated in the 11th or 12th century when it was the seat of a guarding unit. Its Hungarian name suggests it. The word beg which means lord is from Pecheneg language. The first reference to the family village is from 1456. It belonged to several yeoman families. The Rosenberger owned large lands near this village in the 19th century. The plots were mostly wetlands rich in reed and waterfowl. The people were mostly farmers. They cultivated potatoes and raised cattle. The Slovak name of the village has been used since 1948. The village also has a pond called **Boheľovský rybník.**

PADÁŇ (Padány in Hungarian, population 800) was first mentioned in 1265 as Padan. It was an old guarding Pecheneg settlement. Its owners alternated. The rich Amade family also owned a part of its administrative territory. **Earthen houses** with brick gables under saddle roofs are of interest. The dominant feature of the village is the Neo-Classical Reformed **church** built in 1787 and adapted later. Its pulpit is from the time when the church was built.

Many visitors to the Danubeland choose the town of **VEĽKÝ MEDER** (Nagymegyer in Hungarian, population 9,200) as their destination. It lies in the south-eastern part of Žitný ostrov, only 12 km from the border with Hungary and 20 km from Dunajská Streda. Archaeological finds indicate the presence of a Neolithic settlement. Meder acquired its name by modification of the name of its leader Meger, family of whom lived in Žitný ostrov. The first reference to the village as *villa Meger* is from 1268 when it was a property of the County of Komárno. King Matthias granted it municipal rights in 1466. The royal favour brought more privileges to the town. It enjoyed the right of capital punishment and organized fairs. Use of the capital punishment is also suggested by the local nomenclature, for instance, Šibeničný vrch or the Gallows Hill. Komárno Castle owned the settlement between the 16th and 18th centuries. The Turks completely sacked the town and surrounding villages. Nature disasters also tortured the town. Lightening burnt down the town including the town hall with precious documents in April 1702, cholera in 1831 and again fire in 1852 were further blows. The flood of 1965 seriously affected the life of the population of this town, though the firm dike built around the town prevented even greater damage. The town had a small wool-cloth manufacture in the early 18th century,

brickyard and oil-pressing plant were operating here in the 19th century.. At the turn of the 19th and 20th century several guilds were active in the town while that of weavers was the best known. Cemetery commemorates the sad events of the First World War, it contains the graves of 6,000 Serb war prisoners who died in a camp near the railway station. The town belonged to Hungary in the years 1938-1945. It was called Čalovo in the years 1948-1990. Veľký Meder was the district seat in the years 1949-1960. Preserved folk architecture from the 19th century is represented by **clay houses**. The town also has its **pheasant hunting ground**. The **fair** is a traditional event held every year in August on the day of St. Stephen. Veľký Meder has a recognized mixed ensemble of singers founded 108 years ago. But the biggest tourist attraction of this little town is the **thermal swimming pool**.

Therapy and relaxation

The popular and well-equipped thermal swimming pool in Veľký Meder opened in 1973. It makes use of natural mineral hot

spring with a temperature of 54 degrees Celsius from a well 1,500 m deep. The 100 ha large area of swimming pool is situated amidst forests. A combined indoor pool connected with outdoor pool is open all the year round. It has a toboggan, playing grounds and minigolf. The chemical composition of the local hot spring is suitable for the therapy of disease of joints, muscles and back and it contributes to overall regeneration of the human organism.

The Baroque Roman Catholic **church of St. Michael the Bishop** built before 1460 is the oldest sacred monument. It was destroyed in the course of history and a new one had to be built. The new church was built in 1900 in the Neo-Classical style. The Neo-Classical Reformed **church** from 1785 with a tower added to it in 1801 is also interesting. The sacred monuments also include the **Synagogue** from the first half of the 19th century and St. Mary's pillar from 1898 standing in front of the church.

The village of **Ižop** (Izsap) situated next to Čiližský potok brook was added to Veľký Meder in 1976. In its environs are archaeological finds from the period of settlement of the territory by the Old Magyars. The first written record of its existence is from 1297 and the settlers were most probably the Pecheneg guards of the road from Komárno to Bratislava. The villagers were mostly fishermen in the past as the Čiližský potok brook contained abundant fish. The village was property of Komárno Castle, later it was owned by the Esterházy and Zichy families. The village and its

church were destroyed during the Turkish raids. The new Reformed **church** was built by the beginning of the 19th century.

In the immediate environs of Dunajská Streda are several villages with the word Kračany in their names. There were as many as 12 villages called Kračany in the 18th and 19th centuries. As the contemporary documents cite all twelve villages were lying side by side, within an hour's walk from Dunajská Streda. Moravské and Pinkove Kračany were yeoman villages owned by the vassals of the Archbishop of Esztergom, the remaining villages with Kračany in their names were owned by noble families. They gradually merged into two existing villages Kráľovičove Kračany and Kostolné Kračany. The village of **KOSTOLNÉ KRAČANY** (Egyházkarcsa in Hungarian, population 1,100) originated, as we know it now in 1940 by joining with Amadeove Kračany. **Earthen houses** from the late 19th and early 20th century have saddle roofs covered with reed. The only sacred monument and simultaneously a significant architectural monument of Žitný ostrov is the Roman Catholic **church of St. Bartholomew the Apostle.** This Neo-Classical building with Baroque elements was built on the site of an older church in 1820. The main altar bears a painting of the Crucifixion while pictures of the Pieta and St. Stephen the King from the 19th century are found on the side altars. The Neo-Classical font bears the group of statues of the Baptism of Christ from the early 19th century.

The neighbouring **KRÁĽOVIČOVE KRAČANY** (Királyfiakarcsa in Hungarian, population 1,000) originated in its present form in 1940 by joining the villages of Kráľovičove, Etreho, Jastrabie, Klúčiarove, and Lesné Kračany. There are several solitary homesteads in its administrative territory. **Clay houses** with saddle roofs covered by reed survive here from the second half of the 19th century. Some houses have wooden and brick gables, part of them in Baroque style. An **exhibition of nature history** is placed in the peasant house No. 111. The county administrator Aurel Bartal built the now reconstructed **manor house** in the Neo-

Left: Rural architecture
Right: The church in Holice

Classical style in 1830. The manor house was repaired in 1956 and now it shelters a social institution. The **park** in Kráľovičove Kračany is a **protected area**. It contains rare plane trees. North-west of Kráľovičove Kračany is the village of **VIESKA** (Kisfalud in Hungarian, population 100). The oldest reference to this village is from 1291. It was a yeoman village in the Middle Ages and in the 19th century the Nagy family owned its greater part. The only sacred monument is a stone road statue of the Pieta from 1814. The village of **LÚČ na Ostrove** (Lúcs in Hungarian, population 700 not far from Kráľovičove Kračany originated in 1960 by joining villages of Malá Lúč and Veľká Lúč. Both are documented for the first time in a document from 1222 as *terra Luche*. Malá Lúč was owned for a long time by Bratislava Castle before it belonged to the Pálffy family. The well-known Dóczy family was from Veľký Lúč. Both villages have previous examples of folk architecture. **Earthen houses** with saddle roofs are covered by reed. **Malá Lúč** has an originally Renaissance **curia** with four little towers and fortifications built in the early 17th century, adapted in Neo-Classical style in 1833. Now it houses archives. Sacred monuments consist of the **chapel** of St. Anna from the end of the 18th century with a statue of this saint from the end of the 18th century with a Baroque-Neo-Classical altar dedicated to St. Anna. The Late-Classicist **manor house** built in the early 19th century, later adapted is in Veľká Lúč.

The route of the trip includes another interesting village: **HOLICE** (Egyházgelle in Hungarian, population 900). Its historic name was Gala. The oldest reference to the village is from 1250, when Bratislava Castle owned it. Two villages developed from Gala during the rule of King Ladislav I. They were Kostolná Gala and Stará Gala. King Matthias I granted the municipal rights to Kostolná Gala in 1466, which merged with Stará Gala in 1938 and adopted again the name Gala in 1940. Kostolná Gala derives its name from the Roman Catholic **church** (kostol means church in Slovak) of **Sts. Peter and Paul** built in the first half of the 13th century in

the Late Romanesque style. The church contains unique remains of exterior wall paintings from the Late Middle Ages. In the last third of the 14th century, the church was rebuilt in the Gothic style. Renaissance adaptations were made in the 17th century. It was repeatedly reconstructed in the course of the 20th century. Near the church is a Late Renaissance statue of the Virgin Mary from the 17th century. The St. Mary's pillar bears a stone statue of the Immaculate Conception from 1689. The Baroque **church** from the years 1736-1739 was built to the design of the architect T. Haffenecker. The local **roadhouse Kondoroš** and **car-camp site** offer refreshment and haven for passing tourists.

The village of **BLATNÁ na Ostrove** (Sárosfa in Hungarian, population 800) was first mentioned in historic documents in 1286 and later in 1328 as *Sáralja*. The name derives from the Hungarian expression for swampy and muddy lands – *sár* or *sáros*. The village acquired its Slovak name in 1927. In the Middle Ages several yeoman families owned it. It was owned by the Földes family at the beginning of the

17'h century and later by the Bittó family, who lived here until the disintegration of the Monarchy. Two Neo-Classical manor houses from the beginning of the 19th century and the Roman Catholic **church of the Most Holy Trinity** from 1721 represent the cultural monuments of the village. The single-nave building of the church lacking tower contains a semi-circular chancel. In the interior of the church is a precious main altar from the time when the church was built with a painting of the Most Holy Trinity from the 19th century, pulpit from the end of the 18th century with a relief of Resurrection and a Gothic statue of the Madonna, one of the Madonnas called Beautiful, from around 1400.

Many interesting things can also be seen on the way from Dunajská Streda to Gabčíkovo. The modest village of **VRAKÚŇ** (Neékvárkony in Hungarian, population 2,500) possesses many remarkable landmarks. It originated by joining the villages of Vrakúň (Várkony) and Nekyje (Nyék).

Vrakúň was an old property of the Amade family who had their family manor house in this village. It was mentioned for the first time as *Warkun* in a document from 1260, some sources also quote earlier dates. The village enjoyed municipal privileges in the 16th century. Count Tadeáš Amade had a pheasantry here and raised famed cattle in the 19th century. The most powerful landlord who lived in Vrakúň at the beginning of the 20th century was Mate I. Pfeifer who also owned a distillery and steam mill. The local people were farmers and cultivated rye and wheat. **Nekyje na Ostrove** (Csallóköznyék) is documented as *Nee* in a document from 1165, which mentions it as a property of Bratislava Castle. Later several noble families owned it. The villagers were mostly farmers. In the past a mighty brook, which is now regulated and it is part of the Gabčíkovo-Topoľníky channel separated the above mentioned villages.

An old ford

An important ford used to exist on the route Győr – Medveďovo ford – Gabčíkovo – Dunajská Streda – Šamorín – Bratislava

Left: The lock chamber in Gabčíkovo
Right: The church in Gabčíkovo

The road connected the estates of Ráb (Győr) and Bratislava Castle. The ford and the toll were guarded by Pechenegs and Muslim toll-keepers. A fort, the predecessor of the manor house in Vrakúň, used to stand on the bank of what is today the channel.

The villages of Nekyje and Vrakúň joined in a natural way in the course of centuries. Officially they merged in 1940 under the name Nyékvárkony. Nekyje na Ostrove has used its Slovak name since 1927. The most important sacred monument of the village is the 14th century Roman Catholic **church of St. James**, originally Gothic, later adapted in the Renaissance style and restored in 1928. Only some remains of the original ornamentation on windows and on the dome of the church survive. Valuable paintings of saints around the main and side altars, paintings of the Madonna, of the Virgin Mary of the Rosary and of St. Stephen the King in interior of the church are of interest. The present font with a group of statues of the baptism of Christ dates from the late 19th century. In front of the church entrance is a pillory used until 1870. The local Baroque **chapel** of the Most Holy Trinity from 1740, the road cross with the statue of the Virgin Mary under the Crucifixion from the 19th century and the Baroque statue of John Nepomuk from the mid-18th century are the reminders of the religious life of the local people. The local **manor house** from 1904 was built on older foundations. The staircase leading from the manor house will bring the visitors to the **park**, protected area with oak growths and other rare wood species. The manor house now shelters a social institution.

The folk architecture in Vrakúň and the neighbouring villages matches the romantic character of the Danube landscape. The preserved clay houses look as if they grew from the ground also thanks to ingenious construction technology. They reflect the way of life of the local people and tourists can learn more details about it visiting the house No. 458, which contains an **exhibition**. This structure was made from unburned clay bricks in

the 19th century. It contains a furnace for baking bread and in the main room are various objects documenting the way of life of villagers in the past.

GABČÍKOVO (Bős in Hungarian, population 5,000) is 12 km away from the district town and 61 km from Bratislava. It is situated on the banks of the Čiližsky potok brook. It is an archaeological locality with a rich history. Slav, Avar and Roman burial places were found here. The first references about settlements on the left bank of the Danube are fairly old. It was first mentioned in 1102 as *Beys* in the years 1262-1276. It was a settlement in the environs of a water castle called *Bews*. The original name suggests that it might have been a Pecheneg settlement (in Hungarian Besenyők) that was guarding the ford on this then mighty brook of Čiliz. The settlement belonged to Amade family from 1264 until the mid-19th century.

King Matthias granted the village permission to hold weekly markets in 1468. An influx of German colonist meant a positive stimulus for the development of the village in the 16th century. Gabčíkovo was referred to in the 18th century as a little town. It ex-

perienced a battle between the Imperial army and the rebellious Hungarian troops in the revolutionary year 1849. One of the biggest sugar refineries in the County of Bratislava was precisely in Gabčíkovo in the years 1855-1878, the lords of the village had their distillery and brewery in the village. Several water mills worked on the Danube. Various yeoman families owned the village until 1945. Clay houses with saddle reed houses existed in the village until recently. The name of the village was *Beš* and after 1948 it was renamed after Jozef Gabčík, who participated in the assassination of the Reich Chancellor R. Heidrich. The little town recently became famous for its **water works Gabčíkovo**. The Danube always played an important role, and often a negative one, in its history. This was the reason why the local people founded an association with the mission of protecting it against floods. As the floods occurred almost regularly, the gigantic water works were built in Gabčíkovo in 1980-1990 and became its new symbol.

Left: The manor house in Gabčíkovo
Right: Baka

However, the town also has other attractions. It contains numerous cultural monuments. The former **Amade manor house** was built in its outskirts. Before there was a Gothic water castle surrounded by a moat. The palace was situated on the site of today's south-eastern wing of the manor house and castle walls fortified it. The old castle was reconstructed into a Renaissance manor house in the 17th century. Tadeáš Amade had the manor house rebuilt in the Late Baroque style in the 18th century. It is a four-wing building with a courtyard and some rooms contain Renaissance cross vaults. Valuable artistic objects and the family archives were destroyed and stolen by the end of the Second World War. This historic building served as a school after 1948 and now it shelters a home for elderly people. The manor house had an extensive park, which is now a **protected area**. Apart from twelve exotic wood species it contains rare specimen of oaks, diameter of some of which is up to 120 cm. Another manor house of Gabčíkovo, which used to stand about 3 km from the village in the place called Veľké Vranie was also owned

by the Amades. They had it built amidst thick wood in the second half of the 18th century. It was used as hunting manor house and a temporary residence of some family members. It was demolished when the wastewater channel of the Gabčíkovo dam was constructed in 1980.

Visiting Gabčíkovo one cannot miss the church standing in the centre of the town. It was originally the Gothic Roman Catholic **Church of St. Margaret of Antioch** church reconstructed by the end of the 18th century in the Late Baroque style. The original Gothic window and the Late Gothic portal are worth seeing. On the wall is a precious coat of arms of Amade family. Interior of the church is decorated by frescos from the beginning of the 20th century made by painter Teodor Székházy from Nové Zámky. Three altars are of interest in the interior of the church. The main Late Baroque altar with pillar architecture is from 1770. The central painting of Margita Antioch is by Michael Fay of Nitra from 1929. The side altars are dedicated to the Virgin Mary and Jesus Christ. Reliefs lavishly decorate the Neo-Classical pulpit from the second half of the 18th century. The walls of the church bear 14 paintings of the Stations of Cross, which were moved here from the Calvary built on an old cemetery in 1904. The village had a fairly large Jewish community in the past and the **synagogue** from the end of the 19th century built originally in romantic style with pseudoromantic and pseudogothic architectural elements was completely reconstructed. In the northern part of the village is a Jewish cemetery with marble tombstones from the late 19th and early 20th century. Recent monuments include the one commemorating the victims of the First World War and another dedicated to the Holocaust, which stands in front of the municipal office. The **Festival of songs and dances of Žitný ostrov** and the Feast of St. Florian are the attractions of the place every year in June, and the Grand Prize of Žitný ostrov in wrestling is also known abroad. A hot spring with a temperature 51 degrees Celsius feeds the local swimming pool. Two tree trunks 8,000 old conserved under a 10 m thick alluvium of gravel were found here, when the Gabčíkovo dam was constructed. Today these tree trunks together with

other natural and historic exhibits are part of the permanent exhibition of the local **Vlastivedný dom ľudovej architecture** (House of Natural History and Folk Architecture.

The village of **BAKA** (Baka in Hungarian, population 1,100) was mentioned for the first time in 1274 as the settlement of the royal court chamberlains of Bratislava Castle and a property of the Buken family. Then in 1445 it was mentioned as two settlements of Dolná and Horná Baka, which existed until 19th century on the bank of the Čiliz brook. The settlements joined in 1810. Several noble families owned the village. The local people were farmers and raised cattle, horses, and sheep. Original **village houses** built from clay unburned bricks with saddle roof exist in the village. On the Danube not far from Baka were numerous water mills. There were 28 of them in 1881, at the beginning of the 20th century only three of them were left, while none of them survived until the present time. The domi

Left: A fisherman at the Danube
Right: The Danube's delicacies

nant feature of the village is the Late Baroque Roman Catholic **All Saints church** built in 1762 on the site of an older church. It was restored in 1935. The main altar is in the Late Baroque style with pillar architecture and a painting of Assumption of the Virgin Mary from the 18th century.

TRSTENÁ na Ostrove (Csallóköznádasd in Hungarian, population 500) is 12.5 km away from Dunajská Streda. The first written document from 1250 referring to the village mentions the name *Nadast*. Swamps and wetland surrounded the village in the past and its original Hungarian name is related to the fact. *Nád* means reed and *nádasd* the place overgrown with reed. The Slovak name has been used since 1927. In the past it was owned by different yeoman families from the 18th century it was the family of Bartal. The villagers were living on farming, fishing and haulage. The **clay houses** still existing in the village are from the 19th century. The only sacred monument is the stone road cross with a relief of the Virgin Mary under the Crucifixion. It is a folk work of art from the early 19th century.

Not far from Trstená na Orave is the village of **JUROVÁ** (Dercsika in Hungarian, population 400). It was first mentioned in a document from 1253 as *Gursuka*. The village was a royal property of Bratislava Castle and the largest estates belonged to the Méhes and Balogh families. The people lived by cattle and sheep raising. There are several clay houses with open fires from the 19th century still existing in the village. The Slovak name Jurová has been used since 1948. The most important sacred monument of the village is the Neo-Classical Roman Catholic **church of the Assumption of Virgin Mary** from 1778 adapted in 1927. In its interior the main altar with a painting of the patron saint from the first half of the 19th century, a pulpit from 1778 and font from the late 18th century attract attention. Next to the village is the **nature reserve of Jurovský les**, protecting remains of floodplain forest amidst agricultural landscape.

Another farming village is **HORNÝ BAR** (Felbár in Hungarian, population

1,000) mentioned for the first time in 1245 as *Baar*. It was a royal property of Bratislava Castle. Later the greater part of it was owned by the Amade family, the rest belonged to other yeoman families. Each family had its manor house in the village. Matej Bel, the historian and geographer, mentions the manor house of the Amade family in Horný Bar, he allegedly wrote some of this books while staying here. The villagers lived by farming, cattle and sheep raising and fishing. Bodíky used to be part of this village. The local part called Šuľany (before Süly) was first mentioned as *Suul* in 1237 and it was also a property of Bratislava Castle. Sacred buildings include the Roman Catholic **church of St. Stephen the King** from 1774, built in the Baroque-Neo-Classical style, on the site of an old Gothic church. In its interior the side altars of St. Emerich and the Virgin Mary from 1780 are of interest. Another important sacred monument is the Roman Catholic **church of St. Anna** built in the Gothic style in the 14th century in Šuľany. The main altar is in the Baroque-Neo-Classical style from the late 18th century. The folk imitation of the Pieta of Šaštín from the late 18th century situated inside a glass cabinet on the side altar is unique. The castle manor house from the 17th century was rebuilt as a granary at the turn of the 19th and 20th centuries.

The village of **ŇÁRAD** (Csiliznyárad in Hungarian, before Topoľovec, population 600) is only 7 km away from Gabčíkovo. It was first mentioned as *Nyárad* in 1468. Then the Dóczy family owned it. The references to it from the 15th century also mentions other names. Various noble families owned it, mainly the Illésházys and Báthyánys. It was part of the County of Győr. After 1948 it was renamed to Topoľovec and the name Ňárad has been used since 1990. The villagers were almost exclusively farmers famed for horse breeding.

At the point where the wastewater channel of the Gabčíkovo dam enters the original channel of the Danube is the village of **SAP** (Szap in Hungarian, formerly Palkovičovo, population 500). The name of the village was changed to Palkovičovo to

commemorate the Slovak poet Juraj Palkovič (1769-1850) and then again in 1990, when the village acquired its historic name Sap. The first written reference to the village is from 1255 as *Zap*, when it belonged to Bratislava Castle. The owners were yeomen, first Ján from Sap, then the Dóczys and other families. The people of Sap were farmers, and the typical craft of the village was weaving.

The believers from Sap and the neighbouring village Ňárad renewed their Reformed **church** built on the site of the original Neo-Classical one from the late 18th century, which burned down. The interior of the new church is more recent, it is from the 20th century. There is also a **chapel** from 1973. The situation of Sap is very advantageous, it lies next to the Gabčíkovo dam and the beautiful natural setting is complemented by maintained folk traditions. The village is surrounded by numerous lakes and ponds, where the storks nest on top of telegraph poles. **Haláščárda** and the **daily bar called Pri jazere** with traditional reed roof are havens for tourists. Sap was chosen as the stop of the participants in the Inter-

national Danube Tour of canoeists organized in the years 1985-1995.

Leaving Sap in the direction of Veľký
Meder one comes to **BALOŇ** (Balony in
Hungarian, population 700). It was mentioned for the first time in 1252 in the
time of the rule of King Belo IV as *villa
Bolon* or *Bolun*. Baloň, the same as the
surrounding villages is one of the few villages of the present day Slovakia, which
were part of the County of Győr. The
Chapter of Győr directly owned it after the
13th century. Bell-founders of the Győr
cathedral lived there and their duty was to
service the bells in the Hungarian town of
Győr. Baloň and surrounding villages
were sacked and burned down by the
Turks in 1500 and Napoleon's troops destroyed them in 1809. When the Čabian-
sky and Báčsky canals were constructed,
the territory of the village was drained,
which resulted in more arable land for the
villagers, who mostly lived on fishing and
hunting. They sold fish and game in the
markets of Bratislava, Budapest and Vi-

enna. Baloň and other villages suffered a
lot from repeated floods. They tried to protect their houses by building them on artificially made hills. The village cemetery
church and municipal office are situated
on such hills. The dominant feature of the
village is the Roman Catholic **church of
the Visitation of the Virgin Mary** built
in 1835 in the Neo-Classical taste. The
inner furniture of the church is from the
same period and the wooden statue of the
Madonna is from the late 18th century.

The name of the contiguous village of
ČILIŽSKÁ RADVAŇ (Csilizradvány in
Hungarian, population 1,200) appeared
for the first time in documents from 1252
as *villa Rodouan*. Bratislava Castle owned
part of it and the rest belonged to Zobor
Abbey. Some historic sources assert that
its name derives from yeoman family Rád
who owned it sometime in the 15th century. The Slovak name has been used since
1927. Its owners alternated and in the
first half of the 20th century Count Aladár
Bethlen finally owned it. Its inhabitants
were farmers. The Danube broke the protective dikes in the village several times
and the most destructive flood was that of

Left: The church in Čiližská Radvaň

1965, when a great part of one of houses were demolished. A notable cultural monument of the village is the originally Gothic Reformed **church**. It was rebuilt in the Neo-Classical style in 1794. Fire destroyed it in 1861, when almost the whole village burnt down. A priest of the Reformed Church **Mór Kóczán** is the famous native of the village. He won a bronze medal in javelin competition at the 1912 Olympic Games of Stockholm. Čilizská Radvaň is the centre of the region called **Medzičilizie**. This name denotes a picturesque territory in the south-eastern part of Žitný ostrov. It originated around Čiližský potok brook, which created several little sand islands. Seven villages are situated in this area: Baloň, Čiližská Radvaň, Pataš, Kľúčovec, Sap, Ňárad, and Medveďov.

PATAŠ (Csilizpatas in Hungarian, formerly Pastúchy, population 800) is situated between Gabčikovo and Veľký Meder. It was first mentioned in a document from 1268 as *Pothouch*. It was one of those Danube villages, which guarded the border. It was owned by Bratislava Castle, then by the nuns of the Margaret's island in Budapest and in time of Turkish wars it passed into the hands of Clarist order. Gabriel Bethlen occupied the estates, which belonged to the nuns in 1621. Later the village belonged to one of Zichy family and other local yeomen. The administrative territory of Pataš is a kind of cemetery of disappeared settlements and villages, the existence of which is mentioned in historic documents from the 13th century. They included Für or Fyur and Zelebeg, seat of the royal hauliers. The villages probably disappeared in Turkish wars. The only sacred monument of Pataš is the Neo-Classical Reformed **church** from 1794, later rebuilt. The pulpit in its interior is worth seeing.

One of the ways how to cross the border and visit Hungary is the road border crossing Vámosszabadi next to the village of **MEDVEĎOV** (Medve in Hungarian, population 600) situated not far from the Danube dike. The village is 26 km away from Dunajská Streda. The past of the village is connected with the Danube. The river branched here into uncountable arms, separated from each other by sand islands and shallows.

The ford over the Danube

One of the Danube fords was situated lower down the stream, near Kľúčovec in the Roman times. In the Middle Ages there was a settlement called Negeven, in which, as a legend says, forty (negyven in Hungarian) royal hauliers were waiting for the royal clerks who crossed the Danube via the ford in Kľúčovec. Then the hauliers took them to Komárno or Bratislava. The ford was later shifted nearer to Medveďov and became part of the mail route leading from Buda to Bratislava. In the 19th century there was a steam ferry and today a bridge facilitates the communication between the riverbanks. The bridge was the one crossed by the Hungarian troops, which occupied Žitný ostrov on November 5th 1938 following the Vienna Arbitrage.

The first reference to the village is from 1252 when it was mentioned as *villa Medwe* and Bratislava Castle owned it. Its name presumably derives from the Slovak word for "bear", which is also depicted on the municipal seal though it is not probable that bears lived in this area. A family name could also have given the name to this village. The Turks destroyed it. After the Turks were driven out, German colonists repopulated the village and called it The White Church. Some of Germans left and the Hungarian population assimilated the ones that remained. In the 17th century Medveďov belonged to the Chapter of Győr. Beyond the settlement was an island called Cholera, as it was the place where the sick were moved until the 19th century. The villagers were living on farming, haulage, and milling, and from the beginning of the 20th century the majority of them found employment in industry. The only cultural monument of this settlement is the Roman Catholic **church of St. Anna** from around 1800. After a fire in 1855 it was renowned. The Neo-Classical building has a single nave sacred space with chance. In the administrative territory of the village is the **Nature Reserve of Opatovské jazierko lake** with floodplain forest, which contains protected plant and wild life species.

The village of **KĽÚČOVEC** (Kulcsod in Hungarian, population 400) was first mentioned in historical sources in 1252. It was the settlement of the royal court chamberlains and thanks to donation of King Belo IV it became the property of the Premonstratesian monastery in Turiec. The name of the village derives from the Hungarian word *kulcs* for key, which could have also meant the key to the ford as a ford existed there in the Roman era. A settlement existed here as early as in the 11th century populated by the Pechenegs, the guards of the ford and the frontier, together with Moslem tollkeepers. The villages was in the ownership of Komárno Castle from 1268 and the Benedictine monastery owned it from the 16th century. The 1876 and 1880 floods destroyed it. Population were mostly farmers cultivating wheat. Many of them were hauliers. The village was often destroyed by natural disasters, namely the floods

Left: Danube near Kľúčovec
Right: The Malý Dunaj
The weir of the Malý Dunaj

when the Danube inundated its territory in the years 1850, 1924, and 1926. Especially the ones of 1954, when the dikes on the Hungarian side of the frontier broke and of 1965 when the Danube waters flooded the prevailing part of Žitný ostrov are unforgettable for the locals. The only cultural monument of Kľúčovec is the Neo-Classical Reformed **church** with the Baroque elements rebuilt in 1885. The single-nave church contains interior furniture from the 19th century.

Visiting the Danube region one can also choose the route leading through the centre of Žitný ostrov, avoiding the main communications. **VEĽKÉ BLAHOVO** (Nagyabony in Hungarian, population 1,300), one of the oldest settlements in Žitný ostrov. It was first mentioned in a document from 1161 as *terra Oboni*. It was owned by Bratislava Castle and then by petty aristocratic families. They are recalled by the Rococo **manor house** with Neo-Classical elements from the years 1760 to 1765. The sacred monuments of the village include the Baroque Roman Catholic church of the Most Holy Trinity. Its main altar bears the painting of the Most Holy Trinity. The side altar of the Holy Sepulchre is adorned by a sculpture of the Virgin Mary of the Seven Sorrows. The **chapel** next to the church inspired in the Neo-Classical style from the 19th century is also interesting. A recognized Gypsy violinist **János Bihari** was born in this village in 1764. One of the hotels of Dunajská Streda bears his name. A solitary homestead called Trstinový hrad, in Hungarian Nádvár or the Reed Castle used to exist in the administrative territory of the village in the direction of Orechová Potôň, mentioned in historic documents from 1422. It disappeared in the time of Turkish raids and only the name survived which now denotes a place amidst the fields. The **protected area of Plytčiny** contains the rows of willow trees skirting the road.

VYDRANY (Hodos in Hungarian, population 1,300) was first mentioned in 1245 as a royal property of Bratislava Castle. Later it acquired the name *Hodus*. This name probably derives from the Hungarian word for beaver, which inhabited

the river arms. Various representatives of the petty aristocracy later owned the village. The people lived on farming; they cultivated wheat and maize and raised cattle. The sacred monument of the village is the Reformed **church** built as a toleration church lacking tower in 1786. The missing tower was built in the 19th century. The interior of the church contains interesting items, such as tin vessels from the 17th and 19th centuries. A short retour from the main road will bring you to another of the villages of Žitný ostrov that bear the name Potôň. There used to exist nine villages in the area bearing the word Potôň (Patony in Hungarian) in their name. The denomination appeared for the first time in a document from 1250 as *villa Pothun*. The settlements must have originated in the 10th to 12th centuries and their function was that of suppliers. At least seven of them were situated between Dunajská Streda and Lehnice. The origin of the name Potôň probably derives from the word *Potun* that meant "a branch off the main family or bastard". Bratislava Castle owned the serf villages. Only Predná Potôň was a yeoman village. The inhabitants were farmers, and raised cattle and horses. Their territories with abundant meadows and pastures stretched as far as the Malý Dunaj river. The village of **ORECHOVÁ POTÔŇ** (Dióspatony in Hungarian, population 1,600) was first mentioned in 1367 as *Gyospothon*. It was a royal property, later it was owned by Michal Csiba, in the 19th century it was part of Lehnice estate and then it was in the ownership of the Pálffy family, the same as neighbouring Förge and Dolná Potôň. Before the villages originated there was a shallow lake and swampy terrain

and this is why no large settlement exists in this area. Dolná Potôň included some solitary homesteads and a mill. The sacred monument of this village is the Neo-Classical Reformed church from 1870.

The first reference to **HORNÁ POTÔŇ** (Felsöpatony, population 1,900) is from 1255 as *Potun*, later *Pathon*. But the name rather referred to the place and not the village. The village, as we know it now, originated when Benkova Potôň was added to it in 1940 and Čečínska Potôň in 1960. The people were mostly farmers and raised cattle and horses. The Neo-Classical Evangelical Reformed **church** represents the sacred architecture from 1816, which originated by reconstruction of a school building. **Lögerská Potôň** was personal property of the Arpads, then it was owned by the Archbishopric of Esztergom. The Pálffy family owned some estates here until the 20th century. The majority of the original houses with reed roofs burned down in 1877. **Benkova Potôň** was owned by the Archbishop's County of Holice and Bratislava Castle. There is a Neo-Classical Reformed church built in 1816. **Čečínska Potôň** is known

from 1441. It was a royal property and later a property of the Pálffys.

The first written reference to the village of **MICHAL na Ostrove** (Szentmihályfa in Hungarian, population 700) is from 1337, and it is mentioned as *Zentmihal*. As a serf village it had several lords. Its people were farmers. Some **clay houses** with reed roofs survived in Michal na Ostrove. The most important sacred monument is the Gothic Roman Catholic **church of St. Michael the Archangel** from the 14th century. It was rebuilt in the Neo-Classical style in 1787. In its interior apart from the main altar, also the side altars of the Baptism of Christ with a painting from the early 19th century, the Baroque-Neo-Classical pulpit from 1790 and a round stone Early Renaissance font from 1538 are of interest. The 14th century frescos are unique. Next to the church

is a stone cross with sculpture of the Crucifixion from 1657. The village also has a road Neo-Classical **chapel** of the Holy Family from the beginning of the 19th century and sculptures of St. Michael and St. Vendelin placed in front of the church.

LEHNICE (Lég in Hungarian, population 2,300) originated as *Lég* in 1940 by joining the villages of Veľký Lég, Malý Lég and Sása. Later Masníkovo was added to them. The first mention of the settlements of Veľký and Malý Lég is from the first half of the 13th century when they were owned by Bratislava Castle. Later they were known as two villages and their inhabitants acquired yeoman privileges. They were owned by several aristocratic families. The people were active in agriculture and sheep raising. The administrative territory of Malý Lég was always considered the most fertile in the whole Žitný ostrov. Sása was first referred to in the documents from 1239 as *Zaz* and in 1239 as property of Bratislava Castle called *Zás-Város* (the Saxon Town). It was owned by different yeoman families. Masníkovo (the former Predná Potôň) was first mentioned as *villa Pothun* in 1250.

The English park of Veľký Lég contains a Late Renaissance **manor house** from the early 17th century. It was rebuilt in 1930 by Count Rudolf Benyovszky in the romanticizing pseudo-Gothic style imitating English and Scottish manor houses. Today it houses a hospital. The **park** of Lehnice is a **protected area**. The important sacred monument of the village is the Baroque Roman Catholic **church of St. Elisabeth the Widow** from 1679 built on the site of an older Gothic church. The visitors will be certainly intrigued by the Baroque main altar with group of statues of St. Elisabeth the Widow, the side altars with paintings of St. Stephen the King, the Pieta and the Virgin Mary from the early 19th century. The Neo-Classicist **curia** in Sása is from the mid-19th century.

Left: The manor house in Lehnice

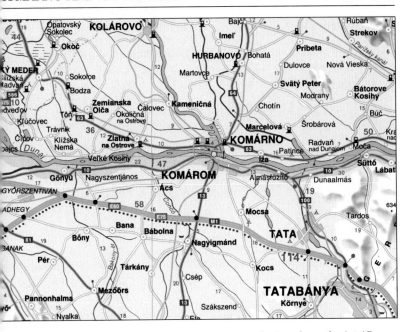

KOMÁRNO AND ITS ENVIRONS

Komárno and its environs spread on the left bank of the Danube in the southern part of the Danube lowland. The western part of the territory lies on the Danube plain. Numerous locust woods, and willow and poplar growths next to the Malý Dunaj, Váh, Nitra and Žitava rivers refresh the flat plain. Going east the character of landscape changes into the undulating landscape of the Hronská pahorkatina hill land with typical wide valleys separated by flat ridges.

The centre of the Slovak part of the Danubeland, the town of **KOMÁRNO** (Komárom in Hungarian, population 37,700) lies on the confluence of the Váh and Dunaj. It is one of the oldest towns in Slovakia. A primeval settlement existed on the territory of the town as early as the Lower Stone Age. Archaeological finds suggest that this place has been continuously settled since the early Bronze Age. Celts settled here at the end of the 4th century BC. Roman Empire extended its frontiers up to the Danube in the 1st AD century and on its left side near Komárno, the Romans built the military camp *Kelemantia* at the beginning of the 2nd century. Barbarian tribes gradually pushed out the Romans of Pannonia at the end of the 4th century and the following migration wave brought here the nomadic tribes of Avars. Archaeologists have discovered eight cemeteries from the Avar period, prevailingly from the 7th to 8th centuries. The great number of equestrian graves (103) with abundant finds indicates that this must have been a strategically important and powerful military centre of the Avars. When the Avar Empire collapsed, the population probably merged with the Slavs. Old Magyar tribes led by Ketel who constructed here the first castle in the 10th century then settled the territory around the confluence of the Váh and Danube. Komárno with its castle resisted the Tartar raid.

Three market settlements originated around the castle which stood on the site of the existing fort, a piece of land squeezed between the arms of the Váh and Danube: *villa Camarum, villa Kezw,*

and *villa St. Andrae*. The oldest written reference to Komárno from 1037 comments collection of fees in the port of Komárno and fishing carried out in the area. Other sources from 1075 mention Komárno as a village with market, called *Camarum*. The settlement next to the castle obtained the right to storage of all goods transported on the Danube in 1244. The merchants were obliged to unload all their goods for several days in Komárno and offer them for sale or pay duty. Komárno was enjoying and profiting from this privilege until 1751 when it was abolished. King Belo IV granted municipal rights to Komárno in 1265. King Charles Robert confirmed them by the privilege from 1331 which exempted the town from jurisdiction of the main *comes* (elected administrator of province). The castle of Komárno was also owned by Matúš Čák Trenčiansky for a while. The medieval town lived through its greatest prosperity in the 15th century when the rulers and court of Kingdom of Hungary frequently stayed in Komárno. The widow of King Albrecht of Habsburg even gave birth to her son, later King Ladislav V. the Posthumous in Komárno in 1440. King Matthias I liked to stay in Komárno and apart from building several important houses in this town he also founded its park and an orchard. The Diet of the Kingdom of Hungary held its session in the town in 1510. On the other hand, the town suffered a lot during the period of Turkish expansion. The castle of Komárno became the main supporting point of the defensive system constructed against the Turks, after they occupied Buda and Esztergom in the years 1541-1543.

The defensive system of Komárno

The fort of Komárno is the largest bastion fortification in Central Europe. It originated in the years 1546-1557 by reconstruction of the 13th century castle. A new pentagonal fort with star-shaped fortifications widened the old fort in the years 1663-1673. A bridge connected the forts over the moat and along with bridgeheads of the bridges of St. Nicholas and St. Peter they formed a compact defensive system.

Left: The system of forts in Komárno
Right: The bastion of the system of forts

The fort resisted practically all Turkish attacks. Only the 1783 earthquake damaged it to such an extent that it lost its strategic significance. However, this system of forts was again rebuilt in the early 19th century as a result of the Napoleonic wars. An outer defensive ring consisting of two bastion lines – called the Váh and Palatine lines – and four little advanced forts were added to it. The tip of the western bastion of the New Fort, which is turned to the town bears the inscription: NEC ARTE, NEC MARTE (Neither by wile nor by force). The inscription placed under the allegorical female statue called the stone virgin, emphasizes impossibility of assailing the fort and indeed, it resisted for centuries. Some attribute it to the stone virgin..

The fort also played an active role in the years 1848-1849 when it resisted the siege and attacks of the Imperial troops led by General J. Klapka. It is a historic monument of European significance and a **national cultural monument**. Bastion VI of the Váh line was restored in 1991. There is a tablet on its wall, which was awarded by the International Association *Europa Nostra* to the fort as the most significant monument of the kind in Europe. The Old and the New forts are situated at the point where the Váh flows into the Danube and the Slovak army uses them now.

The local population also lived through bad times in time of anti-Habsburg rebellions. The Imperial army occupied the Evangelical church and drove out the priest in 1672. Protestants were persecuted and their church pulled down. Serbs, known as good merchants settled here in time of the Turkish assault. They built here a large Orthodox church and a cemetery of their own. Their descendants kept the Serb name but they are prevailingly of Hungarian nationality today. When the Turks were driven out of the country the town thrived on the quickly developing river navigation. A bridge over the Danube was built in 1741. Water mills also complemented the typical panorama of Komárno.

Komárno obtained the privileges of free royal borough from Empress Maria Theresa in 1745. It ranked then among the five largest towns in the Kingdom of Hungary with approximately ten thousand inhabitants, and well-developed trade and crafts. The trade in corn, fish and timber was especially successful. There were about 650 different workshops in Komárno in 1784 and the flour made in this town was widely reputed. The merchants of Komárno supplied fish to the royal court from the 16th century. By the end of the 18th century there were 145 fishermen working in the town. Cabinet-makers who produced painted cabinets of Komárno were also famous. The craftsmen were associated in their respective guilds and the most important guilds were those of the millers, goldsmiths, boot-makers and boat carpenters. Haulage was special category as owners of horses dedicated themselves to pulling the boats up the river stream before the steam engine was introduced. Ship-building was another common craft and the boats made in Komárno were considered of high quality. The favourable economic situation lasted until the early 19th century. This was period in which the famous Hungarian novelist Mór Jókai was inspired to write his novel *The Golden Man*. **Society of the Scientists of Komárno** was founded in the town in the late 18th century. It published *Mindenes Gyüjtemény* (General Miscellany) from 1782. Frequent earthquakes, floods, plague epidemics, and fire hindered further development of the town. Great part of the town and 19 boats on the Danube burnt down in an extreme gale on September 17th 1848. The greatest floods occurred in the years 1800, 1876, and 1880. After the last quoted one the Danube dike was built and an iron bridge over the river was constructed in 1892.

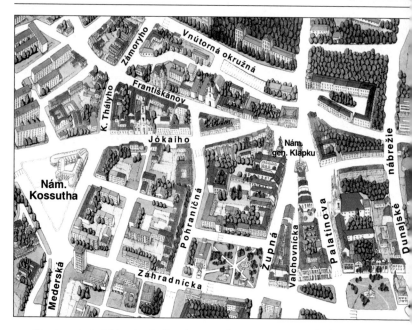

You can start sightseeing in Komárno at the centre near the former **Zichy Palace,** which is one of the dominant features of the Námestie gen. J. Klapku square. Count Zichy had the palace built in the late 17th century. This, originally Baroque, building was severely damaged in the 1763 earthquake, rebuilt in the Neo-Classical style and widened by addition of two lateral wings in the 19th century. The palace was restored in 1989 and one part serves as the Podunajské Museum. There is a **permanent exhibition of the modern history of the town** in the rooms on the first floor of the palace. Its courtyard recently adapted as a park is reached through the vaulted passage around the Baroque group of statues of the Most Holy Trinity. The **Podunajské Museum,** which is not far from Zichy Palace and is a notable pseudoromantic building from 1913, offers a permanent exhibition of **old and medieval monuments**. Another collection called the Roman Lapidarium presenting the Roman

stone monuments of Slovakia is in Bastion VI of the fortification system on the northern edge of the town. **The complex of buildings of the former pavilion of officers** situated only several tens of meters from the Námestie generála J. Klapku square, was built in the Neo-Gothic style in the years 1858-1863 and resembles English Gothic. The statue of the Muse of Arts by sculptor Peter Gáspár native of Bátorove Kosihy stands in entrance hall of the pavilion.

The secular landmark of the town is its Neo-Renaissance **town hall** standing in the Námestie generála J. Klapku square. It was built in 1875 on the foundations of an older building from 1756, from which the ground plan and peripheral walls were preserved. The disasters accompanying the town in its history also struck the Late Baroque Roman Catholic parish **church of St. Andrew** built in the years 1748-1756 now standing on Palatínova ulica street. The now disappeared parish church stood here sometime around 1268. This church was destroyed along with the village in the Turkish raid of 1594. The tower was repaired in the 17th century for the military

---

Right: The Námestie gen. J. Klapku square

guards. The old church was renewed only in 1624, and a hundred years later a nave was added to it, but it fell down later. After the Jesuit order took over the church, construction of today's church started. Wall paintings from 1760 were damaged by the earthquake and finally completely destroyed by fire in 1848. They are known only from descriptions and preserved sketches in the Baroque Museum of Vienna. The church renewed after the 1848 fire has a single nave with lateral chapels. The main altar of St. Andrew made of marble is from the second half of the 19th century and early 20th century. There are twelve Neo-Classical candelabras from the second half of the 19th century on the main altar.

Sightseeing of other churches of Komárno may start as well by the Roman Catholic **church of St. Rozália**, a Neo-Classical building from 1848 situated on what used to be the market place, now Námestie sv. Rozálie square. The central building with dominating dome resembles the works of the architect P. Nobile. The main altar is from the time, when the church was built. Closer to the town cen-

tre on Jókai street is the Neo-Classical Reformed church built in 1788 without a tower. The tower as added to it in 1832. One can admire Rococo pulpit from the second half of the 18th century ornamented by wooden carvings and the Neo-Classical stone font in its interior. Not far from this church the former **military church** stands in the Ulica františkánov street. This Late Baroque church from 1769 was originally the Franciscan monastic church. It was built on the site of the old monastery and church from 1677, which fell down in the 1763 earthquake. The army occupied the contiguous bulky building built around central yard of monastery after the Franciscans left in 1809. On the same street and near Námestie generála Klapku square is the **Evangelical church**, a Neo-Classical building from 1796 with a tower built in the late 19th century. The exterior of the church was changed when the tower was added to it and a Roman sarcophagus was built to its outer side. In its interior the altar with the painting of the Crucified, the pulpit and font from the late 18th century and a Neo-Classical chalice from the

same time are of interest. Another important sacred monument is the originally Baroque **church of the Serbian Orthodox Church** from 1754. It stands on Palatínova street and was restored in the years 1849-1851. Its interior contains a collection of 23 Orthodox icons from the 17th and 18th centuries and a voluptuous iconostasis from 1770. Two large bronze candelabras, Baroque church banners and various chalices, a golden cross with small icons from the 16th century, a copper plate with Oriental motif from the 18th century, an oriental scarf with golden rings are the interesting items in the interior of the church. The Rococo pulpit is from the time when the church was built, while the carved pews were brought here from a monastery in Hungary. The church was built on the site of a former Late Gothic church from 1511, which was pulled down when the New Fort was constructed. The church was given to the Orthodox Church in 2000.

Left: The Courtyard of Europe
Right: The former Officer's Pavilion
       The statue of gen. J. Klapka

The former Jesuit college next to the parish office is a Baroque building and its oldest parts date from 1654. When the Society of Jesus was abolished, the college passed to Benedictines who created here the Calvinist college in 1812. The Late Baroque **chapel of St. Joseph** from the second half of the 18th century, later adapted in the Neo-Classical style and the Baroque **group of statues of the Most Holy Trinity** built in 1715 as a reminder of the plague epidemic and anti-Habsburg wars complement the sacred monuments of the town. The above mentioned group of statues stands on Župná ulica street on the spot, where the Protestant priest Ján Száki was burnt to death in 1670.

The Courtyard of Europe

The Courtyard of Europe is the name of a unique project of the architects grouped in the studio Europa in Komárno. It is in fact the intention, now implemented, to build historic architecture typical for the individual regions of Europe in a styled form on a new square of Komárno. The historic core of the town will be connected with the Courtyard of Europe by historic entrance gates. The gate of St. Stephen commemorating the first King of Kingdom of Hungary and propagator of Christianity closes the ulica Spievajúceho mora (The Singing Sea street). The gate of King Belo IV who granted Komárno municipal privileges is on the western side of the square. The next gate is dedicated to King Ladislav V the Posthumous, a native of Komárno and it provides the entrance from Jókaiho ulica street to ulica Spievajúceho mora street and it will serve to pedestrians and car traffic. It will bear the coat of arms and statue of King Ladislav V. On the northern side of the Courtyard of Europe is the gate of Queen Maria Theresa inspired by the Czech Baroque. On the inner side of the park adjacent to Zichy Palace the gate of King Matthias I, the most important ruler of our history, who had a great affinity to this town, will be placed. With its colours and shape it will resemble the buildings from the reign of Matthias I, including his family castle Hunedoara. There will the royal coat of arms and a commemorative table above the gate. A copy of the original well will be made in the centre of the square. The well used to stand on Hlavné námestie square in front of the town hall of Komárno from 1878. Ornamental bars adorned it. The town donated the upper part of the well to Archduke Salvator. who had the well built again on the courtyard of his manor house in Gmunden, Austria. In a park of statues in the front part of the courtyard of Zichy Palace will be a copy of the music pavilion standing in the Anglia Park of Komárno.

Komárno is widely known as a town with rich cultural and social life. Every two years in April **International Competition of Singers of F. Lehár**, as well as the **Lehár Festival** staging musicals and the June **Days of Jókai** (survey of amateur theatre ensembles) are organized. Cultural events include the **Days of Constantine and Methodius** held in July, **Days of European Heritage** in September and **Days of Matica** in October. In Bastion VI Jokai's theatre presents a survey of theatre ensembles under the title **Theatre Bastion**. By the end of April and beginning of May **Days of Komárno** jointly organized by the towns of Komárno and Komárom in Hungary attract numerous visitors. Their tradition is connected with the International running race commemorating the anniversary of granting municipal rights to Komárno and that of the victorious battle of the 1849 emancipation efforts. The days include pop concerts, a beer feast, navigation on the Danube, days of open doors to the forts in both towns, various exhibitions, a ceremonial Mass and fireworks. The **motor boat race** is also one of the attractions held in July.

Bastion V contains the private Gallery "T". International meetings of Church music under the title *Harmonia Sacra Danubiana* is also one of the important cultural events held in Komárno.

Komárno is the native town of many famous figures. The two best known are the writer **Mór Jókai** (1825-1904), author of many romantic historic novels (The Golden Man, The White Lady of Levoča or The Black Diamonds) and the composer **Franz Lehár** (1870 - 1948), who wrote popular musicals such as The Merry Widow, The Land of Smiles, Paganini, Giudita, etc.

The town enjoys a several centuries old tradition in ship-building. In the past rafts were transporting timber on the Váh river and the timber was used for building ships called "supery" in Komárno. The boats were of very good quality and the ship-builders enjoyed a good reputation recognized all over Central Europe. At present Slovenské lodenice share-holding company is the biggest producer of ships in Central Europe. Komárno is still an important river port and the seat of Slovenská plavba dunajská, the company deal-

The part open all the year round contains two saunas with a cold water basin, a sitting basin with thermal water, a gymnasium and fitness centres. Near the confluence of the rivers Váh and Nitra on an island next to the settlement of Lándor is the **National Nature Reserve of Apáli island**. This conserved floodplain forest is home to rare species of water fowl, which is nesting there.

The administrative area of the town includes the small settlements of Čerhát, Ďulov dvor, Hadovce, Kava, Lándor, Malá Iža, Nová Osada, Nová Stráž, Pavel, and Veľký Harčáš. **Nová Stráž** is the most important one. It was first referred to in 1387. Komárno Castle owned it. After the Turks destroyed it in 1577 it was restored in the 18th century. The name of the village (The New Guard) expresses the function it fulfilled in the past. Military guards, who controlled the access to Komárno until the 20th century were stationed here. Cultural monuments include the originally Neo-Classical manor house with English **park**, which has a Roman sarcophagus at is entrance, remains of a little Romanesque church, and a Neo-Classical church from 1815. The manor house was built in the early 18th century, presumably on the foundation of an older structure from 1785. The village park of Nová Stráž was founded in the 18th century and is a protected landscape park. The manor house served as the summer residence of the Darányi family.

The tourist route leads from Komárno to the west in the direction of the village of **ZLATNÁ na Ostrove** (Csallóközaranyos in Hungarian, population 2,400). It is 8.5 km away from the district town. Southern border of its territory coincides with the Danube with two islands: the larger Veľkolélsky and smaller Zlatý ostrov islands. This village is an archaeological locality with finds from the Stone Age, Roman period and a Slav-Avar burial place. It was first mentioned in 1094 under the name *Locus Aureus* when Prince David donated it to Tihányi Abbey. Later, in 1268 it is documented as the royal village of *villa Oronos*. In the 13th century it was the property of Komárno Castle. Various royal visitors, King Belo IV

ing with Danube navigation. The area of port is 21 hectares, the surface of water basins is 45 ha. The port has the **only balance bridge** in Slovakia opened in 1968, which provides access to the border crossing to Hungary. There is also a railway border crossing to Hungary. The town is an important cultural centre of the Hungarian minority in Slovakia. It is the seat of bishop, the board of the Synod of the Reformed Church in Slovakia and a branch of the Slovak Technical University of Trnava.

The water sports area and boathouse is on a dead arm of the Váh. The visitors to the town are attracted by its **thermal swimming pool**. It exploits two hot springs with a water temperature of 37 degrees of Celsius. They are 1,224 m and 1,040 m deep. The water is beneficial for the therapy of rheumatic diseases and overall recreation. The part of the area used in summer contains a sport swimming pool, one for children, one for non-swimmers and a sitting swimming pool.

Left: The statue of Mór Jókai
Right: The port of Komárno

in 1267, King Ladislav IV in 1277, and King Charles Robert in 1327 visited it. The village of Felaranyos, which also belongs to Zlatná, is referred to in historic sources as a settlement as early as the 13th century. Felaranyos was known for the from the Middle Ages until the 20th century. Gold brought here by the Danube had its origin in the Austrian Alps. Apart from milling, **gold washing** was one of the typical occupations of the villagers for many centuries. Zlatná na Ostrove was struck by numerous disasters. Floods and fires were topped by the Tartar and Turkish raids. The Turks burnt down the village in 1676. Local chronicle mentions an untypical natural disaster in 1847. Swarms of locusts came here from Transylvania and destroyed everything in their way, including the reed roofs of the village houses. Two years later the Austrian Imperial army, which attacked the ford of Komárno also "visited" Zlatná. The two World Wars took their toll as well. The victims are commemorated by two monuments at the cemetery and the one from 1995 at the Jewish cemetery is a reminder of the Holocaust. Extensive orchards around the

village used to exist. The names of the places prove it: The Pear Tree Row, The Cherry Orchard or Below the Gardens are some of them. **Houses built of unburned clay bricks** with saddle roofs covered with reed to be seen in the village are from the late 19th century. There were water mills on the Danube and the first steam driven mill called Katinka was installed here in 1921. The mill was closed down after it was nationalized, but the original owner renewed it in 1995 and it is operating again.

All that is left from the past "gold rush" glory of the village is the local nomenclature and several curias witnessing to the secular life of the local petty aristocracy. Michal and Štefan Magyary-Koss had built the Neo-Classical **curia** from 1769 on older foundations. The reconstructed building now houses a health-care centre. East of this curia is another smaller, and today considerably altered **curia** from the second half of the 19th century. The Reformed Church from 1794 is one example of sacred architecture. The Table of the Lord from 1714 in its interior is of interest. The Roman

Catholic **church** built only in 1935 on the site of an old belfry serves the local Catholics. A car-camping site next to the **roadhouse Drop** is ready to accommodate visitors to the village. Several solitary homesteads existed in environs of Zlatná na ostrove. What is now part of it called **Veľký Lél** is known as an archaeological locality. In the Roman period a guard tower stood there. A legend says that Prince Lehel broke his camp here after his victorious battle with the Czechs. The settlement is referred to in the years 1245-1255 when it belonged to Counts of Fraknó, later its owners alternated. A small fort outside the village was part of the Komárno defensive system. Among the most important owners of the settlement were the Ruttkay and Karcsay families. Baron László Karcsay had built here a Neo-Classical **curia** as a solitary building in the mid-19th century. It is a simple kind of rural curia, now decaying, in many aspects similar to folk architecture. In the northern part of the settlement is a

Left: The Nature Reserve of Veľký Lél
Right: Bodzianske Lúky

manor house from 1935 around which remains of its original park survive. Now it is used by farmers. In the settlement of **Horná Zlatná**, which was first mentioned in 1268 as property of Komárno Castle the family Zichy had built a small and ground floor Neo-Classical **curia** in 1800. A wonderful park around it has been conserved. **Ontopa** is another solitary settlement mentioned in 1449 as a yeoman village, where Matej Ghyczy had built a one floor Neo-Classical **manor house** in the early 19th century, now owned by its original owner.

The administrative territory of Zlatná na Ostrove contains several landmarks. It is the **Nature Reserve of Veľký Lél** with gray herons and other water fowl species nesting there. Herons nest in small colonies counting 25 to 30 nesting pairs usually on poplar trees at the height of 20 m. The protected territory is on the southern edge of the eastern half of the island created by the Danube and its dead arm. The proper island Veľký Lél lies in an inundation area, part of which is covered by water in times of high water levels. North of the village is another natural landmark of Žitný ostrov (The Rye Island): the **protected area called Dropie** where bustards live.

Bustard

This biggest bird of Europe similar to the turkey is a symbol of Žitný ostrov. Its numbers are constantly decreasing and this is the reason why it is protected species in Dropie over an area of 9,218 hectares. Additional birds live dispersed in its environs. The bustard is a very shy bird and large fields are an ideal home for it. About 700 bustards lived in the territory of Žitný ostrov at the beginning of the 20th century. Their number was gradually dropping from 250 in 1955 to today's level of only about 80.

On the route Komárno-Veľký Meder is also the village **OKOLIČNÁ na Ostrove** (Ekel in Hungarian, population 1,500). Archaeologists found a Roman milestone probably from the 2nd century and Slav-Avar burial places in this village. It was mentioned for the first time as *Villa Ekl,* part of Komárno Castle, lying amidst swamps in 1268. In the Middle Ages it was property of petty yeoman families. Its people were mostly farmers raising cattle or growing wine. **Clay houses** from the end of the 19th century made of unburned bricks with saddle reed roofs and wooden gables, as well as the Neo-Classical **curia** of the Erdély family from the 19th century survive in the village. Sacred buildings are represented by two churches. The Roman Catholic Neo-Classical **church** from 1816 was built on the site of the old Romanesque church. The Neo-Classical Reformed **church** from 1804 was restored in the early 20th century The interior of the church with rebuilt tower contains a Late-Renaissance chalice from 1618 and a tin pitcher from 1718.

The village of **ZEMIANSKA OLČA** (Némesócsa in Hungarian, population 2,600) is located not far from the main Bratislava-Komárno road, 1 km from the turn off to Kolárovo. It is 35 km away from Komárno. Archaeologists found here an Old Magyar cemetery from the 10th century and other from the 11th and 12th centuries. The first reference to the village is in the document of King Belo IV from 1264 as *Oucha*. The village was surrounded by solitary homesteads, which gradually merged with it. In the following centuries several yeoman families lived in Olča and its name was changing with the owners. The villagers were farmers, they raised cattle and cultivated vines. Later they worked in the local industry, in a distillery plant, dairy, brickyard or the gravel pit. Several typical **clay houses** covered by reed survived here from the 19th century. Curias and manor houses are reminders of the life of yeoman families. The **curia** standing next to the mill built by the Holczer family by the end of 19th century is the most interesting. The family was killed in the war and the building was abandoned after 1945. Today it houses the home for elderly people. The Neo-Classical building has the remains of its original park. Spiritual life of villagers is symbolized by the Neo-Classical Reformed **church** with Baroque elements built in the late 18th century. It was repeatedly adapted, for the last time in 1924, when

the tower was reconstructed and its interior changed. The interior of the church is made of wood. The pulpit and the Lord's Table made from white Carara marble, as well as a chalice from 1525, most probably moved here from the damaged Calvinist church in Trávnik, are the interesting items of its interior. The Neo-Classical **parsonage** is connected with the church by a low wall. It dates from the turn of the 18th and 19th centuries. The Roman Catholic **chapel**, originally a school from the 19th century, is now used for services after it was adapted. Another **chapel** is in the cemetery. It is a little romantic building from the second half of the 19th century. It was a burial chapel of the yeoman family Galambos. Visitors to the village will certainly like its neat square with a little lake and a fountain. There is an is ecumenical **chapel** with a wooden belfry used for various events in the park on the square.

The village also has a technical monument. It is a **roller mill** built by Adolf Holczer in 1910 not far from his curia. The mill was first steam-driven and then after a fire in 1930 adapted to power en-

gine. It was modernized and produces good quality flour.

In environs of the nearby village of **BODZA** (Bogya in Hungarian, population 300), on the border with the district of Dunajská Streda, some Roman-Barbarian historic settlements and Slav-Avar graves were found. The village originated in the administrative territory of Hradná Bodza by joining two settlements separated by the road leading from Komárno to Bratislava. Its name was *Bogha* in 1268 and it belonged to the Komárno Castle. Later it was property of several yeoman families, including Zichys and Zabrans, who owned it in the 19th century. The villagers lived off agriculture and traces of their farming past can be still seen as the village has several examples of **folk architecture**. The settlement of Bodza-Lúky, which is now the independent village of **BODZIAN-SKE LÚKY** (Bogyarét in Hungarian, population 200) also used to be part of Bodza.

The neighbouring village of **HOLIARE** (Gellér in Hungarian, population 400) is one of the Danube villages known for its archaeological finds from the Neolithic period. It also has a cemetery of the Magyar Culture from the Older Bronze Age, a La Téne settlement and burial place from the 10th and 11th centuries. The village originated by joining two independent settlements of Dolné and Horné Holiare, which used to be the serf villages of Ráb Castle mentioned for the first time in 1257. The sacred monument of the village is the Neo-Classical Reformed **church** from 1786 adapted in 1841. A pulpit from mid-19th century and marble font from 1911 are the interesting parts of its interior. The village was part of Bodza until 1994.

North of Zemianska Oľča in a shallow wet depression is the small village of **LIPOVÉ** (population 200). Its administrative territory is drained by the Okoličné-Komárno channel. This village originated only in 1926 by joining the villages of Bodza and Tôň colonized by people from environs of Trenčín. The villagers lived on farming. The village was annexed to Hungary in the years 1938-1945 and the Slovak colonists were driven out. The neighbouring **SOKOLCE** (Lakszakállas in Hungarian, population 1,300) originated in 1940 by joining two independent settlements Túriszkállas and Laskszakállas, the first of the two was mentioned as early as 1268 and the latter was first referred to in 1332. Both villages were property of petty yeoman. The Neo-Classical **manor house** from the first half of the 19th century represents the secular monuments of the village while the sacred buildings are the originally Late Gothic Reformed **church** and the Neo-Classical Roman Catholic **church of Exaltation of the Holy Cross** from the 19th century. The neighbouring village of **BRESTOVEC** (Szilas in Hungarian, population 500) is known for finds of Old Magyar burial place from the 10th century and a Slav burial place from the 10th and 11th centuries. It was first mentioned in the late 13th century. Brestovec was a serf village of the Archbishopric of Esztergom and it was populated by aristocratic estate owners. It had to be recolonized after it was damaged by the Turks.

Along the main road communication

Left: The church in Sokolce
Right: Tôň

connecting Komárno with Bratislava is the village of **TÔŇ** (Tany in Hungarian, population 900). Remains of mammoth bones and archaeological finds from the Bronze Age and Roman era were dug out in its administrative territory. The village was referred to in the oldest document as *villa Than* (serf village in the property of Komárno Castle). Its name derives from fishermen settlement (Tanya). The first settlers were fishermen. In 1460 it was a serf town with toll point. The original village was situated at the present homestead called Malý Tôň on a hill out of the reach of the Danube waters. Today's Tôň is situated somewhat lower and in spite of anti-flood measures, it is often threatened by high level of underground water and floods. People were farmers, fishermen and hunters.

The industrial aspect of this village is interesting. The local sugar refinery processed about 40,000-50,000 metric tons of sugar beet harvested in its fields a year. The plant employed about 160 men and 100 women at that time. It closed in the time of the 1873 crisis. In 1894 a flax processing plant was put in operation and the first flax turbine made in England was installed here. The flax processing factory employed 250 workers at the beginning of the 20th century. In May 1931 the plant was destroyed by fire. It was later restored and equipped with new machinery. The factory was changed to produce firearms during the Second World War. In 1960 it processed hemp and produced textile. Two brickyards in the village from the 18th and 19th centuries also deserve attention . The roller mill Aranka was also built from the bricks produced in local brickyards by the end of the 19th century. Originally it was built as a store building for the sugar refineries. Sacred monuments in the village include the Late Neo-Classical Reformed **church** from 1834. One of its bells is from 1693 and it was moved here from the old church in Malý Tôň. The villagers of the Roman Catholic religion built the dedicated to the Blessed Virgin Mary. The village is the birth place of an important scientist and writer **József Baranyai**.

The living encyclopaedia of Žitný ostrov

József Baranyai was born in 1876 in Komoč. After he graduated in Budapest and he assumed the career of journalist and writer. We worked as director of the library in Komárno until 1945. He edited the journal Komárňanské listy (The Komárno Papers), Brázdy (Furrows), Žitnoostrovné listy (The Papers of Žitný ostrov) and Žitnoostrovný kalendár (The Calendar of Žitný ostrov). He researched and studied the etymology of the local nomenclature and was a recognized connoisseur of Žitný ostrov. He wrote numerous books and studies, some of them were published. Baranyai spent the last years of his life in Tôň, where he died in 1951.

TRÁVNIK (Füss, population 700) is situated 5 km south-west of village Tôň near the Danube. It was mentioned as *Fys* in 1216 for the first time as property of the Benedictine monastery of Pannonhalma. The name used after 1927 was *Fíš* and its present name is used since 1948. It was property of the Benedictine order on the Pannonian hill, which acquired it from the Arpád rulers as a gift in the Middle Ages. The Abbot Stephen promoted the people of Trávnik for their loyal military service to the estate of the church aristocracy in 1383. The village became an independent yeoman seat. This status existed until 1848, the year, which brought about big changes. One of them was that the village did not belong to the abbey any more and it was annexed to the district in Zemianska Olča and later to that of Komárno. The Second World War was disastrous for Trávnik. When it finished, soldiers occupied the village and deported the poorer

villagers to Bohemia, while all the rich peasants were moved to Hungary and the Hungarian school was closed. The disastrous flood of 1965 caused great damage to Trávnik. Its inhabitants were evacuated as 116 of the total 209 houses fell down and 52 were severely damaged. In the past the inhabitants lived off farming including cattle and horse raising. The village was prevailingly Catholic as it used to belong to the Benedictine order. But its inhabitants together with those of Kližská Nemá and Číčov converted to the Calvinist religion. However, this Protestant religion was abolished in 1737, their priest was driven out and all villagers, who did not want to give up their religion moved to Zemianska Olča. The church fell in decay and its remains were covered by the Danube dike.

The village contains several well-preserved **houses** from the mid-19th century and typical village wells. The dominant of the village is the Roman Catholic **church of St. Beňadik** from 1762, which was re-

peatedly adapted. To the northern side of chancel of this single-nave building a sacristy, **chapel of the Virgin Mary**, was added. Preserved lordly houses, curia and manor house testify to the secular life of the local yeomen in the past. The Neo-Classical **manor-house** from the 18th century is a storied rectangular building mentioned as a monastery, where the estate administration of the abbey and parsonage were located. Today it shelters the parsonage office and the municipal library. Matej Bel, famous Slovak historian and geographer wrote that there existed twelve curias owned by yeomen estate owners in the first half of the 18th century. Only two substantially younger ones survive. Next to the main road is the **curia** of the Balogh family built in the second half of the 19th century and next to the homestead Almáš stands the **curia** of Hriastélys from the early 20th century.

Among many personalities who were born or lived in Trávnik was **Fabián Szeder** (1784-1859). He was involved with promoting Hungarian literature. Szeder entered the Benedictine order in 1804 and studied at Pannonhalma in Hungary. He

Left: The Dead Arm of Číčov
Right: The Dead Arm of Číčov

was the librarian and simultaneously the administrator of the Benedictine order. A **commemorative room** was established in his honour in the manor house in 1996. Apart from the cultural monuments visitors to the village can also admire its wonderful natural setting around the Danube. A remarkable **peat bog** with protected plant species is situated north of the village. Not far from the road to Číčov is the **Rybné jazero** lake (Halastó in Hungarian), a favourite of fishermen.

ČÍČOV (Csicsó in Hungarian, population 1,400) is a village interesting for archaeologists with its finds from La Téne, Roman and Roman-Barbarian era. The village was donated to the Benedictine monastery at the Pannonian Mountain in 1172. From 1268 until the 17th century it was the serf village of Komárno Castle. Several yeoman families owned it. Two villages existed from the 14th century: Horný and Dolný Číčov. The villagers were farmers. The 1965 flood broke the Danube dike near this village with disastrous consequences not only for Číčov but for the whole region.

The cultural landmark of the village is the **manor house** built in the Late Baroque style in 1776 and adapted in the late 19th century. This two storied building with four corner towers was originally the seat of the Zichy family. The **park** around it, founded in the second half of the 19th century with some precious specimen of broad-leaved and coniferous wood species, is a **protected area**. It also used to have a lake fed by a channel. The last owner of the manor house was Adéla Kálnoky and she used it as a summer residence. The manor house was rebuilt as a school after 1945. Sacred architecture in the village is represented by the originally Baroque Roman Catholic **church of Assumption of the Virgin Mary** built after 1677 and adapted in Neo-Classical taste in the late 18th century. The Neo-Classical Reformed **church** is from 1784. The monuments include also the historicizing building of the former **nunnery** from 1889 with a saddle shingle roof. Visitors can also use the **instructive path** along the **Číčovské mŕtve rameno or the Dead Arm of Číčov**. Instructive path is 6 km

long and it has 12 stops. It leads around the Lion lake and it takes about 5 hours to see it all.

The Dead Arm of Číčov

The arm is one of the best conserved and most precious places, from the point of view of natural history, of Žitný ostrov. The National Nature Reserve is situated 2 kilometres west of Číčov and stretches along the bank of the Danube up to the village of Kľúčovec. The dead arm was once a lateral arm of the Danube, but part of the water complex, which is the Lion lake originated in 1899 during floods when the Danube antiflood dike broke. The lake is 3-7.5 m deep. Its shores are dissected with uncountable little peninsulas and bays. It is surrounded by numerous little lakes. The typical willow-poplar floodplain forest and shore vegetation composed mostly of hygrophilous plant species creates an ideal environment for more than 100 fowl species. Flowers of water lilies cover the water table. Twenty four fish species live in the lake, including the original wild form of the Danube carp. Strolling around the floodplain forest, which in places resembles tropical jungle including the "tropic rain" which consists of foam and saliva of millions of cicadas sucking the juice of willow and poplar trees, is an interesting experience.

In the administrative territory of the very old village of **KLÍŽSKA NEMÁ** (Kolozsnéma in Hungarian, population 500) archaeologists dug up a Slav-Avar burial place. It was first mentioned in a document from 1226 as *Nema*. It was originally the property of Komárno Castle and later it passed into the hands of petty aristocracy. Its inhabitants suffered from

repeated Turkish raids. Its **peasant houses** represent a rare evidence of 19th century folk architecture. The Romanesque core of the Reformed church with a part in romantic style added to it in the 19th century is the testimony to the medieval era of the village. The Roman Catholic **church of the Holy Angels Guardians** from 1884 is also an interesting sacred monument. The Neo-Classical curia was built in 1859 on older foundations. The village was always known for **gold-washing** and an old-year tradition of fishing. **Folk song and dance festivals** are held here every year in August.

From Kližská Nemá one gets easily along the Danube to the village of **VEĽKÉ KOSIHY** (Nagykeszi in Hungarian, population 1,000). This village contains archaeological sites with a settlement from the Neolithic era and an Old Magyar burial place. The village was first mentioned in 1247 as *Kesceu* and was owned by Komárno Castle. Later it was the property of several yeomen. Part of the village

called Arcibiskupský Lél was mentioned as early as 1075 as Lela. It was the seat of one of the four archbishop's estates which were joined into one and assumed the name Vojka nad Dunajom in the 16th century. Houses made of unburned clay bricks from the 19th century consisting of three rooms and with reed covered saddle roofs represent the folk architecture. In the centre of the village is a Late Neo-Classical **manor house** from the 1830's. An important sacred monument is the Roman Catholic **church** in the settlement of Arcibiskupský Lél from 1865. It originated by reconstruction of a Baroque chapel from the 18th century. The interior of the Neo-Classical Reformed church from 1819 contains valuable silver Baroque chalices, tin jugs, Neo-Classical plates and the Late Baroque christening set from 1755.

An alternative route runs eastward along the Danube. The first village on the route, **IŽA** (Izsa in Hungarian, population 1,600) 7 km away from Komárno is an attractive tourist point. Neolithic settlement, cremation graves of the North Pannonian culture from the Bronze age

Left: Kelemantia-Iža
Right: The Danube near Patince

unique bronze objects from the Younger Bronze Age and above all the Roman military camp from the 1st to 4th centuries are the landmarks of this village. The first reference to Iža is from 1172. Originally it was property of the monastery of Pannonhalma and after 1268 it was owned by Komárno Castle. King Belo IV donated it to the Clarist order seated on Margit sziget island in Buda. Later Gáspár Somogyi and the Provost of Esztergom owned it. The Turkish wars also affected Iža and the raids lasting 150 years eventually caused the people to flee and it fell in decay. Repopulation of Iža took place in the late 17th century. The foundations of new houses and the well were built with stone from the remains of the Roman fort, which stood nearby. It was a guard castle next to an important Danube ford. The population lived on farming. **Clay houses** with reed roofs still exist here. Several **water mills** were operating on the Danube. The village was stricken by earthquake in the years 1763-1773 and fires and floods did not avoid it either. The 1965 flood was the greatest tragedy of the village. It destroyed 267 houses and damaged 199. The monument from 1965 with its three pillars symbolizing the districts which helped Iža to restore its houses (Trenčín, Uherské Hradiště and Šumperk) commemorates the disaster.

The most important sacred monument of the village is the Roman Catholic **church of St. Michael the Archangel**. The original Gothic church mentioned in 1599 disappeared and in 1763 was rebuilt in the Baroque style. But the 1773 earthquake damaged the new church and it needed repair. Another earthquake caused that the vault of the nave fell down in 1822. It was replaced and the lateral walls of the church were made taller. The Late Baroque Reformed **church** was built in 1871. In its interior the wooden pulpit made in taste of the romantic Neo-Gothic style is of interest. The village is the venue of annual **Equestrian days**. Small beaches on the Danube bank invite the lovers of bathing. The recreation **area of an Artesian well** and the archaeological site **Kelemantia with instructive boards** are also worth visiting.

Kelemantia

The Roman fort called Kelemantia is situated on the left bank of the Danube. Up to 2.2 m thick peripheral walls of the fort of rectangular shape survive in this archaeological site. The corners of the walls are rounded. In the middle of each wall there was a double gate guarded by towers. The also walls had other gates. A triple moat with bridges at each gate skirted the fort. Judging from the location of commander's building the main road must have connected the northern gate with the southern. A bath was presumably situated in the south-eastern part of the structure. The whole area is cut by a dike of more recent date. Only the towers between the south-western corner and the western gate and profiles of the moat on the northern and western side jut out of the earth.

In the administrative territory of Iža is the **Nature Reserve of Bokrošské slanisko saline area**. The saline area contains a large saliferous "window" surrounded by fields. In some parts of this saliferous window are small salt lakes with an open table of underground water

where salt accumulates. Some notable salt-loving plant species grow here.

PATINCE (Pat in Hungarian, population 400) is the next village and also archaeological site settled since the Neolithic era. An Old Slavic barrow with inhumation graves from the 9th century, but also older settlement and a burial place from the Bronze Age were found here. The village originated in 1957 by separation from Marcelová. In the past it was owned by Komárno Castle. In the second half of the 16th century the Turks destroyed it. It formed again around the Pálffy estate in the 18th century. Several **clay houses** made from burnt and unburned bricks are still existing in Patince. The only sacred monument of the village is the Roman Catholic **church** situated on its edge. It was restored in 1776 and its facade changed in the late 19th century. But Patince is known mainly for its hot springs.

Hot springs and medicinal mud

Sulphurous hot springs were discovered in Patince almost 50 years ago. Hot spring Hévíz with temperature 27 degrees of Celsius, which springs up from the depth 200 m created a 620 square metres sized lake. The villagers knew about the therapeutic effects of the local mud and always used it. Hévíz is one of the chain of hot springs existing along the Danube. They occur in the area, which starts in Patince and ends in Margit sziget island in Budapest. Additional and richer springs were found near the old hot spring, which gave origin to a car camping site and recreation centre with swimming pools fed by thermal water, suitable for bathing and boating.

The village of **VIRT** (Virt in Hungarian, population 300) is situated between Patince and Radvaň nad Dunajom. It was first mentioned as *terra Werth* as early as 1256, when King Belo IV donated it to the German knight Sebrit. It was part of Komárno Castle from 1268. A 19th century historic document reported the occur

Left: The thermal swimming pool in Patince
Right: The re-pumping station in Virt

ence of remains of some unknown Roman structure in the territory of this village. **Pyber's manor house** standing in the village, originally a two-tower curia from the first third of the 18th century was built in the Renaissance-Baroque taste. The manor house in situated in a wonderful natural setting. Its builders planned it as a guarding manor house, part of the guarding system on the Stará Žitava river at the point where it flows into the Danube. Frequent floods on the Danube and Stará Žitava were the reason why a **steam re-pumping station** was built in its vicinity. It consists of a structure with outlet and inlet regulators, a pump, coal store and an independently placed stack. Its contemporary equipment is fairly conserved and it represents a precious **technical monument**. Originally the Baroque Roman Catholic **church of the Most Holy Trinity** and the cemetery **chapel** from the first half of the 18th century are the sacred monuments of the village.

The village of royal equerries and barrel-makers **RADVAŇ nad Dunajom** (Dunaradvány in Hungarian, population 700) is known as an archaeological site. Aeneolitic settlement, graves from the Bronze Age, Halstatt, La Téne, and Roman eras, the remains of the Roman, Barbarian and Slavic settlements were found here. While excavating near one of the best known Danube fords, which existed in the village of Žitava, the archaeologists also discovered an Avar-Slavic burial place from the 8th century. Its 49 graves contained equestrian equipment, objects of daily use and a great amount of animal bones, remains of food for the dead warriors. Women and children had only an offering vessel put at their feet. Radvaň was first mentioned in 1260 as Rodoan. King Belo IV donated land called Rodowan including the royal equerries, island and fishing area to the canon Sixtus of Esztergom in 1267 for excellent services. Matúš Čák occupied and burned down the village in 1303, the Turks came in the 16th century and did the same. The village and its environs were in the centre of Turkish wars in the 16th and 17th centuries.

The Peace of Žitava concluded with Turks

Not far from the village and next to the place where the Stará Žitava flows into the Danube, the Emperor Rudolf II's brother Matthias, later King of Hungary, representing the Emperor concluded a very disadvantageous peace with the Turks for 20 years. He accepted the condition of paying 200 thousand guldens and leaving the occupied territory to them. This event is known in history as the Peace of Žitava. It was signed under an enormous oak tree, which does not exist anymore.

Radvaň nad Dunajom was also a renowned centre of millers who had **water mills** on the Danube and a guild of their own which existed until 1874. The milling disappeared as late as 1945. Typical **folk architecture** of clay construction with reed roofs and viticultural huts from the 19th century testify to the past of the village. In the territory of what used to be the medieval settlement of Žitava, between the cemetery and the former port of Radvaň are the remains of a Gothic church

from the 15th century. The monuments of sacred architecture include the Neo-Classical Roman Catholic **church of the Virgin Mary** from 1833. The main altar with the painting of St. Stephen the King is from the time when the church was constructed. The Reformed **church** was built in the second half of the 17th century, reconstructed in the 18th century and adapted in Neo-Classical taste in the first half of the 19th century. The arms of the Danube and Žitava rivers offer excellent opportunities for water tourism. The **Nature Reserve of Mašan** is situated on elevated dunes, which are slightly higher situated than the surrounding agricultural landscape. This reserve contains one of the best-conserved localities of vegetation thriving on sand.

The neighbouring village of **MOČA** (Dunamocs in Hungarian, population 1,200 is also an archaeological locality. The finds documenting settlement are from the Neolithic, Lower Bronze Age, Roman-Barbarian, and Slavic periods.

Left: The Bulcsua's monument
Right: The swamp near Búč

The first reference to the village as *villa Moch* is from 1208. Part of the village belonged to the Báthory family from the 16th century, then it was plundered by the Turks. In 1602 eight water mills were working on the Danube near Moča. The villagers lived by farming, viticulture, fishing and haulage. The guild of the local millers was mentioned in 1821. Eighteen mills worked on the Danube near Moča until 1945. The sacred monuments of the village include the Roman Catholic **church of the Most Holy Trinity** from 1764, later repeatedly rebuilt. The Reformed **church** in Neo-Classical style was built in the years 1856-1860 and rebuilt by the beginning of the 20th century. The village has ideal conditions for the development of water tourism. One can visit the local inn called Rybárska krčma (Fisherman's Tavern) and the local beaches.

The road leading along the Danube dike will bring you to the village of **KRAVANY nad Dunajom** (Karva in Hungarian, population 800). In the administrative territory of the village, which was settled as early as the Neolithic period, Roman settlement was also discovered. The first written reference to the village is from 1245 under the name *Korwa*. The local yeoman families owned it. In 1300 when it existed under the name *Kysseukorva* it was destroyed by Matúš Čák, and by the Turks in the 16th century. It was completely abandoned in the 17th and 18th centuries, but repopulated in the 19th century. It had 417 inhabitants in 1828. The local people were mostly farmers and cultivated fruit trees and grapes. Mills were also a common phenomenon and in 1876 a society dedicated to anti-flood measures was founded here. The sacred monuments are represented by the originally Late Romanesque Roman Catholic **church of the Virgin Mary** from the mid-13th century. It was later adapted in the Baroque taste and restored in 1936. Around the local **manor house**, the former summer residence of businessman Gustáv Lank is a historic **park** founded by the end of the 19th century. It contains some precious wood species. The present appearance of the manor house is the result of reconstruction after 1926, when two individual buildings were connected into one with two lateral wings, with a well and another building in the yard which contains technological equipment. After the Second World War the manor house served as an agricultural school with accommodation facilities for the students. The village boasts a wonderful view of the **Gerecse Mountains** in Hungary. Orchards and vineyards frame the foothills of this mountain range. The Danube flows slowly here and this is the place where its channel is widest in Slovakia.

Interesting history and monuments also invite visits to the northernmost village of the region **BÚČ** (Búcs in Hungarian, population 1,300). One gets there through Moča. Archaeological finds confirm that Búč was a settlement of the Old Magyar tribes. It was mentioned for the first time in 1208 as *villa Bolsou*. It was a property of Archbishop of Esztergom until the abolition of serfdom. The followers of Matúš Čák destroyed it in 1311. The village did not avoid partial destruction during the Turkish occupation either. The population lived by farming, cattle and goose keeping. The road between Moča and Búč is skirted by a row of cellars suggesting a viticultural tradition. The dominant of the villages is the Neo-Classical Reformed **church** built under the Toleration Patent in 1784. It was widened in 1791 and made longer in 1817 and restored. The sacred monuments of the village also include the Roman Catholic belfry, a slim square-shaped brick building from 1914. The headmaster of the local Calvinist school built a **curia** at the end of the village in 1924. It was recently restored and the original architectural details were removed. The mill of Jókai and Szaly families built in the 1940's now houses the **restaurant Mlyn Attila** or Attila malom that means in English Attila's Mill. Búč and its environs are also interesting for the tourists for their natural features. In the south-western edge of the village in direction to Moča is a protected row of poplar trees. In the western part of the villages is the pond Halastó and in the southern edge of the village is remarkable for **Búčske slanisko** or the Saline Area of Buča.

BÁTOROVE KOSIHY (Bátorkeszi in Hungarian, population 3,600) is situated 5 km north-west of Búč. Its administrative territory was settled in the remote past as archaeological finds prove. Aeneolithic channelled pottery, Avar-Slav burial place from the 8th century, Slav finds from the Great Moravian period and an Old-Magyar cemetery from the 10th century were found here. The village was mentioned for the first time in 1156 as *villa Kesceu*, in the ownership of Zachej the Archbishop of Esztergom. At the beginning of the 16th century it became the property of the Báthory family, who endowed it with its present name. Between the 17th and 19th centuries the Pálffy family owned it. It obtained the market privilege in 1783 and became a little town, while its character also changed from agricultural to industrial. A sugar refinery was built here, two distilleries and a brewery soon followed. A still operating mill survived in the middle of the village. A small oil plant, which processed plant oils from 1935 and a brickyard also contributed to the development of Bátorove Kosihy.

The most valuable monument of sacred architecture is the Baroque Roman Catholic **church of the Visitation of the Virgin Mary**. Count Nicholas Pálffy had it built in the years 1720-1728 on older foundations. The tower was added to it in 1735 and a sacristy was built in 1795. The church was rebuilt in the Neo-Classical style in 1797. The storied oratory was added to it in the late 19th century while the church was simultaneously adapted in the Neo-Gothic style. Next to the church stands an iron **Obelisk**, the tombstone of Pálffy family from 1872. It is one of the first metal-founding works of the kind made in the 19th century, in pure Empire style. The Reformed **church** was built in 1785, first without a tower, which was added to it in 1878.

Not far from Bátorove Kosihy is the village of **MODRANY** (Madar in Hungarian, population 1,400). The first document mentioning it dates from 1260 when it was owned by Marcel de Modor from the Posádka castle. Later it was part of the

Left: The blown sands of Marcelová
Right: The pond in Chotín

Svätý Peter estate, and it was the time when its territory was forested. The village was almost destroyed by earthquake in 1763 . Its people were farmers. Their spiritual life is symbolized by the Reformed church standing on a hill over the villages. It originated in 1691 by reconstruction of the Gothic church. This church fell down during the mentioned earthquake and was built again. Today it is the Neo-Classical building with a pulpit in the romanticizing style. The wooden **belfry** standing in front of the church contains a bell from 1749. In the neighbouring village of **MUDROŇOVO** (population 100) the archaeologist found Old Magyar graves from the 10th century. The history of the village started only in the years 1921-1923, when it originated from a subordinate part of Modrany (Újpuszta). Slovak immigrant families arrived here from Zvolen, Liptovský Mikuláš, Martin, Východná, and Topoľčany. They built new houses. The contiguous village of **ŠROBÁROVÁ** (population 500) is also a young village. It was constructed in 1919 by the Slovak colonists on the site of an estate of Marcelová and Modrany. In 1925 stood 82 new houses there. The dominant feature of the village is the Roman Catholic **church of the Virgin Mary**. The inscription on the portal of the church bears the year of its construction: 1929.

MARCELOVÁ (Marcelháza in Hungarian, population 800) has a longer history than, for example, Šrobárovo. Archaeologists discovered there the Neolithic settlement, North Pannonian cremation graves from the Bronze Age, inhumation burial place from the La Téne period, an inhumation grave from the Migration Period, and some Old-Magyar graves. The first written reference to it dates from 1353 and it is mentioned as *Nogkezeu*. It was owned by the local yeoman families. In 1552 it was mentioned as an abandoned settlement with 19 houses. In the 17th century the Pálffy family re-colonized Marcelová and it became the centre of their estates. The inhabitants were farmers. In 1784 a liquor plant and in the 19th century a distillery were founded here. Old architecture survived in the form of clay houses with saddle roofs. The subordinate village of **Krátke Kesy** was first mentioned in 1256. The ruler sold the village to the Archbishop of Esztergom in 1264. It almost disappeared after Turkish raids in the 17th century and was resettled by serfs from the counties of Trenčín and Nitra.

The Reformed **church** is a sacred monument from 1803. The original church got a tower later. Another sacred monument is the Roman Catholic, originally Gothic, **church of St. John the Baptist**, which was severely damaged by an earthquake in 1731. Part of the old building was used in the reconstruction. There is also a nice **park** in the village founded in the mid-19th century. On an elevated terrace stands a **curia** from the first half of the 19th century adapted in the romantic style by the end of the 19th century. The curia and park served to the family Baranyi in the 19th century. More than 70 species of fowl such as heron, white stork, etc live on the **nature reserve of Pohrebište** not far away from the village. Protected area consists of a water body and surrounding reed growths, willow and poplar trees. It is the remains of extensive and gradually drained swamps. There are several elevations formed by blown sands with pines and locust trees in stark the environs of Marcelová.

The blown sands of Marcelová

In the Quaternary period this area was stricken by frequent sand storms. Strong winds blew tiny particles of sand from the river alluvia and created dunes. These blown sands in contrast to those that occur in the Záhorie region contain a great share of limestone particles. The Nature Reserve of Marcelová protects sand-loving plants and thermophile insects.

The village of **CHOTÍN** (Hetény in Hungarian, population 1,400) is an important archaeological site. The finds confirm the existence of settlements and burial places from the Neolithic period, Bronze Age, La Téne, and Roman periods up to the Great Moravian Empire. Old Magyar and Slav burial places from the 10th - 11th century were also found here. The village was first mentioned in 1138 as

villa Hetten. The Provost of Dömös owned it, later it passed to the property of the Archbishopric of Esztergom. The Turks destroyed it in the 16th century and it revived only with the arrival of settlers from the Považie and Gemer regions in the 18th century. Clay houses contained three rooms, they were covered by saddle roofs made of reeds. The centre of village life is the Reformed **church** from 1792. The single-nave building with added tower contains in its interior an interesting Baroque-Neo-Classical pulpit from the time of construction of the church. The environs of the village contain numerous sand dunes. Two kilometres north-east of the village in **Nature Reserve Chotínske piesky** can one see protected sand-loving and xerophile plant and animal associations. The blown sands are 2 to 3 metres tall in places.

Within the administrative territory of **SVÄTÝ PETER** (Szentpéter in Hungarian, population 2,600) only several kilometres away from Chotín a burial place of the Carpathian Barrow Culture from the middle Bronze Age was found. It also contains settlements from the younger Bronze Age,

La Téne inhumation graves, Slav burial place from the period of the Great Moravian Empire and an Old Magyar burial place. The village originated around St. Peter's church built in 1332. It was referred to as *Sanctus Petrus* or *Zenthpeter*. But the territory was settled as early as 1200. A couple of houses existed around Harsány as well. The Komárno estate owned it. It decayed and remained abandoned in the time of the Turkish raids. Svätý Peter the same as other villages of the region was donated to the Zichy family in 1659. The 1763 earthquake partially demolished it. In the revolutionary year 1849 big fighting between the troops of General J. Klapka and the imperial army took place near the village. On the edge of the forest between Chotín and Svätý peter is the place where Russian troops camped while waiting for the results of peace negotiations. This place is called "the Russian stone". Wine production enjoys long tradition here. The wines of Svätý Peter were consumed not only in the village and its environs, but the Budapest restaurants also purchased them. Numerous wine cellars still exist in the village.

Three churches represent the sacred monuments. The originally Baroque Roman Catholic **church** was built in 1730 on the site of the former Gothic church. It was restored in Neo-Classical style after earthquake. The Neo-Classical Calvinist **church** from 1784 was built as a Toleration church lacking a tower. The sacred buildings also include a modern Evangelical **church**. The mill built in 1926 is also a historic building. One of notable landmarks of the village is its **park** next to the house of Zichy family from the late 19th century. It is a kind of garden with landscape arrangement, grass areas, broadleaved and coniferous trees.

On the south-western protuberance of the Hronská pahorkatina hill land, 4 km away from Svätý Peter is the village of **DULOVCE** (formerly Nová or New Dala, population 1,900). Originally it was a settlement within Stará (Old) Ďala, today's Hurbanovo. It became independent in the

14th century and assumed the name Nová Ďala. The name Dulovce has been used since 1948. It was alternatively the property of the crown and the Archbishopric of Esztergom, Komárno Castle and of various yeomen. It lived through difficult times during the Turkish wars. After the Žitava peace was concluded in 1606 it was completely dominated by the Turks. In 1669 the villagers refused to supply the Turks during the siege of the fort of Nové Zámky and were completely plundered at the order of Kara Mustafa. The village disappeared and only in 1690 it was re-settled by Slovaks from the Váh basin and the Moravian-Slovakian boundary area. Magyarization (i.e. imposed adoption of Hungarian nationality) of the Slovaks living in the area started after Austria settled with Hungary and included Dulovce. Its people were mostly farmers who also produced top quality wines while petty crafts such as embroidery were alternative sources of living. Many villagers emigrated to America and France in the early 20th century.

The most important sacred monument is the Neo-Classical Roman Catholic **church** of St. Luke the Evangelical from 1872 with the Late Neo-Classical and romantic elements. It is a single-naved building with presbytery and an in-built tower. The **old houses** made from clay with reed roofs and carpentered gables did not survive. In front of the open yards **weigh-beam wells** used to stand, but only one of them was survives. The newly built amphitheatre is the place, which contains a summer cinema and also hosts the **Southern-Slovakia children's and youth festival**.

PRIBETA (Perbete in Hungarian, population 3,200) is a village known for the finds of remains of settlements from the Younger Stone Age, Slav graves from the period of the Great Moravian Empire from the 10th to 12th centuries and a disappeared monastery with a church from the 13th century. The first written reference to Pribeta is from 1312, when the village owned by the Esztergom Archbishopric was occupied and destroyed by the followers of Matúš Čák. There are documents proving the existence of a castle in the vil-

Right: The observatory of Hurbanovo

lage. The village and the castle disappeared in the time of the Turkish raids. It was settled against in the 17th century. The most important sacred monument is the Baroque Roman Catholic **church of the Most Holy Trinity** from 1733 restored in the Neo-Classical style and rebuilt by the end of the 19th century. The valuable interior contains a Rococo pulpit and marble font from the second half of the 18th century. the Reformed **church** from 1784 was built as Toleration church without tower; by the beginning of the 19th century it was widened by a perpendicularly situated new nave and a Neo-Classical tower. The Baroque-Neo-Classical **chapel** of the Virgin Mary is from 1762. It was built on the site of the former hermitage and the painting of the Madonna was placed here in commemoration of the 1763 earthquake.

The destinations of the tourists roaming in the Danube area should perhaps also comprise the town of **HURBANOVO** (formerly Stará Ďala, population 8,000). It lies in the central part of the district, on the left bank of the Žitava river. It is 20 km away from Komárno. Archaeological finds prove a settlement and burial place from the Bronze Age, Halstatt cremation graves, La Téne cemeteries, Roman-Barbarian settlement and a Slav cemetery from the Great Moravian period. The finds of a disappeared Romanesque church from the 12th century with burial place and 11th to 13th century medieval village are unique. Hurbanovo was first mentioned as *Gyala* in 1329. The Turks destroyed it in the 16th century, it was resettled by serfs from the Counties of Hont, Trenčín and Nitra in the 18th century. The village was always inhabited by farmers who grew tobacco above all. A tobacco factory existed there in the years 1820-1860. Several surrounding small villages were gradually added to Hurbanovo and it was a district town in the years 1923-1960.

Sacred monuments are represented by two churches. The Roman Catholic **church of St. Ladislav** was built in the years 1912-1913 on the site of an old Baroque church from 1718, which was restored after the earthquake in 1763. The church standing there today is the an Art Noveau building inspired by Transylvanian Gothic architecture. In its interior the

main altar with painting of St. Ladislav from the mid 19th century and the lateral pseudo-Neo-Classical altar from the time when the church was built bearing the picture of Calvary will certainly intrigue visitors. The Reformed **church** is from 1796, it was later rebuilt and a built-in tower was added to it along with new Late Neo-Classical facade. It interior is from 1940. In front of the church is the Late Neo-Classical **Trinity Pillar** from the mid-19th century. Recognized figures born in Hurbanovo include the painter Arpád Feszty and Mikuláš Konkoly Thege, an astronomer is buried here. Hurbanovo is famous for astronomy.

Opening of the planetarium in 1983 contributed to promotion of astronomy among the public. Since 1962 it has been called **Slovenská ústredná hvezdáreň** (Slovak Central Observatory). It co-ordinates 15 observatories, seven astronomic cabinets, and six planetariums. The observatory is a multi-storied building with large and small glass domes, a communi-

cation tract and single-storied wings. The small dome was built at the same time when the summer-house, the large one was built in the thirties. There is a wonderful protected **park** around the observatory from the mid-19th century. The **manor house** built in historicizing style and inspired by the French Baroque-Neo-Classical style is from the beginning of the 20th century. The brewery existing in Hurbanovo also became famous. Now it is a part of the multinational company Heineken, but it still produces the beer **Zlatý bažant** or Golden Pheasant exported to numerous countries of the world.

Bohatá, first mentioned in 1571 as *Bagota* is also part of Hurbanovo. It was depopulated in Turkish wars and re-settled in the 18th century. The sacred architecture of the settlement includes the Late Baroque Roman Catholic **church of St. Anna** from 1739 with a Neo-Classical adaptation from the late 18th century. Bohatá has two wonderful **parks**. The older one of them was founded in the mid-19th century and its basis are coniferous and broad-leaved wood species. On its edge is an L-shaped **curia** built in the 2nd half of

Left: The manor house in Hurbanovo
Right: Golden Pheasant

the 19th century in the Neo-Classical style. Next to the entrance to another historic park is a small rural curia from 1840 with the Late Neo-Classical architectural elements. In the **Nature Reserve of Révayovská pustatina** on the north-western edge of Hurbanovo is a finding place of precious species of mushroom amidst a locust grove. For some species it is the only site in the territory of Slovakia..

Also the village of **BAJČ** (Bajcs in Hungarian, population 1,200), 5 km north of Hurbanovo, boasts some remarkable archaeological localities. Its Romanesque church from the 13th century has disappeared. The village was first referred to in 1312 as *Boych*, a property of the Archbishopric of Esztergom. It was destroyed by the Turks, but resettled in the 18th century. Archbishop Batthyányi had drained the extensive swamps around the village and a road constructed. The most significant buildings of the village is the Neo-Classical **curia** from the second third of the 19th century and the Neo-Classical Roman Catholic **church of St. John the Baptist** built in the years 1827-1831. Next to the village is one of the most significant **pheasantry** in Slovakia and its environs contain hunting grounds specializing in hare.

North-west of Hurbanovo is the typical village of **MARTOVCE** (Martos in Hungarian, population 800). This territory was settled in remote history. Not far from the village on the hill Aba, an Avar settlement existed in the 6th century and some finds also prove the presence of the Old Magyar tribes. The hill Aba was probably renamed after the leader Aba Samuel or after the name of the Avar tribe, the name of which had the variation Abar. A legend says that the first villagers hid in the swamps between the rivers Nitra and Žitava in fear from the Tartars. The Marthos family were the first settlers, who built six houses in the part of today's Martovce called Hatháza. The village was first mentioned in 1438 as *Marthos*. Then it was referred to as property of Archbishop of Esztergom in 1487. Extensive swamps protected the village in time of Turkish raids when it was an advanced defensive point of the fort of Nové Zámky. Turks discovered and

sacked it in spite of this in the 16th century. The Primate of the Kingdom of Hungary, S. Rudnay wanted to move the village because of repeated floods, which regularly struck the village, but the people did not want to give up the good fishing. They were also farmers, tobacco growers and raised cattle. In the early 20th century a company for draining the territory was founded here.

Martovce was fairly isolated from the surrounding settlements in the consequence of its situation. This is probably the reason why its has preserved some features of folk culture. A clay farm house built in 1871 now contains an **exhibition of folk furniture** and documents the way of living in the past. The residential part of the house has three rooms: a front room with stove, a corridor with separated kitchen part with an open chimney and the back room. The farm buildings followed, while the roof was common for the whole house. The inner furniture is from the 19th century and it includes painted peasant coffins, canopied beds with painted frames and numerous ornamental cushions with typical red embroidery. As

the people of Martovce were Calvinists, the walls of their houses were not adorned by pictures with biblical scenes. Normally they were covered by painted plates. The villagers wore the typical folk costumes until long after the Second World War. It was only in this village that the women fashioned typical embroidered cloths with red applications. The Reformed **church** from 1732 was widened and rebuilt in the Neo-Classical style in 1898. In its interior are the Late Neo-Classical pulpit, pews and chancel.

In the administrative territory of the village also lies the **Nature Reserve of Gémeš**, which protects several species of swamp and water fowl. In the inundation area of the Žitava is the **Nature Reserve of Allúvium Žitavy** with several protected plant species where fowl nest. **Nature Reserve of Listové jazero lake** is in the administrative territory of **VRBOVÁ nad Váhom** (Vágfüzes, population 600) which likewise, contains protected water fowl and plants in environs of the lake.

Left: The Nature Reserve of Gémeš
Right: The rural house in Martovce

IMEĽ (Imely in Hungarian, population 2,200) is the village lying north-west of Hurbanovo. Archaeological finds document settlements from the Neolithic, Bronze Age, La Téne and Roman periods. There are many finds from the Migration Period, Old Magyar graves and settlement from the 11th and 12th centuries were found here as well. It was then owned by the Archbishop of Esztergom. After the Turkish occupation it was resettled by the colonists from the County of Nitra. It was a typical farming village. Old building techniques are documented by **clay houses** from the later half of the 19th century. They contain typical reed saddle roofs and gables made of osier, normally there were three rooms and an open fire place with chimney.

Clay houses
The typical appearance of the villages in the Danube lowland is caused by the material used for their construction. First of all it was sandy clay, straw and reed. Clay was used in several ways. Small cylinders or bricks were formed and were dried by the sun. The walls built from this material were then covered by a straw roof and left to dry for a year or two. The walls were then rough-hewn by an axe, openings were made and the truss built. The walls of the house, which usually had three rooms, were finally whitewashed.

The most important sacred monument of this village is the Roman Catholic **church of St. John the Baptist** from 1799-1800. This single-nave building has an interesting Neo-Classical pulpit from the time of the church. the Neo-Classical Reformed **church** is from 1888. The **vintner's huts**, here called "hajnochy" also attract the attention of tourists with their typical architecture.

The neighbouring village of **NESVADY** (Naszvad in Hungarian, population 5,200) is known as archaeological locality with remains from the Neolithic, Bronze Age settlement with Magyar culture, Roman-Barbarian settlement, a Slav cemetery from the time of the Great Moravian Empire and from 11th-12th centuries. Old Magyar graves were also found here. The first written documents referring to the village are from 1258, in which it is mentioned as *Nazwad*. It was owned by the Archbishop of Esztergom. The village was completely destroyed by the Turks, and re-colonised in the course of the 18th century by colonists from the County of Nitra. It also suffered by frequent floods. The local people were known as excellent fishermen and artisans. The village houses are typical examples of the lowland type of **popular architecture**. The Roman Catholic **church of St. Joseph the Guardian** was built in the 18th century in Late Baroque taste. The original Gothic church was severely damaged in Turkish wars. It was restored in 1780 in the Neo-Classical style. The stone font is the only item preserved from its interior furniture. The Reformed **church** was built by the end of the 18th century and modernized in 1950-1951.

The route of the next trip from Komárno to Kolárovo leads through the village of **KAMENIČNÁ** (Keszegfalva in Hungarian, population 1,800), situated on the right bank of the Váh. The settlement of Vodný hrad was joined to Kameničná in the 19th century. It also includes the settlements Balvany, Lohot, and Sady. Frequent floods are the reasons, why today's village moved from its original place. It was first mentioned as a property of Komárno Castle in 1482. The royal servants, courtiers, and marshals inhabited it. The village fell in decay after Turkish occupation. King Leopold I had a water castle built here in 1681 and entrusted its administration to young Stephen Zichy. The remaining parts of the territory were owned by different yeomen. The people were mostly farmers and the village was known for production of hay and tobacco. In the course of the 19th and 20th centuries two channels with pumping stations which drained groundwater out of the land and back to the Váh were built, a measure, which aimed to drain the swampy terrain of Kameničná and its administrative territory. Emperor Joseph I with his suite also took part in the opening of one of the channels. A tablet on the wall of the structure commemorates his visit. The disastrous flood of 1965 inundated the whole village. It reached the

height of 2 to 3 metres in places. In a week 251 houses fell down and 200 were severely damaged. The village was built again in two years. The sacred buildings are represented by the Neo-Classical Roman Catholic **church** from 1755. The subordinate village of **Balvany** boasts the foundations of a Romanesque church mentioned in historic documents as St. George's Church in 1268.

The administrative territory of the village contains several nature reserves. The **Nature Reserve of Lohótsky močiar** north of the village is a nesting locality of water fowl. The swamp somewhat animates the monotonous character of the surrounding farm land. The **Nature Reserve of Vrbina** lies south of the village and it is linked to a water body surrounded by wood species and shrubs with "soft" and "hard" floodplain forests with abundant water fowl and other precious animal and plant species. Amidst the floodplain forest and close to the village between the Váh river and its now dry dead arm is the **Nature Reserve Malý ostrov**. It protects the water and wood fowl nesting there.

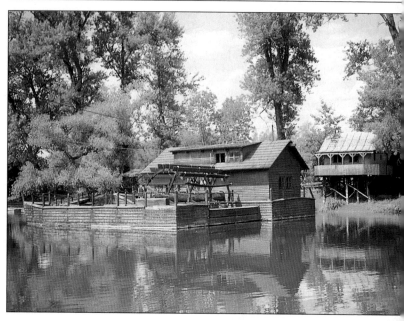

Not far from Kameničná is another archaeological locality **ČALOVEC** (Megyercs in Hungarian, population 1,200). This locality has been continuously settled since the Bronze Age. Archaeological finds prove Celtic and Roman-Barbarian settlements, a Slav-Avar cemetery and Slav settlement from the period of the Great Moravian Empire. The first written reference to the locality is from 1268 as *Megers*. It was owned by Komárno Castle until 1592 and later it was in the hands of different yeomen. The people lived on farming, cattle raising and fishing. They suffered from floods for centuries because the village lay in the inundation area between the Váh and Danube. Houses of burnt and unburnt bricks survive from the beginning of the 20th century. Their saddle roofs are made from reed. The most important building of the village is the originally Neo-Classical Reformed church from the early 19th century adapted in romantic taste by the end of the same century. In its interior the chalice form 1652 is of interest.

The town of **KOLÁROVO** (Guta until 1948, population 11,000) lies on the confluence of the Váh and Malý Dunaj. It is 18 km away from Komárno. The village of Malá Guta was first mentioned in 1268. This settlement was also called Stará Guta in the past and the Archbishop of Esztergom owned it. In the 14th century the village of Veľká Guta was founded. After the battle at Mohács the people fearing the Turks moved to a safer place, the site of today's Kolárovo.

The Frog Castle

A castle mentioned in 1349 existed in the territory of the village. Queen Mary had it built and its task was to protect the fords and trade road. It was rebuilt as a Baroque fort aimed to protect the area against the Turks in the years 1662-1664. In July 1708 it was conquered by the rebellious general Ján Bottyán. But when the fighting finished the fort was destroyed and the soldiers driven away with the following words: "Let the fort be the dwelling of frogs from now on." The fort was later restored but its mocking name Békavár (The Frog Castle) survived. Now there are only its

Left: The water mill in Kolárovo
Right: The recreation zone in Kolárovo

uins left above the confluence of the Malý
Dunaj and Váh.

Villa Gutta obtained municipal privileges in 1551, among them the right to
markets. The document of King Ladislav
V also granted other privileges included
the right to hold fairs, exemption from
toll, customs and other fees. The people
were farmers and specialized in growing
fruit, cattle raising and above all fishing.
They also produced fishing nets. Famous
fishing for sturgeons (some of them are as
much as 8 m long) was very lucrative and
it brought to King of Hungary 340
guldens every year in the 1570's. For example in November and December 1578
in Kolárovo 142 sturgeons were caught.
The fish was sent to Vienna or even to
France as a special delicacy for royal
feasts. Fishing on the Danube was profitable and played a significant role in the
world trade in fish. The village was plundered and eventually completely destroyed by the troops of the Beg of Esztergom in 1576. The Archbishop of Esztergom owned Veľká Guta until 1848, when
the retreating Austrian army burned the
village. In the late 19th and early 20th century five kilometres long of protective
dikes against floods and a bridge were
constructed near Kolárovo. The railway
and a steam mill were also built and an
anti-flood association was founded. The
flood in 1956 severely damaged the town.
The modern history of the town in fact
started on October 14th 1967 when
Kolárovo was again declared a town.
There are several 19th century burnt brick
houses with masonry gables in the
Baroque style surviving in the town.

The sacred monuments of the town
are represented by the Baroque Roman
Catholic church of **Ascension of the Virgin Mary** from 1724. It originated on the
site of an older Gothic church, which
burnt down in 1715. The interior of the
church is from the early 19th century. The

Neo-Classical main altar bears a painting
of Assumption of the Virgin Mary from
1832. Also the Baroque **chapel** from the
18th century with a tower from the late 19th
century standing in the former cemetery
also contribute to the spiritual life of the
villagers. It is a small rectangular sacral
structure with statue of the Virgin Mary.
Visitors to the town may be surprised by
the well maintained municipal park and
the greenery. Advantageous position of
the town at the confluence of two rivers
makes it an ideal centre of water sports
and fishing. The floating **water mill** on
the Malý Dunaj river with preserved
equipment from the early 20th century is
the only technical monument of its kind
in Slovakia. The town also has the
longest log bridge in Central Europe and
remains of a Baroque fort housing the
Museum of water milling (Múzeum vod-
ného mlynárstva).

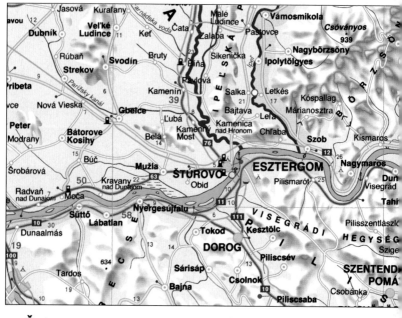

ŠTÚROVO AND ENVIRONS

The territory is under administration of the district town of Nové Zámky. Its prevailing part lies in the Danube hill land. The rock faces of Burda mountain range tower above the plain and hilly relief along the Danube and the lower reaches of its tributaries the Nitra, Žitava, Ipeľ and Hron.

The only town in this part of the district is **ŠTÚROVO** (Párkány, population 13,300). It is situated on the left bank of the Danube, in the southern part of the Danube Hill land. Its rich history is closely connected with that of Esztergom lying on the opposite bank of the Danube in Hungary. It was settled as early as the Stone Age. Archaeologists discovered here settlements from the Older and Younger Bronze Age and a burial place with cremation graves from the Hallstatt period. In time of the Romans a guard station *Anavum* existed here. A Slav-Avar burial place and a Slav settlement from the 11th

Right: The church in Štúrovo
The Maria Valeria Bridge

and 12th centuries have also been proved. The Turks eventually succeeded in conquering Esztergom in 1543 and occupying Kakath. West of the destroyed Kakath, approximately on the site of today's Roman Catholic church fortifications were constructed and the change of the settlement's name to Parkan is related to these fortifications.

Why precisely Parkan?

The Turks built a fort in 1546 on the site of castle documented in 1304 and called it "a fort clawing the enemy's liver". The garrison of the Parkan fort in the 16 century consisted of 200 men and the for was equipped with cannons. Parkan became along with Esztergom an important starting point for the Turkish raids and e. forts to obtain new territories.

The Turks introduced weekly markets at Parkan in 1589 and their tradition has survived up to the present days. The settlement was promoted to a town with market right in 1724. The Emperor Charles III granted market right to the town and the most important market day was tha

Simon and Jude. Queen Maria Theresa endowed Parkan with municipal privileges in 1740. Repeated heavy fighting took place in the environs of the town. The Hungarian army conquered the castle and the Turks plundered the town village in 1592, in 1663, a year later imperial army of General Souches and in 1683 the army of Jan Sobieski of Poland sacked it again. A "shuttle bridge" was built in 1762. It was a kind of ferry, which crossed the Danube in 6-8 minutes. A pontoon bridge replaced it in 1842. It was soon (1849) destroyed. The government of Hungary decided to build a new bridge over the Danube. The bridge connecting Parkan with Esztergom was finished in 1895. Retreating troops of the Hungarian Soviet Republic destroyed part of the bridge in summer 1919. The bridge was restored again in the 1920's. By the end of the second World War the German troops blew up the three central parts of the bridge. Its reconstruction is under way now and it will mean further opening of the town to the world. When the railway from Budapest to Bratislava in 1857 and further to Levice in 1887 was finished, Parkan became an important railway junction. After the 1876 flood the Danube dikes were built here. During the First World War Parkan obtained its port. It was adjudicated to Hungary in the years 1938-1945. Štúrovo is today an important industrial centre. Above all the paper and pulp industry (Assidomän Packing) are developed, although the food, textile, building material and machinery industries are also represented in Štúrovo. It has a border crossing to Hungary, a river port and ferry connecting it with Esztergom in Hungary. After the town of Čierna nad Tisou Štúrovo is the second largest railway junction used for transports coming from the north to Rumania and Bulgaria.

Cultural monuments worth seeing include the Late Baroque Roman Catholic **church of St. Emerich** from the end of the 18th century. New side chapels were added to the main nave. Seeing the interior the visitor must notice the valuable paintings on the main and side altars, the Late Baroque pulpit with paintings of four

Evangelists on a windowsill from 1760 and a Rococo organ from 1790. The Late Baroque Calvary from 1760 and the statue of St. John Nepomuk, carved in stone by folk artists from 1807 are also interesting. Recently the nice building of what was once a bank built in the Art Nouveau style was renewed and it serves the purpose it was built for as it now houses the Všeobecná úverová banka. One of the main attractions of Štúrovo is the three day lasting **fair of Simon and Jude** held in October every year now for the past 450 years.

Štúrovo is the southernmost town of Slovakia, which hosts many visitors from

Left: The thermal swimming pool in Štúrovo

up to 395 m above sea level. The nature of Burda is protected by two National Nature Reserves. One of them is the **National Nature Reserve of Kováčovské kopce-juh** (Kováčovské hills-south).

The gems of nature

Protected territory offers its riches to everybody and satisfies even the most demanding visitor. It contains steep andesite rock faces on the southern slopes known under the name Skaly (Rocks), forest steppe flanks of hills under the top of Burdov Mt., former pastures above the vineyards near Kamenica nad Hronom, but also old abandoned orchards next to the village of Chľaba. Several species of plants and animals living in the territory of the park are protected.

A trip to the Burdov Mt. is a kind of adventure as no marked footpath leads to its top. Start on the red-marked hiking path, which leads from Kamenica nad Hronom to the edge of the National Nature Reserve of Kováčovské kopce-juh. After a nice walk across meadows with fine view of the Danube and its confluence with the Hron, the Pilis mountains and the Basilica of Esztergom the footpath enters the wood and continues along the ridge parallel to the **instructive path of Kováčovské kopce-juh**. The linear, medium demanding instructive path 4.9 km long and with elevation difference of 220 m has existed since 1996. Six information panels accompany the visitors to the landmarks. The salient point of the instructive path is Kamenica nad Hronom or Kováčov. The rocks on the southern side of the mountain range originated through frost weathering in the Quaternary period. Wonderful views of the Danube and hills on its opposite bank accompany the hiker most of the time. The path joins the blue-marked route after a while, descends and turns right. After passing the crossroads of forest roads it runs along feeders for game, beyond which you have to turn right to reach the top of the Burdov Mt. The top is forested and consequently with no views. To go back return to the blue-marked footpath and descend by the asphalt road to the Ipeľ cottage. The blue

home and from abroad attracted here by its beautiful natural setting. The meander of the Danube starts here and provides wonderful view of the dominant feature of the surrounding landscape: the Neo-Classical basilica of Esztergom from 1856. The gorge-like reach of the Danube between the Slovak mountain range of Burda and the Hungarian mountain range of Pilis is called the Vyšehradská brána Gate. The Danube makes use of a depression in the earth crust, which originated on top of a fault line. An incised meander of the river proves tectonic uplift of the surrounding mountains. Dead arm of the Hron, which flows into the Danube beyond the town, is a much sought out fishing site. Burda is volcanic mountain range, origin of which dates to the Tertiary Age. The river Ipeľ separates it from its geological twin mountain range Börzsöny and the Danube separates it from the Pilis mountains. **Burda** is composed of firm andesite volcanic rock consisting of dust, ashes, sand and boulders. Andesite also shows in places. The height of the mountain is

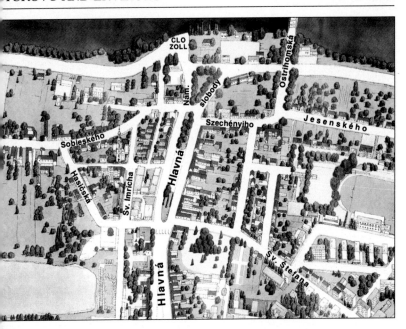

marked route runs through Veľká dolina alley to Chľaba where you can see old vintner's cellars with ornamented facades.

Štúrovo also has one of the biggest bathing complexes of Slovakia, **Vadaš**, its area is 24 hectares, and it uses the natural hot spring with a temperature of 38 degrees Celsius. There are four swimming pools, a water slide, playground for children and various sport facilities. The area also has its car camp. Next to the Danube is the Dom vodných športov or House of Water Sports and more thermal swimming pools. A visit to the venerable Estergom is also attractive. It offers not only some remarkable cultural monuments but you can also ascend the 404 metres tall Vaskap hill. The view from its top is worth the toil as it includes the whole of Esztergom, Štúrovo and the Burda Mts. Lovers of wine can use the occasion and visit the Belianske kopce hills, which contain the **Nature Reserve of Ťršok.** Vineyards with their corresponding wine cellars cover the slopes of the Belianske kopce hills.

The town does not administer the village of **OBID** (Ebed in Hungarian, popula-

tion 1,150) anymore. It is known for a remarkable find of silver Celtic coins from the 1st century BC, as well as the burial place and settlement of the Carpathian Barrow Culture. A Slav-Avar burial place and one from the 11th-12th centuries were also found here. The village was first mentioned in 1237 when the yeomen living here guarded the castle of Hlohovec. It is known from 1259 as *villa Ebed.* The Chapter of Esztergom owned it. In the years 1542 and 1663 it was sacked by the Turks. In the late 17th century it disappeared and its people moved to Esztergom. The medieval village of Obid lay nearer to the Danube channel and the villages were farmers, vintners and fishermen. The houses were made by the technology traditional for the region, which used clay bricks for masonry and reed for the roofs. Only foundations of the elongated nave with a semicircular apse survived from the 12th century Romanesque church. The originally Baroque Roman Catholic **Church of St. Stephen the King** dates is from 1732. Its facade was rebuilt in the Neo-Romanesque style. The main altar with wooden pillar architecture bear-

ing in its centre an oil painting of St. Stephen the King is from the first half of the 18th century . The pulpit and the font are in the Neo-Classical taste. There are also thermal springs in Obid.

Two kilometres north-west of Štúrovo is the now independent village of **NÁNA** (Nána in Hungarian, population 1,100). It used to be a part of Štúrovo for some time. It is a well-known archaeological site with finds from the Neolithic, Hallstatt, La Téne, and Roman periods. King Gejza II donated the salt toll station of Nána to the Chapter of Esztergom in 1157. Its owners were yeomen of Berka in 1228. The village already had its church at that time. There are no references to the village of the period of Turk raids. It was resettled only in the second half of the 18th century. Its inhabitants were farmers. Its most important sacred monument is the Roman Catholic **church of St. Vendelín** of 1791, which originated by reconstruction of an older Baroque chapel. The single-nave

space has a cross vault. The original presbytery of the chapel is now the sacristy. The road statue of St. Vendelin and the stone Baroque cross from the 18th century at the cemetery also symbolize the spiritual life of the village.

On the main road communication Štúrovo-Levice lies the administrative territory of the very old village of **KAMENNÝ MOST** (Kőhidgyarmat in Hungarian, population 1,100), continuously settled since the Younger Stone Age. The coat of arms of the village contains a stone bridge as its name suggests (Kamenný most means stone bridge in English). A collective find of numerous bronze objects, La Téne settlement and cremation graves, Roman Barbarian settlement and Slav settlement from the time of the Great Moravian Empire were found here. The first written reference to the village is from 1271 or 1282. The village was property of the Archbishopric and Chapter of Esztergom, which owned it until the abolition of serfdom. Parish presumably church existed here from the Middle Ages. The village was sacked in the years between 1295-1311. King Ferdinand II of Hungary, concluded

Left: Kováčov
Right: Hron

peace with the Turks in this village n 1625. The village was restored only in the 18th century. **Clay houses** with straw roofs represent the folk architecture while the sacred buildings include the Baroque Roman Catholic **church of St. Mauritius** from 1746. Its Late Baroque altar with pillar architecture and sculptures of St. Stephen the King and St. Ladislav are worthy seeing. The left side altar displays the painting of the Holy Family from the early 19th century. The Late Baroque side altar on the right side dedicated to St. John Nepomuk with pillar architecture, the central painting and sculptures of bishops from the late 18th century are also interesting. The church also has a pulpit from the 18th century with four sculptures of Evangelists and a Neo-Classical marble font from the first half of the 19th century. The village was adjudicated to Hungary in the years 1938-1845.

On the south-western foothill of the Burda mountain range, two kilometres from the place where the Hron flows into the Danube is the village of **KAMENICA NAD HRONOM** (Garamkövesd in Hungarian, population 1,400). Finds of the Želiezovce and Lengyel Cultures, inhumation and cremation cemeteries prove settlement in the Neolithic, Aeneolithic, and Bronze Ages.

The first reference to the village is from 1156. Historic documents quote its names as: *Kuesd, Kuued, Keuesd, Kwesd, Kevesd*, etc. Its present name has existed since 1928. It was also mentioned in 1232 along with villages, which were adjudicated to Zvolen Castle, later it was owned by the Archbishopric of Esztergom. The owner paid a lot of attention to the operation of the water mill existing in the village. The local parsonage was mentioned as early as 1397.

The village was recognized in the past for its extensive vineyards producing an excellent red wine. The bridge over the Hron, constructed by Aladár Sebestyén and Rezsö Póka, was in fact the biggest arched bridge in the Kingdom of Hungary, when it was built in 1907-1908. The environs of the settlement were the scene of heavy fighting and a large part of it was demolished between December 1944

and March 1945. The Nazi troops blasted the bridge in 1945 and it was replaced by a temporary wooden one until 1961 when a new bridge was built on the surviving pillars. Kamenica nad Hronom also belonged to Hungary in the years 1938-1945.

The village is the birth place of the writer István Gyurcsó, one of the spiritual fathers and organizers of the Jókai's Days event dedicated to literature and regularly held in Komárno. The nineteenth century **folk architecture made of clay bricks** with saddle roof, wooden gables and straw or reed roofs survives in the village. The Neo-Classical, originally Baroque Roman Catholic **church of St. Michael the Archangel** is from 1734. A tower was added to it in the mid-19th century and later it was repaired. In its interior the Baroque main altar of St. Michael the Archangel, pillar architecture with Baroque statues of St. Catherine and St. Barbara, side altars of St. Ann and the Virgin Mary, the Late Baroque pulpit with a statue of The Good Shepherd and the painting of Assumption of the Virgin Mary from 1744 are the main artefacts.

The village is the destination of canoeists travelling down the rivers Danube or Hron. The peculiarity of this village are its wine cellars dug into the loess rock faces in its environs. The loess profile of Kamenica is registered as a **protected natural phenomenon** and it is a 5 to 15 m tall loess rock face on the south-western slopes of Burda with nests of fowl. The territory of Kamenica includes Kováčov, a recreation settlement located below the picturesque andesite rocks of Burda. It has gravel beaches, playgrounds, accommodation and catering amenities.

Old Kováčov

At the turn of the 19th and 20th centuries Kováčov was the favourite place of trippers and holiday-makers from Esztergom and Budapest. A steamer brought the trippers from Esztergom to the opposite bank of the Danube and the ones from Budapest arrived by train. The railway station was right behind the port and visitors then walked to their respective pensions and hotels using the hiking footpaths.

The village of **CHĽABA** (Helemba in Hungarian, population 700) is set into the picturesque nature of the confluence of the Ipeľ and Danube. As an important archaeological locality its settlement is documented from the Neolithic times until the Middle Ages. Cremation graves of the North-Pannonian Culture from the Older Bronze Age, a settlement and cemetery of the Carpathian Barrow Culture, as well as the La Téne graves were found here. In the fourth century the Roman guard tower,

Left: The vineyards of Bajtava
Right: Pension in Mužla

burgus, stood here. It was referred to as a fisherman's village called *villa Helenba* in 1138. Remains of disappeared medieval villages from the 11th to 16th century were discovered in the administrative territory of Chľaba. It was owned by several Church institutions. First of all it was the Provostship of Dömös and after 1523 the Chapter of Esztergom owned it. In 1234 it is mentioned in connection with orchards existing here and in 1339 it had a hunting ground. It belonged to Hungary in the years 1938-1945. The villagers were mostly farmers and vintners in the past and their **wine cellars** boast a 300 year history.

The Late Baroque Roman Catholic **church of St. Emerich** in Chľaba is from 1769. It was reconstructed in the Neo-Classical style in the early 19th century. This single-nave building with in-built tower contains a Late Neo-Classical font from the middle of the 19th century. Viticulture, fruit-growing and fishery are also the prevailing occupations of the local people at present. South-east of the village is the railway bridge over the Ipeľ to the village of Szob in Hungary. In the administrative territory of the villages of Chľaba and Leľa is the **National Nature Reserve of Kováčovské kopce-sever** (Kováčovské kopce-north) with occurrence of rare species of bugs and some wood species.

The route of a the trip also may lead from Štúrovo through Kamenica nad Hronom to the village of **BAJTAVA** (Bajta in Hungarian, population 400). The first written mention of Bajtava is from 1261 when it was called *villa Beyta.* It was owned by the Archbishopric of Esztergom until 1848. It was known for good wine in the past. Its dominant feature building is that of the Roman Catholic **church of the Birth of the Virgin Mary**. The original chapel from the second half of the 18th century was widened and rebuilt in the Neo-Neo-Classical style in 1872. The facade of the church has a gable and little wooden tower. In its interior the Gothic stone font from the 15th century is of interest. The stone road cross dates from 1782.

In this part of the Danube basin also the village of **LEĽA** (Leléd in Hungarian, pulation 400) is also worth visiting. Ae-olithic and La Téne settlements were und here. It was mentioned for the first ne as *Leled* in 1262. Its people were rmers and vintners. The Roman atholic Baroque church built in the ars 1752-1774 represents sacred mon-ments. In the interior the main Late-aroque altar from the second half of the 3th century with pillar architecture and ulptures of St. John Nepomuk and St. aul are interesting. The stone font is om 1879 and the pulpit dates to the sec-nd half of the 18th century. Leľa, like her villages in the eastern part of the anube hill land and Burda is known for s typical folk architecture.

The typical folk architecture

In the area of Burda people dug cel-rs in the ground, which survived up to e present time. The roofs of farm build-gs were given a double saddle form; the ofs of houses were hipped. Straw, reed shingles originally covered the roofs. ow they are all covered by shingles. ences were also made of natural materi-: wood, stone or wicker. The wells were ug in the yards. Houses more than hun-red years old made of clay and still in-abited were found here. The majority of e preserved buildings are made from w clay. They were covered with plaster ter. The houses were divided into a om, store room and third room with en fire. The adapted historic houses ow have two rooms and a stove has re-laced the open fire.

MUŽLA (Muzsla in Hungarian, popu-tion 2,000) is another village situated est of Štúrovo. Not far from it, in the set-ement of Čenkov, the Neolithic burial lace and settlement was found. In close cinity of the Danube the archaeologists iscovered the remains of the **Roman ontier military fort** from the 4th centu-. It is the type of fort called "burg". This mall and bulky tower had a square 0x10 m) ground plan and meter thick alls. An earthen fort also found at the cality is from the 10th to 11th century. he village was first mentioned in 1156 as osula. It was in the ownership of Trenčín

Castle and from the 15th century the Arch-bishopric of Esztergom owned it. Yeomen are mentioned in connection with *Musla* in 1255 but the Primate of Esztergom owned it again from 1388. Two settle-ments existed here in the 16th century side by side: Dolná Mužla later destroyed by the Turks and Čenkov referred to as early as 1243 as the property of a Spanish no-bleman Simon. The villagers were farmers and vintners. **Earthen houses** with sad-dle straw roof from the late 19th century existed here until recently.

As far as the sacred monuments are concerned, the Roman Catholic Neo-Clas-sical **church of the Virgin Mary** is the one to admire. Its construction started in the 18th century but finished only in 1817. After fire in 1862 it was restored and by the end of the century also fur-nished. Its decoration in the Art Noveau style with Byzantine elements is interest-ing. A sculpture of the Pieta is a Late Baroque folk work of art from the early 19th century.

Peculiarities of this village are the well preserved wind wells from 1920 and **sul-phur springs** known from the 16th centu-ry near the church. In the territory of the village next to the disappearing settlement of Čenkov are two **National Nature Re-serves: Čenkovská steppe and Čenkovská forest-steppe areas.**

There are also other protected territo-ries in the environs of the village. Rare species of flora and fauna found in the **Mužliansky potok** and its immediate en-virons are also protected. Near the settle-ment Jurský Chlm is the **Nature Reserve of Jurský Chlm**. The object of protection is the unique occurrence of several plant species.

The village **BELÁ** (Béla in Hungarian, population 400) is situated further north. It was first mentioned in 1138 as *villa Bela*. In the 13ᵗʰ century the crown and the Chapter of Esztergom alternate owned it. In the late 14ᵗʰ century the local yeomen clear cut the forest owned by the Archbishop. Two settlements were mentioned in the 16ᵗʰ century, Malá and Veľká Belá, though they disappeared after the Turkish raids. Belá was resettled only in the 18th century. Vineyards, **viticultural huts and cellars** surround the village.

The centre of Belá is the originally Late Baroque **manor house** built together with the church in the years 1732-1755. It was adapted in the Neo-Classical taste in 1834, in the late 19ᵗʰ century, and again in the 20ᵗʰ century. The interior of the manor house contains the Late Neo-Classical frescoes. It is in decay. After the reconstruction now under preparation it should become the site of a viticultural association called VINO VERITAS SLOVAKIA. The manor house has a **park** of its own, which is also a **protected area**. The Roman Catholic church stands close to the manor house. Its central nave has an oval dome. The generously decorated interior contains unique wall paintings from the second half of the 19ᵗʰ century, a Rococo cabinet with the statue of Maria of Mariazell and there is a crypt under the church from 1850. The sacred monuments of the village include the Late Baroque Roman Catholic **church of the Exaltation of the Holy Cross** from the years 1748-1760 and a **chapel** in the

vineyards from the late 19ᵗʰ century wit statues of St. Urban and St. Nicolas fro the 18ᵗʰ century.

If you continue northward you will a rive at the village of **ĽUBÁ** (Libád in Hu garian, population 400). Archaeologist found here Neolithic and Slav settlemen the latter being from the period of Grea Moravia. The first references to the villag as *Libad* or *Lobad* were in documen from 1294. From the mid-16ᵗʰ century th Chapter of Esztergom owned it, but it wa completely abandoned in the late 17ᵗʰ cer tury. The village was repopulated in th 18ᵗʰ century and its people were farmer and vintners. The dominant feature builc ing and the only sacred monument Ľubá is the Roman Catholic **church of S John Baptist** from the second half of th 18ᵗʰ century. It was built in the Lat Baroque taste and its presbytery contair two interesting Baroque niches with shell. The painting of St. John Baptist o the main altar is from 1882.

Leaving Ľubá and going in the direc tion of Gbelce you can visit the village c **ŠARKAN** (Sárkanyfalva in Hungariar population 400). Neolithic settlement from the Older and Younger Bronze Ag were found here. The first reference to th village is from 1247, when King Belo IV c Hungary donated it to noblema Bechend. In 1409 the priest Zigmud fror Karva (Kravany) owned it. It was de stroyed in the 17ᵗʰ century and later grad ually restored. The inhabitants were farm ers and vintners. The proof of their reli gious life is the Neo-Classical Roma Catholic **church of the Virgin Mary** fror 1710 and the Late Baroque **statue of th Pieta** from the second half of the 18ᵗʰ cer tury at the local cemetery.

The village of **GBELCE** (Köbölkút population 2,400) 14 km away fror Štúrovo is also an important archaeologi cal site, settled since the Neolithic perioc Archaeologists found here the Volute Cul ture settlements, Hallstatt and La Tén settlements and inhumation graves, bu also the Roman-Barbarian settlemen with cremation burial place. It was firs mentioned in historic sources as *Cabulcu* in 1233. The family of Kobulkúti owned i until the 14ᵗʰ century, later its owner

---

Left: The church in Ľubá
Right: The Nature Reserve of Parížske močiare

vere various yeoman families. The local parish church was first referred to in 1397. The village was destroyed during the Turkish occupation, later repopulated by the people from Nová Vieska and Bešeňová. The aristocratic Pálffy family founded a big pond here.

The Pariž brook and Count Pálffy

The Pariž brook created a lake, or better said a swamp north of the village, which spread as far as Nová Vieska. The Pariž brook forked there into two branches. One flowed through Gbelce in direction to the south-east to Mužla and went into the Danube. The other arm headed to the east to the villages of Diva and Kamenný Most and ended up in the Hron. In the years 1819-1826 the lake was partially drained, when Count Pálffy had a canal dug here.

There are interesting **wine cellars** in the territory administered by the village. The houses and farm buildings are mostly from the early 20th century and are arranged in a long row. A pillared gangway is their typical feature. The dominant feature building of the village is the originally Baroque Roman Catholic **church of St. Bartholomew** from the 17th century, rebuilt in the Neo-Classical taste in the early 19th century. It has got one nave and an in-built tower, which bears a coat of arm above its entrance. Also the Baroque-Neo-Classical **curia** testifies to the presence of yeomen in this village in the past.

NOVÁ VIESKA (Kisújfalu in Hungarian, population 800) is 4 km away from Gbelce. Although the archaeologists found here a Neolithic settlement, the territory of this village was settled probably only in the 15th century. Ján Keglevich owned it in the early 17th century and in the 18th century it belonged to various yeomen. Polish troops destroyed in 1683 and when the Turks were driven out, it was re-settled by

the people from Gbelce. The reformed **church** built in 1878 provides for the spiritual life of the local people. It was restored after a fire in 1874.

Not far from the village is the **Nature Reserve of Drieňová hora**. It includes part of a small oak and locust wood and the rest is a non-forested part on blown sands and loess. It protects rare species of thermophilous insects and plants. The administrative territory of the villages of Gbelce and Nová Vieska on the alluvial plain of the Pariž brook is the **Nature Reserve Parížske močiare swamps**. This area is one of the most valuable localities for water fowl and rare swamp plant and animal associations. Another similar reserve is the **protected area Alluvium of Pariž** in the administrative territory of Strekov and Nová Vieska.

THE HUNGARIAN DANUBELAND

SITUATION AND DIVISION

The Hungarian part of the Danube region is situated in the western part of the Republic of Hungary and occupies the northern part of the Transdanubian region. From the natural point of view it lies in the northern part of the Little Hungarian Lowland and particularly the **Győr Basin**. The eastern part of the territory contains the **mountain ranges of Gerecse, Pilis and Visegrád**. The territory is limited by the stream of the Danube in the north and in the east. In the west the country borders on Austria and in the north-west on Slovakia. Its southern edge is formed by the line Hegyeshalom — Mosonmagyaróvár — Győr — Tatabánya — the frontier of County of Komárom-Esztergom — Visegrád.

The territory is administered by the Counties of Győr-Sopron-Moson and Komárom-Esztergom and partially the County of Pest.

Right: The Danube near Nagybajcs

NATURAL SETTING

The Little Hungarian Lowland or Kisalföld occupies the western section of the Hungarian part of the Danube region. It is the largest lowland of the Transdanubian region and includes the Danube lowland in Slovakia. The **Győri-medence** (Győr Basin), **Komárom-Esztergomi-síkság** (Komárom-Esztergom lowland) and the **Dunazug-hegyvidék** (Mountains of the Danube's Meander) including the **Gerecse, Pilis** and **Visegrád mountain ranges** are the orographic features of the country.

The Győr Basin consists from the island **Szigetköz** squeezed between the main stream of the Danube and the Moson branch of the river, and the **Moson plain**. Szigetköz with its area of 372 square kilometres is part of the County of Győr-Sopron. Its relief is flat and in the past it was frequently flooded. Its altitude above sea level oscillates between 110 and 126 metres and it drops in the direction from the north-west to the south-east. The original surface with

numerous valleys was silted and planated by sediments. Only some parts of the original river beds survive. Szigetköz is a young, still sinking territory and its geothermal potential, compared to other parts of the country, is above average. It is not sufficiently exploited although water with a temperature of 80 degrees Celsius is feasible here. The Quaternary sand and gravel form 100 to 250 m thick layers here. The old Pannonian layers of mud thicker than 2,000 m with enormous reserves of ground water are under them. Some strata of fine sand used to have high contents of gold, which was transported here from the Alps. However, construction of various water works on the Danube interrupted the flow of gold to Hungary.

It is a warm and dry territory. The length of solar radiation varies between 1,900 and 1,950 hours a year. The sun shines 770 hours in the summer season here. The mean annual temperature varies between 9.5 and 10 degrees of Celsius, and rises in the eastern direction. A mean of 185 days a year are free from frost, mostly in the period between 15th April and 18th October. Record temperatures are usually 33.5 degrees Celsius above zero and 15.5 degrees Celsius below zero. The mean annual precipitation total is 590 mm. The highest daily precipitation total was taken in Hédervári: 78 mm. Continuous snow cover lasts about 40 days in winter and the maximum of its thickness is 28 cm. The prevailing winds blow from the north-west.

The main stream of the **Danube** flows around the island on a track 57.6 km long in the north and in the south the meandering **Moson branch of the Danube** long as much as 121.5 km long flows around the island. The discharge of the Danube near Dunaremete is 2.025 cubic metres, but it is influenced by the Gabčíkovo Dam on the Slovak side of the frontier.

The Danube

The Danube is the river with the highest content of water in Central Europe

---

Left: The Danube near Ásványráró
Right: The Moson branch of the Danube

and it flows through the highest number of countries in the world. It carries a great amount of sediments from the area above Komárom and deposits them beyond the same town. It flows in mild meanders between the towns of Komárom and Esztergom. Passing trough Esztergom where the river Hron flows into it, the Danube is forced to deposit new sediments. The width of the bed Komárom and Esztergom varies between 330 and 450 m. However, immediately before Esztergom the Danube together with its islands and branches is more than 2 km wide. The bottom of its channel is covered by gravel, sand and clay. The inclination of the river in this section is 2.83 m. The river has the greatest amount of water in June, the least in October and December. Regulation of is bed was made in the Hungarian part of the Danube region in the years 1886-1896. The velocity of the stream beyond Komárom doubled after these adjustments. The depth of water varies, in average 6 to 8 metres. It is estimated that the Danube's sediments contain a million kilograms of gold in tiny grains. But its extraction is not economic, although it brought profit to some people until the early 20th century. Due to low banks and insufficient flood control the people suffered from frequent floods of the Danube. Gradually the dikes were built and made firmer and the life along them became safer. There is a territory along the dikes that can be periodically flooded and it is mostly agricultural land.

Water comes to the Moson branch through the floodgate in Rajka. The Danube usually contains the greatest amount of water in the early summer. The territory is safeguarded by good quality anti-flood dikes. The area within the dikes occupies 28.8 square kilometres and it is covered by alluvial forests, meadows and pastures. The route of navigation must be constantly cleared and deepened and the result is that annually almost 200,000 cubic metres of gravel and sand are extracted. The dead branches of the river occupy an area of 35.6 hectares. They are five in total and the area of biggest one in Dunaszeg is

25.6 ha. The other branches are the Cikolasziget 29.3 km, Bodac 20.3 km, Ásványráró 35.2 km and Bagomér 19.8 km long.

There are several Artesian wells on the island. They are up to 100 m deep and yield 150 litres of water a minute Hot water is used only near Lipót where its source yields 2,000 litres of water a minute with temperature between 61 and 76 degrees Celsius. The island is a reserve of drinking water of national significance. The flora is Pannonian, thermophilous and the wood species are represented by willow, ash, poplar, and in places oak trees. The island is mostly covered by arable land (65%), forests cover 16 %, built-up areas occupy 6 %, water bodies spread on 5.7%, meadows and pastures are on 3% and the flooded area makes up for 3% of its total area.

The **Mosoni-síkság** (Moson plain) stretches over an area of 425 square kilometres in the County of Győr-Sopron. River sediments and sporadic wind sediments (loess) form it. It lies 110-130 metres above sea level. Its surface slightly decreases from the north-west to the

south-east and it is interrupted only by canals and river beds. The main asset of this territory apart from gravel and sand extracted as building material, is peat and geo-thermal energy, which is not fully exploited yet. The warm and dry territory has 1,900 hours of solar radiation, out of which 770 occur in the summer months. The mean yearly temperature oscillates between 9.5 and 10 degrees Celsius. Frost is absent 185 days a year, mostly between April 17th and October 19th. The highest temperature reaches 33 and the lowest drops to mean -15.5 degrees Celsius. Precipitation amounts to 580-600 mm a year. The most abundant rainfall was recorded in Lebényi-Mosonszentmiklós. Snow cover occurs here for 40 days, its thickness normally does not exceed 29 cm. North-western winds prevail in this area.

The major part of the territory is drained by the Moson branch of the

Danube, which limits the territory in the north for a distance of 104 km. The Lajta is another important river, which flow from Austria. Its 20 km long left-bank canal and 7.5 km long Rét-árok flow into the Moson branch of the Danube. The lowest and the highest discharge of the Moson branch are 10 and 150 cubic metres per second respectively; those of the Lajta are 4 and 100 cubic metres per second respectively. The territory is covered by artificial canals, the task of which is to drain groundwater, which often rises to the surface and threatens the fields and settlements. The ground water contains iron. Thermal wells were drilled and used only in Mosonmagyaróvár and Lebény where water with a temperature of 76 degrees Celsius is exploited.

The surface of the Moson plain is changed, thanks to its highly fertile soil chernozem, to arable land, which covers here as much as 85% of the territory. In the woods stretching along the streams and canals willow, poplar, alder, oak and hornbeam trees grow. Remains of the original willow-birch wood associations still exist in this area.

Left: The confluence of the Rába and the Moson branch of the Danube
Right: The flora of Szigetköz

The **Komárom-Esztergom lowland** is divided to the **Győr-Tatai-teraszvidék** terraces, **Almás-táti-Duna völgy** valley and **Igmánd-Kisberi-medence** basin. The Győr-Tatai-teraszvidék with an area 550 square kilometres lies in two counties: Győr -Sopron and Komárom-Esztergom. It is slightly dissected and undulating terraced lowland. The territory is bordered by the Danube in the north and its water level gradually drops in this area from 120 m to 110 m above sea level. The floodplain of the river is regularly flooded. Along it terraces reaching 150 to 180 m a.s.l. were formed. The highest situated place, west of the town of Tata is at 201 m above sea level. The relief is refreshed by valleys of the little rivers flowing into the Danube. The sediments of the Danube and its tributaries cover the territory, while gravel and sand of different size prevail. The whole territory is very sensitive in terms of seismology. The town of Komárom is sometimes referred to as the town of earthquakes.

The earthquakes

The greatest natural disasters that occurred in this area are floods and earthquakes. One memorable earthquake with its centre on the Slovak bank of the Danube was in Komárno on June 28th 1763. After this experience the people became extremely sensitive to any suspicious movement of the earth and only in 1784 280 such movements were recorded. The last intensive movement of the earth occurred in 1822. As a result of the 1815 earthquake part of houses in Dunaalmási fell down. The traces of the past earthquakes are still visible in some places and buildings; for instance the Romanesque-Gothic church in Zsámbék. Earthquakes also entered fiction. Baróti Szabó Dávid wrote the poem Komáromi föld indulás (The Movement of Earth in Komárom), the writer Jókai Mór in his book Elátkozott család (The Cursed Family) described the horror and anxiety of people during the earthquake with a particular degree of imagination.

The climate is moderately warm and dry. The inhabitants and the visitors of

the area enjoy 2,000 hours of sunshine a year, in summer about 780 hours. The mean annual temperature moves around 10 degrees Celsius. The maximum temperature reaches 34 and the minimum - 16.8 degrees Celsius. The annual precipitation total is about 580 mm. Snow cover lasts on average 35 days and reaches a maximum thickness of 26 cm. North-westerly winds prevail. The climate is especially suitable for growing thermophilous plants and crops, such as grapes or sunflowers.

The Moson branch of the Danube flows through the territory and its length here is 15 km, the reach of the Danube is 42 km long here. The Danube has several tributaries: Cuhai-Bakony-ér 11 km long, Concó (12 km), Fényes-patak (14 km), Mikovínyi-árok (11 km) and Által-ér (14 km), the last mentioned being its longest tributary. The highest discharge of the Danube occurs in spring and early summer. The area of the floodplain of the Danube and its tributaries equalling 35.5 square kilometres is occasionally inundated. Consequently this area is not settled. It is used for meadows, pastures or as floodplain forest.

There are many water bodies in this area. Two natural lakes occupy the area of 242 hectares: the **Öreg-tó** (The Old Lake) in Tata spreads on 209 hectares. The area of five artificial lakes is 74 ha and the **Névtelen-tó** (The Lake with no Name) in the village of Mocsa is the largest of them (20.5 ha). There are also several Artesian wells next to the Danube more than 100 m deep and their performance is 100 litres per minute. They contain hard water with higher contents of iron. There are also two ther-

mal wells with temperature 42 and 60 degrees Celsius in Komárom.

On the banks of the rivers soft and hard alluvial forests prevail. They occupy about 10 % of the territory. Willow, alder, oak trees and blackberries are the typical species growing there. Also the locust trees are frequent. As much as 70 % of the area was changed to arable land, on which mainly wheat, barley, maize and sugar beet are cultivated.

The **Almás-táti-Duna völgy** valley is situated between the northern slopes of the Gerecse Mountains and the stream of the Danube. The altitude above sea level of the territory is between 110 and 150 m above sea level while the terraces are somewhat higher. The terraces consist from gravel and sand and sporadically loess. The territory is moderately seismically active and as far as the climate is concerned, it is classified as moderately warm and dry. Its climate is similar to that of the neighbouring Győr-Tatai-teraszvidék terraces. The highest daily precipitation total was

Left: The Gerecse Mts.

taken in Nyergesújfalu (51.8 mm). The mean duration of snow cover is 35 days a year and its maximum thickness is 24 cm. Westerly winds prevail.

The axis of the territory is the 33 km long reach of Danube. It has several small right side tributaries flowing into it from the Gerecse Mountains. The greatest of them is Bikali-patak. The mean discharge of the Danube next to the settlement of Lábatlan is 2.290 cubic meters per second. The soils near the Danube are mostly of alluvial type, in higher position on loess chernozem prevails. The territory is suitable for growing cereals and root crops, which must be irrigated. Exploitation of the area corresponds to the above-mentioned assets and consequently 51 % of the area is represented by arable land while the most frequently grown crop is maize. The inundation area of the Danube is 17 square kilometres and woods and meadows cover it. The prevailing wood species growing here are the willows, poplars and alders. Coniferous species were also introduced in this territory. Big dikes were constructed especially around Esztergom. **Dunazug-**

hegyvidék (The Mountains of the Danube's Meander) are divided into the mountain ranges of Gerecse, Biske-Zsámbeki-medence, Budai-hegység and Pilis-hegység. The **Gerecse** and **Pilis** ranges stretch into our area of interest. The Gerecse Mountains consist of limestone and dolomite and they are triangle-shaped. They are divided into four parts - Western Gerecse, Central Gerecse, Eastern Gerecse and Gete. All of them run from the south to the north towards the Danube. The higher parts of the mountain range steeply drop by the lateral rocky slopes (visible from great distance) into several inter-mountain basins.

The **Western Gerecse Mts.** run from the village of Neszmély up to Tatabánya and its character is that of a plateau. It spreads over an area 200 square kilometres in the County of Komárom-Esztergom. Its tallest mountain Öreg Kovács (The Old Kovács) rises to 556 m. Sun shines in this region 1,970 hours a year, 770 hours in summer. The mean annual temperatures oscillate between 9.5 and 10 degrees Celsius, though the maximum temperatures can reach as much as 32 degrees. The minimum temperature is 16 degrees Celsius below zero. The mean annual precipitation total is around 650 mm. The winter and snow lasts mostly 40 to 45 days while the snow cover has a maximum thickness of 30 cm. The greatest river of the region is Által-ér 38 km long with a mean discharge 1 cubic meter per second near the town of Tata. Forests cover the greater part of the territory (57 %); arable land occupies only 30 %. Twenty percent of the territory is protected area.

The **Central**, also called the **High Gerecse Mts**. is the tallest part of the mountain range. Its has an area 50 square kilometres in the County of Komárom-Esztergom. The tallest mountain Gerecse reaches 634 metres. There is a TV tower on its top, visible from any place in the mountain range and consequently a point of reference as far as orientation is concerned. The Pisznice (544 m) is another mountain in the central part of the mountain range and in its

flanks red marble is extracted, the same as in the Bánya hegy Mt. The Pes kő Mt. (401 m) is notable for its steep rock faces and the Somlyóvár (448 m) offers an excellent panoramic view from its top.

The inhabitants and visitors to the area enjoy 1,980 hours of sunshine a year, in summer about 760 hours. The man annual temperature varies around 10 degrees Celsius. The maximum temperature reaches 32 and the minimum - 16.0 degrees Celsius. The annual precipitation total is about 650 mm. The maximum daily precipitation total was taken in Pusztamarót (118 mm). Snow cover lasts on average 45 days and has the maximum thickness of 50 cm. The central part of Gerecse is forested landscape. Oak-hornbeam woods occupy as much as 88 % of its area. Only one tenth of the total area, namely the lower situated places, is arable land.

The Eastern Gerecse Mts. compared to the mountain ranges described above and the Gete mountain range are somewhat shorter as its tallest mountain Öreg kő (The Old Rock) is only 374 m tall. This eastern part of the Gerecse mountain range lies in the County of Komárom-Esztergom and its climate is similar to that of its western part. The maximum daily precipitation total 96 mm was recorded in the village of Bajna. The geological base is a feature, which distinguishes the eastern part from the western. Wind-blown deposits, loess, cover the majority of the territory of the eastern part. Consequently, the local soils are more fertile than in the western part where the rock base is mostly limestone. Man has changed 64 % of the territory to arable land and woods cover only a fifth of it.

The remote past of the Gerecse Mts.

The oldest rocks appearing on the surface of the mountain range are 200 to 220 million years old. Limestone and dolomite are the remains of sea sediments and also the imprints of the Triassic round organisms, algae. The algae need sunshine for their life and it means that the sea was shallow there. A great

amount of imprints and fossilized remains of plants was found in limestone rock in Dunaalmás. The limestone near Tata and Vértesszőlős contain evidence testifying to the life of primeval man in this area. During earth works and extraction of building material near the village of Süttő a skull and teeth of a huge mammal similar to an elephant about million years old from the Ice Age were found. At that time hot springs existed there with high contents of Calcium carbonate and created a system of lakes in the area of today's Süttő. Deposition of the mineral component of warm water created conditions at the bottom of the lakes, which favour the conservation of organic remains. Looking for food this enormous mammal must have fallen into the lake and got drowned. The sediments of Calcium carbonate conserved its body. The finds are deposited in the Hungarian National Museum and the public was able to admire this spectacular mammal on the occasion of the World Hunting Exhibition.

Left: Visegrád
Right: The Visegrádi hegység Mts.

The parts of the mountain range consisting of limestone also contain numerous karstic forms or caves. Only four caves were known in the area in 1847. Today there are more than 80. The best known caves are the ones in the environs of the town Tatabánya: Szelim-barlang, Turul-lyuk, and Denevér-barlang (The Cave of Bats). The higher concentration of carbon dioxide in the Lengyel-barlang cave is the reason, why it is also called the Gas Cave. Visits are not recommended. Caves are also concentrated around the mountain Oreg-kő near the village of Bajót. More caves are locates near the villages Bajna, Tata, and Dunaalmás. The water regime in Gerecse is partially similar to the karstic regime. In some plateaux there is no surface water. It gets lost under the surface where it creates a dense network of underground rivers. On the other hand, the northern slopes of the Gerecse Mts. suffer from heavy erosion and the area is one of the 18 most affected areas of Hungary. The mountain range has remarkable and diverse vegetation, as a result of the climatic and soil conditions. Specific plant associations originated on limestone and dolomite in the south and south-east or on the blown sands on the western edge of the mountain range. As the climate is somewhat similar to the Mediterranean, the area has several species, which can be found, for instance in the Balkans. Special plants survive on the loess faces of the deep valleys. Near the springs around the town of Tata the thermophilous swamp flora grows. Willows called sad willows brought here from China were planted for the first time in Hungary in the town park of Tata.

The **Pilis Mountains** lie partly in the County of Komárom-Esztergom and partly in the County of Pest. They form a triangle limited by the Danube in the north and east and by the Pilisvörösvár valley crossed by the railway track connecting Budapest and Esztergom in the south-west. It is a markedly dissected mountain range, which the morphologists divide into Pilisi-hegyek Mts. and Pilisi-medencék Basins. The taller part the mountains occupies an area of 30 square kilometres and mostly consts of limestone and dolomite. The Pilis asins stretch over an area of 120 quare kilometres and the Pilisvörös, Ilisszentkereszt, and Dorog Basins are ie largest. Thick sedimentary layers lso containing brown coal fill them.

The sun shines in this region 1,950 ours a year, 770 hours in summer. The iean annual temperatures oscillate beveen 8.5 and 9.5 degrees Celsius, iough the maximum temperatures can each as much as 34 degrees. The miniium temperature is 16 degrees Celsius elow zero. The mean annual precipitaon total is around 700-800 mm. Snow over in higher and shaded position lasts p to 90 days while the snow cover has maximum thickness of 50 cm. Arable und in the Pilis mountains covers a uarter of the territory, half of it is covred by woods, in contrast to the Pilis Iasins where arable land prevails and roods survive only on 15% of the terriory.

Visegrádi hegység or the Visegrád ountains as the only mountain range n the right bank of the Danube are part f the Észak-Magyarországi közepegység (North Hungarian Middle Mounains), which represent the highest iountain ranges of Hungary running long the frontier with Slovakia. Morhologically they are classified into the **'iségradi Dunakanyar** or Visegrád forge of the Danube and Visegrád iountain range.

The origin of the Visegrád Gorge of the Danube

One of the most popular and also most beautiful natural setting in Hungary s the Danube gorge near Visegrád. The iorge between the villages of Dömös and 'isegrád has got a horseshoe shape not eaching more than 8 km of length. The taiered river stream squeezed between ocks with the spectacular ruins of Visegád castle on top of one of them provides a harming visual experience, which, as ome tourists assert, equals that of the iorge of the Rhine. Andesite rocks on both anks represent the evidence that they

are of common origin. After they were separated, the river found its way to the south between them. Originally the scientists believed, that it was the Danube, which deepened its bed across the mountain range. But now they offer a different explanation. In the time when the Visegrád mountain range originated the Pannonian Sea covered the Danube region, with numerous volcanic islands, similar to those that still exist in Indonesia. The Visegrád mountain range was a part of a very active volcano, which broke into two parts precisely in the area of Visegrád. The breaking line of the volcano, as seen in Vesuvius, is never straight. The Danube has to slow down its stream before it zigzags through this tapered section and continues on its way to the south.

The Visegrád mountain range in the Counties of Komárom-Esztergom and Pest has an area of 240 square kilometres. The Danube separates it from the Börzsöny Mountains situated nearby. It is 220-700 m high and it is a Tertiary volcanic mountain range changed by the posterior tectonic movements. Parts of the territory surpassing 600 m above sea level fall into the cold and moderately humid climatic zone and the ones under 600 m a.s.l. are in the cold climatic zone.

The territory has 1,950-2,000 hours of solar radiation, out of which 750 - 800 occur in summer months, in winter 150 hours in lower positions, and over 200 hours in higher positions. The mean yearly temperature at the foothills of the mountain moves between 9 and 9.8 degrees Celsius; on Dobogókő it is a little less than 8 degrees Celsius. The highest temperature can rise to 32 degrees in

lower situated places and to 29 degrees Celsius in higher positions. The lowest temperature drops to -16 degrees Celsius. Precipitation amounts to 600 mm, in mountains 800 mm a year. The most abundant rainfall per day is 73 mm and it was taken in Dobogókő. Snow cover maintains here for 35-90 days, its thickness normally does not exceed 50 cm. North-western winds prevail in this area.

The larger tributaries of the Danube on this territory are: the Szentélek-patak and Bükkös patak brooks. With regard to geological composition of the base rock the springs are temporal and yield less than those in karstic areas. The richest spring is Kinizsi-forrás near Pilisszentkereszt (260 litres per minute). Vegetation adapted to the sea level altitude, while forests represent 86 % of the territory. Oak and hornbeam woods prevail. Two thirds of the territory are protected. Arable land is only on 6 % of the surface. The local orchards contain above all cherry trees and fruit-bearing shrubs, such as raspberries.

The Visegrádi Dunakanyar o Danube's Meander at Visegrád lies in th Counties of Komárom-Esztergom an Pest. The place consists of the Tertiar limestone rocks and andesite tuffs or ag glomerates covered by river sediments As far as the climate is concerned, it is a transitory area between the moderatel warm and moderately cold zones. The colder parts are situated north and south of the gorge and the warmer part are situated in the eastern and western sides of the gorge. Considering precipita tion (600 mm) the territory is moderate ly dry. On the banks hard alluvial forest with a prevalence of willows alternate with various species of oak and chestnu trees. The gorge is a protected area with in the **Pilis protected area**.

The Danube near Visegrád

The reach of the Danube flowing trough the Visegrád Mountains is 39 km long, which is the distance between Esz tergom and Vác. The Szentendre branch of the Danube separates from the main stream below Visegrád, its length is 31.5 km and it creates the island of Szentend

---

Left: The Danube near Visegrád

re. *The mean discharge of the Danube at Nagymaros is 2,375 cubic metres per second, the maximum and minimum discharge is 7,570 and 1,045 cubic metres per second respectively. This section of the Danube is easily navigable, but the Szentendre is not navigable in time of low water. Nagymaros was the place where a part of the Gabčíkovo water works was planned and some of it also built, but when the Hungarian party withdrew its participation in the project, all that was constructed before is now being pulled down.*

HISTORY

The oldest settlement of the Hungarian part of the Danube region followed the streams of smaller rivers, which flowed into the Danube. The remains of the first settlements were found for instance, next to the Únys brook. On the western slopes of the Gerecse Mountains was a dense network of hot springs, which also offered a warmer climate. Ape-man made use of this natural wealth. Remains of the oldest man, who settled the Danube area about 400,000 years ago, were found there.

The ape-man in the Danube region
The village of Vértesszőlős is known for a unique find of part of the skeletons of two individuals. The skull of one of them was probably used as a vessel for water. Groups of the first predecessor of man probably lived in this area. Their way of maintaining fire was particular. They covered embers with grease bones and then with earth, which was quite an efficient way to keep them alive.

Younger finds from the Middle Palaeolithic period (100-40 thousand years ago) were found near Tata, Tatabánya, and the Szelim cave, while objects from the Younger Palaeolithic were dug out at the meander of the Danube between Esztergom and Pilismarót. Man also lived near the Danube on selected elevated places and protected against the floods in the Neolithic era. The excavations point to settled man rather than nomadic people. What is called "an earthen castle" surrounded by moats is a Neolithic settlement found near Esztergom. People originally used the local resources, produced tools and bartered their products. Wandering food gatherers, hunters and fishermen gradually settled down. They grew crops and kept domesticated animals. In the area of the Gerecse Mountains tools made of stone, bone, copper, and bronze were found. Remains of a smith's workshop from the Bronze Age were even found near the village of Szomor. Tools used for controlling horses of the same period were conserved in the Hungarian part of the Danube region. This fact confirms the assumption that the people already knew how to tame and utilize horses. Use of horses facilitated travelling longer distances, which in turn opened the way to barter trade with larger region. They came to the Danube region from the northern coast of the Black Sea. They were followed by the Celts, which occupied their former territory. The Celts had an advanced culture and brought it with them to the Danube area in the 5th - 4th century BC. They settled on the whole of the Hungarian Lowland up to the gorge of the Danube meander as proved by the archaeological finds and monuments, such as one found near Pilismaróty. The Celts also founded a settlement called **Arrabona** on the site of today's town of Győr. Its name survived in the German name of Győr and to the river Raab.

The Celtic settlement meant progress connected with several innovations, including use of the potter's wheel, production of tools, weapons, use of iron and later introduction of money. Celts were also gradually occupying higher situated localities, which provided an efficient protection. Such was the castle hill in Esztergom, which became the centre of craft production and the seat of administration. In the loess rock face near Esztergom weapons and tools of Celtic origin were found.

Construction of fortifications proves that expansion of Dacians from their territory in Transylvania reached the meander of the Danube. The Dacian kingdom entered into an argument with the Roman Empire in 60 BC. The arrival of the **Romans** in the Danube area was probably motivated by the wish to push the Dacians out of the region. The Roman Empire expanded to the Danube area from the south in the first decades of our era. Occupation of this territory started during the reign of the Emperor Augustus and was completed after long fighting during the reign of Tiberius. The original Illyrian and Celtic population mostly stayed in their territories and submitted to the new rulers. The whole territory was a part of the province of Pannonia. The Emperor Marcus Aurelius called "the Philosopher Emperor" led the fighting against the Quadi and Markomans personally. He wrote part of his philosophical reflections, which were published in the majority of the world languages in his seat near Esztergom. In his memoirs he mentions for instance, the river Hron, near which he was writing.

The Romans built a chain of fortifications along the Danube called **Limes Romanus** in order to protect their territory against the Barbarian tribes penetrating from the north. The best known forts in the territory of today's Hungary were Arrabona (Győr) and Brigetio (Szőny). Then there were the camps Ad Flexum (Magyaróvár), Quadrata (Barátföld), Ad Status (Gönyű), Ad Mures (Ács), Azaum (Alásfüzitő), Crumerum (Nyergesújfalu), and Solva (Esztergom). Remains of the Roman fort, situated on the highest point of the town, Káptalan domb (the Capitol Hill) were found in Győr. It was the seat of legionaries of Emperor Trajan, who controlled this part of the northern frontier of Empire. In the 4th century the Romans, compelled by the ever more frequent attacks of the Barbarians, retreated to the south and left Pannonia to the coming waves of Germans, Huns, and Avars. The symbol of the end of the Roman rule in this area

was the death of the Emperor Valentinian on November 17th 375 in Brigetio. He died during peace negotiations with the Quadi.

Several monuments survive from the Roman period. For example, the Romans extracted coal from the 3rd century AD in places, where the layers were on the surface and used it in more than forty plants for smelting bronze and iron and for the production of glass and pottery. Archaeologists arrived at this conclusion, when they researched the sediments at the bottom of discovered remains of these plants. Especially the excavations carried out near the settlement of Tokod brought numerous proofs. Remnants of pig bones and carbonated corn confirming existence of an advanced economy were also found. The building activity of the Romans is proved by parts of buildings, water mains roads, and mines. A smith's forge was found in the village of Bajna.

The **Avars**, who came from Central Asia, were the successors of Romans in creating a longer lasting rule in the Hungarian part of the Danube area. Their decay started after the defeat they suffered in battle with the Frankish King Charles the Great in 795, and in the 9th century Pannonia was already completely controlled by the Franks. Also the raids of the Great Moravian Prince Svätopluk, who attacked the territory from the north and also plundered Győr, influenced the development of the area. The campaigns of the Great Moravian troops fostered the settlement of the territory by Slavs, who left their traces here in the form of place names.

The Magyar tribes arrived at the Danube area from the Tisza basin around 900. Led by Árpád they found the Franks fighting against the Great Moravian soldiers and they alternately supported both parties. The Danube area was an important place for the beginning of Magyar settlement. Prince Gejza chose Esztergom as his residence and figuratively Hungarian civilization was born in the area of the Pilis Mountains. In the time of King Stephen (1000-1038) Esztergom was a luxurious

---

Right: The window of Visegrád Castle

royal seat of European significance. The king's wife Gizela of Bavaria brought here priests and craftsmen, who helped to found a town around the royal seat. Belo I ascended the throne in 1060 and with the help of his relatives in Poland rid the country of German influence. Though the court stayed in Esztergom, Belo I spent most of his time in Dömös, where he also founded a monastery. Dömös, lying between Visegrád and Esztergom was important for him as the salient point for hunting in the Pilis Mountains. A royal curia existed there as early as the 11th century.

After fighting, which affected the life of population as a result of depopulation in the 11th and 12th century the territory was ever more frequently repopulated by Germans. Especially during the reign of the **Árpáds** many immigrants arrived in the country, among them craftsmen and merchants. New churches and palaces were built, masonry and stone extraction revived. Marble, or better said hard limestone extracted in the area, became an important building material also used for buildings in Esztergom, Visegrád, Buda, even Vienna and Kraków. Historical records prove that the boats of King Emerich transported marble to many Danubian towns in the 13th century.

The marble of the Danube area

The oldest marble quarries in the Danube area are known from the period of King Ladislav's rule in the 11th century. Their position near the Danube was decisive for their development, as marble was transported on this important water communication. Most of the stone was hauled to Óbuda and Visegrád for the construction of the royal palaces. Marble extracted near the village Piszka was used in the Middle Ages for tombstones. In the Renaissance period it enjoyed popularity among builders not only in the Kingdom of Hungary, but also in the surrounding countries (for instance the Jagelonian chapel in Kraków is made of it).

In this period, Esztergom experienced the most active building in the Hungarian part of the Danube. The first public bath

making use of the local hot springs was opened in Hungary precisely in Esztergom. They were built following the Byzantine design. It was destroyed by the Tartars in the 13th century and reconstructed by the Turks later. The greatest building work of King Belo III was that of the royal palace, remains of which along with the Basilica are the greatest attraction of the town. The royal court of Esztergom also hosted the German Emperor I Barbarossa, who came on a boat leading the Crusader Army in 1189.

The **Tartar raids** caused enormous damage to the territory of the Hungarian part of the Danube region in the 13th century. After they left, the castles in Moson and Magyaróvár were occupied by Přemysl Otakar II, King of Bohemia, while that of Moson was completely destroyed. Craftsmen specializing in construction of castles and forts were invited to the country in the same century. They helped to build the upper and lower castles in Visegrád and the joint fortification of both of them. **Visegrád** became the capital as its position and environs were the best for this task.

The Visegrád meeting

The 1335 meeting, in which besides other guests, King Kazimír III of Poland met John of Luxembourg, King of Bohemia with the aim of seeking possibilities for creating a new trade road, which would avoid Vienna, was an interesting one. The chronicler Thuróczy recorded the occasion and noted that the Czech king with his suite consumed daily 2,500 loaves of bread while the Polish king with his companions consumed 1,500 loaves of bread.

King Louis I the Great (1342-1382) moved his residence from Visegrád to Buda, but the town maintained its importance. The King kept the beautiful castle of Visegrád for his summer residence and foreign guests were accommodated there because the woods surrounding the castle offered excellent hunting. The Hungarian royal crown remained in Visegrád even after Louis moved to Buda and his death, a fact proving the importance of Visegrád. The

Left: The fort in Komárom

Polish crown was also deposited there after King Louis I was crowned King of Poland in Kraków in 1370. King Matthias I Corvinus (1458-1490) maintained the glory of Visegrád during his reign. He reconstructed both the upper and lower castles. For this aim German craftsmen from Transylvania were invited. The reconstruction was in the Gothic and Renaissance styles. The king also cared for the town and its modernization. He moved here 100 German families, which changed the demographic structure of the town.

In the 16th century after the battle at Mohács and the following disintegration of the country into three parts, the area of the Pilis mountains found itself on the border between the Habsburg and Turkish Empires. Great part of population fled from the Turks and many plundered and burnt villages disappeared. Especially the year 1529 was hard for the people. Turkish troops advancing to Vienna sacked the Danube region and many medieval villages from Győr eastward were victims of this campaign. Their population either fled or were taken into slavery.

The town of Győr, for example, was burnt down and its new Turkish name Janik Kala (The Burnt Town) best illustrates its destiny. The expanding Turks repeatedly tried to conquer Esztergom Castle and finally succeeded in 1543. The castle became an important advanced fortification of the Turkish rule for the next long 140 years. The Turks used the castle as the seat of their administrative unit and built a pontoon bridge between Esztergom and Štúrovo.

The Turks residing in the eastern part of the Hungarian Danube region were defeated on October 12th 1683 by Jan Sobieski, the King of Poland. His troops crossed the Danube and conquered Esztergom Castle on October 27th. But the Turks were not giving in and tried to re-conquer the lost territory. Only the battle of August 16th 1685 at Tát meant the final defeat of the Turks and the victory of the Christian army meant the complete liberation of Esztergom.

The greatest problem of the region at the turn of the 17th and 18th centuries after the long rule of the Turks, several rebellions of the Estates and repeated plague epidemics, was depopulation and the end of many villages. Population number started to increase only after 1711 by re-settling the abandoned territory. The majority of the immigrants were Germans and Slovaks. The Germans brought here their mining technology and new methods of cattle, sheep and horse raising. They built water mills and production of ceramics was introduced in Tata. Emperor Joseph II's reforms brought more profound changes to the areas of Pilis and Visegrád than to the rest of the country. The Church and monasteries owned most of the estates in this region. Emperor's resolution ordered confiscation of this property, which was used for construction of village schools and parsonages and obligatory school attendance was enacted. The orders nursing the sick and educating children were exceptions to the reform.

In the 19th century the impulses of development determined by the onset of a new historical stage for the Kingdom of Hungary were becoming ever more obvious. The biggest contemporary structure in the country was started in Esztergom in 1822. It was the basilica. Győr was also one of the towns that developed rapidly to become soon a prosperous and busy town. It was here that the appeals concerning recognition of the Hungarian language as one of the official languages of the Kingdom were proposed. Komárom also played an important role in the revolutionary year 1848. Even after the uprising of the Hungarian revolutionaries was defeated at the battle of Világos, Komárom did not give up and continued the fighting. The patriots led by General Klapka kept their position for another month and a half. The capitulation was signed only in September in Herkálypuszta near Komárom. In spite of the lost fight and thanks to the persistence of the patriots, Komárom became the symbol of the struggle for emancipation.

The capitalism found quite acceptable conditions in this territory with the last traces of feudal prejudice after the 1848 revolution finished. The area we are talking about became one of the most advanced in what is now Hungary. As much as 15 per cent of population was working in industry, in Győr it was even 46 per cent, and the town ranked among the ten most industrialized towns in the country.

Importance of agriculture also increased in the region in the 19th century. More arable land was obtained by draining and fertilization. Horse breeding was one of the popular and widely spread branches of farming. The most successful horse breeding station was in Bábolna, where the horses were bred for army from 1807 and became the symbol of the village.

Transport communication of the area with the rest of the county improved a lot by construction of railway, for instance of that from Esztergom to Buda and in 1895 the bridge over the Danube between Esztergom and Štúrovo, or **The Maria Valeria Bridge** was finished. It was the second most important bridge after Elisabeth's Bridge at Komárom was finished in 1892, which helped to re-

move the barrier effect of the Danube in the south-north direction.

The transport routes in the past

Various trade roads have crossed the Danube region since the time immemorial. They mostly ran on the right bank of the Danube in the direction of Bicske-Komárom and Esztergom-Komárom. Komárom was an important port on the Danube and the main junction of corn trade. Esztergom was also important as it was the place where merchants from various countries met. Navigation on the Danube existed practically from the Roman era and it developed further during the reign of the Árpáds and Matthias Corvinus who especially loved boats and navigation on rivers. His big boat looking like a castle was anchored at Komárom. When going up the stream the boats were driven by rowers and there were pulling mechanisms on the banks as well. The first steamer appeared on the Danube on October 6th 1818. The trip from Pest to Komárom took 71 hours. The regular navigation started only on February 1st 1831. The development of the road transport was slower. Also the roads with milestones, resting areas and post stations existed from the Roman times. One of them lead from what is today Budapest to Albertfalva, through Bicske and Tata to Brigetio. Today's roads were partly built on the original Roman roads. They exist on the routes Budapest-Esztergom and Esztergom-Székesfehérvár. The route Budapest-Dorog-Dunaalmás was used by the main post service to Győr and Vienna. The task of this service was not only to carry the post but also personal transport, which started its regular operation between Buda and Vienna in 1752. Irregular transport existed even earlier.

Economic decay followed the end of the First World War. The Monarchy disintegrated and it meant that the factories were cut off the resources, markets disappeared and military production was in depression. The Paris peace settlement ordered separation of several villages north

Left: The Maria Valeria Bridge
Right: Esztergom

of the Danube and more territorial losses followed he Second World war when Jarovce, Rusovce and Čunovo were adjudicated to Czechoslovakia. Consequently the traditional road to Vienna was cut and a new road in through Hegyeshalom had to be built. In Hungary as in neighbouring Czechoslovakia a communist regime was established after the war. The events of October 23rd 1956 in Budapest culminated in an uprising and Győr became the second centre of the revolution. The army of the then ruling communist regime, for example, shot at a popular assembly held in Mosonmagyaróvár and killed more than hundred people. The events of autumn 1956 ended with the arrival of Soviet troops in November 1956.

The life in the region after 1956 had to adapt to the centralized political system under the ideological pressure of the former Soviet Union. The frontier regime became extremely strict and the boundary areas isolated. Mosonmagayróvár, which immediately borders on Austria was especially stricken by the new situation. Following the growth of the 1960s and 1970s recession in heavy industry manifested in the eighties. Its brought decline of the mining and other traditional industries in the environs of Tata. After the fall of Iron Curtain in 1989 the first free parliamentary elections held after the long 43 years in spring 1990 created the premises necessary for the origin of democracy, private enterprise and local and regional self-government. Opening of the frontiers and development of business activities resulted in intensified building and construction in the region, communication improved and services and travel industries received the needed impulse. The origin of small and medium sized private companies distinctly improved availability of services connected with tourism. The Danube region joined the most important developing areas of Hungary and opened its gate to tourists above all from Austria and Slovakia.

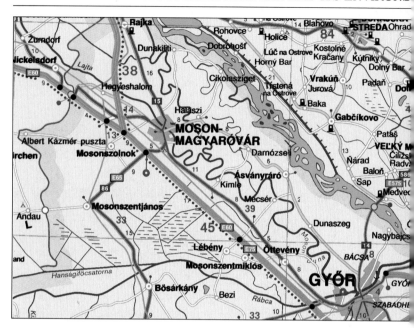

MOSONMAGYARÓVÁR
AND ITS ENVIRONS

The region is part of the Small Hungarian Lowland. It is filled by the Moson plain and the upper north-western half of the Danube's Szigetköz island. The main stream of the Danube and the frontier with the Slovak Republic limits it in the north and north-east. The southern and south-western limits of the territory reach the line of the motorway from Győr to Vienna. The north-western border of our territory coincides with the frontier with Austria. The south-eastern limit of Mosonmagyaróvár and its environs is the natural border, which divides Szigetköz into upper and lower parts between the villages of Hédervár and Ásványráró. The territory is administered by the County of Győr-Moson-Sopron and occupies its north-western part.

MOSONMAGYARÓVÁR (population 29,900) lies in the northern part of the

Small Hungarian Lowland. It is situated on one of the main European railway tracks from Paris to Istanbul. The road from Budapest heading to Vienna and Bratislava crosses the town. Mosonmagyaróvár is 34 km from Bratislava, 39 km from Győr and 54 km from Vienna. The river Lajta which originates in Lower Austria at an altitude above sea level of 1,264 m flows through the town, it forks into three branches and flows into the Moson branch of the Danube. From its total length of 182 km only a short lower part of its stream flows in Hungary. The Moson branch of the Danube separates from the main stream of this river near Čunovo on the Slovak territory and flows back to the Danube after 125 km creating the inland island of Szigetköz.

The territory of the town was always a crossroads of important routes between the north and the south, and the west-east. In time of the Roman Empire it was part of the defensive line Limes Romanus reaching from Vindobona (today Vienna) to Aquincum (now Óbuda). It included the fort of Ad Flexum on the territory of the modern Mosonmagyaróvár. This locality

Right: Moson Castle

was especially important in the past because on its southern side a swampy area spread through which only one road heading to north led. This road was part of the famous Amber road connecting the Baltic Sea with the Mediterranean area.

The first man lived here about 5,000 BC. However, proofs of settlement are only from the time of the first cultures: the Celtic and Illyrian. The Roman Emperor Augustus annexed this territory to the Roman Empire as a part of the province of Pannonia. The first camp originated on the site of today's Mosonmagyaróvár. The need to found this camp was caused by the excessive distance between the forts of Carnuntum (now Petronell-Carnuntum in Austria) and Arrabona (today Győr). The forts could not control the comparatively large and swampy terrain covered by thick woods. The task of the fort Ad Flexum was to prevent penetration of the tribes coming from the north. This fort was also a trading centre as the goods were bartered between the Romans and the Barbarian tribe north of the Danube. The Danube was also used as a transport road, as prove the remains of a port found near the point where the Lajta flows into the Moson branch of the Danube in 1970. During the rule of the Roman Emperor Hadrian (76-138) the situation along the Limes Romanus changed. The Emperor visited Pannonia in 124 and proposed construction of a paved road network in this area. Instead of wooden and earthen forts ones made of stone had to be built. Settlements sprang up around the forts and trade and craft activities became more intensive.

Between the years 169-171 the Germanic tribes living on the left bank of the Danube, who possessed a fairly powerful army, started toward the borders. They achieved one of their greatest successes precisely near the fort of Ad Flexum. One of the most frequently attacked camps on the border was destroyed in these years. It is probable, that the contiguous settlement was also destroyed and its population fled further inland. Restoration of Limes Romanus started during the rule of Emperor Caracalla (211-217). Ad Flexum was also restored. The crafts, especially pottery and metal works, were flourishing

again. The houses were mostly built from unburnt clay bricks and stones. Bronze jewellery, utility objects and kitchenware are the finds from this period. The situation calmed down and protection of the frontier was again secured. It is estimated that about three to four thousand people lived there in the 4th century. However, the attacks of the Huns were increasing and they gradually ruined the Roman administration of this territory after the Emperor Valentinian died in 375. Part of Pannonia fell into their hands. The importance of Ad Flexum as a guard place diminished. Only a part of the settlement survived. The territory was annexed to the Frankish Empire when the Frankish King Charles I the Great ended the rule of the Avars.

The territory between the Danube and the swampy Hanság (region lying southwest of the town in the direction to the modern Austrian border) became important again in time of King Stephen I. This best known King of Hungary promoted Moson to one of his strategic towns, had the seat of a county established there and built a royal castle with the aim of protecting the Hungarian frontier along the Lajta river.

The castle of Moson and the crusaders

The chroniclers describe Moson as one of the strongest castles and the busiest trade towns of the time. The castle fulfilled an important task in time of crusades in 1096. King of Hungary Koloman I did not allow the crusade troops led by Emerich Leiningen consisting of 30,000 men enter the castle as he had bad experience with them. The crusaders besieged the castle

Left: Magyaróvár in the 19th century

and almost occupied it. The defenders of the two contiguous castles, those of Moson and Óvár, united and drove the crusaders out to the swamps of Hanság.

In time of the Árpáds the medieval town lying nearby also developed. Moson became the political, military, and economic centre of a wide area. The original Roman roads were used for transport. The settlement consisted of stone houses, a market place and a church built of stone. The castle, which resisted the Tartar raids was conquered and destroyed by King Přemysl Otakar II of Bohemia. The kings of Hungary did not feel any need to restore the castle and consequently the centre moved to Óvár Castle. From then Óvár Castle developed. The first settlement existed on the territory of Magyaróvár, after the destruction of the Moson Castle the inhabitants of Moson also moved here. Moson had houses with fixed foundations already in the 14th century. In the 15th century there were several storied houses made from unburnt bricks on the main

street. It was also the time when the existing ground plan of the town originated. The townlet had a busy trade and there existed several mills. It obtained the privilege of a free royal borough in 1354. The castle and its estate was acquired by noble families after 1364. When it became again a royal property, King Louis II donated it to his wife Maria and from then it was a part of the Habsburg property. After the battle of Mohács the town and its castle became an advanced bastion of the Austrian defence.

The life in the 16th century town was extremely influenced by Martin Luther's reform. The majority of its citizens adopted Luther's Reformed religion by 1546. Gál Huszár founded the first school in the town in 1555 and three years later he opened the first printing plant where religious books were printed. As he was pursued he moved to Košice and later to Debrecen. In the meantime the Catholics won back the reformed church and the reformed confession was forbidden in 1672. The Turks burnt down the town and the castle on their way to Vienna in 1529. Many precious buildings and the munici-

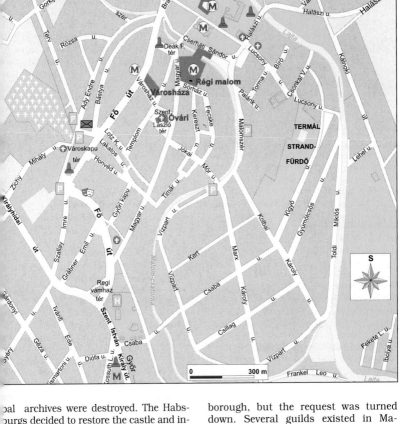

pal archives were destroyed. The Habsburgs decided to restore the castle and invited Italian craftsmen into the country for that end. After Győr was conquered, Moson with its castle was better fortified. The retreating Turks damaged the castle and town again in 1683. The castle lost its military importance in the early 18th century and its military equipment was moved to Bratislava in 1712. Magyaróvár fought incessantly for more independence from the royal power from the end of the 17th century. Especially the Mayor András Kehrling was the one who was brave enough to resist the will of the ruler. The town was struck by a cholera epidemic in 1713 and it was also the year when the town asked for the privilege of free royal

borough, but the request was turned down. Several guilds existed in Magyaróvár, such as the tailors, tanners, etc., and in 1760's the town had more than 400 craftsmen registered. The cattle and corn markets of Magyaróvár were also famous. The first grammar school was opened here in 1739. The Empress Maria Theresa donated the estate of Magyaróvár to her daughter Maria Christina. In 1818 her husband Kazimír Albert founded and economic university in the town.

Moson and Magyaróvár successfully developed in the later half of the 19th century. Regular railway transport between the village of Hegyeshalom and Győr was opened and the town also got a new railway station on that occasion. The new

house of county administration was finished in 1893, and the first municipal newspaper started to appear the same year. Construction of the largest military plant in the Austro-Hungarian Monarchy was started in 1913. The plant was dismantled and converted to a factory producing fertilisers and synthetic fibres (the first in Hungary) after the First World War finished. The Moson county disappeared as an administrative unit in the consequence of the Treaty of Trianon, because two thirds of it were adjudicated to Austria. Moson and Magyaróvár united into one town in July 1939. Its population was 17 thousand people, out of which 83 % were Hungarians, 13 % Germans and 3 % Jews. The Second World War did not affect the town too much, but the destroyed bridges and railway made the town rather inaccessible. The greater part of the German population was displaced in 1946 and the town lost many of its educated and rich citizens.

Today Mosonmagyaróvár offers many interesting landmarks. Its centre has partially preserved its medieval character with traces of **fortifications**, and 42 of its houses are included among the protected cultural monuments. The former market place, now the Deák Ferenc tér square opens from the Fő utca or the main road leading to Bratislava. One of the most important monuments of the town stands on the square: the **castle** with an irregular rectangular ground plan. A brick bridge leads to its gate over the Malom-csatorna canal built on the site of the former drawbridge. The gate is rather a small tunnel

10 m long. The bust of the Austrian poet Nicolaus Lenau who lived in house No. of Fő utca street in the years 1822-1823 stands in the castle courtyard. The castle now houses a school. There are monuments to the victims of both wars, including those of the 1956 revolution, standing in front of the castle. The English **park** founded in the early 19th century, a protected area is behind the castle going northward and crossing the river Lajta. East of the castle is the Lucsony street with its romantic single-floor **Baroque houses**. On the upper part of the street is the **chapel of St. Anna** from 1714, which commemorates the plague epidemic. The sacred monuments of the town include two Roman Catholic churches: the **church of St. Mary and Gotthard** and **St. John Nepomuk's Church.**

The town centre was protected by walls until 1809. An interesting Baroque building from the 18th century is the **Draskovich-Hegedüs house** on Fő utca No. 7. On the Ferenc Deák square is the U-shaped Habsburg **manor house**. It was built in the 18th century in the Baroque taste. Its most beautiful part is the arcaded courtyard. The guests to this manor house included Count István Széchényi and Lajos Kossuth. The Baroque **statue of St. John Nepomuk** stands on Ferenc Deák square. The statue situated on a tall obelisk is surrounded by three figures. The **County House** on Fő utca street was built in 1892 in the Neo-Renaissance taste. Since the County Moson was abolished in 1924, it has served as the town hall. The building of the Piarist grammar school from 1793 stands opposite. It adjoins the Neo-Classical building of the original town hall from 1827. **House No 19** on Fő utca is the oldest building in the town. Research carried out in 1975 showed, that the wing of the house turned to the street was built in the second half of the 15th century. The house was enlarged in the 16th century, rebuilt in the 1730's and restored again in 1885 in eclectic style. Since 1982 it has sheltered the **Hanság Museum**. Hanság is the area lying south-west of Szigetköz. The Museum contains artistic works of the region and also collections of the natural history

Left: Near the canal in Mosonmagyaróvár
Right: A shop on the main street

thnography and history of the area. Visitors are attracted here by the **thermal swimming pools.**

The thermal swimming pools

The well of hot water yielding 1,800 litres per minute is a sufficient source to feed the local swimming pool area. The water is extracted from a depth of 2 thousand metres. Its temperature is 75 degrees Celsius; it contains carbon, chlorine and sulphur, a composition that entitles it to be classified as medicinal water. It cures the locomotion apparatus, rheumatics, and respiratory problems. Drinking of this water is recommended to patients with digestive disorders. The total area of swimming pools is 3 hectares. It includes four pools for adult, 1 for children, and 1 therapeutic pool. They operate the whole year round and the rate of visitors is more than 250 people a year, while the daily rate is about 3.5 thousand people.

The water areas in the immediate vicinity of the town are also of interest to visitors. They are the two branches of the Lajta river, the Moson branch of the Danube, and the lake, which originated after extraction of gravel. But their environs are still not prepared for a greater number of tourists. Horse riding offered by the **riding school** in the town, is a favourite pastime. The largest and oldest park of the town is **Wittman's Park**, which has been a protected area since 1990. The local people and visitors always like to go to the banks of the Moson branch of the Danube covered by a narrow belt of floodplain forest on the eastern edge of the town called Sziget-erdő (the Island Wood). It provides charming nooks ideal for outdoor activities or simple relaxation.

RAJKA (population 2,700) lies on the frontier with the Slovak Republic, 12 km away from Mosonmagyaróvár and 20 km from the centre of Bratislava. International railway and road communications from the Balkans to Western Europe cross this settlement.

The first written reference to Rajka is from the 13th century. Its first inhabitants settled here on the higher bank of one of

the Danube branches. They sustained themselves by fishing and catching crayfish. This was the origin of its name Rákfalva (rák, rak Hungarian and Slovak for crayfish) or Rača dedina in Slovak and Krebsdorf in German. Crayfish is also depicted in the coat of branches of Rajka. Its population dramatically declined in the time of the Tartar raids and then German colonists repopulated it. They called the village Raggen or Ragendorf.

King Louis I the Great donated the lands on the site of the existing village to Herman Schwarz in the later half of the 14th century. Schwarz became the first known inhabitant of *Villa Rajk* as one of the documents calls it. The village possessed market privilege from the Middle Ages. The retreating Turkish troop burnt the village but as the legend says they were punished as they got drowned in the surrounding swamps. The village was comparatively quickly restored and it was mentioned as a little yeoman town in 1721. Two rich noble families, the Zichys and Hennins built manor houses and founded orchards in the restored village. Fruit cultivated near Rajka was sold at

the markets in Bratislava, Magyaróvár and Burgenland in Austria. The population of the townlet was a mixture of nationalities, mostly Germans, Hungarians and Croatians.

Rajka became a district town in 1867. Noblemen, craftsmen and merchants lived there and cared for the prosperity of their town. But the best time of Rajka's history was interrupted by the First World War and its consequences. The origin of Czechoslovakia within newly drawn frontiers meant that Rajka became a peripheral settlement with limited opportunities. It remained in Hungary as it lies on a strategic spot near the place where the Moson branch separates from the Danube's main stream. After the Second World War 864 German citizens were moved out and Hungarian families which lived until then in Žitný ostrov in Slovakia replaced them.

The Roman Catholic **church of St. Martin** is the most important sacred monument of Rajka. It was built in the Gothic

style from the remains of the material of the former Roman guard tower around 1350. Its interior was adapted in the Baroque style in the 18th century. The Baroque **Calvary** from the 18th century is also an important cultural monument. **Stahrenberg's house**, no the Evangelical parsonage is from the 17th century. The centre of the spiritual life of the local Evangelical congregation is the church built in the late 18th century. Another remarkable building, the **manor house of the Zichy family** was built in the Late Baroque style in the same period.

Ancestors of the outstanding composer Ferenc Liszt lived in Rajka. His great grandfather Sebestyén Liszt, a poor villager, and grandfather of the composer Ádám Liszt, were born in this village. The painter Gábor Modrovich was also one of the famous natives of Rajka. The administrative territory of Rajka also includes a secluded homestead called Zichypuszta situated about 2 kilometres from the centre of Rajka in the south-western direction. It is separated from Rajka by the motorway. The village has lost its position on the periphery of the country. Just the op-

Left: The manor house in Rajka
Right: The church in Rajka

osite occurred after the frontiers were opened and the contacts improved, it acquired an excellent position for development of cross-frontier co-operation in different areas of social life. The closeness of the capital of Slovakia, Bratislava also plays an important role in various cultural or business activities of the local population.

BEZENYE (population 1,600) spreads on both side of the road from Mosonmagyaróvár to Bratislava. It is 9 km away from Mosonmagyaróvár and 6 km from the state frontier with Slovakia. It is limited by the Moson branch of the Danube from the one side and the Lajta's canal from the other. The first inhabitants of the territory were Germanic tribes. Archaeological finds prove their presence. In the locality Pap-rét objects of Longobard origin with inscriptions in Old German were found. Remarkable finds are exhibited in Hanság Museum in Mosonmagyaróvár. After the Magyar tribes settled here the place became a guard point. The village was sacked by the Turkish troops. Depopulation provoked the need to resettle the locality. Croatians from Dalmatia and Germans came and imprinted a new ethnic character on this part of the Danube region. Germans called the village Palersdorf and the Croatians used the name Bizonja. The origin of the name Bezenye however, derives, as some sources assert, from the Slav word for the European elder (*Sambucus nigra*), "baza". The Germans dealt with production of saltpeter. At the beginning of the 20th century about 880 Croatians, 300 Germans and more than 100 Hungarians lived in the villages. After the Second World War the majority of poorer Germans were displaced to Germany. They were replaced by several families from the surrounding Szigetköz villages and Hungarian families displaced from Slovakia.

The village has got a little **museum** with an exposition about the life of the local population in the past. It was established in the oldest house of the village on Ady Endre street No. 11. In the western part of the village is the Roman Catholic **church of the Blessed Virgin Mary** from 1812, which was enlarged, in the late 19th

century. The village has a Croatian self-administration, which is trying to maintain the ancestral traditions of the minority.

HEGYESHALOM (population 3,550) lies on the Moson plain north-west of Mosonmagyaróvár. It is the largest railway and road border crossing from Hungary to Austria. The village acquired this position of border crossing as a result of border changes when the villages of Čunovo, Rusovce, and Jarovce were adjudicated to Czechoslovakia after the Second World War. At the present moment it represents an open gate for the Hungarians to Western Europe. An access road to the motorway of Budapest-Vienna is now under construction near the village in the direction of Rajka.

The village was first mentioned in the donation document from 1197. The territory of the village was always a transit area. The Romans crossed it and they were followed by various ethnic groups in the time when the nations were moving. The destiny of Hegyeshalom was closely connected with that of castles in Bratislava, Moson and in Magyaróvár. The local population lived through the most cruellest times during the Turkish raids in the 17th century.

German population prevailed in the village in the 15th and 16th centuries, but later as the records show, the number of craftsmen with Hungarian surnames was increasing. Imperial troops deprived the local Evangelical congregation of its church in 1673. This situation lasted more than hundred years before the religious tolerance was restored. A new wave of German immigration started at the beginning of the 18th century. Then the Hungarian families represented only around 2 %.

The villagers were prevailingly farmers. Some of them also practised crafts and in time of Maria Theresa's rule many found jobs in processing of saltpeter and production of gun powder. After the First World War Hegyeshalom became a frontier village with a customs office and bank. The Second World War brought it enormous damage, especially in March 1945 when American air force bombarded the village. After the war the ethnic composition of the village changed by the forced displacement of 569 Germans in 1946. Hegyeshalom is now a developing frontier village as its transport function and situation near the most important road communication of Hungary allows.

As far as the cultural and historic monuments of the village are concerned, the most interesting is the Roman Catholic **church of the Virgin Mary.** It stands on a small hill of the Fő street on the site of what used to be a cemetery. It was built in the Romanesque style in the 11th -12th centuries. In the 13th century a Gothic sanctuary was added to it. Medieval frescoes were discovered in the tower. The western part of the church is in the Baroque taste from the 18th century. Above the side entrance a statue of Jesus and in the interior paintings from the 15th century are of interest. The Baroque altar, pulpit and pews are from the 18th century. There is also an **Evangelical church** in the village. Károly Bendl built it in the Neo-Classical style in 1850. The altar contains a remarkable painting Jesus and St. Peter by F. C. Stetter. Pleasant natural setting of the village attracts fishermen

and fans of water sports. In the territory of the village is a large artificial lake (7 hectares), which originated after extraction of gravel. A special feature of the local climate is its windiness. In fact the locality is the most windy one of Hungary with prevailing north-westerly winds. The settlement of Márialiget, closed between two branches of motorway from Budapest to Vienna and Bratislava, also belongs to Hegyeshalom.

LEVÉL (population 1,650) also lies in the north-western corner of Hungary 7 km east of the Austrian border and 5 km west of Mosonmagyaróvár. The first written reference to this village is from 1410 when it was mentioned as *Kalt hostan* from which the name *Kaltenstein* developed. The origin of the Hungarian name is probably connected with the word lövő or lövér, which means a shooter. The motif of a shooter is connected with protectors of frontiers in this area. The first inhabitants of the villages were messengers and hauliers of the Óvár Castle. After the rule of the Turks finished in the region the settlements were resettled by Germans from Württemberg. The Germans then acquired the dominant position in the village and the German name of the village; Kaltenstein is used even today. The people were mostly farmers and concentrated on bee keeping, sheep and cattle raising and viticulture. The village flourished especially by the end of the 19th century. By the incentive of the teacher at the Agricultural academy in Magyaróvár, Imre Újhelyi, the Siementha breed of cattle was introduced in the local farms and the village became famous for its breeding. The chronicles also recorded the cultural and social life of the village at the turn of the 19th and 20th centuries During the Second World War, the German and Russian troops damaged the village. The nationality structure of the village completely changed after the war, as 1,500 Germans, which accounted for 91 % of the total village population were displaced. They were replaced by the Hungarians from Transylvania and southern Slovakia. The Evangelical priest Lajos Gulyás became the local hero, active member of the revolutionary events of

Left: Dunakiliti
Right: The branch of the Danube

1956. He is buried in the local cemetery and a **tablet** in the village commemorates his heroic deeds.

The surviving **connected and closed rows of houses** on the main street; remains of German architecture are interesting. The village has the Roman Catholic **church of St. Ladislav** from the 17th century. The Evangelical **church** built in 1789 is much younger.

DUNAKILITI (population 1,750) is the westernmost village of the Szigetköz island. It lies on its north-western edge in a very dissected territory of the Danube branches, today marked by anthropic effects. The environs of the village with woods, bays and river branches are very interesting. The relief of the landscape bears traces of the preparation works connected with the larger project of the water works Gabčikovo-Nagymaros, which should have included also our area. Especially in the north of the village are the remains of unfinished earth works the aim of which was construction of the Dunakiliti reservoir.

The first written reference to the village is from 1165. There are several theories about the origin of its name. It allegedly derives from the family name *Kelud,* the name of the Bratislava noble *Kilit* or the name of the patron saint of the first chapel, St. Kelos Kilit. The key position of the village on the Danube could have been also decisive as kilit means key in Turkish. Germans resettled the area after the Turks left. The village was then called Frauendorf (The Village of Women). Dunakiliti was administered by the County of Bratislava until 1883 and it was also referred to as Moson-Kiliti.

The Danube had dozens of branches here in the past. They were constantly moving and changing their channels. Maybe also the present main street of the town was water in the past. Finds of fishing tools in the wells of the houses, comparatively far from today's river branches prove it. The local population lived on fishing, logging and burning charcoal, which was why the forests disappeared from the area. The original activities of the villagers are symbolized by the coat of branches of Dunakiliti, which bears the water of the

Danube, a deer as symbol of hunting, an oak tree as symbol of logging and a cross as symbol of Catholic religion. The most important monument of the village is the manor house originally owned by the Bátthyány-Strattmann family. This family had a hunting **manor house** with park built in the village in the years 1858-1862. But the villagers destroyed the original furniture, including the library of the manor house after the Second World War. The building serves now as school. The village has the Roman Catholic **church of Exaltation of the Holy Cross** built in 1910. The settlement Tejfalusziget, about 2 km east of Dunakiliti is also part of the village.

The village is now one of the main centres of recreation in Szigetköz. It is the salient point to the Doborgaz-sziget island, which is often referred to as a tourist oasis on the Danube. Nice woods survive along the whole stream of the Danube. They stretch up to the village of Dunaremete and provide the ideal environment for strolling or bicycle riding. It is protected for its rare species composition. The place is most beautiful in spring when the willow, ash, elm, and oak trees are in flower.

FEKETEERDŐ (population 350) is a small village on the border of the Moson plain and Szigetköz island. It lies near (5 km) from the centre of the Mosonmagyaróvár area. The administrative territory of this village is limited by the meanders of the Moson branch of the Danube on three of its sides. The surrounding floodplain forests full of wild life are protected areas.

The first written reference to the village is from 1274 and the second is from 1323. The name of this village was similar to that used now: *Fekete Erdeu, Feketewedeu* (Black Forest). The name was not accidental as the chronicles mention the fact that the village was hidden in thick woods. Thanks to it the local population could hide and survive the Turkish and Tartar raids. Feketeerdő persevered even the worst period, which was when the Turks retreated in 1683 when almost all villages in the area were sacked and burnt down. But the real disaster came only after, in 1730. It was a plague epidemic. The village remained without population.

Its isolation was advantageous in war time but in terms of development and trade it was a clear handicap, which was partially overcome by construction of a wooden bridge over the river at the beginning of the 20th century. Thanks to this bridge the village became the "gate" to Szigetköz and the people obtained more business and communication opportunities.

Feketeerdő was part of Dunakiliti until 1990 and then it became independent. In spite of diminished woods, compared to the situation in the Middle Ages, it still possesses a wonderful natural setting. Apart from the woods, meadows and water bodies there are also numerous rows of trees planted by man. There is, for example, a 700 years old oak tree in the village, one of its natural attractions. It is a small and quiet settlement with about 100 houses. Its vicinity to Austria makes it a sought after spot for those who flee from the busy cities. An interesting event in the life of this village are the annual feasts held on Sunday after September 8th.

DUNASZIGET (population 1,500) lies near the main stream of the Danube in the upper part of the Szigetköz island, 15

Left: Dunasziget

km away from Mosonmagyaróvár. The Danube branches there into several branches, which create islands. Settlements named after the one of the island on which they are situated, originated here: Cikolasziget, Sérfenyősziget, and Doborgazsziget. These parts of the island form together the village of Dunasziget (The Danube Island), but the individual parts retained their names. The centre of the village is in Sérfenyősziget. The village was formed as we know it now, in 1969.

The first settlements originated here in the 13th and 14th centuries. They were small and literally had to fight for space with the omnipresent water. But the river with its branches provided them sustenance. The villages were linked with the settlement of what is today the northern Slovak bank of the Danube. They were in fact founded by the inhabitants of the neighbouring Slovak villages Vojka and Dobrohošť in form of loose farmsteads, solitary farms called "tanya" in Hungary. The nobles gradually became owners of the land obtained from the Church. This closely linked and coexisting area on both banks of the Danube however, was separated by the frontier after the First Word War. The settlements on the right bank were compelled to develop independently and since then one can talk about their proper history. Construction of efficient dikes against floods accelerated the development of the villages. Woods and arable land prevail in their territory. The Danube branches with forested banks offer a pleasant ambience for relaxation, recreation, and water sport. Almost all of it was damaged by the great Danube flood in 1954. New adjustments of the Danube's channel were made after this disaster. Further modifications were made when the Gabčíkovo Dam was finished on the Slovak side. Part of the Danube's water was deviated to the feeding canal of the Dam. But the branches near the village are still sufficiently fed by the water of the main channel of the Danube.

Tourism in Dunasziget

Dunasziget is an increasingly popular holiday centre. Tourists from Hungary and from abroad are relaxing on the banks of the Danube branches in summer. The recreation area is well prepared with all kinds of amenities especially around the Danube branches of Zátonyi-dunaág and Gázfűi-dunaág. Its area is more than eighty thousand square meters, it includes water bodies, a park, camping site, cottage quarter with more than 300 private and four company cottages and a youth camp. Daily as many as 5,000 people can relax here. The interest in purchasing of houses in the village is increasing. Old and abandoned houses are reconstructed and sold at ever higher prices to buyers from Hungary, Germany and Austria. The renewed houses with preserved original architecture contribute to the neat and cosy appearance of the village.

HALÁSZI (population 2,950) lies on the bank of the Moson branch of the Danube, five kilometres away from Mosonmagyaróvár. The community was situated on a busy trade road in the past and is also now one of the crossroads of the Szigetköz island. The original thick alluvial woods were clear cut in the past, while their small remains can be found near water bodies. In spite of it, rich fauna including red deer, heron, boar and pheasant survive here. The best known and most popular is the wood called Salamon erdő (The Solomon's Wood). The wood bears the name of the pursued King Solomon who found shelter with the local fishermen. When he ascended to the throne he rewarded the villages with this wood. The name of the village derives from the Hungarian for fisherman (halász). The local fishermen supplied fish to the Magyaróvár estate. The first written reference to the village is from 1335 as *Halaz* and its form *Halazy* is from 1497. The village was expanding and acquired the character of a small town. It obtained town privileges from the King Louis II Jagelonsky at the beginning of the 16th century and in 1550 also the right of seal from King Ferdinand I. The seal bears the picture of St. Martin (Szent Márton) with grey beard and wearing the Hungarian folk costume. Halászi also gradually obtained the right of toll collecting and that holding markets. The villagers were even exempt from tax paying for some time.

Halászi was the seat of the Reformed Bishopric administered by János Samarjai in the years 1635-1649. The village suffered a lot during the Rebellion of the Estates and it was struck by plague epidemic in 1713, which completely depopulated it. After it retreated, Croatian and German colonists settled here. They gradually merged with the Hungarian population and nowadays they are small ethnic groups. The village was known for cattle and goat raising as there were abundant pastures in its administrative territory. It was connected with the southern part of the Moson region thanks to the bridge over the Moson branch of the Danube, built in 1906. A great blow for the village was when the Germans destroyed it during the Second World War. The new bridge was built from parts of the destroyed Kossuth's bridge of Budapest. But the new bridge did not last either and in the 1990's it was replaced by the one, which is there today.

The most remarkable building in Halászi is the Roman Catholic **church of St. Martin** from 1777. The church in the Baroque style is the biggest of the Szigetköz island and it takes up to 1,200 believers. The altar painting is probably by the pupils of the outstanding artist A. F. Maulbertsch. The impressive building is frequently visited by tourists. The interesting objects of the village include folk architecture, represented by two Baroque **peasant houses** standing near the church.

The favourite place for tourists and visitors to Halászi is the Moson branch of the Danube used for water sports. The recreation area is on its bank. Arak, a small community with 1,800 inhabitants is part of the village. Arak was formerly an independent settlement situated 3 km from Halászi. Its name derives from the Hungarian word for ditch (árok).

Not far away from Halászi on the left bank of the Moson branch of the Danube is **MÁRIAKÁLNOK** (population 1,350). It lies 5 km from Mosonmagyaróvár and it is connected with this county town by an iron bridge built in 1928. According to the oldest documents, the settlement existing here was called *Kaal* in 1264 and *Kalnuk* in 1357. It is supposed that the origin of the name derives from the Slav word *kal*, which means mud. The word Mária symbolizes the pilgrim character of the place. The German name of the village *Gahling* also appeared in 1381. The local people lived on hunting, fishing, farming and viti culture. They were subjects of the Magyaróvár estate. The village was a widely known place of pilgrimage.

The pilgrims in Máriakálnok

Máriakálnok has been a favourite place of pilgrimage since the mid-16th century. People came here annually to visit the healing spring called Szent-kút (The Holy Source). Many legends connected with the spring existed along with rumours about hundreds of healed people. One legend says that the local fisherman pulled a little statue of the Virgin Mary carved in lime wood out of the Danube. A chapel was built near the spring and it was consecrated to the Blessed Virgin Mary. Count János Viczay had a larger chapel built on its site in 1663. Around the chapel an individual parish originated after 1701. Fire destroyed the chapel in 1873 and a year later the one standing there now was built. Visitors can visit the chapel from the Easter Monday to October. The Szent-kút spring originally sprang in the corner of the chapel. Later it was taken out to allow easier access. A statue of the Virgin Mary stands above the stone altar.

The village was the only one in Szigetköz island where an important German minority lived. This was the difference between this village and the rest. The village was isolated in the 19th century. Its economic development stagnated. Regular floods even worsened the situation. For instance, the 1829 flood almost completely destroyed Máriakálnok. Then a plague epidemic followed in 1851. After the Second World War 900 Germans out of the total 987 inhabitants of the village had to leave their houses and go to Germany. Máriakálnok became the symbol of unjust and forced displacement in the post-war

Right: The floodplain forest near Halászi

period. Hungarian families from the surrounding villages and from the Slovak Žitný ostrov replaced those who left. Older generation still keeps contacts with the emigrants.

Visitors of the village mostly go to the **chapel**. Especially the special masses served in the open air near the chapel and under the lime trees at the time of religious feasts are abundantly visited. Near the chapel is what is now the most important building monument of the village: the **Marsow manor house** (now used as asylum).

The village of **PÜSKI** (population 650) lies not far from the right bank of the Danube, 13 km east of Mosonmagyaróvár and 28 km west from the county seat of Győr. The first written reference to it is from 1314. It was mentioned as *Piski* in 1397 and as *Pysky* in 1488. It was a property of the Bishopric of Győr. A legend says that the name of the village coincides with that of Bishop of Győr, János Püski who once hid in the local oak wood when he was pursued. After he became the Bishop in the mid-17th century he admitted many refugees here. But the name probably derives from the word püspoki (Episcopal in English). Püski was presumably owned by the Bishopric the same as the today's urban district of Bratislava Podunajské Biskupice, and the abbreviation of the word püspoki gave origin to the name of the village.

The ownership of the village was frequently a subject of argument between the noble families of Pálffy, Héderváry, and Bakics with the Bishopric of Győr. The village was probably destroyed at the time of the Turkish siege of Vienna. At the end of the 17th century the judge of the County of Moson, Ferenc Bacskó, received the village in pawn. András Vályi described the quiet life of the village in the 18th century in his historical work: "Püski, a Hungarian village in the County of Bratislava, the people are Catholics, it lies near Remete, and the farmers grow rye and barley, there are woods, less meadows and the villagers go to the markets in Moson and Győr". The village burnt down in 1797. After it was constructed again the passing Napoleonic troops sacked it.

In 1894 it was taken out of the County of Bratislava and included in that of Moson.

The most important cultural and historic monument of the village is the Roman Catholic **church** built in the years 1778-1780 and reconstructed after fire of 1797. The **statue of St. Florian** erected as a token of gratitude for protection against fire stands in front of the church. The village is full of visitors especially at the time of the local feasts, which are annually celebrated on the Sunday following the St. George Day (April 24th). Wonderful and romantic environs of the village above all on the Danube dike are suitable for walks and bicycle tours. Nature enthusiasts will certainly like the protected areas of **Salamon-erdő** and **Járai Duna.**

Only several kilometres northward on the right bank of the Danube is the village of **KISBODAK** (population 400). It is 15 km away from Mosonmagyaróvár and 30 km from Győr. According to a legend the fishing settlement of Bodak or Bodajk was founded on a territory of a thousand islands on a slightly elevated spot among them. The name is probably of Slav origin and means swampy place overgrown with

water plants. Bodak was first mentioned in 1330 as a property the of Héderváry family. Other sources assert that the first reference to the village is from 1400. While today there are two villages Kisbodak and Nagybodak, only one village existed in the 15th century as proved by the Héderváry family documents from 1429-1548. Two villages, *Kys Bodak* and *Nagy Bodak,* are referred to for the first time in 1591. The repeated floods and incessant movement of the Danube branches were presumably the cause of their separation. A situation on waterlogged land was an advantage in war time. But what was saved from war, was destroyed by water. The village chronicles mentioned above all the floods of 1712 and 1736. Owners of the village alternated and the best known are the families of Amade or Viczay.

The villagers lived on fishing in the past. The river branches were recognized as the best fishing areas in the Szigetköz island. Several water mills existed near the village. Many adventurers tried to extract gold from the Danube sediments in

Left: Rural architecture in Szigetköz

the past. Napoleonic troops visited the village and sought food in 1809 and when they did not find it they burnt the village The following event, which struck the restored village in 1851, was fire. The 1954 flood also destroyed a great part of the village. After the flood retreated, earthen works started, the roads were paved and better dikes constructed. In connection with opening of the water works of Gabčíkovo on the Slovak side of the river the amount of Danube water flowing into the branches is controlled. The environs of the village are rich in natural beauty. Pálffy's wood is a part of the protected territory of Szigetköz island. Fishing and boating are the favourite pastimes of visitors to this village. Construction of a camping site and swimming pool is planned.

The villagers maintain their folk usage, maybe because the village is somewhat more isolated then the rest of the villages situated on the Szigetköz island. There is a **stone cross** in the middle of the village erected by the Countess Mária Khuen-Viczay. She originally planned to build a church, but the villagers were afraid they would not be able to maintain it financially. The modern Roman Catholic church of **Sts. Balázs and Ladislav** was built in 1993. It is the largest church in the districts.

Near the Danube dike, 13 km east of Mosonmagyaróvár and 26 km west of Győr lies the village of **DUNAREMETE** (population 250). Fishermen founded this village. The origin of its name stems from the Hungarian word *remete* which means a hermit and the first part of the name Duna refers to the river. Allegedly, two hermits lived here in the past. They provided shelter to the people pursued for various political or religious reasons and then became the founders of the village.

The first written reference to Dunaremete is from 1456. It was quoted as *Remethe,* and the seat of the Héderváry family. The locals were mainly fishermen. The village was probably repeatedly destroyed by fire and changed its face after each reconstruction while it always moved to a safer place. In 1521 it became a property of the Bakics family and the inhabitants became Evangelical. The village was re-Catholicized at the end of the 17th century when the Viczay and Széchényi families became the local landlords. Historic sources from the 18th and 19th century recorded that the land around the village was not too fertile and they emphasize its position and beautiful meadows, groves and pastures. The village passed under the administration of the County of Moson. The population was of Hungarian nationality. Dikes around the village were finished in 1929 and a year later a post office was opened. The port improved the position of the village as it removed the isolation caused by the state frontier and speeded up the transport. But situation got worse after the Second World War. The victims and damage of war and closure of the port made that the village was isolated again. On the other side it contributed to the conservation of folk usage and tradition. The most important building of the village is the Roman Catholic **church of St. John Nepomuk** from 1775. The material of the original Protestant church was used for its construction. On the feast of St. John Nepomuk, the first Sunday after May 16th the local **village feasts** are also celebrated. The village has a **port** for fishing boats and the road to the port is rimmed by a beautiful **row of plane trees** planted in the period between the two World Wars.

LIPÓT (population 700) lies in the middle part of Szigetköz island near the main stream of the Danube. It is situated 15 km east of Mosonmagyaróvár and 25 km west of Győr. The first written reference to the village is from 1216. The name of the village derives from the name of the original owner of the village, Lipót. Historians assert that King Béla IV donated this territory to Lipót in 1264. The village was mentioned in several documents, for example as *Lypóthfalva* in 1377 when it was property of the Hédervárys. The following owner was the Bakics family. The Hédervárys owned it again in 1542 and the population, as was usual then, converted to the Protestant religion and were re-Catholicized in 1630. The population was often obliged to flee to the surrounding islands because of floods and wars

only to construct their houses again on the original or an apparently safer place. This was how the village shifted in the course of centuries. The original and oldest community is on the other bank of the Danube's branch now in a locality called Falusziget. One of the sites of the village was on the bank of the now dead branch near the Macska-sziget island. Remains of the original houses and church were found here The village was repeatedly struck by cholera epidemics: in 1658, 1784, 1831, 1849, and by plague epidemics in 1684 and 1688. During the last mentioned one, for example, 200 people died. The Napoleonic troops sacked it 1809 and a great flood destroyed what was left. Lipót, like the surrounding villages, became part of Moson County in 1884. The local population originally lived from fishing. The most frequent fish caught here was eel, which was sold in the markets of Bratislava or Vienna. Historic sources mentioned that in 1831 39 inhabitants were living on washing for gold. In 1885 six water mills existing in the locality were mentioned. Part of the villagers sustained themselves by haulage and dragging of boats. The works connected with regulation of the Danube in 1885 greatly influenced the life of the locals. Many people lost their original jobs and had to dedicate themselves to farming. The First World War, disintegration of the Monarchy, and the change of frontiers resulted in the village finding itself on the periphery of the state and even losing some territory, when parts of its forests and pastures were annexed to Czechoslovakia. The 1954 flood, the reason why we find prevailingly recent architecture there, heavily struck the village. The houses are now mostly built on top of deposited earth and the streets copy the tracks of the former channels of the lateral river branches. The most important monument of the village is the Roman Catholic **church of St. Clement** from 1722 (or 1777, as some sources assert). Its interior is decorated by a wonderful fresco painted by A. F. Maulbertsch.

But the main attraction of Lipót is the **thermal swimming pool** the water of which comes from the local 2,215 m deep

well. Its temperature is 65 degrees Celsius at the source. It is open only in summer. The **dead branch of the Danube**, the nesting locality of different bird species, spreads north of the village over an area 68 hectares is also very attractive. The road to Darnózseli is rimmed by a **row of protected chestnut trees**. Its length is 2,050 m and it occupies an area of 2.5 hectares. The huge tree crowns create almost a continuous cover and provide romantic nooks in any season of the year.

HÉDERVÁR (population 1,100) is situated further to south and next to the centre of the Szigetköz island. It is on half-way between the two main centres of the region: Mosonmagyaróvár and Győr. The village is one of the oldest in the region. The Knight Hedrych Héder who helped King Gejza II, received the island lying near Győr where he built a wooden castle in 1142. This is how the history of the village and the Héderváry family started (váry in Hungarian means "belonging to a castle"). The first written reference to

the village is from 1210. From the 14th century the village is mentioned as the one next to castle ruins. Hédervár obtained the privileges of a town and maintained them for several centuries.

The **Héderváry manor house** was originally built between the 2nd and 13th century, probably on the ruins of a Roman fort and was repeatedly damaged and restored in the course of the centuries. On the site of the present manor house stood a Renaissance manor house damaged in 1534. The family built a larger and bulkier one with corner towers in 1578. The manor house was rebuilt again in the 18th century. Its present form contains elements of different building periods. The facade of the manor house is in the Baroque style. A three-storied tower with hexagonal ground plan is the remnant of the tower of the medieval castle and two smaller towers with rectangular ground plan are from the 17th century. There are two sphinxes on the gate from the 19th century. The square courtyard has Neo-Gothic tiles. Only the original chapel is decorated. The manor house is a

Left: The manor house in Hédervár
Right: The park in Hédervár

otel today. Behind the manor house on the northern edge of the village is a **park** spreading over an area of 9 hectares. The larger part of the park, the planting of which started in the 19th century, contains the original wood species typical of the hard alluvial forest. Oak and beech trees and other wood species were added to it later. Hidegkúti-ér brook crosses the park. In its south-eastern part the archaeologists discovered remains of a 13th century settlement. It is supposed that this was the place where the residence of the Hédervárys stood. The park has been a protected area since 1965.

The Roman Catholic **church of St. Michael** near the manor house obtained its Baroque form in the 18th century. In its interior the statues of Sts. Florián and Vendel in Tyrolian folk costumes are of interest. Statues of Sts. Ladislav and Stephen carved in wood stand at the sides of the altar and between them is a painting of Bratislava painter J. Zallinger depicting the fight of St. Michael with Lucifer. The side altars and the Gothic font of this church are also remarkable. Not far from St. Michael's church is also the Roman Catholic **church of the Blessed Virgin Mary**, originally a tomb with a chapel where the members of the Héderváry family were buried. The tower was built in the Romanesque style in the 13th century. In 1348 Gothic naves were added to it. In the second half of the 17th century on the northern side a chapel was built. This structure was reconstructed in the 19th century in the Neo-Gothic taste; its interior consists from three naves and there is a crypt underground. The lateral chapel is adorned with a statue of the Virgin Mary carved in wood from the 15th century. An **oak** more than 700 years old stands in front of the church.

Another famous **tree** stood next to the road in the direction of Darnózseli. It was a poplar tree under which allegedly István Kont met with his partners to prepare a conspiracy against King Sigismund of Hungary. They were betrayed and beheaded. Another tree grows on its site now. In the middle of the village is what is called the Zsidódomb (Jewish Hill), in fact, the **ruins** of a medieval castle. According to a

legend it was damaged by the Tartars, but it was recently confirmed that it disappeared several centuries later. On the road to Darnózseli is the **chapel of St. Pelegrin** with an octagonal ground plan. It was built in honour of the protector of the pilgrims and wanderers in 1709. Beyond the Hársfa utca street is a protected **landscape park** with an area of 57 hectares. In the past it was a pheasantry of the Hédervárys, now it also contains other animal species such as red deer, rabbits, wild geese and ducks. In its middle is a clearing with benches and tables. Its territory is crossed by the Kárászos-ér brook, which flows into the Moson branch of the Danube on the edge of the wood. From the point of the confluence one gets a fine view of the river's meanders.

DARNÓZSELI (population 1,600) is the village situated further west in the central part of the Szigetköz island, 16 km away from Mosonmagyaróvár and 28 km from Győr. Darnózsely consists of two originally individual communities: Zseli and Mosondarnó. A continuous floodplain forest survives in its administrative territory. The territory of the village was set-

tled in the 12th century. King Gejza II donated the area to the German Knights Héder and Wolfger. Farmers and shepherds of Slav origin settled there under the protection of the two knights. Part of the village's name Darnow meant grassland and the second part Selew meant cabbage in the Slav language. During the Turkish rule in Hungary, the Héderváry estate, which also included this village, was almost depopulated. The territory was further devastated during the Rebellions of Estates and in 1809 the passing Napoleonic troops plundered the village. Imperial troops erected gallows in the village to intimidate the local population in the revolutionary year 1848. Natural disasters did not avoid the villages either, they were floods in the first place, cholera epidemic in the 19th century and fires. The 1954 flood destroyed the majority of houses in the village. The two villages united into one in 1934. By the end of the Second World War the Germans deported the small Jewish community from Darnószeli.

The dominant feature of the village is the Roman Catholic **church of St. Joseph** from 1936. The most important native of the village was Dr. Mihály Karácsony (1800-1869), one of the founders of technical university learning in the Kingdom of Hungary. The village maintains folk traditions and it has a dance ensemble of its own called **Szigetköz**. The situation of the village in the central part of the Szigetköz island is an asset in terms of accessibility to the main stream of the Danube and its Moson branch. Near the road to Hédervár is the floodplain forest Zseli-erdő with willow, oaks, elm, ash, and alder trees in-

cluding the Tartar maple, which grow only in this locality of Szigeköz. The envi rons are excellent for bicycle trips. The vi lagers provide accommodation in privat houses accompanied by the tasty loca cuisine.

South-west of Darnózseli on bot banks of the Moson branch of th Danube, 10 km away of Mosonma gyaróvár and 30 km of Győr lies the villag of **KIMLE** (population 2,800). This villag originating by merging of four settle ments: Horvátkimle, Magyarkimle, Ká rolyháza and Novákpuszta in 1966. Th main railway line Budapest-Vienna cross es the village and the motorway Bu dapest-Vienna passes it as well.

Archaeological finds prove, that th territory has been settled for a long time Fragments of pottery from the Roman pe riod were found around the church i Magyarkimle. A Roman guard tower pre sumably stood in this place. The loca names testify to the presence of Slavs i this territory, for example the name Nová derives from the Slav word for new (nový) in this case, new land, and new settlers The first reference to the village was a Kamana, which can be also associate with the Slav word for stone (kameň) Opinion exists that the name of the villag derives from the Magyar phrase kém-les which means observation point for ob serving alien spies. Part of the villag Novák(puszta) was first mentioned i 1210 when King Andrew II donated thi settlement administered by the County o Győr to Comes Poth of Moson. The nam of the village changed from the 13th centu ry to *Kemen* (1274), *Kynkemme* (1365) *Kempne* (1403). In the early 15th centur both parts of the village bearing Kimle i

Left: Souvenirs from Szigetköz

heir names existed as two names are quoted: *Kilsukempne* (1409) and *Belseukempne* (1429). Owners of the settlements alternated. Novák was owned by the Hédervárys and Andrássys from the second half of the 19th century. The Andrássy family built here a lovely hunting castle. Kimles were gradually owned by the Seide, Tankházy, and Nagylucsai families. Two settlements, *Nagykimle* and *Kiskimle*, on the site of today's Kimle were mentioned in the 16th century. The Turks destroyed them on their way to Vienna in 1529. Depopulation of the villages called for resettling. Croatians moved here in the 16th century. After it was plundered again in the 17th century, Hovátkimle was referred to as *Puszta Kémlye* (Abandoned Kémlye). More Croatian families from the areas around the rivers Mura, Dráva and Száva came in 1685. The name *Horváth Kemle* was used from 1696. The village maintained its Croatian character until the 18th century. In Magyarkimle the number of Hungarian speaking inhabitants was increasing. Matej Bel wrote in 1740 that Magyarkimle was called so to distinguish it from Horváthkimle as the first was Hungarian and the second a Croatian speaking village. Several German families from Bavaria moved to Magyarkimple around 1767 and gradually came to form half the families. In that time Magyarkimle was referred to as a German-Croatian settlements and its people lived by cattle and sheep raising. After the First World War the village had a distillery, starch factory, and mill. In 1929, 385 Croatians and 447 Germans lived in the village. After the Second World War 70 Germans were forced to move out from Magyarkimle and many others left voluntarily. The most important sacred monuments include the Roman Catholic **church of the Blessed Virgin Mary** in Magyarkimle from the 13th century. It was widened in 1699 and adapted in the Baroque style. When it was restored in 1992 several original Romanesque elements were discovered. Next to the church stands the **statue of the Most Holy Trinity**. The local cemetery contains several precious **tombstones**. Apart from the Roman Catholic church of the Holy Spirit in Novákpuszta there is also interesting Roman Catholic **church of St. Michael** in Horvátkimle. It acquired present form in 1780. Many Gothic elements were preserved in its interior. A **memorial** to Mate Mersich Miloradič from 1993 stands near the church.

Close to the monument of Mate Mersich-Miloradič is another **monument** dedicated to the 450th anniversary of the arrival of the Croatians at the village. The **obelisk** from 1949 and the **row of chestnut trees** with pillars commemorate victims of the Second World War. The most important secular building is a well-preserved **manor house** in Novákpuszta. In the local part of Károlyháza is the **protected nature territory**, which stretches on both banks of the Moson branch of the Danube with remains of the original floodplain landscape.

The varied nationality structure of the village consisting of Hungarians, Croatians and Germans is a kind of enrichment of its cultural and social life. Interesting folk traditions and customs survive here. Village feasts are held on May 1st and August 20th. There are several amateur folk ensembles and music bands, cultural clubs, and a library containing eleven thousand volumes in three languages. A **Croatian club** was founded here in 1980.

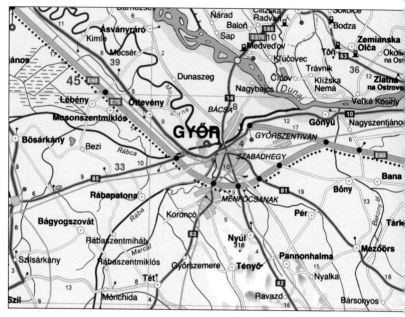

GYŐR AND ITS ENVIRONS

The region is part of the Little Hungarian Lowland, and particularly the Rába Basin. It is filled by the south-eastern half of the Danube island Szigetköz and the alluvium of the Danube between Győr and Komárom. Its north and north-eastern frontier constitutes the main stream of the Danube and the frontier with the Slovak Republic. The border of the County of Győr-Moson-Sopron limits the east. The southern and south-western limits of the territory reach the line of the motorway from Budapest to Vienna. The north-western limit coincides with the natural border dividing the Sigetköz island into the upper and lower parts running between the settlements Hédervár and Ásványráró. The County Győr-Moson-Sopron administers the territory.

GYŐR (population 127,300), centre of trade, transport and culture, is the most important settlement of the County of Győr-Moson-Sopron. It lies in the Little Hungarian Lowland and the Győr basin.

Right: The town of rivers

Two rivers, Rába and Rábca, flow into the Moson branch of the Danube in the town the reason why it is also sometimes referred to as "the town of rivers".

The city of rivers

In the territory of the city is a comparatively bulky terrace out of the reach of the floods in the past. It meant that the core of the city with a castle could freely develop. The core of the city is 9 km away from the main stream of the Danube while the river is only 3 km away from the city's edge. The Moson branch of the Danube joins the Rába and Rábca and the branch becomes navigable from the confluence up to the main stream of the Danube. Consequently the city always had a river port. The width of the branch is 100-120 m and its depth reaches 3.5 m. The bed of the branch seems larger compared to the amount of water, which flows in it. The Moson branch diverted the flood waves of the Danube before it was regulated and dikes were constructed.

Traces of early settlement were found in the territory of the town. Celts lived ere in the time between 350 and 400 BC nd gave it its first name: Arrabona. In ime of the Roman Empire the town was ne of the most important in the province f Pannonia. Several trade and military oads met in the town: the one leading rom Vienna, others to Sopron or Szombathely, Veszprém, or Székesfehérvár. The osition of the town was advantageous. It vas founded next to the trade route leading from Vindobona (Vienna) to Aquincum Budapest). The road headed to the south, is the natural conditions were better south of Danube than on its north side. The main asset was that on this side of he Danube there were not so many great ivers to cross. The only serious barrier n this route was the river Rába. The ford across this river was in the territory of oday's Győr. Apparently the situation of he city next to the Moson branch of the Danube and off the main stream of the iver was not too profitable, but it was not a problem in the past, because before the period of extensive works connected with he control of the Danube's channel in 1886-1894 all navigation ran on the Moson branch. Nature predetermined this place to become the main crossroads of he Little Hungarian Lowland. At the beginning of the 5th century when the Romans were gradually loosing their influence, they concluded an agreement with he Huns leaving them the province of Pannonia. This was how the Huns subdued the Transdanubian territory in around 430. The original inhabitants of Arrabona on the territory of the present Győr probably fled and the Huns established a burial place there. It is proved by he find of twenty Hunnish graves under what is today Széchényi tér square. The rule of the Huns ended shortly after their leader Atilla died in 453.

The Germanic tribes took over control of the territory. The Avars came in 568 and pushed out the last of the German tribes, the Longobards. The territory of the city probably became one of the Avar centres. It was surrounded by protective ramparts in form of rings which have probably also given origin to the present name of the city (Hungarian word gyűrű means a ring). But there is no evidence for

this presumption. The origin of the city's name was not reliably explained so far, while three different theories exist. One of them is that the name Győr derives from the name of some old ethnicity or tribe, another attributes it to some Avar word with uncertain meaning and the third theory asserts that it derives from the word denoting fold or furrow (in Hungarian gyűrődés). The archaeologists discovered 900 Avar graves here. The rule of the Avars broke down under the attacks of the Franks in the 8th and 9th centuries. The Frankish chronicler Einhardus describes how the Avar fortifications of Győr were conquered by the troops of the Frankish King Charles I the Great a in 791. But the Avars stayed in this territory and gradually merged with Slavs.

By the end of the 9th century the Old Magyar tribes arrived in the territory of the city. The first crowned King of Hungary, Stephen I paid a lot of attention to Győr. He had a Bishopric established here and developed the city as a strategic fort. A castle was built in the 10th century. Attacks by the Czech, Austrian and German troops between the 11th and 13th centuries were always stopped at the river Rába. The city was an important trade junction already in the 11th -12th centuries, as it possessed advantages connected with toll paid in Hainburg. The renowned Arab geographer and cartographer Al Idrísi also mentions Győr as a busy and developed city. When the Tartars plundered the territory north of the Danube in 1241-42, Győr was attacked by the Austrian troops of the Emperor Friederich. The enemy occupied the castle, but it was won back. Renovation of the city was carried out during the rule of King Belo IV. The expe-

rience with Austrian troops meant that Belo IV decided to built a stronger and better fortified castle. The army of Přemysl Otakar I, King of Bohemia, was also stopped at Győr in 1271 although it was successful everywhere. The brave defence of the city won it the title of a free royal borough in 1271 and its citizens were granted the corresponding privileges.

Several church orders gradually settled within the castle walls in the 13th century. A Franciscan monastery with church was built in 1235. Both were destroyed in the 16th century. The town thrived in the 14th century. Houses of craftsmen and merchants were built around the castle and Győr developed into a prosperous medieval town. Guilds originated in the 14th century. But the boom was followed by a break down at the beginning of the 15th century. Győr lost the position of a free royal borough when the followers of King Sigismund of Luxembourg occupied its castle in 1403. It was

then owned by different owners and became a free royal borough again only in 1743. The Turkish invasion into the Danube Basin resulted in that Győr was a well-fortified settlement for another 200 years. By the end of the 15th century the majority of houses in the town were made of mud, wood and osiers. Some streets were formed then and acquired their names. The trade route crossing the town from east to west was becoming ever more important especially for the cattle and food trade. But the developing town thriving on crafts and trade became a marginal frontier town with defensive function as it had been during the Árpád period, as a result of the division of the country. The first Habsburg ruler Ferdinand I occupied Győr Castle in 1527 and left his guards there. During his campaign to Vienna the Turkish sultan Süleyman I also occupied the town and castle abandoned by the Habsburg soldiers who fled fearing the Turks. The castle was burnt down and population annihilated. Reconstruction was planned in the mid-16th century but fire, which broke out on September 29th 1566, hindered it. Eventually the whole

Left: Győr in the 19th century
Right: Győr Castle
     The Moson branch of the Danube

)wn burnt down, though the castle was ne least damaged. The settlement exist- ng below castle acquired a different char- cter after the fire. Italian, Spanish and ·erman builders came to the town and neir buildings showed traces of styles sed in their homelands. Tuscany pillars r decorated loggias surviving in Győr rove it. The town maintained its trading pirit although it was now situated on the order. It became the place where goods vere exchanged between the occupied nd free parts of the country. The castle vas besieged again by the Turkish troops n 1594. The defenders of castle, mostly ne German and Italian soldiers, ex- hanged the castle for the possibility of aving their lives. The fall of this strategic ort of utmost importance provoked panic n the whole of Central Europe and the opulation of Győr fled. The castle was re- overed four years later.

Conquering of Győr Castle

In March 1598 the troops of experi- nced leaders Nicholas Pálffy and Adolph chwarzenberg gathered secretly. It was a uitable moment for the attack, as part of he soldiers of the Turkish garrison settled n the castle counting 6,000 men was out nd the rest were relaxing. Pálffy and chwarzenberg set out to the Győr reach- ng the castle in the night of 28th March. everal soldiers disguised in Turkish lothes were sent to the Féhérvár Gate to heat the guards. The disguised soldiers sked the guards to open the gate with the xcuse that they were bringing food. The urks were so careless that they did not ven bother to lift the drawbridge. While he guards talked with the disguised sol- liers, their companions entered. The sur-

prised Turks were not able to resist and the castle was liberated in several hours.

In the first half of the 17th century the town began to develop again. Its picture gradually changed, as the poor simple huts in the immediate vicinity of castle started to disappear and the rich mer- chants built storied houses in the Renais- sance style. Several guilds, such as shoe- makers, tailors and innkeepers were founded. Historic sources quote as much as 1,500 craftsmen living in Győr at that time. Empress Maria Theresa granted Győr again its privileges of free royal bor- ough in 1743 and it was the great im- pulse, which spurred further development of the city. Thanks to new architecture ap- plied in the 18th century Győr acquired an urban appearance. The city was occupied by the Napoleon's troops in June 1810. They stayed for several months. The last day of August the same year Napoleon himself arrived to check his soldiers and he had the castle towers destroyed. After the French soldiers departed, the city be- came the most important centre of corn trade in Kingdom of Hungary. The cheap- est means of transport to the port of Győr was still the Danube. Oxen pulled the loaded boats up the stream to the port of Győr where there were 150 storehouses. The goods were later hauled further to the west by smaller boats or carts.

The cultural life of the city at that time was also remarkable. Several au- thors of fiction lived there, for instance Miklós Révay or József Rajnics, who were the pioneers of the reforming movement in the 19th century. The first theatre building in the country, except for the capital, was built in Győr in 1798. The building was

constructed in the Neo-Classical style and financed by voluntary collections from the local population. Also Streibig's printing plant played a significant role in the cultural life of the city, as it helped to propagate reformed thinking. In the mid-18th century scientific academy providing for higher education in the field of law and philosophy was founded in the city. Maria Theresa nationalized it in 1776. The academy was closed in the revolutionary years 1848-1849, as the city was the centre of revolutionary moods. Győr was the stage of the revolutionary efforts of Hungarian intelligentsia. In the 1820's the protagonist of the Slovak national emancipation, Ľudovít Štúr, studied in this city. In October 1948 Lajos Kossuth, the first figure of revolution, visited Győr with the intention to form an army and to prepare an attack on Vienna. The situation finally completely changed and the Austrian General Alfred von Windischgrätz's troops occupied the city on December 27th 1848.

The development of the railway meant decay of the corn trade transported

on the rivers in the second half of the 19 century. The guilds were also disappearing and the first factories were opene The most important one, along with th textile industry, was the plant producir railway cars. While at the beginning of th 19th century the share of the Hungaria and German population was equal, by th end of the century. As much as 94 % population adhered to Hungarian nation ality after the First World and Győr lost i hinterland on the left bank of the Danuk War, which was annexed to Czechoslov kia. Many business contacts, which hav existed within the boundary area, wei lost. For instance, the largest factory pre ducing cannons in Central Europe, whic was built in co-operation with the Škod Company of Plzeň and the Krupp Concer was also closed. In spite of the losses i the time between the two World War Győr was still the second most industria ized city in Hungary following Budapes In 1920 more than 50,000 inhabitant lived in the city. As far as their religion i concerned, three quarter were Catholic the Jews represented one tenth, while th Evangelical and Reformed Churches mad up the rest. The city had to face mor losses and suffering when the Secon World War finished. Renovation of builc ings and bridges was necessary. The situ ation stabilized, the villagers, who los their lands in the process of nationaliza tion, started to move to the city. Indus tries developed and new housing estate were built in the socialist era. The popu lation surpassed a hundred thousanc However, isolation of the country from th Western Europe also caused the loss c historic cultural and business linkages They were renewed after the fall of th communist regime and Győr started t flourish again. Foreign capital is being in vested and it shows also in the appear ance of the city. The close vicinity of thre capitals, Budapest, Bratislava and Vien na, makes Győr a very attractive place The city and its environs are becomin one of the economically perspective an most quickly developing spaces in Centra Europe. The sectors of services an tourism are the two industries, which ar indeed thriving. The city provides suffi

Left: Pedestrian zone

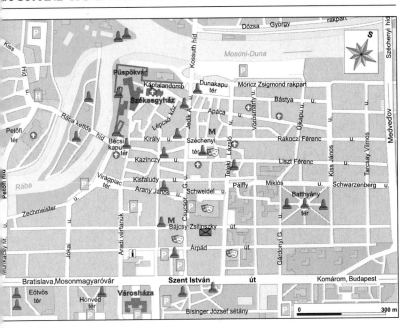

cient accommodation and catering capacities for its visitors and numerous opportunities for relaxation. Many like to visit Győr for its thermal springs.

The hot springs of Győr

The first thermal spring with temperature 66.4 degrees Celsius yielding 720 litres per second was drilled to a depth of 2,000 metres in 1962. In 1966 the second spring from the same depth was drawn onto the surface and its temperature was 69 degrees Celsius. Its performance was 1,100 litres per second. The third probe was carried out in 1973. The result is water with a temperature of 68 degrees Celsius and yield 1,500 litres per second. The alkaline water is used for therapy and provides an excellent opportunity for swimming and recreation in the local area of thermal swimming pools.

As far as the number and quality of cultural monuments are concerned, Győr is the third richest city in Hungary following Budapest and Sopron. Its inner town (Belváros) was skirted by town fortifications until 1830. When they were pulled down and the moats covered, the inner town merged with its suburbs. The majority of the historic and protected buildings of Győr are situated inside the original **town walls** built in the 16th century. In the western part of the old town is the **Bécsi kapu tér square**, one of the most beautiful Baroque squares in Hungary. Its western side has opened towards the Rába river since the mid-19th century. The Bécsi kapu or the Viennese Gate limited it before. The square is named after this gate, though during the communist regime it was called the Republic Square. It was also the most beautiful closed square in a town with an inimitable ambience. **Medieval houses,** reconstructed in the Baroque and Neo-Classical styles fill the eastern side of it. Extensive ruins of a Roman house stood on this square until the 16th century. They were probably used as building material for the construction of the castle. In the middle of the square stands the bronze **statue** of the poet Károly Kisfaludy (1788-1830) by Lajos Mátrai. The **Carmelite church** from the years 1716-1725 built by Martin Witwer also stands on the square. Its shape is

oval and three statues decorate its Baroque facade. The main Baroque altar made in the 19th century by the Viennese artist Johann Kastner bears the paining of the Immaculate Conception of the Virgin Mary. F. Richer made the statues on the main altar. The painter Martino Altomonte of Naples painted the side altars. The fresco to the motif of the Last Supper on the wall attracts attention. The Dark Chapel built in 1718 is the copy of the Nazareth chapel. It contains the statue of the Virgin Mary. A large crypt with a single supporting pillar is hidden under the church. In the adjacent **Carmelite mona-stery** is now a hotel. On the right side of the main entrance stands one of the most beautiful statues representing the Virgin Mary. This statue from the 18th century was placed here only in the 19th century.

Opposite the Carmelite church are the remains of **castle**. The origin of the castle dates from the end of the 10th century. It was repeatedly destroyed and restored in the course of centuries. The Napoleonic

troops finally blew it up in 1809. When they left only the **courtyard** and the **Sforza tower** existed. The tower now shelters a **museum** containing interesting exhibits connected with the town history. Part of one of the former town gates called the Fehérvári kapu can be seen here. Count Pálffy blew it up in 1598 when he liberated the castle from the Turks. The **statue of St. Stephen** on a horse stands on the square next to the tower on the bank of the Rába. On the opposite side of the square is **Altabak's house**. Canon Altabak rebuilt this house from 1520 in 1620. The building displays the typical traits of the Baroque style. Near to it, on the Király street, is a two-storied Baroque **house** called **Napoleon's** built in the 1770's from three older houses. It became famous when Napoleon stayed overnight there on August 31st 1809. Not far from the Napoleon's house the **house Rozália** stands on Kazinczy utca street. It is a well-conserved building from the first half of the 18th century. It bears the picture of St. Rozália, the first victim of a plague epidemic, placed under the window at the first floor. A pelican with spread wings adorns the facade of the roofed balcony.

Káptalan-domb or the Chapter Hill is on the confluence of the Moson branch of the Danube and the Rába. A centre of spiritual life was founded here in the Middle Ages: **Püspökvár** (The Bishop's castle) and the **cathedral**. Houses from the 18th and 19th centuries surround the cathedral. The cathedral stands opposite the Bishop's office on the **Apor Vilmos püspök tér** (The Bishop Vilmos Apor Square). It gained the title of a **Basilica Minor** after it was visited by the Pope in 1997. Originally a little Romanesque church from 1030 stood here. Later it was rebuilt in a three-nave basilica. In had to be reconstructed in the 13th and 14th centuries because it was damaged during the wars. In the 15th century it was adapted in the Gothic taste. It was used as a stable, cannon position or gunpowder store during the Turkish occupation, which caused a lot of damage to the building. The local Bishop György Draskovich entrusted its restoration to the Italian master Battista Rava in the years 1639-1645.

Left: Entrance to a burgher house
Right: Bécsi kapu tér square

The tower was finished in 1680 and the interior was made in the 1770's. The interior was made in the 1770's. The cathedral was restored at the beginning of the 20th century and again in the years 1969-1972. The facade of the cathedral is in the Neo-Classical style. The church acquired its original Romanesque form after the reconstruction made at the beginning of the 20th century. Bandi Shim made the bronze gate in 1938. The vault of the main nave bears the **fresco** of F. A. Maulbertsch and it represents Jesus Christ, his disciples are depicted on the smaller side vaults. The main altar is a monumental work of art, created to the design of Menyhért Hefele. It bears a painting representing the Assumption of the Virgin Mary by master F. A. Maulbertsch from the years 1772-1781. An interesting part of the interior are the two lateral tin "black altars" on the two frontal pillars of the sanctuary from the 1770's. They are the work of Jakab Müller (Mollinarolo) and depict St. Stephen with the royal crown and St. Ladislav at the grave of St. Stephen. The most beautiful altar is the Baroque altar of the Virgin Mary in the northern aisle of the cathedral, brought here from Ireland. The Bishop's chair in the sanctuary was originally made on the occasion of the coronation of Maria Theresa and bought by the Bishop Zichy. The **Chapel of St. Ladislav** from 1404 is the main attraction of the southern aisle. It contains a unique example of the Hungarian gold-smith art, a gilded silver **helmet of St. Ladislav** with Byzantine enamel ornamentation. The probable authors of this work were the brothers Kolozsváry from the beginning of the 15th century. A **sarcophagus** of the martyr Bishop Vilmos Apor who gave the name to the whole square is also deposited in the chapel. A cemetery used to exist near the cathedral with the grave of the White Lady of Levoča, the main protagonist of the eponymous novel by Mór Jókai. When the cemetery was liquidated in the early 18th century, the tower was damaged and it had to be repaired and fixed with a new wall with the Neo-Classical elements. The sacristy contains the Baroque furniture and a valuable crucifix made of ivory, the only one in Hungary. A set of precious clerical garments is also displayed in the chapel. Several stones from the former Roman

military camp Arrabona are inserted into the corner of the building of cathedral.

Győr and the White Lady of Levoča

The sad legend about the White Lady of Levoča dates from the 18th century. A burgess of Levoča by the name Júlia Géci-Korponay betrayed her own town and husband when Levoča was besieged by the Imperial troops. She managed to pass the key of the town gate to the enemy and let the soldiers in. Her betrayal was motivated by a fatal passion for the commander of the Imperial troops. Later she returned to the rebels and her former lover had her imprisoned in the castle of Červený kameň. She ended up in Győr and spend the last days of her life before execution in 1715, as the legend says, in the cellars of the original building of the old town hall on the Szechényi tér square. There used to be a scaffold for the people of higher ranks on the eastern side of this square. The White Lady of Levoča was also executed there in 1715. Her story was immortalized in the

novel of the world-famous Hungarian novelist Mór Jókai.

Opposite the cathedral is the Bishop's Castle. It contains a chapel sometimes called the Dóczi's Chapel although Bishop Orbán Nagylucsei had it built at the end of the 15th century. Underground structures were found under the northern wing of the castle and were taken for escape corridors, but recent research showed that they are remains of the original buildings built for Bishop Omodé after the Tartar invasion in the 13th century. On the corner of the building several stones from the original Roman fort can be seen. The Bishop's garden is near the castle. A Baroque **statue of St. Michael** stands in front of the church from 1764. It was erected by a local nobleman who was sentenced to do so by the town hall, because he allied with criminals in order to get richer. On the corner of the Apor Vilmos püspök square is a permanent **exhibition** of the sculptor Miklós Borsos. On the **Gutenberg tér square** further to east stands the **group of statues Frigyáda** carved by Antonio Corradini to the design

Left: The Town Hall
Right: The Virgin Mary's pillar

of J. E. Fischer von Erlach to the order of Charles III in 1731. In the building of the former seminary near the statues apart from the theological college also the **Church museum and a library** reside. This building from the 17th century contains more than 40,000 volumes of books and old prints, while the most valuable of them are from the time of Matthias Corvinus. The symbol of the town is the well **Vaskakas** (The Iron Cock) located on the bank of the Moson branch of the Danube in the **Dunakapu tér square**. Its original is situated in the Museum of János Xantus. The symbol of the cock originated in Turkish times. According to a legend the Turks asserted that the Hungarians would recover the castle only if an iron cock crowed above the Danube. The original main square of the town was that of **Széchényi tér**. Markets, popular feasts and social meetings were held there. The buildings from the 17th and 18th centuries frame the square. **Esterházy's house** stands on the western corner of the square, its facade overlooks the Király utca street. The precious Baroque palace was built on the site of several smaller houses. Its first known owner was the merchant of Italian origin, Lajos Angarano. Today it houses a **gallery**. The house No. 3 originated to the design of Antal Frümann in 1850 in the Neo-Classical style. The contiguous No. 4 is called **Zittrisch house**, **Vastuskós house** or the Turkish house because the local people erroneously believed that a Turkish harem resided in it. A merchant in cattle Orbán Gindl built the house at the turn of the 17th and 18th centuries in the Baroque style. Mátyás Zittrisch also merchant trading in spices bought it in 1833.

The most beautiful Baroque building on the square is No. 5, the **Apátúr house**, which originally accommodated the Benedictine abbots. Now it houses **the Museum of János Xantus**. Abbot Benedek Sajghó from the Pannohalma Abbey had it built. Its most precious room is the former refectory decorated with the frescoes by István Schaller. The building contains the collections of history and homeland studies. It bears the name of János Xantus (1825-1894), a famous Hungarian geogra

pher and researcher of the American continent. The core of the collections consists of archaeological artefacts of the former Benedictine grammar school founded in 1858. It also contains the most detailed documents on 39 town guilds.

The southern side of the square is occupied by the Benedictine **church of St. Ignatius** built in the years 1634-1641 as a Jesuit church. The church has two towers. A fresco on the vault and the altar paining represent St. Ignatius. Paul Troger made both in 1744. The **pulpit**, a work of master Ľudovít Gode of Bratislava, is a Baroque jewel from 1744. The **Benedictine monastery** (1667) and the **Benedictine grammar school** (1627) owned by the Jesuits until 1803, were built simultaneously with the church on the southern side of the square. Opposite the church of St. Ignatius towers a 16 m tall Baroque **pillar of the Virgin Mary**. Lipót Kolonits, Bishop of Győr had it built at the end of the 17th century in the honour of liberation of Buda from the Turks. On the pillar made of red marble stands the statue of the Virgin Mary with the infant Jesus in her arms. Below it are smaller statues of

St. John Baptist and another three saints standing on four shorter pillars.

The **old town hall** on the Rákóczi Ferenc utca street was built in the 16th century. It was severely damaged during the Turkish wars. A new building was erected only when Győr became again a free royal borough in 1743. The building served as a town hall only until 1898. It is now an admired Baroque single-storied palace. Its balcony above the gate is supported by two Tuscany pillars and a stone console. The railing of the balcony is also interesting for its artistic form. The present town hall on **Városház tér** (Town Hall Square) is built in the eclectic style with a tower and semicircular balcony. It was built in the years 1896-1898 to the plans of the architect Jenő Hübner. In its hall stands a statue made by the glass-blower József Bisinger and the building was financed from his legacy.

The house called **Kreszta** from the 18th century on Apáca utca street No. 1

Left: The old nooks of Győr
Right: A rural house in Ásványráró
The Moson branch of the Danube

lying further north from Szechényi tér square is also valuable. It acquired it present Neo-Classical appearance in th 19th century. Today you will find there permanent **exhibition** of Margit Kovács ceramics. The building called **Hungarian Ispita** on the Rákóczi utca street No. was built in 1666 on the site of several old houses as a hospice for the old and sick and it was financed from the foundation of Bishop György Széchényi. It is a one storey house with two statues in its facade. It has two courtyards with balconies supported by Tuscany pillars. It is generally accepted as one of the most beautiful Renaissance monuments in the town. The Ispita also had an 18th century church connected with the **church of St. Anna**. I was severely damaged in the Second World War and only the altar of St. Elizabeth survived. The painting on the altar is by István Schaller who painted it in 1740. The building now contains the collections of Péter Váczy who donated them to the town. Not far from the Hungarian Ispita a **Franciscan monastery** was built in the 17th century and rebuilt in the Neo-Classical style in 1826. **Ferenc Liszt** gave concert in this building on January 16th 1840 The tablet and the bust of the famous composer on the building commemorate the event. There is another tablet dedicated to Jan Sobieski, King of Poland, who participated in the defeat of the Turkish troops in the northern part of the Danube Basin in 1683. At Liszt F. utca No. 20 stands the **House of Zichy,** one of the most wonderful buildings in the town. The building was built in 1720 by Ferenc Miller for the Count István Zichy. A group of statues of Mary with Joseph and Jesus Christ stands in the niche. A **bridge** over the Rába leads to the island, which is part of the districts of **Sziget** (Island) and **Újváros** (The New Town). The island is limited by three streams: the Moson branch of the Danube, Rába and Rábca. It has been inhabited since the Middle Ages The district of Újváros originated only in the 16th century. Next to the bridge is a boatyard from 1886 still in use. The **synagogue** standing on the island was built in the years 1866-1870. It is under repair now. As the island has a special atmos-

phere it became the regular venue of various international cultural events. The **Music Festival Mediawave** is one of the most popular. Another sacred monument of the town is on the **Petőfi tér square** — the Evangelical **church**. It was built in the years 1783-1785. The Evangelicals were allowed to build this church only under the condition that it would be erected within a closed yard and without tower. The structure consists of three naves and the altar is created in the Rococo style. Visitors to the town like to stay on the island because of its recreation area with thermal swimming pool. Next to the confluence of the Moson branch of the Danube and Rába stands the **Cziráky pillar** (Cziráky oszlop) built in honour of the Count Cziráky, who greatly contributed to the regulation of the Rába river.

South of the inner town (Belváros) is a more recent quarter called Nádorváros. It originated in the 18th century and its name derives of Palatine, administrator of the country (nádor in Hungarian). **Nádorváros** has a **Calvary** on the street with the same name and there are the stations of the Cross along this street. Győr has also absorbed the former independent villages of **Bácsa** and **Győrszentiván**. Bácsa especially is a favourite destination for weekend trippers. It lies immediately on the bank of the Moson branch of the Danube. Groups of **old willow trees** growing there create pleasant and original scenery. They are protected. On the Szent Vid hill not far from there an old settlement used to exist in the time of the Árpáds.

ÁSVÁNYRÁRÓ (population 1,950) lies on a small island created by depositions of the Danube in the central part of

Szigetköz on the right bank of the Danube, 20 km north-west of Győr. At the place where this settlement lies, Szigetköz divides into two parts, the upper and the lower, which are different in terms of fauna and flora.

Originally there were two independent settlements: Ásvány and Ráró. The contemporary village originated by their joining in 1936. The name of the first part Ásvány (mineral in English) derives, as the historians assert, from the fact, that its first inhabitants extracted gold from the river sediments. Ráró is an older word for falcon, which was a sacred bird of the Old Magyars. Some linguists though are convinced that Ráró was a family name or denomination of the local wood while Ásvány was the word for a ditch in the local dialect. The territory has been settled for more than 5 thousand years. The earliest settlement is documented by finds of fragments of worked stone tools, a lance from the Bronze Age, a Celtic grave from the Iron Age, and a Roman coin from the period of Antoninus Pius' rule. Ráró became part of the Héderváry estate in the 14th century as proved by references in the documents from various periods. The first written mention of Ásvány under the name *Assowan* dates from 1443. The owners of both settlements alternated and included the Bakics, Révay, Clobber and Pálffy families. Bishop George Széchényi of Győr also had some property here in the 17th century. Several destructive floods struck Ásványráró in the past like the majority of settlements existing on the Szigetköz island. The chronicles recorded the fact that the 17th century flood almost carried away Ásvány. The territory of the village was inundated for the last time in the years 1954 and 1965, in 1954, 360 houses were severely damaged. At the beginning of the 19th century 500 and 1,300 people lived in Ráro and Ásvány respectively. Most of them lived on fishing, gold washing or haulage. There were numerous mills on the Danube then. Both villages were known for cabbage growing, raising of farm animals and eel fishing. The villagers sold their cabbage in such remote places as for instance the Vojvodina region in the territory of today's Yugoslavia.

In 1938 more than 25,000 inhabitants mostly of Hungarian nationality lived in this village. The most important monuments of Ásványráró are the two Roman Catholic churches. The **church of St. Andrew** from the 14th century is in the part Ásvány. After it was destroyed in the 16th century it was built again in 1658. In the years 1820 and 1904 it was reconstructed and widened. The font of this Baroque church is made from red marble and it dates from 1430. **St. Rochus' church** in Ráró is originally from the 17th century. It acquired its present appearance in 1903 when the family of Count Wenckheim widened and reconstructed it in romantic style. On the edge of the village in the direction of Győr stands a **Calvary** built in the Baroque style by the Count Lázár Apponyi in 1738. It is surrounded by a poplar **grove**. The circumference of the thickest poplar tree in this grove measures 520 cm. Not far from the Calvary and near the entrance to the cemetery is the **monument** to the victims of the Second World War, the work of sculptor József Somogyi, who spent his childhood in this village.

MECSÉR (population 650) lies on the right bank of the Moson branch of the Danube precisely in the place where the river meanders. It has existed here only since 1564. The village moved according to the shifting bed of the Moson branch. The origin of its name is probably connected with one of the Slav languages. It was referred to under the name *Mecher* in historic documents from the years 1208 and 1359. Its first inhabitants were prob-

ably Slavs who lived from fishing and cattle raising. A cholera epidemic killed half the village's population in 1862. The village obtained its independence in 1937 when it separated from Mosonszolnok. It was then double its present size. This low situated village was often flooded in the past. During the great flood of 1954 half of the inhabitants were evacuated for a week to more distant villages. While it was connected with the opposite bank of the river by a ferry until 1946, nowadays there is a new bridge. The most important building of the village is the Roman Catholic **church**. Originally a small oval church or chapel must have stood on its site. The Count Ferenc Zichy built a bigger church in 1679. In 1744 an independent parish also originated here. But the new church did not escape disaster either, so the Countess Krisztina Wenckheim had another church built in the Neo-Romanesque style in 1900 and it is the one, which exists there now. The villagers maintain folk usage and traditions and the initiation of young boys is one of the most popular.

Initiation of young boys

At the time of the local feasts the young boys are initiated, which means they are admitted among the adult men. The boys who reach the age of 16 choose their godfathers on that day. Godfathers submit the boys to various tests and their fulfilment is the condition necessary to pass the initiation. The boys are then obliged to buy ten litres of wine as the entrance fee. Naturally it is all accompanied by fun and the whole village ends up enjoying itself in a dancing party.

Only several kilometres away from Mecsér, on the left bank of the Moson branch and 15 km north-westward from the centre of the County, Győr, lies **DUNASZENTPÁL** (population 600). The terraces of the Moson branch have been inhabited since the time when the Old Magyars came. However, the first written reference to the settlement is from as late as 1391, when it was part of the Héderváry family property. The name of the village is composed of the name of the Danube

Right: The church in Dunaszeg

(Duna) and St. Paul, the patron saint of the local church. The village was joint to the village Győrzámoly until 1926 and Dunaszeg until 1945.

The 16th and 17th centuries were of great suffering to the local population. King donated the local lands to Pál Bakics after the battle at Mohács in 1526. The Turks passed through the village in 1529, set fire on the church and houses. In 1594 the village burnt to ashes again. Slovak families were invited to repopulate the area after this event. They settled in the northern part of the village near the Moson branch of the Danube. The Turks passed through the village for the last time in 1683 leaving their bloody and glowing traces behind. The 18th century was calmer. Chronicles recorded that the population lived on pasturing, growing of wheat and rye, and forest economy. The owners of the lands were alternating and the families of Viczay and Héderváry were the best known of them. Nevertheless, there were some more disasters in the 18th century. After the troops of Napoleon passed through the village, it was stricken by repeated epidemics of cholera in the

years 1806, 1831, and 1849. Fire damaged the village in 1845.

Steam boats introduced in 1860 improved the transport communication of the village with its environs The bed of the Moson branch was substantially altered in 1888 and it prevented further floods until 1954. Many families moved out of Dunaszentpál when co-operative farming was imposed after the Second World War. This is the reason why it does not rank among big villages at the present. The most important cultural and historic monument here is the Roman Catholic **church of St. Paul** built in 1847. The Moson branch of the Danube attracts tourists and it is the favourite place of fishing and water sport fans. There is a **camping place** on its bank, which is full of trippers in summer.

DUNASZEG (population 1,650) lies on the left bank of the Moson branch of the Danube about 12 km away from Győr. The legend says that the villagers are the descendants of the Magyar tribe which came here led by chieftain of the tribe, Huba. The first inhabitant of the village was allegedly a man called Pata who built

his house on the place of today's Pataháza street. The first written reference to Dunaszeg is from 1435 as a property of Héderváry family. It was gradually mentioned in other documents as *Dunazegh, Dwnazegh, Dunazeg* and *Dwnasegh*. The owners of the village alternated quite often. The Bakics, Pálffy, Révay and Czobor families owned it. In the late 17th century the village ended up in hands of the Viczay family and then it was inherited by the Khuen-Hédervárys. There is a reference to the village from the 18th century as one populated by Catholics who made their living by farming. In the mid-19th century it was referred to as well-kept territory where arable land prevailed over the forest. About 900 people lived in Dunaszeg in 1900. A fire of 1911 destroyed half the village, but in spite of it 1,000 people lived there after the First World War. The 1954 flood destroyed a great part of Dunaszeg. During renovation its ground plan was modified, roads were paved and the protection against floods

Left: The church in Győrzámoly

improved. Although Dunaszeg was under the common administration of Győrzámolyi until 1925 and in the years 1968-1990 under that of Dunaszentpál and Győrzámoly, it is now independent again.

The most important building of the village is its Roman Catholic **church of the Sacred Heart of Jesus**. The original church was destroyed in 1658. Family Viczay built the new church in 1720. This Baroque church was later adapted but its furniture from the 18th century survived. Especially the main Baroque altar from the 18th century is remarkable. On the outer wall of the church is the **tablet** commemorating the victims of both World wars. There is also a **monument Kis kép** built in the honour of the four patron saints of the village: Florian, Vendel, Borbála and the Blessed Virgin Mary. There are several wonderful spots around the village amidst the nature of the Moson branch frequently sought after by hikers and above all cyclists. Two independently situated homesteads, the smaller called Bolgányi puszta, west of the village and the second more popular Gyulamajor lying north-west of the village are also interesting.

Travelling from Dunaszeg to Győr one passes through three villages, which bear the name of their corresponding county seat in their names. The first of them is **GYŐRLADAMÉR** (population 1,150) and lies on the left bank of the Moson branch, 10 km away from Győr, the county seat. The village probably acquired its name from that of Ladomer, Bishop of Esztergom who held the office in the years 1279-1297. According to another version its name derives from the Ladomer brook, which flows not far from the village. The first reference to the village dates from 1146 when The Knight Hedrych Héder owned it. Other reference mentions that during the reign of King Stephen V the territory was the property of the Kurig family. The village was later mentioned in various documents as *Ladamer, Ladomeer, Ladomér,* and *Lodomér*. Various noble families who lived on the Szigetköz island successively owned it: Héderváry, Amade, Révay, Pálffy, Czobor, and Viczay. The Turkish troops caused a lot of damage in the village in the 17th century. When they left it was almost depopulated. The new settlers came only after 1719 when several families were moved here from the County of Veszprém. However, it was never a big village and its population did not reach a third of its present number in the 19th century. The records about the life of the locals talk about fruit and corn growing. The flood in 1954 caused a lot of sorrow and damage to the village. It was built again as so many times in its history. The population number has increased in the last decades of its existence. As it is close to the county seat and has a pleasant ambience, new houses are being built and citizens of Győr buy the old and empty ones. The most important monument of the village is the comparatively recent Roman Catholic **church**. Győrladamér became an independent parish only in 1946. Until then it was administered by the neighbouring village of Győrzámoly. The new church, converted from what was originally a granary was consecrated in the same year.

But tourists prefer the environs of this village. The vicinity of the main stream of the Danube and its branches is the main feature of the territory. There is the wood called Somos-erdő and a lake Nádas tó (The Reed Lake) and the remains of the dead branch of the Danube in the administrative territory of the village. A small **port** was built on the bank of the Moson branch. The fans of horse riding also come into their own as there is a **riding school** in the village. A **cycling route**, which crosses the whole of the Szigetköz island, passes through Győrladamér.

The neighbouring village of **GYŐRZÁMOLY** (population 1,450) also lies in the eastern part of the Szigetköz island, near the western edge of Győr. The origin of its name derives from one of the Slav languages as it means the "place beyond the shallow point". Another theory explaining the origin of the name asserts that it derives from the name of one of the Héderváry family, Samuel. The first written mention of the village is from 1271. It was a property of the Héderváry family in the first half of the 15th century. In the years 1443-1548 it was mentioned in sixteen documents in different forms: *Zámoly, Zamoly, Zamol*. The Szemere, Nagylucsei and Rozgonyi families successively owned it. At the beginning of the 17th century the Héderváry family owned it again. The local population lived on farming and fishing. The cabbage cultivated in this village was sold at the markets of Vác and Pest. The village lived through hard times when Napoleon's troops burnt it at the beginning of the 19th century (1809).

The village was quickly restored and it had as many as 920 inhabitants in 1836. In 1869 part of the village, including the school and church fell victims to fire. The floods were a permanent danger. The last destructive flood struck the village along with others in the wider environs in 1954. In spite of the fact that Győrzámoly was in a safer place than the lower situated villages straight on the Danube's bank, the damage was great. Water carried away the majority of the older and more interesting houses. Today more recent houses built in the second half of the 20th century prevail. The dominant feature of the village is the Roman Catholic **church of St. Ladislav** built in 1779 in the Baroque style on the site of a smaller church burnt by the Turks. It burnt down in 1869 and was built again in its original form. The side altar, pulpit and baptistery are its interior items that were moved here from the original church. The victims of the two World Wars have their **monument** here. The village also has its social life. For instance, a competition of amateur singers of folk songs called Daloló Szigetköz (The Singing Szigetköz) is organized here. The local **museum of homeland studies** documents the interesting history of the village and landmarks in its fine natural setting. The Moson branch of the Danube is suitable for water sports. There is also another branch of the Danube in the administrative territory of the village called Remencei-ág. It contains the largest reed growth in the lower part of the Szigetköz island. In turn the locality Zámolyi tölös is known for its best-conserved hard alluvial forest in the region with prevalence of oak, elm, and ash trees.

Near the north-western edge of Győr and south-eastern edge of Szigetköz is the

village of **GYŐRÚJFALU** (population 1,000). The first written reference to this village is from 1341. Later it was mentioned as a part of the Héderváry estate and object of their property argument with the Bakics family. During of the Turkish occupation it was completely destroyed. Under the supervision of János Héderváry and Imre Czobor it was re-populated in 1609. The records from the 17ᵗʰ century reveal that the village was suffering from the presence of the Turks. The villagers also lived in constant fear from the floods. The local people were farmers and earned an additional income by haulage and trade. During the revolutionary events of 1848 the village burnt down. In spite of its vicinity to Győr, Győrújfalu was completely isolated by the Danube and its branches. The river Rába also represented an almost insuperable barrier. The only link with Győr was the narrow and poorly maintained bridge near Győrsziget. At the turn of the 19ᵗʰ and 20ᵗʰ century a plan to build railway from Győr

to Szigetköz was prepared. The negative stance of the owners of lands, the Hédervárys, and the beginning of the First World War hindered its realization. Only when the iron bridge between Győr and Révfalu was finished in 1958, was connection with the town improved. The village was severely damaged by the 1954 flood, which washed away the oldest farmer's buildings. At the present the most recent architecture is spreading here thanks to the well-to-do immigrants and weekend trippers from Győr. The most important building in Győrújfalu is the Roman Catholic **church** from 1848. Its interior is decorated with wonderful **frescos** by Antal Borsa.

Three villages lie west from Győr and on the side of transport communication heading to Mosonmagyaróvár. The first of them is **ABDA** (population 2,750). It spreads between the river Rábca and the Moson branch of the Danube. Originally it was situated several hundred metres further south, on the site now commemorated by a chapel. The first man probably appeared on this territory some 5,000 years BC. In the first century the Romans ar-

Left: The market days in Abda
Right: The market days in Abda

rived. The territory of the village was part of defensive line of their empire. In the second half of the 6th century the Avars occupied the territory and in 803 the river Rábca was the frontier of the Frankish Empire. In 883 the ruler of the Great Moravian Empire, Svätopluk plundered the area. The Magyar tribes arrived at this area in 900. The Rábca and the Moson branch of the Danube then had uncountable small and interwoven branches, which created numerous islands. Abda was lying on one of them and represented the gate of Győr to the west as the village possessed the only ford over the Rábca.

The first written reference to the village under the name *Abada* dates from 1221. Swamps protected the village from the north and the west, but it was open from the eastern side. The Tartars used the fact and plundered it in 1242. Toll was collected here from the beginning of the 13th century. King Belo IV personally stipulated the amount of the toll for the merchants passing by and heading to Germany. A battle between King Stephen V of Hungary and King Přemysl Otakar II of Bohemia took place near this village in 1271 and ended with the victory of the Hungarian troops. The village became a property of the Bishopric of Győr in the 15th century. Due to its strategic position a castle was built in this village in the 16th century. Turkish plundering and floods caused that Abda decayed in the late 17th century. Only 60 inhabitants lived there in 1698. During the Rebellion of the Estates the bridge over the Rábca was destroyed, though it was rebuilt six years later. One of the legends about **Rákóczi's monument** is connected precisely with the period of the last battle of the Rebellion.

Rákóczi and a fish

The monument depicts the event when, as the legend says, one of the soldiers gave a recently caught sheat-fish to the Prince of Transylvania, Ferenc Rákóczi who was then transported as a prisoner of war. Rákóczi threw the fish in water with the following words: If only Rákóczi who gave you freedom, could follow you and be a free man! But the freed sheat fish was not perhaps a common fish because

Rákóczi indeed won his freedom back. The monument was erected in 1940 near the bridge over the Rábca.

In 1829, when two floods completely destroyed the village a new one was constructed on an elevated place called Pityerdomb. A battle between the imperial troops and rebels took place in the village on June 18th 1849. The patriots could not resist the Imperial soldiers, who outnumbered them and were defeated. They are buried near the **chapel**. Allegedly also the young Emperor Francis Joseph I participated in this battle. One of the most important Hungarian writers, Miklós Radnóti, also perished as a hero near the village in spring 1945. A **monument** standing on the bank of the Rábca commemorates this event. There is also a statue of the writer made by Miklós Melocco in 1980. The most important cultural monument of Abda is the Roman Catholic **church of St. Joseph**. It was built in 1845 in the Neo-Classical style. Behind the church stands the **statue of St. John Nepomuk**, a Baroque monument from the mid-18th century.

If you continue in the direction of Mosonmagyaróvár, you will arrive at the village of **ÖTTEVÉNY** (population 2,600) lying between the Moson branch of the Danube and the Rábca river, 14 km west of Győr. It is a former post station on the route Vienna-Budapest. The name of the village probably originated in connection with the activity of the rivers, which flooded the area and deposited sand and mud there. The material (öttevény) became the root of the name of the village. It was also called Öreg Öttevény (Old Öttevény) in the past. In the time of the Roman Empire there was a guard station on the site of today's village called Quadrate. The oldest written reference to the village as *Villa Wetewjn* is from 1321. In 1379 it was part of the Héderváry estate. In the document issued by King Sigismund in 1421 it was mentioned under the name *Eyteven* and later as a property of the Szentgyörgy family. In 1619 the village burnt down and a request of the villagers for tax exemption exists from that time. The villagers aban-

doned their houses in fear of the Turks advancing to Vienna in 1683. When the Turks left, the village became the property of Archbishop Széchényi. Imperial troops camping in Abda sacked the village in 1688. A toll on the rivers and roads was collected in this village for centuries. German families moved to the village in 1701. As the village was always situated on the main road, it also suffered during the Rákóczi rebellion and during the revolution in the years 1848-1849. In the 19th century it belonged to the families Viczay and Sándor, and one of its last owners was the widow of Miklós Földváry who had several storied manor houses built in the village. Destructive floods repeatedly struck the village. The most fearful flood was that of 1899. The village started to develop after 1867. Öttevény was always known for the vegetables grown there. This activity and trade in vegetable still exist and the villagers offer their products in tasty little shops along the main road. The village with numerous shops and service is well-prepared for tourism.

The most interesting buildings in the village are its **two churches and manor house.** The Roman Catholic **church of St. John the Baptist** was built in 1786 in the Baroque taste on the site of the original church. In the park next to the church is the **monument** to the victims of the Second World War erected in 1992. The Evangelical church was built in 1929. The manor house of the Földváry family dates from the 19th century. It was reconstructed for the last time in 1993 and it is now used as a hotel and restaurant.

KUNSZIGET (population 1,200) lies on the right bank of the Moson branch of the Danube in the historic region called Tóköz. It is 15 km away from the county seat of Győr. The village lies on the original northern frontier of the Roman Empire known for its chain of fortifications under the name Limes Romanus. The remains of a guard tower from that period were found in the village. The first written reference to the village dates from 1443 when it was mentioned along with the neighbouring villages as Öttevény sziget and a property of the Hédervárys. Its own-

Left: The church in Kunsziget
Right: The Danube in Vámosszabadi

ers alternated and included the Bakics and Czobor families. In 1594 when Győr fell into hands of the Turks, the population of the surrounding villages including Kunsziget fled to remote places. The document from 1602 mentions an abandoned and decayed village. The family Viczay-Héderváry decided the resettle the village by the beginning of the 18th century. In 1728 the local parish registered 600 inhabitants and at the end of the 19th century the number of inhabitants reached almost its present number. At that time the village separated from the neighbouring settlement of Öttevény and changed its name to Kunsziget. The village was struck by a great flood in 1899. The villagers were farmers and the carrots grown here were sold in many towns of Hungary. Apart from the Roman Catholic **church of St. Lawrence** the chapel of **St. Antal** built in 1830 to commemorate the victims of cholera epidemics is of interest. The chapel was widened in 1910.

The tourists travelling by car from Győr to Slovakia pass through the frontier village of **VÁMOSSZABADI** (population 900) lying on the right bank of the Danube, 7 km north of the county seat Győr. This village originated by joining the villages Alsóvámos and Győrszabadi in 1950. Both medieval settlements were part of the large property of the Héderváry family. The old name of **Alsóvamos** was *Vámos*. The name derived from its position and function, which was collection of toll (vám in Hungarian) and duties. The first written reference to the village dates from 1268 when it was mentioned as *Villa Vamus*. It suffered from wars in the 13th century. The Tartars and troops of Přemysl Otakar II King of Bohemia damaged it. A wooden church was built here in 1330. The Turks destroyed it along with the whole village in 1594. Alsóvamos was owned by several families, for example the Héderváry, Viczay and the Bishopric of Győr. In the second half of the 17th century its inhabitants were mostly Evangelicals and that was the reason, why the landlord János Héderváry asked them to convert to the Catholic religion or to move out. Those who decided to go, left for Győrújfalu, Čiližská Radvaň or other villages of the Rye Island in the territory of today's Slovakia. Napoleon's troops pass-

272

GYŐR AND ITS ENVIRONS

ing through the village in 1809 consumed all that the villagers had. By the end of the 19th several floods inundated the village. The worst of them came in 1896, when, as chroniclers put it, it was possible to go to church only using boats. **Győrszabadi** was originally called *Zabadi* or *Zabodi*. The name derives from the Hungarian word for freedom (szabad) and it is connected with the privilege of the inhabitants to free hunting and fishing. The destiny of this village was very similar to that of the neighbouring Alsóvámos. The Tartars and the Turks destroyed it. In 1727 only 12 families lived here. In the second half of the 19th century the village was completely flooded five times. It burnt down in 1924. But the worst natural disaster that has struck the village in its modern history was undoubtedly the 1954 flood.

As far as the cultural monuments are concerned, the Roman Catholic **church** from the mid-19th century is of interest. It was built on the site of the destroyed medieval church. Its frescoes and the altar painting are the work of an unknown Italian artist. The environs of the village provide numerous nooks for fishermen and bikers. There are three ponds surrounded by floodforest near the village. The dead branches of the river were gradually silted and created swamps with specific hydrophilous vegetation.

Not far from Vámosszabadi is **KISBAJCS** (population 700). It lies on the eastern edge of the Szigetköz island, 3 km north-east of the county seat of Győr. This settlement originated in a swampy terrain not far from the confluence of the Moson branch of the Danube and the Rába flowing into the Danube. The first written reference to the settlement is from 1252 when it was mentioned as *Baych*. The name derives from a family name Baj and with the suffix "cs" added to make a diminutive. According to the document from 1657 the settlement belonged to the Győr Bishopric. After the battle at Mohács at the beginning of the 16th century it was mentioned as an important fishermen's settlement. Along with the neighbouring

villages of Nagybajcs and Bácsa its duty was to protect the Danube ford against the Turks. When the Turks besieged Győr in 1594, the Christian troops built a defensive line with cannons in the territory of the village. The Turks destroyed the village a hundred years later (1683). The population fled to the surrounding swamps. The village started to develop only in the early 18th century. There were several mills working in its administrative territory. The caught fish was sold well in the surrounding settlements. The waterlogged soil was not suitable for growing cereals, but vegetables thrived and the humid atmosphere also favoured pastures.

Floods and two World Wars in the 20th century slowed down the development of the village, which is a small one. After the Second World War many people lost their jobs when the steam boat transport on the Danube disappeared. Also the 1954 flood was a great blow for the village as it washed away seventy percent of the houses. This sad event was the reason why better flood dikes were constructed in the environs of Kisbajcs. The level of groundwater also dropped by melioration. Nevertheless, Kisbajcs is now a lively little village. For example, the local newspaper *Szigetköz Csüke* (The Szigetköz Corner) is published here. Several cultural events are organized in the course of the year. The most important events of the village are the **feasts** celebrated on the first Sunday of October and The **Day of the Village** celebrated in summer.

The neighbouring **NAGYBAJCS** (population 850) lies on the right bank of the Danube in the north-eastern part of the Győr-Moson-Sopron County, 5 km north of the county centre of Győr. The first written reference to the village is from 1252 as *Boych*. The administrative territory of the village spread on the left bank of the Danube and on the territory of today's Slovakia in the past. The most important owner of the village was the Bishopric of Győr. The villagers together with the inhabitants of the neighbouring villages Kisbajcs and Bácsa defended the access to the Danube against the Turks, who advanced towards the north after

they won the battle of Mohács. As a results of the Turkish invasion some nobles from the south of the country also found a refuge in Nagybajcs. Thanks to them the village obtained several royal privileges in 1720. Nagybajcs was free from duties and could live on fishing and gold washing.

The village lived through a considerable economic development in the 19th century. Several water mills were working here and the river was used for transport. A port still exists near the village. Corn milling was also famous in this village. The last water mill worked on the Danube near Nagybajcs until 1935. But the floods always limited the growth of the village. The last one damaged the village in 1954, when out of 264 houses, 64 were completely destroyed. From the architectural point of view, the Roman Catholic **church** built in 1869 is of interest. Next to its wall is a valuable **statue of the Virgin Mary** from the 17th century. The varied cultural life of the village is remarkable. There are active amateur theatre groups and folk ensembles. The local **feasts** held on St. George's day, April 24th are very popular. The village is now trying to profit from

tourism. The favourite spot is that of the local **pond** situated right in the centre of the village. Nice trips can also be enjoyed hiking along the Danube. Interesting reed growths full of nesting birds are found in the inundation area beyond the dike, which protects the village against the floods.

The small village of **VÉNEK** (population 150) lies on the eastern edge of the Szigetköz island directly at the confluence of the Moson branch with the Danube. It is one of the oldest settlements in this region and was mentioned as early as 1003 when King Stephen I of Hungary donated it to the Pannonhalma Abbey. The name of the village derives from family name Vének, the written form was often varied as *Weinuch, Weinick* or *Wének*. The population lived through cruel times in the late 16th century. The Turks managed to cross the Danube near the village and started to besiege Győr. They sacked the whole of the Szigetköz island then. Vének was also completely destroyed and the population fled. It was resettled again in 1713 thanks to German settlers who called the village Apfeldorf (Apple Village).

Gradually Hungarian families from the surrounding villages of Szigetköz and the Žitný ostrov also moved here. However, several families left for America in the early 20th century trying to escape misery, because the village did not offer means of sustenance. The mills closed, the transport on the Danube was gradually disappearing and the repeated floods and groundwater damaged the fields.

The dominant feature of the village is the Roman Catholic **church** built in 1906. Its Baroque **organ** is a cultural monument and there are organ concerts regularly held in this church. The **statue of St. John Nepomuk** is also interesting. The natural setting of this small village is very nice. On the north-eastern edge of the village near the dike is a **park** called Aranykert (The Golden Garden). At the end of the 19th century the villagers planted here 12 oaks to commemorate the millennium and 5 in honour of Queen Elisabeth. A continuous alluvial forest survives on the bank of the Moson branch of the Danube.

Left: The embankment of the Danube

It is the richest one in species in the lower past of the Szigetköz. There are also excellent fishing spots in the environs of the village. Vének is full of visitors above all on the 1st of May, when there is competition in cooking of the typical Hungarian fish soup called **halászlé**.

The contiguous village of **GÖNYÜ** (population 2,800) also lies on the right bank of the Danube on the main road from Győr to Komárom. Evidence of early settlement of the area exists in the territory of the village. Stone tools from the Neolithic period and a mile stone from the Roman period were found here. A permanent settlement with paved roads existed here in the Roman period. The fort of Ad Status as part of the defensive line Limes Romanus was located the area of today's village. The settlement also continued in the time of the Avar presence in the Danube region. After the arrival of Magyars during the rule of King Stephen I a castle was built in the area of the village. The first written reference to the village is from 1222, when King Andrew II donated it to Pannonhalma Abbey. King Belo IV gave the castle to Mihály Bolunducsy for his heroic fight against the Turks. The village repeatedly changed its owners. It was destroyed during the Turkish rule and remained abandoned for a long time. Only several dozen people lived here in 1729. However, in the course of the 18th century the village revived and in 1784 70 houses and 7 mills were mentioned.

Great changes in the life of village took place in the 19th century. From 1830 steamboats were navigating on the Danube. Original fishermen, hauliers, and workers who were dragging the boats became fair-weather sailors. A port was built there. The village lived through hard times in the revolutionary years 1848-49 when the Hungarian patriots shot at an Austrian boat loaded with gunpowder anchored at the local port on April 23rd 1849. The blast also destroyed a great part of the village. In the ruins of the original **church of Sts. Peter and Paul** valuable documents were burnt. The new church, which is the dominating building of the village has stood there since 1880. In the late 19th century after repeated floods dikes were constructed. The works were finished in 1896. At the turn of the 19th and 20th century the village developed thanks to the port. But the situation changed with the onset of the Second World War. The greatest loss for the village, apart from the war damage, was moving of the port to Komárom.

The present inhabitants of the village have to commute to Győr. But the population is not diminishing, all the contrary, in the recent times several families have moved here from Győr. Many inhabitants from the surrounding towns and foreigners spend their weekends or holidays in the attractive environment of Gönyű. There are good conditions for water sports, fishing and relaxation in the quiet romantic woods stretching between the river branches.

South-east of Gönyű is the village of **NAGYSZENTJÁNOS** (population 1,850). In lies on the north-eastern edge of the County of Győr-Moson-Sopron, on the railway track from Győr to Komárom. Nagyszentjános has been an independent village since January 1st 1985. Before that it co-existed administratively with the neighbouring Gönyű. After the change of social and political situation self-administration was introduced here in 1990. The first written reference to the village is from 1216, when it was in the ownership of Pannonhalma Abbey as *Zászló* or *Zazlon*. In the administrative territory of today's village and on the site of the homestead called Krémer-major the settlement of Öreg Szentjános (The Old Saint John) used to exist. It had a church, which was later rebuilt in a fort. According to a legend the building had an underground corridor which connected it with the castle in Pannonhalma. It sounds like a fairy tale, as the distance is enormous. This village was probably destroyed like many other villages in the time of Turkish rule in the Kingdom of Hungary. It was resettled only in the mid-17th century thanks to the farmer families attracted here by the noble Esterházy family. Two settlements originated here: Nagyszentjános and Kisszentjános. When the Esterházys sold part of their lands to the Lichtenstein family, another settlement called Majkszentjános was founded. A **manor house** was built here at the beginning of the 19th century and Napoleonic officers lived in it in 1809. The village managed to obtain a railway station on the track Budapest-Vienna, which was a great event in the history of the village. It determined its further development. A mill was opened here in 1880. More families from eastern Hungary moved here in the course of the 20th century. The dominant building of the village and a centre of the spiritual life of the local people is the new Roman Catholic **church.**

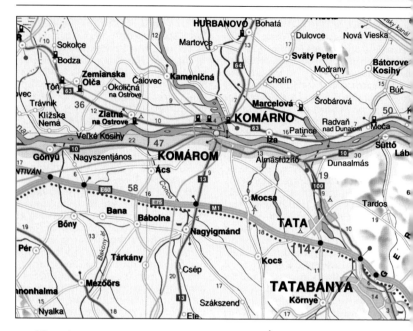

KOMÁROM AND ITS ENVIRONS

From the geographical point of view the region is part of the Little Hungarian Lowland and Transdanubian Middle Mountains, particularly the Gerecse mountain range. From the administrative point of view it fills the central and north-western part of the County of Komárom-Esztergom. The stream of the Danube limits the western border of our territory, in the south it is the section of the motorway Győr-Tatabánya and the southern border of the County. In the west it is limited by the County border with the County of Győr-Moson-Sopron and the eastern border runs through the central part of the Gerecse Mts. As far as the natural setting is concerned, the region consists of two parts: the western lowland and the eastern hilly parts. The biggest town of the region is Tatabánya, smaller though historically more important towns are Komárom and Tata.

Right: The port in Komárom

KOMÁROM (population 19,600) lies on the right bank of the Danube. The town originated by separation from the town of Komárno, which is situated on the Slovak bank of the Danube, after the First World War. A bridge built in the years 1891-1892 destroyed in the Second World War and reconstructed after, connects the two towns. The bridge is important for the international road and railway transport also due to the fact that the next railway bridges over the Danube are in Bratislava and Budapest and next to Medveďov in Slovakia is the only one border road bridge. Although the history of the town is rich, most of the events took place in the northern Slovak part of the original settlement (see the chapter on Komárno in the Slovak part of the Danube region). Komárom acquired its present face in 1977 when the village of Szőny was annexed to it. The western suburb of the town called Koppánymonostor was annexed to Komárom in 1932. The territory of today's town became famous in the past because of the existence of one of the most important Roman forts on the northern border of the Roman Empire, known as Brigetio.

Brigetio

The Romans constructed their camp on the site of a Celtic settlement and also used their name "briga" which meant an elevation or fort in the local Celtic language. Brigetio lay on an elevated section of the Danube's bank. In the north the stream of the Danube represented the natural defence and in the south swampy terrain provided another guarantee of safety. The ground plan of the camp was rectangular with dimensions of 540 x 430 metres. A stone wall with guard towers and moats skirted it. It was gradually rebuilt into a fort with four gates. The dimensions of the structure were intended for 4,000 to 6,000 men. For better security another advanced fort on the northern bank of the Danube known as Kelemantia was built. South of Brigetio a military fortified settlement gradually originated and the wives and children of the soldiers and veterans inhabited it. The settlement had its amphitheatre, churches, public buildings and houses. The water was brought to Brigetio by a pipeline from what is today the town of Tata. West of this settlement another fortified settlement also sprang up, where tradesmen and craftsmen resided. Both settlements gradually merged and created the town of Brigetio at the beginning of the 3rd century. Thanks to the advantageous central position on the defensive line between Vindobona (Vienna) and Aquincum (Budapest) the town became a busy trade centre. Paved stone roads lead from it to the west, east and south. The stones of the Gerecse Mts. were used for their construction. The distances were calculated from Brigetio and a milestone marked each mile. The Romans also made use of the Danube's navigability and had a military fleet. Komárom was the place, from which the Roman Emperors Marcus Aurelius and Valentinianus I led their military campaigns against the Germanic tribes of Marcomani and Quadi.

The settlement of Rév-Komárom originated in the Middle Ages on the southern bank of the Danube opposite to the Slovak Komárno near the Csillag-erőd fort. Monasterium de Koppan was the monastery founded west of this settlement in the 12th century. The Monastery of the Blessed Virgin Mary belonged to Pannonhalma Abbey. It was referred to as Koppanmonostor in 1413. It disappeared around 1529. The southern part of Komárom expanded in the 17th and 18th centuries even in spite of several disasters, which struck it. For example, the plague epidemic killed the major part of its inhabitants in 1710. Then in 1763 and 1783 the town lived through two severe earthquakes, which caused great damage. And we have to add the 1767 fire, which extended over the whole town. Komárom became the seat of the Austrian Emperor for a short time at the beginning of the 19th century. The Austrian Emperor Francis I with his court found refuge here from Napoleon in 1809. The Emperor decided it was necessary to built extensive fortifications, which could take 200 thousand soldiers on both banks of the river, including Komárom. His intention was to create an advanced bastion to Vienna in case of attacks from the east and an alternative refuge if the capital was attacked from the west. But the plan was not completely realized. Komárom became an important

strategic point during the revolutionary years 1848-49. The fort Csillagvár (Csillag-erőd) now in the territory of Komárom also played an important role in the successful defence of the town.

The opening of the Elisabeth's Bridge by the end of the 19th century helped to unite the two banks of the town. However, the two parts were divided again by the state frontier after the First World War in 1920. Three quarters of the original inhabitants remained in the Czechoslovak part of the town. Amenities, which were missing in the Hungarian Komárom, were rapidly finished then: the town had electricity in 1920 though the water main was not available. It was finished in 1927 by constructing a pipeline under the Danube bridge from the Slovak Komárno. The towns united again for a short time in the years 1938-1945. Komárom developed independently after the Second World War.

Komárom is often referred to as the town of forts. The forts were constructed in this town in the years 1809-1877. Out of the three forts the **Monostori-erőd** (the Monostor Fort) next to the Danube is the largest. It was built in the years 1850-1871 and served military purposes until 1990. Imperial troops resided in it and they also had a canteen and a bakery on the premises. Moats and underground passages also ensured the fort, stretching on an area of almost 60 hectares. Now it is opened to public and it can be visited with a guide. On the southern end of the town is the **Igmándy-erőd** (the Igmánd

Fort) built in the years 1871-1877. It is much smaller than Monostor fort and served the army until 1945. It is a part of the **György Klapka Museum** with ex hibits from the Roman period. The oldes fort of Komárom is the **Csillag-erőd** (the Star-Shaped Fort), the task of which was to control the passage over the Danube. I played an important role during the revolutionary events of 1848-49. This fort surrounded by moats lost its original function in the 20th century and is now used a a warehouse.

Among the most important sacred monuments of Komárom are the Roman Catholic **church of St. Stephen** from 1891 and the Reformed church in the Neo-Romanesque style from 1927 built to the design of Kálmán Dudás. A **statue of soldier** stands in front of the town hall and commemorates the war victims of Komárom. Komárom has more recent, 20th century churches. The Reformed church was built in the Neo-Romanesque style in 1927 and shortly after also the Roman Catholic **church of the Sacred Heart of Jesus**, an interesting work of the modern sacred architecture designed by Nándor Körmendy, was finished. Sport fans visit the town on the occasion of the **International Running Race Komárom-Komárno** and lovers of relaxation and recreation prefer the **local thermal swimming pools**.

Thermal water

The town has several hot springs. The first of them was drilled in 1965 and thanks to it 930 litres of water with temperature of 62 degrees Celsius emanates from a depth of 1,250 metres. The second spring was drilled in 1968 and its parame-

Left: The fort of Komárom
   The in-door swimming pool in Komárom
Right: The thermal swimming pool in Komárom
   The church in Ács

ters are: 930 litres of water, temperature 42 degrees Celsius and its depth is 1,268 metres. Hot water is used for the local bath and the municipal swimming pools. The water is medicinal and it heals the nerves, women's diseases, rheumatics, skin diseases, physical and mental exhaustion, and it is also used for general rehabilitation. There is a belt of greenery framing the swimming pool and its area of 40 thousand square metres makes it the largest recreation area in the territory of Komárom.

East of the centre of the modern town and on the ruins of the Roman fort of Brigetio the settlement Szőny originated (it has been part of the town since 1977). Szőny was first mentioned in a document from 1211 as *Sun*. Then it was mentioned as *Seun* and was a property of the Archbishop of Esztergom in 1249. Later the presently used name Szőny was adopted and it is probably derived from the Hungarian word for fair-haired "szőke". The Turks destroyed the community known for growing vines in 1529. It was in the neighbouring island, where the Turkish Sultan and the ambassadors of the King of Hungary signed the first and second Peace of Szőny in the years 1627 and 1642. When Hungary got rid of the Turks, Szőny started to develop. The surrounding swamps were drained and dried and more arable land was made available. One of the greatest engineers and geographers of the time, Samuel Mikovíny, led the drainage works. Mikovíny simultaneously mapped and described the Roman monuments in this locality. The community lived its best times, when it was owned by Count Miklós Zichy's widow, Erzsébet Berényi in the second half of the 18th century. She financed several buildings in the village, helped with renovation after the 1783 earthquake, and dedicated to its memory the statue of the Most Holy Trinity. She also helped with construction of the two Catholic and Reformed churches, which testifies to her exceptional religious tolerance in a time when rather the opposite was normal in the Kingdom of Hungary. The dominant feature of the present urban district of Szőny is the Roman Catholic **church of the Blessed Virgin** Mary from 1777 presumably designed by Jakab Fellner.

The town and its environs boast several protected localities. **Ácsi-erdő** or the Wood of Ács, situated in the west is widely used for trips and walks. There is a **pheasantry** in the same locality. The Danube created the Monostori sziget island near Komárom. The original Szőnyi-sziget island, where the Szőny Peace was signed in the 17th century disappeared as a result of the river's activity and regulation.

ÁCS (population 7,000) is situated south-west of Komárno near the Danube in the north-western part of the County of Komárom-Esztergom. It has a very advan-

Left: The Danube near Almásfűzitö

tageous position on the main railway line from Budapest to Vienna. It spreads over a moderately undulating landscape in the valley of Concó brook. The territory of the village was settled already in the Roman period. It was mentioned as *Ad Status* and later a shorter variation *Ads* was used. The first written reference to the settlement is from 1138. Counts Pál and Vilmos owned it in 1434. The settlement disappeared in the time of Turkish rule in 1540. In 1590 it was mentioned as *Ácsi* and only four families inhabited it. In the 17th century Hungarian Protestant families moved here from Komárom. The village was subsequently owned by different noble families, for example the Lengyels, Poglányis, etc. Later the Eszterházy family acquired large estates here. The settlement expanded in the 18th century, and the census of 1787 documents 2,895 inhabitants in Ács. In the 19th century the village became part of a Zichy property. In 1809 a battle between the Napoleonic and Hungarian troops led by the Count Batthány took place near the village. The

village became the scene of important fighting again during the revolutionary events in summer 1849. When businessman Konrád Patzenhoffer, motivated by the fact that Komárom lay on the main railway line, founded a sugar refinery here, the first in the whole of the County of Komárom, the village lived through a period of development.

The most important secular building in the village is the Zichy **manor house** with its park. The oldest part of the building is from the 13th century and its largest part is from the 17th century. It was originally owned by the Esterházy family, the reason, why it is also called Esterházy's manor house. For the time being it houses the cultural centre and the local library. Ács has the Roman Catholic **church of Assumption of the Virgin Mary** from 1844. Its altar bears the painting of the Assumption of the Virgin Mary by Friedrich Schildner. Four valuable Rococo pews are placed in the sanctuary. On the site of the old Roman Catholic church from the 13th century a Reformed church was built in 1640. On the edge of the village is the **Malom-tó** (The Mill Lake), a favourite spot for local fishermen. Ács also boasts a partially conserved water mill. More than 250-year-old oaks, conspicuous among the planted locusts and conifers, grow in the village. There is also a hot Artesian spring in the administrative territory of the village with a temperature of 71 degrees Celsius which is used only for heating the green houses at the moment.

MOCSA (population 2,250) lies between Komárom and Tata, in the terraced part of the Little Hungarian Lowland south of the Danube. The first written reference to this settlement is from the years 1237-1240 when it was mentioned as *Macha*. A document from 1291 mentions it as Mocha. Some historians assert that the name is of Slav origin and probably derives from a personal name. Others believe that it derives from the Hungarian word for swamp, which is mocsár. In the time of the Árpád dynasty the village was a royal property. It was then inhabited by the royal hunters. Wife of the King Andrew III donated Mocha to the Archbishopric of Esztergom and from then for a long time, in fact until the end of the Second World War, it remained in its hands. The village was destroyed by the Turkish troops in 1543. It was resettled only in 1622 by the Hungarian families of the Reformed Church. The Archbishop of Esztergom prohibited the Reformed Church in 1715 and the believers were included in the Roman Catholic parish. Immediately after he had a Roman Catholic church built. In 1782 the parish of the Reformed Church was restored, and a year later the Reformed church was built. The village counted then 2,456 inhabitants. Mocsa was damaged during the Napoleonic wars and similar destruction was caused by the revolutionary years 1848-49. The Reformed church was destroyed during the Second World War. Mocsa has an extensive administrative territory. Several settlements existed on the lands administered by Mocsa, but they disappeared in the time of Turkish invasion. Extensive fertile fields were cultivated by the locals who were excellent above all in growing corn, grapes, and fruit and in sheep and horse keeping. Later they were also dedicated to cattle breeding and bee-keeping and at the beginning of the 20th century to growing sugar beet.

The most important monument of the village is the Roman Catholic Baroque **church of the Virgin Mary of the Rosary** from 1758, which was rebuilt twice in the years 1851 and after a fire in 1903. The furniture in its interior is mostly from the 19th century. The **statue of the Most Holy Trinity** is also an interesting cultural monument from 1824. On the Kis utca street No. 23 stands a **house** containing collection of old instruments and objects documenting the life in the past. In Tömördpuszta, part of Mocsa, also an original Baroque **monastic house** from 1760 and a **farm building** from 1840 in the Neo-Classical style have survived apart from the Roman Catholic **church of St. Stephen**. The village has its recreation area next to the artificial lakes, which originated by gravel extraction. It offers fishing, water sports and a camping site.

ALMÁSFÜZITŐ (population 2,600) lies near the Danube, east of Komárom and north-west of the town of Tata. It consists of two parts: the original settlement and a more recent industrial part with a housing estate. It developed into a centre of the Hungarian chemical industry. The chemical factory made use of the river as a water source and for communication. The industrial part is located on the eastern edge of the village.

Man has lived in this territory since the Neolithic period. Archaeologists also found remains from the Bronze Age and the Roman period here. The Romans founded here the military fort of *Azaum* and a settlement also existed here in Migration Period. The first written reference to the village as *Fizeg* is from 1005 in a document of Pannonhalma Abbey. The village appeared under the names *Fizic, Fizio, Fyzig, Fizigteu, Fuzegtu*. The name Füzegy probably derives from the Hungarian word for willow (füzfa). Its present name appeared for the first time in 1095 when a joint railway station was established with the adjacent village of Dunaálmás. The Benedictine order owned the village in time of the Árpád dynasty. King Belo IV invited German colonists to renew the village destroyed by the Tartars. It was also owned by Matúš Čák for a short time and then it was again a royal property. It was subject to Komárno Castle in 1422. Turkish troops burned it down in 1529 and historic documents from 1570 show that it was not resettled by then. Count Isztván Zichy purchased the local lands in the 17th century and had Hungarian families settled here. Almásfüzitő became an industrial village in the 19th century. A starch producing factory, distilleries, and sugar factory and a steam mill were gradually opened here. The industrial orientation of Almásfüzitő deepened in the 20th century. A crude oil refinery worked here for a short time in 1904, and in 1934 the flax and hide processing factories were put into operation. The industrial part of the village was bombed during the Second World War. A factory processing bauxite, the most important in Hungary, was founded here after the war. The village does not possess cultural monuments worth mentioning. But the visitors like to attend various cultural and sport events held here. Every September the event Füzitői napok (The Füzitő Days) with varied accompanying programs is a well-known cultural event, and in summer the international race of motorboats is organized on the adjacent reach of the Danube.

NASZÁLY (population 2,250) stretches between Komárom and Tata, on the dunes of the Danube in a slightly undulating terraced lowland. The first inhabitants of the area were the carriers of the Hallstatt Culture from the Iron Age, which left remains of graves here. The first written reference to Naszály is from 1269 as *Keurus*. The variation of its present name, Naszal, appeared for the first time in 1628. It probably derives from a Slav name Nosál. The original medieval settlement was destroyed by the Turks. In 1643 it was referred to as a property of Count Ferenc Zichy. The Count tried to attract here labour and new settlers came to the village only after 1645. The village gradually absorbed the lands of the disappeared settlements such as Billeg and Grébics.

Right: The "puszta" riders

The owners of the village alternated in the 18th century and in 1727 József Esterházy bought the estates on its territory. From then up to 1945 the Esterházys were the bigger owners in the village. Extensive lands provided good conditions for growing crops and farming. The village became famous for cattle and sheep raising, growing of corn, potatoes and for the spirit made of sugar beet. There was also a mill working in Naszály in the 19th century. An important part of its life was viticulture.

The Reformed Church decisively influenced the life in the village. Its **church** was built in 1787. It acquired its present form after the 1859 reconstruction. The former **water mill** with its brick bridge over the brook is a valuable monument. In the part of the village called Billegpuszta is the former **Esterházy curia,** a Baroque building from the 18th century. There are several remarkable Neo-Classical **tombstones** in the local cemetery. Tourists are attracted to the village on the occasion of annually held **feasts**, which take place on the first Sunday after August 20th. The second most important event in this village is the **vintage** connected with the village ball.

The local ponds founded in 1960's are an interesting part of the local landscape. Besides giving fish they also fulfil an environmental function, as there are numerous species of waterfowl nesting there.

DUNAALMÁS (population 1,500) is located east of Almásfüzitő in the northern part of the county, between the northern projections of the Gerecse Mts. and the Danube. As the village lies on the northern slopes of the Gerecse Mts. there are great altitude differences within the territory administered by the village. There is a nice view of the Slovak territory lying opposite the mountains from their tops. The territory of the village has been settled since remote times. Remains of various objects from the Copper, Iron and Bronze Ages, as well as from the Roman period and the time when the Old Magyars arrived were found there. The Romans had a quarry near the Kőpite Mt. where they extracted stones used to build the fort of Brigetio and roads connecting the individual forts. The Magyar tribes arrived in the territory of Dunaalmás at the beginning of

the 10th century. Remains of an earthen castle and burial places from this period were found here.

The first written reference to the village as *Almás* is from 1093. The name of the village derives from the Hungarian word for apple (alma, almafa). The village was first owned by Pannonhalma Abbey. The Tartars sacked and destroyed it. It was mentioned again in a document of King Charles Robert. The Benedictine order owned it in 1405 and two decades later it belonged to the Komárno castle estate. The Turks destroyed it in 1529. The captain of Komárno castle settled Almás with the Magyar families of the Reformed Church in 1570. An important historic event took place in the village in 1606 when after a 15 year war peace was signed near the Almás monastery. When the village was freed from Turkish rule, several noble families including the Zichy owned it. Allegedly King Matthias Corvinus and the Empress Maria Theresa used to bath in the local hot springs, which were also known to the Romans. The Swedish King Charles XII also visited the local spa in 1714. The village was struck by several natural disasters in the 19th century. Earthquake in 1815, which left it in ruins and the 1830 flood, were among them. The village did not escape destructive epidemics and the cholera epidemic of 1831 was the worst. In 1848 the patriots led by General J. Klapka clashed with the Austrian imperial troops near the village. Dunaalmás was known for its high quality wine, quarries and hot springs in the 18th century. The local quarries supplied stone to the construction of the Komárno fortifications, the Basilica of St. Stephen and Elizabeth's bridge in Budapest. Tourism connected with the local spa became the dominant feature of the 20th century village. Restaurants and hotels were constructed next to the local hot springs in the course of the 20th century and in 1933 even a casino was opened here. But the village started to decay after the Second World War. The quarries became meaningless and the hot springs lost their significance as well. The village existed under the common administration with Neszmély and under a new name, Almásneszmély in the years 1977-1991. Now it is independent again.

Dunaalmás has a Baroque Roman Catholic **church of St. John Nepomuk** built in the years 1754-1757. There is a **commemorative room** in one of the village houses, which contains along with other historic exhibits, the objects connected with the relationship of the poet Csokonai to his beloved Lilla. Lilla's (whose real name was Júlia Vajda) grave from 1855 is in the local cemetery. The village also had a **thermal swimming pool** serving the locals and visitors in summer months.

East of Dunaalmás on the right bank of the Danube is the village of **NESZMÉLY** (population 1,500). Remains of almost every historic period were found in the territory of this village. The most abundant finds are from the Iron Age and the Roman period. The first written reference to Neszmély dates from 1240, when it was referred to as a property of Pannonhalma Abbey. Half of the village was a property of the County of Komárom and the County of Esztergom owned another half in 1341.

Toll was collected in this village for two centuries. In 1439 sick King Albert II of Habsburg died here on his way to Vienna. The village acquired municipal rights in 1471. After the lost battle of Mohács, the escaping Queen Mary announced death of the king precisely in Neszmély. It was repeatedly sacked by the Turks and disappeared. At the end of the 16th century, a census quotes only 6 houses in Neszmély. Population adhering to the Reformed Church resettled the village, which was owned by Count Miklós Zichy by the end of the 18th century. The village was famous for its local wine and cereals, especially rye. The local wines were exported and competed with the well-known German wines. When in the second half of the 19th century xylophera damaged the vineyards, the villagers started to grow fruit and nuts. Lipót Hacker and his son founded a brickyard in Neszmély in 1922. The village had 32 businesses before the Second World War. The most important cultural and building monument of Neszmély is the Gothic Reformed **church** from the 15th century skirted by walls with loopholes. On the castle hill near Terekesz-patak brook foundations of the tower of a medieval fort were discovered. The Gothic **Király-kút** (The King's Well) on Szőlő-hegy Mountain from the 15th century also has historic value. On the edge of the village are romantic **wine cellars** dug into a loess rock where the famous wines are matured. The village organizes jazz festivals every summer. The dissected landscape with a narrow belt of alluvial forest creates a pleasant environment for rural tourism. Higher positions in the environs of the village offer nice views of the Danube and the Danube Lowland on the Slovak side of the river. The Danube widens near the village and creates several islands.

The Danube islands near Neszmély

The river widens between Neszmély on the Hungarian side and the villages of Moča and Radvaň nad Dunajom on the Slovak bank of the Danube and forms four larger islands: The Upper (Felső-sziget), The Lower (Alsó-sziget), The Mocsa (Mocsisziget) and Radvaň (Radványi-sziget) Is-

Left: The church in Neszmély
Right: A rural house in Süttő

lands. They are partly forested. In the past fruit trees were planted on these islands. The importance of islands lies in the fact that though no protected plant species occur there, they provide shelter to various species of waterfowl. At time of low water the birds find enough food and quiet spots for nesting here.

East of Neszmély on the northern side of the Gerecse Mts. is the village of **SÜTTŐ** (population 2,000), in the past known for extraction of red and white limestone. Objects and remains of structures from the Bronze and Iron Ages, the Roman period and early Middle Ages were found in the territory administered by the village. Milestones from the Roman period next to the original Roman road survive here, ruins of an earthen castle were dug out in the part called Alsó-Bikol and around the Gerecse mountain the remains of a ditch of unknown origin exist.

The first written reference to the village is from 1295 as *Sédtő*. The name was connected with that of brook Séd, which passes through the village. King Sigismund of Luxembourg donated the village lands to the Archbishop of Esztergom. Two medieval settlements existed near Süttő: Bikol mentioned in 1267 and Alsóvadács with the first written reference from 1138. The village was repeatedly destroyed and depopulated by the Turks. By the end of the 17th century German and Hungarian families resettled it. Historic sources from 1732 mention only German population in the village, which arrived here from Saxony. Several Italian immigrants, who lived on stonemasonry, came here in the course of the 18th century. It was the time, when quarries one after another were opened in the environs of Süttő. The local people were employed in these quarries and apart from it they grew vines and lived on logging. Several water mills were also working in the village. At the beginning of the 20th century the village had 2,200 people and 1,600 out of them were Germans.

The most important cultural-historic monuments of the village are the Roman Catholic **church** in the Baroque taste from 1716, **Reviczký's curia** in Bikolpusta, and an original stonemason's house a with Baroque well on the Vásár-tér

square. The **Millennium Monument** commemorating the arrival of the Old Magyars to the Carpathian region towers above the village. Several precious **tombstones** survive at the local cemetery. A bulky lime tree to which many legends about Rákózci's uprising are connected grows in the village. The dominant structure of the environs of the village is the **TV tower** placed on top of the tallest mountain of the Gerecse mountain range.

In the north-eastern part of the Gerecse Mts. approximately 6 km south of the Danube is **DUNASZENTMIKLÓS** (population 400). In this village remains of the Bronze Age and Roman period were found. Remains of a cemetery date from the time of the Árpád dynasty. The name of the village derives from its patron saint Szent Miklós (Saint Nicholas) to whom also the church is dedicated. The prefix Duna (Danube) was added to the original name in 1913 with the aim of emphasizing the situation of the village to distinguish it from other villages with similar name. The first reference to the village is from 1382 when it was owned by Mihály Zenthmiklósi and his wife Anna Agostyáni. The village was destroyed by the Turkish troops attacking Vienna in 1529. Dunaszentmiklós remained deserted until the 18th century. József Esterházy had it repopulated by Germans in 1739. They were mostly Catholic farmers. The German speaking population prevailed until the Second World War, and founded various associations and clubs here. Some of these Germans was driven out of the country after the war. A chapel substitut-

ed the regular church and on its site a log church was built later. The first church made of stone was erected in 1852 but it did not last long. The existing **St. Nicolas church** is from 1911 and it was built in the Neo-Gothic style. The village is famous for viticulture and quality wines, which are stored in historic **wine cellars**, dug into the loess rocks.

The village of **SZOMÓD** (population 1,950) lies in the western part of the Gerecse Mts. Two smaller settlements, Ferencmajor and Máriamagdolna puszta also belong to this village. The territory of Szomód has been settled since the Copper Age. Archaeologists also found here small object from the Bronze Age, the Roman and Celtic periods. Illyrian tribes lived here at time when the Romans arrived and assimilated with the newcomers. Stones with Roman inscriptions testify to this period. The first written reference to the village dates from 1216. Another mention from 1225 refers to it as *Zumuld*; the name derived from *Szomol* with the Hungarian suffix –d. The name *Villa Zomold* as part of the Tata Castle estate appeared in 1349. From that time it shared a common destiny with Tata Castle. Both became a property of the Rozgonyi family. After the battle of Mohács, the Turks advanced towards the north of the Danube region. They conquered the Tata Castle and destroyed Szomód in 1543. The village revived only in the 17th century after the arrival of the Hungarian families of the Reformed Church from the Tisza Basin. Count József Esterházy owned Szomód in 1727and invited here several Catholic families from Württemberg. The Catholics took over the Reformed church and rebuilt it as a Roman Catholic church in 1775. The Reformed parish was restored in 1784 and its new church was built in 1889. Cereals were grown on the fields belonging to Szomód. Vineyards were founded on the southern slopes. The village also had a mill and pond. Szomód was part of the town of Tata until 1990 and since then it has been an independent settlement. The most important buildings include the Roman Catholic **church of St. James** from 1775 built by Jakab Fellner in the Baroque style. The Baroque **statue**

Left: Processing of stone near Süttő
Right: The castle in Tata

from 1708 of St. John Nepomuk stands in front of the church. On the slopes of the Gerecse Mountains several protected wood and plant species grow.

The town of **TATA** (population 23,700) lies on the western edge of the Gerecse Mts. The territory of the town was settled already in the Bronze Age. In the opinion of some historians the name Tata derives from the one of the founder of the Benedictine monastery Deodata (which means "given by God"). Other sources assert that the name derives from Tata or Tadeus of the founder of the Benedictine Abbey in Tata who lived at the royal court. In the territory of the town and its immediate environs objects from the Bronze and Iron Ages, from the Celtic, Roman, and Avar period were found. The Romans constructed an aqueduct from here to Brigetio on the bank of the Danube. A monastery stood here as early as the 11th century. The Benedictine monastery was first mentioned in the years 1083-95 when Pannonhalma Abbey owned it. Gradually a settlement originated around the monastery. Tata became a royal property after 1326. The first reference to the

settlement is from 1221 as *Nova Villa* (New Settlement). The name proves that an older settlement must have existed here before. In the 14th century there were two settlements with the name Tata and two churches were also mentioned.

The **castle**, which is today an important cultural monument, was the main centre of life for centuries. It was probably built in the years 1397-1409 on a rock surrounded by moats and swamps as the residence of the Lackffy family. King Sigismund of Luxembourg negotiated with the King Erik VIII of Denmark and Emperor of Byzatium, Manuel Paleologos in the castle in 1424. The castle was partially demolished in 1543 and later, during the Turkish invasion; it was fortified with bastions. King Matthias Corvinus rebuilt the castle in the Renaissance style. After this reconstruction the castle was one of the most beautiful Renaissance buildings in the country. During his rule the castle had its best times as the royal summer residence. It was a favourite meeting point of scholars of European importance. In time of Turkish expansion the owners of castle alternated while it was further fortified. The

intention was to make it an advanced defensive bastion for the town of Győr. The Turks damaged the castle several times and eventually it was blown up by the Grand Vizier Kara Mustafa in 1683. The castle became an important bastion of János Botthyán during the Rákóczi's uprising. Count József Esterházy whose property stretched from Croatia to Bratislava owned it. He chose Tata for his main residence. In the years 1765-1769 he had a manor house built south of the castle, in which the Emperor Francis I and Napoleon I Bonaparte concluded what was called the Schönbrunn Peace. An important architect and builder Jakab Fellner designed the manor house in Tata.

Jakab Fellner

The greatest Baroque builder in Tata was Jakab Fellner (1722-1780) a native of Moravia. He studied in Vienna and entered the service with the Esterházy family. His buildings are evidently influenced by the

---

Left: The Gothic windows of the castle
  The church in Tata
Right: The chapel above Tata

French Baroque and Neo-Classicism. His principal works are the Lycée in Eger, churches in Pápa, Tata, Tarján, Császari, the manor house in Tata the Bishop's Palace in Veszprém, the Prince's Palace at Eger, inns and mills in Tata and Tata-bánya. Jakab Fellner architecture played an important role in the character of the towns of Pápa, Veszprém, Eger, and above all Tata. He died in Tata and is buried in the parish church, which he built.

A church college was founded in Tata in 1766 and personalities such as the linguist Miklós Révai or physicist István Szablik taught there. The painter János Vaszary, a famous naturalist and Árpád Feszty lived in Tata. Tata traded in corn, wine and timber, the commodities, which yielded a decent income. There were several mineral springs around the castle, which were regulated and the Nagy or Öreg tó (Big or Old Lake) were created. There was also enough water for artificial ponds situated north of the town. Tata boasted a unique fish breeding industry which matched only that of southern Bohemia in the framework of Central Eu-

rope. Economic development was also spurred by the favourable transport conditions determined by the situation of the town near the Danube and on the main road between Vienna and Budapest. The farmers used this road for driving their cattle from the Great Hungarian Lowland to the western markets, while they made use of the surrounding pastures to make the animals stronger before they were sold. It was near Tata that potatoes were grown for the first time in Hungary in 1745. In Vértessomló, not far from Tata, coal was also extracted for the first time in about the same period. Guilds were flourishing in the 18th century and among them the potters, millers, butchers and cloth-makers were the most profitable occupations. The territory with numerous brooks and lakes provided good conditions for the operation of mills. The historic records reveal that there were six water mills in the territory of the town as early as the 13th century. Tata became famous for production of ornamental ceramics, a lucrative article in the past. The first factory producing cloth was opened here in 1728. The owners invited Mora-

vian cloth makers, recognized masters in the craft, to help them with opening of the trade. The guilds were gradually disappearing in the second half of the 19th century when industrialization started. In 1883 railway transport was introduced. At the end of the 1920's the representatives of what were two settlements then, Tata and Tóváros (in English, the Lake Town), agreed that they would develop joint activities with the aim of attracting tourists. The English Garden (Angolkert) with exotic plant and wood species located on the shore of the Cseke-tó Lake opened its gates for the first visitors. Tata and Tóváros definitely merged in 1938. Although the merging of the Catholic farming population of Tata with more industrialized and Reformed Tóváros was not simple, the new settlement gradually became a recreation centre and one of the most visited places in Hungary. The town acquired municipal rights in 1954.

Among the most important cultural and historic monuments of the town are the castle and the Roman Catholic parish **church** on Kossuth square built by Jakab Fellner and József Grossman in the years

1751-1784 in the Late Baroque style. Esterházy's coat of arms is placed above its entrance. The **statue of Jakab Fellner** stands in front of the church. The Capuchin **church** dates from 1745 and is built in the Baroque style. On the shore of Öreg-tó Lake not far from there is **Esterházy's manor house**, also a work of Jakab Fellner. The manor house is surrounded by the Kastély-park with a row of lime and chestnut trees. North of the manor house towards the narrow part of the lake is the **castle**. The more recent part of the castle is its pseudo-Gothic facade in the courtyard from 1897. The castle houses a **museum** (Kuny Domokos múzeum) with a permanent exhibition of pottery, history and archaeology. Remains of the moats are evident around the castle.

Water mills on the shore of the lake are industrial historic monuments. The oldest is the **Cifra-malom** (Decorated Mill) from 1587 rebuilt in the Baroque style in 1753. The **Nepomuki-malom** (Nepomuk Mill) stands nearby and the **Miklós-**

malom (Nicolas' Mill) built by Jakab Fellner in 1760 stands on the northern side of the lake. In its interior is well-preserved wooden furniture. An ethnographic **exhibition** is installed inside. The Synagogue shelters a **museum** of copies of classical statues. Jakab Fellner built a Baroque **chapel** on the site of the original Gothic church from 1350 on Calvary. By its side stands the Late Baroque **group of statues** from 1770 representing the Crucifixion. Fellner's 45 m tall observation **tower** standing near the chapel offers an opportunity to enjoy the panoramic view of the Danube, the Gerecse Mountains, Vértes, and Bakony. It is a wooden tower with a clock from 1763 and it was built without using a single metal nail. A board on the wall of the tower, now missing, commemorated the session of the Diet of Hungary in 1510 summoned by King Ladislav II because of the Turkish threat. Ambassadors of the Emperor of Germany, King of France, and King of Poland attended this session. An open-air **amphitheatre** on the **Calvary hill** "documents" the 235 million history of the area as the single geological layers, sedimentary rocks of grey-

Left: The Öreg-tó lake
Right: The bridge in Tata

white limestone from the Triassic, red-brown limestone from the Jurassic, greenish limestone containing fossils from the Cretaceous are observable on the sides of the amphitheatre.

Tata: the town of lakes

If Győr is the town of rivers, Tata is the town of lakes very popular in the whole country. The lakes with adjacent park and English garden are the favourites of the locals. Öreg-tó also called Nagy-tó with the area 209 hectares, mean depth 3 metres and volume 5 to 6 million cubic metres of water is the principal lake. The little river of Által-ér feeds it. Unfortunately, the water was polluted by the sewage in the postwar period. In order to improve the water quality fish are no longer kept in the lake, the river was first diverted to a newly built decontaminating basin and the bottom of the lake was cleared of sediments. Water quality is now better and the town became again a holiday resort. The second most important lake of Tata is Cseke-tó. A 2,000 metre racing track for rowers was constructed on the Nagy-tó lake, which is larger and an Olympic training camp for the preparation of the top Hungarian sportsmen is next to the smaller Cseke-tó lake.

Tata is also known for its hot springs. The Romans called this place Lacus Felix (or Ad Lacum felicis), the Happy Lake, precisely because of the high yielding hot springs. The Romans transferred water of the Apácakerti spring via an aqueduct to Brigetio (today's Komárom-Szőny), 15 km away. The water temperature of the majority of the springs is about 20 degrees Celsius. It is karstic water containing dissolved carbonates. The yield of the spring is diminishing in the consequence of mining activity in the environs of Tatabánya. The performance of the springs has been regularly checked since 1919, when 225,000 cubic metres daily were recorded. At present it yields only one quarter of this. The Big Spring and Small Spring dried out in 1960. Problems with supply of drinking water for the town followed. When the scientists researched the Small spring another, called the Angel Spring, was discovered along with a cave where objects from the Celtic and Roman period, and the Middle Ages were found. The

Angel Spring yielded 600 cubic metres of water daily but when the groundwater level dropped, it disappeared. Artificial interventions, drilling and pumping were necessary to obtain hot water for bathing. These works were realized in the first half of the 18th century under supervision of a significant Hungarian scientist, Samuel Mikovíny.

Samuel Mikovíny

Count József Esterházy, the owner of the estate in Tata invited Samuel Mikovíny (1700-1750), a scientist, founder and the first teacher at the Mining Institute, the predecessor of the Mining Academy in Banská Štiavnica in 1727, to Tata. His task was to prepare the plans for regulation of the water regime of the Grand Lake (Nagy-tó.) Mikovíny drained the swamps in the environs of the Ószőny-Almás-Tata and diverted the water into the Danube. He fulfilled the demanding task and successfully solved the problem in spite of animosity, from the estate owners, who incited the lo-

cals against Mikovíny. The common people feared that they would lose the means of sustenance, especially fishing and milling, through the regulation of the water table. A commemorative tablet expresses the gratitude of the town of Tata for his magnificent work.

Agostyán has been a part of Tata since it was annexed to the town in 1985. It lies on the western side of the Gerecse Mountain. In its territory objects from the Bronze Age were found. The first written reference to the settlement is from 1343. The Turks destroyed it in 1543 and it was renewed only in 1733. German colonists resettled Agostyán, but they were displaced after the Second World War. Slovak immigrants replaced them. The dominant building here is the Roman Catholic **church of St. Ágoston** built in 1809. The landmarks include an **arboretum**, three kilometres away from the settlement, in a valley called Bocsájtó-völgy (The Valley of Forgiveness) of the Gerecse Mts. at a height above sea level of 260-320 m. On an area of 25 hectares more than 400 wood species, the majority of them

Left: An open-air museum
Right: Tatabánya

conifers from exotic countries grow. Instructive paths and a little lake were prepared for visitors.

VÉRTESSZŐLŐS (population 2,700) is located on the south-western edge of the Gerecse Mts., between the towns of Tatabánya and Tata. The first written reference to a permanent settlement in this area is from 1244, as *Villa Scelus*. In the time of the Árpáds vintners lived here and the name of the village suggests it, as *szőlő* means vine. The prefix Vértes was added in 1909 and it symbolizes the vicinity of the Vértes Mts. The settlement called *Zewles* belonged to István Rozgonyi in 1440. The village lying on the main communication could not resist the Turkish raids and disappeared in 1543. It remained abandoned for almost two long centuries. But the records mention seventeen Hungarian families of the Reformed confession and five Slovak Catholic families living here in 1717. The Esterházys acquired the village shortly after and came here in 1731. They offered advantageous conditions for settlement and attracted here more Slovaks from the County of Trenčín. Slovaks became the main ethnic component of the settlement. The locals lived from farming, logging and processing of timber and stone, and haulage. A fire destroyed a large part of the village in 1878. When it was restored, the existing ground plan with central square was given to the village.

The dominant feature of the settlement is the Late Baroque Roman Catholic **church of the Blessed Virgin Mary** built in 1792 and renewed after fire in 1878. The last adaptations were made in 1942. Several well-preserved peasant **houses** standing in the village are of interest. One of them contains a **museum** dedicated to the life of a Slovak family in the Hungarian part of the Danube region in the 19th century. The village became famous in 1965 when the remains of the oldest ancestor of man, almost half a million old were found here. This find was so glamorous that other finds from more recent history, which confirmed settlement of the area in the Early Middle Ages were ignored. The Hungarian National Museum established an **open-air museum** on the

site of the archaeological finds displaying some original parts and copies of the finds.

The early man of Vértesszőlős

Thick layers of the fresh-water limestone or travertine, which were extracted until 1965, are on the top of the Kis-kő (Small Rock) Mountain. László Vértés found some traces of pre-historic man there when the quarry was closed. The find is from the period about 500,000 year ago and it concerns Archantropus. Part of his skull, traces of dwelling and fireplace were discovered. The finds of animal bones and plant pollen confirmed abundant representation of plant and animal species in that period. Stone tools testify to the way of life of this ancestor of human kind.

TATABÁNYA (72,000 inhabitants) lies in the valley between the Gerecse Mts. and Vértes on the southern edge of the County of Komárom-Esztergom. The town stretches over an area almost 15 km long. The motorway and railway from Budapest to Vienna passes through the town. Tatabánya is the largest town of the

Left: Modern architecture

County and has been its administrative seat since 1950. It originated in 1947 by joining four settlements: Felsőgalla, Alsógalla, Tatabánya, and Bánhida. The town with oblong ground plan is not homogeneous. Its appearance is influenced by its orientation to industry. Air pollution caused by industry has been reduced recently.

Early man lived in the territory of Tatabánya. He used Szelim-barlang (Selim Cave) in the foothills of the Gerecse Mountains as his living place. Objects from the Iron Age, Celtic, Roman, Avar, and the Árpád periods were found in the territory of the town. Fragments of pottery from the Bronze Age were among the most important finds. On the bank of the Álttalér traces of the settlement from the Late Bronze Age were discovered. The Celts arrived in this territory in the 4th century BC. The area was included in the Roman Empire by the end of the 1st century AD. From this period remains of a stone building were discovered. Small finds also confirm the presence of the Germanic tribes,

including the Goths and Longobards. But the majority of the finds are from the Avar period (burial place, a lance and stirrup). Near the confluence of the Által-ér and Galla patak rivers remains of settlement from the period of arrival of the Old Magyars were found. There is a legend saying that the arriving Old Magyar tribes defeated the troops of Great Moravia led by Prince Svätopluk in a battle on the territory of today's Bánhida in 907.

First mentioned was the settlement of Galla in 1251 when it belonged to Komárom Castle. A document from 1426 quotes that Galla belonged to the castle in Tata. Two settlements containing Galla in their names, Kisgalya (Little Galla) and Galya mayor (Great Galla) were mentioned in an document from 1440. The name Felsőgalla (Upper Galla) appeared for the first time in 1459. The origin of the name Bánhida mentioned for the first time in 1288 is probably derived from that of the original owner of the Bána lands as there used to exist several bridges (the Hungarian word for bridge is híd) around the town. The two words Bána and híd formed the composed name of the village, Bánhida.

In time of the Turkish raids all settlements, which existed in the territory of the present town were destroyed and resettlement took a very long time. Bánhida was the largest of the settlement on the territory of the modern Tatabánya. Toll was collected in Bánhida in the Middle Ages. The cattle bred in the Lower Land were driven to Western Europe along the trade road. The region was repeatedly sacked during the Turkish occupation. Galla was destroyed as early as 1529. Bánhida fell victim to Turkish raids in 1543 after the castle of Tata was taken. Turbulent times did not allow for resettling the territory. The first settlers including several Hungarian families of the Reformed Church settled in Bánhida only in 1622. The settlements fell into hands of the Esterházy family in the early 18th century. The Esterházys exchanged a part of this estate for the one in the County of Turiec in 1629. Count József Esterházy invited German families, above all from Saxony and Bavaria to settle the estate from 1733. They stayed mainly in Alsógalla and Felsőgalla. In contrast to the Hungarian and Slovak population the German enjoyed some privileges, for example, they were exempt from tax for six years and they could freely move, purchase and sell houses. In that time Slovak Catholic and Hungarian Reformed families lived in Bánhida. At the beginning of the 18th century, the recogonized scientist and historian Matej Bel visited the townlet and wrote the following characteristics: "Although the structures of the church and of the town ruins suggest that Bánhida was sometime a prospering town, its days of glory are gone. Only fragments of an old road from Győr to remained here." In time of reign of Joseph II the census recorded 580 people in Alsógalla, 842 in Felsőgalla and 1,144 inhabitants in Bánhida in 1785. While Germans prevailed in all settlements with "galla" in their name, Slovaks represented two thirds of Bánhida's population. The local population actively participated in the revolutionary events of 1848. One of the leading figures was the priest from Bánhida, József Fieba. After the defeat of the revolutionaries he was convicted, served a part of the sentence in

the prison of Olomouc and was released in 1852. Completion of the railway from Újszőnyi to Budapest in 1884 had great importance for the development of the area. The second most important event was the discovery of coal in the environs of the town.

The most important cultural monuments attracting the attention of visitors are the Baroque Roman Catholic **churches** in Felsőgalla from 1798 and in Alsógalla from 1766. The **church of St. Stephen** in old Tatabánya, church of St. Michael and parsonage in Bánhida from 1755 and the mill Lapatárimalom from 1753. Except for the church in Felsőgalla Jakab Fellner built all the above mentioned buildings. History of mining and industry is documented in **the mining museum and museum of industrial history**. The main attraction in the district of Újváros (The New Town) is the **arboretum** near the sanatorium. Above the town on the hill Kő-hegy (The Stone Hill) was a **statue** of sacred bird of the Hungarians, Turul erected by sculptor Gyula Donáth. According a legend it led the Old Magyars from their original homeland to the Carpathian Basin. The place, where the statue stands offers a fine view of the town and the whole basin. The statue is in a **landscape park**, an ideal area for walking and relaxation in nature. Szelim-barlang is a cave in the landscape park, a protected area within the administrative territory of the town.

There are several protected areas, natural landmarks and trees. South of the town is the **Észak-Vértesi Természetvédelmi Terület** (the North Vértés protected area). More than sixty species of protected plants including rare forest associations grow in its territory. Several protected localities and parks are situated within the municipal limits. One of the best known is the **Calvary hill** in Felsőgalla, which towers to a height of 324 m above sea level. In its entrails are two interesting **caves** Csontos-barlang (Cave of Bones), where fragments of big mammals from the Ice Age were discovered, and Réteg-barlang (The Stratified Cave) with varied rock layers and stalactites. The parks of the town are also protected areas:

Jubileumi park on the south-eastern edge of the main square, **Május 1. Park** with protected oaks, **Népházliget park** behind the Jászai Mari Színház (Theatre of Mari Jászai), an **oak wood** near the sanatorium in the Sígvölgy and **arboretum** in Újváros. On Jegenye utca street is a protected **row of poplar trees**, on the Platán tér square an old **plane tree** is the object of protection and near the Ságvári utca street are three protected bulky **oaks**.

BAJ (population 2,650) lies in the western part of the Gerecse Mts. The origin of the name derives from the old Turkish language and its meaning was rich. Objects of the Bronze Age and Roman period were found in the administrative territory of the village. The first written reference to the village is from 1228 as *Bay*. In the Middle Ages the Garai family owned it. It was destroyed in the time of Turkish rule in Hungary. According to the census from 1533 the village was deserted. Hungarian families of the Reformed church gradually settled it from 1622. But the Turks burned the village again in 1683. Baj was given to the Count Jószef Esterházy at the beginning of the 18th century. As he was religiously intolerant and enforced the Catholic religion, the Protestant families were obliged to leave Baj. German Catholics from the County of Moson replaced them. In 1784 they built the Roman Catholic church in the villages. Baj was referred to as a settlement surrounded by fertile arable land and famed vineyards, which produced an excellent wine. The symbol of viticultural pride was the second largest wooden barrel in Hungary, known under the name Rákóczi's barrel manufactured in this village in 1832. Its volume was 74,800 litres. A brickyard was built in the village in 1860. The Germans remained the decisive nationality of the population even in the 20th century. The ethnic composition changed only after the Second World War, when Hungarian families from the village Zemné in Slovakia were moved here in 1946. The local Germans were not deported and preserved their influence. Gradually German cultural and social organisations were founded in the village. A self-administration authority of the German minority has functioned in Baj since 1994.

The most important sacred monument of the village is the Roman Catholic **church of St. Francis of Assisi**, finished to the plans of Anton Gott in 1796. Tourists are mostly interested in the local vineyards with well-equipped cellars. The local owners very gladly open them at any time of the year to host the lovers of this agreeable beverage. A former lordly **wine cellar** called Nagy-pince (The Large Cellar) built by the greatest builder of the region, Jakab Fellner, is situated on top of the Szőlőhegy (Vine Mountain).

TARDOS (population 1650) lies in the central part of the Gerecse Mts. in the Tardos-tolnai medence (The Tardos-tolnai Basin). It is the highest situated village of the Gerecse Mts. It lies at a height of 292 metres above sea level. The village is known for extraction of red limestone, which was sold under the name the marble of Tardos or the Hungarian marble.

Left: The statue of Turul
Right: The grapes of Baj

The red colour is caused by the contents of ferric oxide. The limestone was used for the construction of several buildings in Visegrád, Tata and Buda.

The first written reference to the village is from 1217 as *Tardos*, but the present name was used already in 1266. The name is probably derived from a Hungarian personal name. In the period between 1954 and 1993 it was also called Tardosbánya because of the main occupation of its inhabitants (bánya in English is mine). The village was destroyed in time of the Turkish occupation of the Danube region and deserted until 1720. It revived only in the 18th century. The Archbishopric of Esztergom moved here Slovak Catholics who built a new settlement in the immediate vicinity of the old one. They were living on mining and haulage. A great demand for stone used in many famed Baroque buildings in the Kingdom of Hungary started in the 18th century. Italian craftsmen and merchants moved here to extract and work the stone and their stay left traces in the form of some surnames still existing in the area. The architecture of long closed yards with houses covered by reed roofs is typical of the 19th century. It was quite normal that as many as six or even eight families lived in one yard. Some of those houses still survive though with shingle roofs. Almost 2,000 inhabitants of Hungarian and Slovak nationalities lived here in 1938. Most of the local Slovaks moved to Slovakia after the Second World War. As the village was situated on an elevated place, there is not so much arable land and the locals rather grow vine and fruit.

The most important cultural monuments of the village include the Baroque Roman Catholic **church** from 1775. Its special feature is the shingle dome. A recognized Hungarian historian and expert in Turkish matters, Lajos Fekete, was born in the village and the villagers established a **commemorative room** in his honour in Tardos. In one of the neighbouring house is a **museum**, which contains the original furniture and displays the folk costumes from the beginning of the 20th century. The environs of the village are also interesting for its natural setting. The

Bikol-patak brook passes through the village and flows into the Tardos Lake. The brook flows in a wonderful Malom-völgy valley suitable for walks and relaxation. The environs are rich in karstic forms including springs and sinkholes. Running races and tourist events are regularly held here. The **quarry** near the Pisznica Mountain is a strictly protected area.

VÉRTESTOLNA (Tolnau in German, population 550) lies in the south-western part of the Gerecse Mts. in a beautiful environment of the Tardos-vértestolnai medence valley. In the territory of the village objects from the Bronze and Iron Ages were found. The first written reference to the settlement is from 1247 and the second is from 1337. Vértestolna was not a big settlement in the past and that is the reason it was referred to as "pustza", the word for small settlements or farmsteads. Count József Esterházy bought the local lands at that time and decided to colonize them by inviting German colonists. Several German families from Würzburg and other parts of Germany responded to his offer and moved here because the Count granted them privileges. A parish counting 500 believers existed here in 1742. The people sustained themselves by growing fruit, animal husbandry, and extraction of timber and stone. The promising development of the village was hindered by fire in 1875. In the inter-war period around 580 inhabitants lived here, and the Germans of Catholic confession represented almost 85 %. The German population still lives in Vértestolna, the reason why also the German form of the name of the village, Tolnau, is in use. The village was joined to Tardos in the years 1977-1990, but since 1990 it has been independent again.

The most important sacred monuments of the village are the Roman Catholic **church of St. Antal** and the **chapel of the Virgin Mary** from 1812. The church was built in 1744, first without the tower, which was added to it in 1788. Its interior contains a valuable Baroque font and a Rococo main altar both from the 18th century. Forest prevails over arable land in the environs of the village. The Bikol-patak has its source in the administrative territory of the village and there is also a little natural lake.

TARJÁN (population 2,750) lies in the valley of the Szent László patak brook in the mountain range of Gerecse, 10 km north-east of Tatabánya. Small objects proving settlement of the area in the Upper Stone, Copper and Bronze Ages were found in the administrative territory of the village. The Romans and Avars, who left their graves here were also living in the area. The village was first mentioned in 1240 as a property of Pannonhalma Abbey.

The name originated, according to one opinion, from the Old Magyar tribe named Tarján and according to another version it stems from the Old Turkish word "tarqan", which means His Majesty. In 1426 it was referred to as a part of the Tata Castle estate. The village disappeared as a result of the Turkish raids in 1529. A hundred years later it was settled again by the Hungarian families of the Reformed Church. Tarján became a property of Esterházys who moved here German

Catholic families. Forty families moved here from the area of the German Schwarzwald and outnumbered the natives. A manifestation of religious intolerance also took place in Tarján, when the Catholics occupied the Reformed church in 1747. The villagers lived on fruit growing, viticulture, cattle and sheep raising, logging and haulage. The German colonists introduced a certain form of communal economy here. In the second half of the 19th century the village became known for its markets with animals. The German population was mostly displaced to Germany after the Second World War. Hungarians from the County of Borsod and southern Slovakia replaced them.

The Reformed **church** from 1779 (another source quotes the year 1785) built in the Baroque style is the most important local cultural and historic monument. Famous Jakab Fellner built the Roman Catholic **church** in the years 1779-1783. The main altar is from the 18th century, like the paintings of the twelve apostles on the walls. The Baroque statue of the Most Holy Trinity is also from the 18th century. The **statue of St. Roch** was placed here in 1766 as a token of gratitude when the cholera epidemic finished. Visitors to the village are interested in several peasant **houses** and the circular **cellar** on the edge of the village. A local German ethnographic **museum** was opened in one of the houses in 1975. North of the village amidst fields is a **tombstone** from the Roman period.

Somlyó-hegy is the mountain, which towers above the village and offers a panoramic view of the environs. A castle used to stand there, but only ruins are left. Not far from it is one of the taller mountains of the Gerecse Mts., Pes-kő, with a cave bearing the same name. East of the village is a small pond. Vines are grown on the surrounding deforested slopes. Wines produced by the individual private producers are tasted during the annually held wine competition. But if you visit the village the local vintners are pleased to invite you to their cellars at any time of the year. The **cellars** are concentrated south of the village at a pleasant place where there is also the local dis-

Right: Héreg

tillery. A **music festival** and a youth camp where German is taught are held here annually.

HÉREG (population 950) lies in the central part of the Gerecse Mts. The first written reference to the village is from 1326, which mentions it as a property of the Archbishopric of Esztergom. The name probably originated from the German family named Heric. Several small settlements, such as Fyast at the foothill of Jásti-Hegy existed here in the past. The first inhabitants of the area were probably the Celts followed by the Romans. Foundations of a fort, coins and remains of a Roman road prove it. In the 16th century Turkish troops repeatedly passed through this territory and they plundered the village every time. It was called *Zeregen* then and in 1570 it was mentioned as a deserted settlement. Resettlement started after 1662 when people of the Reformed church from the County of Hont, Catholics from the County of Komárom (from the village of Imel), and from the County of Vas (town of Sombathely) came here. A new settlement was founded in the administrative territory of the former Zeregen. The Reformed Church was prohibited in the years 1716-1787. A plague epidemic broke out in the years 1739-1740. In the revolutionary year 1848 some inhabitants fought against the Imperial troops, who took revenge by burning down a part of the village. The villagers lived on corn and vine growing and by logging in the 19th century.

The village has a Baroque Roman Catholic **church** built in 1794 and enlarged in 1825. The adjacent parsonage and the Late Baroque Reformed **church** from 1787 are also valuable. In one peasant house covered by reed roof with open fireplace from the 19th century a village **museum** was made in the 1980's. It contains the objects illustrating the life of villagers in the past. The top of the tallest mountain of the Gerecse Mts. (633 m) and the **Király kút** (The Royal Well) nearby are the most visited places as they offer **fine views** of the environs.

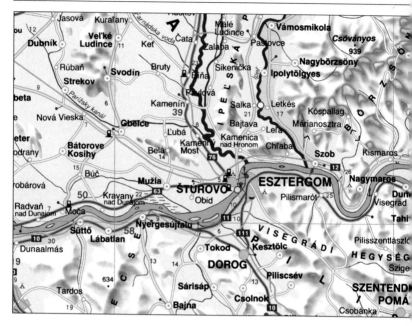

ESZTERGOM AND ITS ENVIRONS

Geographically the region belongs to the Gerecse and Pilis ranges of Trans-Danubian Mountains, and the Visegrádi-hegység of the North Hungarian Mountains. Administratively, the region consists of the eastern part of the County of Komárom-Esztergom and a small part of the County of Pest. To the north, the territory is bounded by the river Danube, to the south, by the southern and south-eastern boundary of the County of Komárom-Esztergom and part of the main ridge of the Visegrádi-hegység Mountains. The western boundary consists of the highest, central part of the Gerecse Mountains, while the eastern boundary follows the eastern ridge of the Visegrádi-hegység Mountains. From the natural point of view, the territory is very divided, varied and interesting, with the unique Danube gorge at Visegrád. The area can be divided

Right: The castle gate

into two parts – a lower western part of sedimentary limestones, and a more mountainous eastern part, formed by volcanic rocks. The largest town is Esztergom. Dorog and Nyergesújfalu are smaller towns.

ESZTERGOM (28,150 inhabitants) lies on the right bank of the Danube, west of the Visegrádi-hegység Mountains, in the north-eastern part of the County of Komárom-Esztergom. The Danube flows past the town in a curve, dividing into two branches to form the island of Prímás-sziget. Esztergom was one of the places of residence of the Kings of Hungary, and is one of the most attractive towns in Hungary for tourists.

The territory of the present town was settled from time immemorial. Paleolithic objects have been discovered on the Castle Hill (Várhegy). The Romans built an important fort on the Castle Hill, which received the name Solva and became one of the main pillars of the defensive northern frontier line along the Danube. Remains of the fort and some sections of Roman roads were preserved for many centuries. The name Esztergom is probably derived from the name of a Bulgar settlement on the Danube. After the coming of the Magyars to the Carpathian Basin, Prince Gejza used their existence and founded his administrative centre here around 970. The first King of Hungary, Stephen I, crowned on 1st January 1001, was born in the town around 969-975. The Archbishopric of Esztergom was also founded in 1001. Esztergom became the centre of a county, the seat of the kings of the Árpád dynasty and the capital of the Kingdom of Hungary, a status it retained until 1256 in the reign of King Béla IV. Until the 13th century the only mint in Hungary was situated here. In 1189, when the German Emperor Frederick Barbarossa passed through, Esztergom is mentioned as a developed capital city. Louis VII also stopped in the city in 1147 during his crusade. The Tartar invasion of 1242 stopped the flourishing of the town. The Tartar hordes did great damage to the royal city, but failed to capture the castle. It was defended by soldiers led by Simon Bajóti. During the siege, the population from the settlement below the castle retreated into the castle. After the withdrawal of the Tartars, King Béla IV transferred the royal seat from Esztergom to Buda. The royal palace was left to the archbishop. The city did not regain its royal lustre, wealth and glory, but it retained an important role in the state as seat of the archbishopric. Apart from the royal castle built by Béla III, the Cathedral of St. Mary and St. Adalbert was the most important building on the castle hill. King Stephen III of Hungary was buried in it in 1172. The finest part of the cathedral - the entrance portal - was built in the reign of King Béla III. It was built of red marble using Byzantine techniques. It was called the *Porta Speciosa*. The city was surrounded by walls with gates and a water filled moat. The city suffered considerable damage in the struggles for the throne after the extinction of the House of Árpád. Their successor Charles Robert was crowned at Esztergom. In 1301, his opponent in the struggle for the throne, Iván Köszegi occupied the city. Charles Robert and Archbishop Gergely Bicskei had to flee. Six years later the archbishop re-

gained possession of the city. Successive archbishops often played important roles in support of the kings. They participated in military campaigns, founded schools, supported the development of culture, established collections and built churches. At the beginning of the 14th century, Archbishop Csanád Telegi built various important buildings on the castle hill. János Kanizsai, Archbishop from 1397, participated in the Council of Konstanz and became Chancellor of the Holy Roman Empire. His successor György Pálóczi helped to organize the struggle against the Hussites. When threatened by Turkish attack after the Battle of Mohács, Archbishop Pál Várady transferred the archbishopric to Trnava in 1541. Soon after, on 9th August 1543, Sultan Suleyman occupied Esztergom. It was held by the Turks until 3rd September 1595, when Karl Mansfeld succeeded in capturing the castle from the Turkish commander Ali Kara. However, ten years later the Turks recaptured the castle and fortified it more strongly. This time they remained in the city for 78 years. In 1683, the united Christian army of King John Sobieski of Poland and Duke

Charles of Lorraine occupied Štúrovo. The Turks abandoned Esztergom on the opposite bank. The soldiers made their ceremonial entrance to the castle on 28th October.

The revived town was formed from 4 settlements – Királyváros, Vízíváros, Szentgyörgymezö and Szenttamás. The settlements were administered separately, but in political, economic, cultural and social life they were joined. In September 1706, Esztergom Castle was occupied by Ferenc Rákóczi. The Kuruc occupation of the castle did not last long, because the French governor of the castle Bonafax opened the castle gates to the imperial army. The new governor of the castle demolished two hundred houses in the area below the castle so that he could use the material to strengthen the fortifications.

Regaining the privileges of a royal borough in 1708 stimulated the development of the city. The city was gradually en-

Left: Esztergom at the beginning of the 18th
     century
Right: Basilica
     Basilica with castle

larged by settlement of people from neighbouring villages, but also of Germans, Czechs and Moravians. In 1700-1716 the Franciscans built the Church of St. Anne in the royal town. By 1720, the settlement below the castle was fully populated by 2,700 people living in 420 houses. In 1822, more than 10,000 people already lived in the four settlements in the territory of the present town. Fifty five guilds operated in the city. In 1851, a commercial chamber was established, especially associating traders in flour, spices and iron. However, the majority of the population worked in agriculture. The construction and consecration of the Basilica in 1856 was an important event in the history of Esztergom. Ferenc Liszt participated in the consecration with a specially composed work called the "Esztergom Mass". At the beginning of the 19th century, the seat of the archbishop returned to Esztergom. In 1853, during the period of absolutism after the fading away of the revolutionary events, the four original settlements in the territory of the present town were united under a common administration. However, in 1868 after the Austro-

Hungarian Ausgleich, they became independent again, at the request of the city and the county. In 1876, the inhabitants were shocked by the news that, since the city had less than 15,000 inhabitants, it had lost the title of royal borough. In spite of the efforts of the representatives of the town, the decision was not changed, and the town was restricted in its development. Development of industry in the town was restricted by its peripheral position away from the main transport routes. Construction of railways to Komárom in 1893 and to Budapest in 1895 brought a partial improvement. The Maria Valeria Bridge over the Danube to neighbouring Štúrovo was opened in the same year. The constant development of the four settlements in the area of the present town led to them gradually merging, and from 1895 they were finally united into one city called Esztergom. However, the town still retained an agrarian character. In 1920 more than 16,000 people lived in it. The break up of the old Austro-Hungarian Monarchy and its position on the frontier with Czechoslovakia also meant a shift to the periphery. The city was severely damaged in the Second World War, but the greatest loss was the destruction of the Maria Valeria Bridge, which joined Esztergom with Štúrovo. After the revolutionary events of 1956, the city was not favoured by the communist government because of Archbishop József Mindszenty, one of the leading participants in the struggle. After the crushing of the revolution, the function of the seat of the archbishop was more or less symbolic.

The most important cultural-historical and architectural monument in the city is the Neo-Classical **Basilica**. It is the largest sacred building in Hungary, built on the site of the original church of St. Adalbert from the 11th century and later cathedrals.

The Basilica of Esztergom

Building started in 1822 on the castle hill in the Neo-Classical style, on the site of the original church from the 11th century. Its construction was initiated by Archbishop Sándor Rudnay. The architect was Pál Kühnel. After his death, the building was completed by János Packh and József Hild. The basilica was solemnly consecrated on 31st August 1856. However, building work and construction of the portico continued until 1869. The church is 118 m long and 40 m wide. The dome has an internal height of 71.6 m. Some foundation walls go down 16 m. The portico of the basilica has eight Corinthian columns, each 22 metres high. There are statues of King Louis I and Archbishop Csanád Telegdi by the main entrance. Statues of Archbishop Dénes Széchy and János Hunyadi are placed a few steps further on the inside. On the west side, facing the Danube are statues of Kings Stephen I and Ladislav I. The high altar was made from marble by Péter Bonani. The altar painting, measuring 13 by 6.5 m is a copy of Titian's Assumption painted by the Italian master Grigoletti. The fresco on the sanctuary vault is a work of the Munich painter L. Moralta. Grigoletti also participated in producing the northern and southern side altars. The statues of Péter Pázmány and János Simor are the most artistically valuable of the statues in the interior. On the north side is the Chapel of St. Stephen, with an altar by István Ferenczy. On the south side is the Bakócz

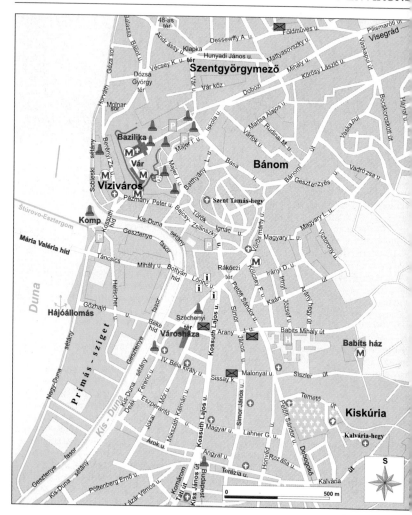

Chapel, which originally belonged to the old church from the 11th century. It was built in the period 1506-1511, as the final resting place of Archbishop Tamás Bakócz. Its builder, an unknown Italian artist gave it a Renaissance character. Its marble altar was made by the master Ferrucci. It is interesting that at the time of the construction of the basilica, the chapel was taken apart into 1600 pieces and re-erected after completion of the basilica on its south side. A separate entrance leads to the Archbishop's Treasury (Föszékesegyházi kincstár), containing a collection of medieval and later sacred objects, including the Renaissance Calvary of King Matthias. The crypt, built in Ancient Egyptian style under the central nave, contains graves of the Archbishops of Esztergom. The foundations of the original church of St. Adalbert are hidden here.

Right: Esztergom seen from Basilica

Next to the basilica is the entrance to the castle complex, with excavated remains of the medieval royal **castle**, destroyed in 1543 during the Turkish invasion. The excavations in the castle started in the 1930s and have continued until today. The most valuable part of the castle complex is the Romanesque **castle chapel** (királyi kápolna) with a rose window over the entrance. Its vault is one of the oldest in Central Europe. The restored palace (Szent István tér 2) contains the **Castle Museum** (Vármúzeum) with exhibits associated with the history of the town and its environs during the Turkish wars and up to 1945. Parts of the *Porta Speciosa* portal of the original cathedral are valuable exhibits in the collection of fragments. The castle is now being reconstructed, with some of its components renewed in modern architectural form.

A number of fine Baroque, Rococo and Neo-Classical houses have survived in the area between the castle and the Danube, in the Viziváros (Water Town) district near the castle hill. A Baroque Roman Catholic parish **church** (Vízivárosi plébániatemplom) with two towers from 1738 stands here. Beside it, on Mindszenty hercegprímás tér (Prince-Primate Mindszenty Square) stands the *Archbishop's Palace*, built in 1870. Today it contains the Christian Museum (Keresztény Múzeum) with rich collections of medieval Hungarian art, 60 valuable paintings by Italian masters, tapestries from the 15th century, examples of faience pottery and a collection of clocks. The archbishop's archives were placed on the upper floor. A Baroque **column in honour of Mary** stands in this part of the town on Bajcsy-Zsilinszky utca. The original county house on Pázmány Péter utca contains the **Bálint Balassa Museum** (Balassa Bálint Múzeum), named after the famous Hungarian poet. The exhibits illustrate the history of the town and include a picture gallery. The nearby park contains a **monument to Bálint Balassa**, who died heroically in the siege of the city by the Turks.

The smaller round Neo-Classical **Church of St. Anne** on Lajos Kossuth utca was built in 1828, according to plans by János Packh. Remains of the medieval **town walls and a bastion** have survived by the Little Danube, on József Attila tér.

A monument to King John Sobieski of Poland stands here. In the centre of the city, south of the castle is the main square – Széchényi tér, with a Baroque **monument in honour of the Holy Trinity** in the centre. The Baroque **Town hall** with arcades dates from the 18th century. It was built according to plans by András Mayerhoffer. The square also has some Baroque houses, built at the time of the Kuruc uprising led by János Botthyány. Near the square, in the so-called Inner Town (Belváros), are two Baroque churches, the **Parish Church of Sts. Peter and Paul** (Belvárosi plébániatemplom) from 1757 and the **Franciscan Church** (ferences templom) from about 1700. The poet Mihály Babits lived in the city from 1924. A house in the street named after him contains his **museum** (Babits Emlékmúzeum). The **Parish Church** built in 1775 in the Szentgyörgymezö district of the city, is an important sacred building.

Esztergom has an active cultural an social life. A real influx of tourists began in 1973, when the city celebrated the mil-

lennium of its foundation. Visitors come here in every season of the year, mainly to see the cultural monuments, but various annual events also evoke great interest. On the first Saturday in May, an annual **national pilgrimage** to the Basilica commemorates the anniversary of the death of Archbishop József Mindszenty, one of the leading figures of the anti-communist uprising of 1956. In July and August, the **theatrical performances** in the Castle Theatre (Várszínház) on the castle hill are popular cultural events. In the first half of August, the **International Festival of Guitar Music** attracts visitors. The **Summer Art University** is organized in summer. The **horse races** in August are the most popular sports event. Tourists also visit Esztergom for the hot springs.

The Medicinal Water of Esztergom

The Spa Hotel (Fürdöszálló), an old building with a modern wing, stands in Bajcsy-Zsilinszky street. As the name of the hotel indicates, behind it is a spa, already mentioned in 1238. The spa area with bathing facilities is in a park by the Little Danube. The hot springs in the area

---

Left: Basilica seen from Štúrovo

of the town were already used by the Romans. In the 12th century, the Order of St. John established the first public spa in the Kingdom of Hungary. New hot springs with a temperature of 28°C were created by drilling in the 20th century. The water comes to the surface from a depth of 323 m, and contains mainly compounds of sulphur, iron and magnesium. It is useful for medicinal purposes.

The territory of Esztergom includes the **Pilis Mountains protected landscape area.** There is a **ferry** between Esztergom and nearby Štúrovo on the Slovak side of the Danube. The Maria Valeria Bridge is now being reconstructed. The city is a tourist centre of international importance. Its cultural monuments and tourist services make it one of the best prepared cities in Hungary.

Since 1985 the administrative area of Esztergom has also included the village of **Pilisszentlélek** south-east of the city in the valley between the Pilis Mountains and the Visegrád-hegység Mountains. In the reign of Béla IV, the village already contained a monastery and a church. The monastery was destroyed during the Turkish wars of the period 1526-1543. The original name of the village was Hutaszentlélek because there was a glass furnace here. At the beginning of the 18th century, some Slovak families settled here. They supported themselves in forestry and the glass industry. In the first half of the 20th century, the village remained mostly Slovak in population (450). In 1948 some of the Slovaks were resettled in Slovakia. Today, Pilisszentlélek is a popular summer resort for people from Esztergom and for tourists from other parts of Hungary.

LÁBATLAN (5350 inhabitants) is situated between the Danube and the northern spurs of the Gerecse Mountains, west of Esztergom. It was formed in 1950 from two settlements – Lábatlan and Piszke, which have now completely merged. Objects from the Bronze Age, Iron Age and period of Celtic settlement have been found in the territories of the two settlements. Remains of a Roman defensive position have been found in Piszke. The first written mention of Lábatlan dates from 1267. According to legend, the name, which means "Legless", is probably derived from a local landlord with one leg. Piszke is first mentioned in a document from 1332. In 1385, both neighbouring settlements were mentioned as a property of Pál Henslini. A church with a cemetery were already situated on a hill above Lábatlan in the time of the House of Árpád. After its destruction, a new Gothic church of St. Michael was built on its site in 1400. In 1732 it became a Reformed church. It acquired its present form from a reconstruction in 1894. A Dominican monastery was founded at Piszke in 1489, but destroyed in the Turkish wars. In spite of the constant danger, the settlements were not entirely depopulated during the period of Turkish domination. During the 18th century, German Catholics were invited to settle in Piszke. Piszke was famous for the extraction of marble, which was exported under the name "Piszke marble". The most important product of the local farmers was wine, which found markets especially at Tata, Esztergom and Dorog. Industry was introduced in the second half of the 19th century. A cement works opened at Lábatlan in 1869 and in 1905 a works for processing "red marble". Both works use the local raw material - limestone. In 1925, a paper factory opened at Piszke. The cement and paper works also survived the change of political regime in 1989 and still exist today.

The most important cultural-historical and architectural monuments in the town are the two churches – the Reformed church from the 15th century, reconstructed in 1894 and surrounded by a wall, and the Roman Catholic church at Piszke from 1792, in front of which is a monument to the inhabitants who fell in the First World War. The original **furnace** for producing cement and the chimneys of the cement works are technical monuments. The environs are also interesting from the natural point of view. In the southern part of the territory, below the highest peak of the Gerecse Mountains – Pisznice (545 m) is a **cave** also called Pisznice. Pisznice belongs to the Gerecse protected area.

NYERGESÚJFALU (7,800 inhabitants) is situated closer to Esztergom, between the Danube and the northern spurs of the Gerecse range. Together with neighbouring Lábatlan, it forms a settled area almost 10 km long. It is part of the Danubian industrial zone extending from Komárom to Esztergom. As a result of the advantageous geographical position, the area was already settled in the Bronze Age. A cemetery of 180 urn graves from this period was discovered during building work. Vessels for storing food and drink were also found in the urns. The area of the town was also important in the Roman period.

A silver denar (penny) from the second half of the 11th century is the most important find from the period of the coming of the Magyars. The first written mention of the settlement is from 1283, and using the name *Nergetscheg*. After the Tartar invasions, the settlement is mentioned in 1285 under name *Nova Villa*. The present name Nyergesújfalu has been used since the 15th century. The name is derived from the Hungarian word *nyereg* (saddle) and *újfalu* (new village). There is disagreement on whether it refers to the saddle of a horse or a saddle between the hills above the town in the northern spurs of the Gerecse range. After Germans came in the 18th century, the name Sattel-Neudorf, an exact translation of Nyergesújfalu into German, was often used. The community belonged to various families. In 1371 it became a royal property. In 1388, King Sigismund gave it to the Archbishopric of Esztergom, which continued to own it until 1945. In 1438 King Albrecht granted it the right to charge tolls on use of the ford across the Danube to the village of Kravany nad Dunajom. The territory of the town remained a strategic place for military campaigns, trade and post. When the Turks besieged Esztergom in 1543, they devastated the wider environs of the city, including Nyergesújfalu. The place was soon resettled and remained inhabited, one of the few places occupied through the whole period of Turkish domination.

The settlement was again depopulated in 1683 during the expulsion of the Turks from Hungary, and it remained unoccupied for a long time. Some German and Hungarian families settled here at the beginning of the 18th century. The Danube crossing was important during Rákóczi's uprising. To guard it, the Kuruc built a small fort on the ruins of the Roman fort on the Sáncs-hegy hill above the village. The remains of the Kuruc fortress can still be identified on the ground.

After the Peace of Szatmár of 1711, a further wave of German settlers from Bavaria came to the village. At the beginning of the 19th century, the population was half Hungarian and half German. They had to face various floods and fires. Various mills, craft workshops and coal mines were established in this period. In 1816, there were 8 mills on the Danube. Some master stone workers from Italy came here to work the well known stone from the Gerecse range. In the mid 19th century, the daily steam ship between Bratislava and Budapest stopped here. In 1862, a brick works began to operate and was followed by a cement works. At the beginning of the 20th century, the town had a Salesian school, at which the well known Hungarian poet József Attila studied for a short time. Various important painters were born at Nyergesújfalu, including especially the brothers János and István Nyergesi. The painter Károly Kernstock also worked here. He was born in Budapest, studied in Paris and Munich, but he spent a large part of his childhood with his grandparents at Nyergesújfalu, and later liked to returned here. Nyergesújfalu has been officially a town since 1989.

The most important architectural monuments of the town include the Baroque Roman Catholic **Church of St. Michael** from 1771 and the **parsonage** from 1780. The parsonage is surrounded by a wall, in which a stone with a Roman inscription can be seen. Another interesting feature is the **stone cross** on Kossuth utca, the **house** of the painter Károly Kernstock, a Roman **column** in the garden of the house at Kossuth utca 5 and the **monument** in honour of the millenni-

---

Right: The church in Bajót

um of the coming of the Magyars, standing above the town. A **monument** to the soldiers who fell in the First World War stands on the Calvary hill. The **Chapel** of Sts. Sebastian, Rochus and Rosalia in the cemetery was built in 1739 after a plague epidemic.

BAJÓT (1500 inhabitants) is situated on the northern side of the Gerecse range, 5 km south of Nyergesújfalu. Finds in nearby caves under Öreg-kö (Old Rock) hill show that people lived here from early times. Fragments of pottery from the Copper Age have been found in the territory of the village. Pot sherds from the Avar period and remains of Roman graves have been found directly in the village. The area was also settled at the time of the coming of the Magyars. The first mention of the settlement dates from 1202, when King Emmerich gave it to a certain Benedek from Transylvania. After his death, Simon and Bertrand Bajót, who were of Spanish origin, inherited it. According to some historians, the name of the village is derived from them. Later, it belonged successively to the royal court and to the Archbishopric of Esztergom. It was depopulated

during the Turkish invasions. After resettlement at the end of the 17th century, the village was again destroyed and depopulated during the Rákóczi uprising at the beginning of the 18th century. Later, Hungarian and Slovak families gradually settled here. At the end of the 18th century, the village already had more than 700 inhabitants. In the mid 19th century, coal mining began in the territory of the village, which led to a number of peasants changing their livelihood and becoming miners.

Bajót originally had a castle. Its **ruins** are partly preserved south of the church. The castle was destroyed in 1332 during a war. The most important sacred building in the village is the Roman Catholic church from the 13th century. In the 15th century, it was reconstructed in the Gothic style, and in 1771 in the Baroque style, so that only a small part of its original Romanesque appearance survives. A Gothic portal from the 15th century is preserved on the north side of its tower. An imitation of the cave at Lourdes, built in the 1930s by the director of the mine Sándor Schmidt, is an interesting feature of the

village. Some elements of folk culture are still preserved in the village. Tours wearing masks in the Christmas and Carnival periods are the most popular. The territory of the village also includes the lesser village of **Péliföldszentkereszt**. It has **remains of a castle** of unknown age and a Baroque Roman Catholic **church**, built by Imre Esterházy in 1735. The village also had a monastery, occupied successively by several different religious orders, ending with the Salesians in the 20th century. Péliföldszentkereszt (Péliföld Holy Cross) is also well-known as a **place of pilgrimage.**

MOGYORÓSBÁNYA (850 inhabitants) is situated in the eastern part of the Gerecse range, only a few kilometres east of Bajót. The territory of the village was settled from early times. In 1959, traces of a Bronze Age hill-fort were uncovered on Óhegy (Old Hill). Smaller finds also confirm settlement in the Roman period. The first written mentions of the village date from 1269 and 1281, when it was called

Left: The "Devil Rider"
Right: Gyermely

Mogyorós (mogyoró means hazel-nut). It belonged successively to several families, the royal court and the monastery of Óbuda (today part of Budapest). It was destroyed and depopulated during the Turkish wars. It was resettled only after the Kuruc uprisings at the beginning of the 18th century, and mainly by Germans and Slovaks. The village has had its present name since 1902. The second part - bánya - means "mine". It is a result of the coal mining in the territory of the village, which started at Szarkás in 1819, and spread to other areas. Coal mining remained the main symbol of the village in the 20th century.

The **Church of St. Margaret**, which originated as early as the 12th century, is a dominant feature of the village. There is a **monument** to the victims of the First World War. The sculptor Gyula Bezerédi, an important representative of Hungarian sculptural Romanticism, was born in the village in 1858. His works were also installed in Budapest, Prague and Vienna. The village has a Slovak minority, which excels in cultural activity and preserves its traditions. The local Slovak **miners' brass band** has gained recognition at various competitions in Hungary. The annual camp for astronomy enthusiasts, called Ég-Föld (Heaven-Earth), is held nearby on Kö-szikla hill.

NAGYSÁP (1,550 inhabitants) is situated further south in the eastern part of Gerecse range and in the Bajna basin. The territory of the village was already settled in the Bronze Age. Fragments of objects from this period have been found at the localities of Kerekdomb-major and Úrisáp. Continual settlement of the territory also continued in the Celtic, Avar and Roman periods. Remains of a settlement from the period of the House of Árpád were found at the locality of Gedás-hegy. The village is first mentioned in writing in a document from 1248. At the beginning of the 14th century, the monastery on Margaret Island in Budapest held the largest property here. The Church of St. Martin already stood here in 1332 and survived until the 18th century. The village was depopulated during the period of Turkish domination in Hungary. In the 18th century, it was settled by Hungarian families, who belonged to the Reformed Church. The Sándor family owned the largest area of land in the territory of the village. Cereals, vegetables and vines were cultivated in the territory of the village and timber was extracted. Large herds of cattle and sheep grazed on the surrounding pastures. In the 20th century, the inhabitants were mostly employed in the surrounding coal mines. In 1890, a new Roman Catholic church was built. The interesting features of the village also include a well, called the Sodor-kút, according to legend dug by the Turks.

BAJNA (2,000 inhabitants) is situated south of Nagysáp in the eastern part of the Gerecse range. Objects from the Bronze and Iron ages have been found in its territory, including pots and remains of burial urns, and goblets. Pottery from the Celtic and Roman periods has also been discovered. The first written record of the village dates from 1293. It belonged to several families in succession. The village remained settled in the time of the Turkish presence in Hungary, unlike some of the neighbouring villages, which were depopulated in this period. However, in 1706 the imperial Austrian army looted and burnt it, because the local people supported Rákóczi's uprising. In the 17th century, the Sándor family owned the greater part of the land. They remained the owners until the 20th century.

The Roman Catholic **Church of St. Stephen** is the most important cultural-historical monument and dominant feature of the village. The original octagonal church was built in the 15th century. The Sándor family built a new church on its ruins. The sanctuary and windows are in the Gothic style, the nave and tower are in the Romanesque style. The church was restored several times. The most important change was the building of the choir in 1751. In 1885, Archbishop János Simor added two side aisles. Apart from the high altar, the church has 3 side altars decorated with paintings and statues. It also has a fine organ and bells. The most important secular monument in the village is the **manor house**. It was originally built in the Baroque style, but in 1834 it was reconstructed in the Neo-

Classical style under the direction of József Hild. The manor house originally had 59 rooms, two reception halls and a chapel. The interior was decorated with frescoes, statues and porcelain. After the Second World War, its contents were dispersed and the building was used for economic purposes. Today it is awaiting restoration. There was a park around the manor house. The village also has a Baroque **stone cross** from 1778. There are remains of a medieval pottery kiln and a small ironworks at the locality of Csimai Kalvária, on the site of the old village of Csimaszombatja, destroyed by the Turks. A **cultural festival** is held every year on St. Stephen's day (20th August). Camps for folk art, at which traditional pottery making can be seen, are also held in summer.

EPÖL (600 inhabitants) lies in the eastern part of the Gerecse range, in the Bajna basin close to the eastern edge of the territory of Bajna. Fragments of pottery and stone weapons from the Copper Age have been found in the territory of the village. Fragments of objects from the early Iron Age were found at the locality of Nagyhegy. However, the largest quantity of finds date from the Roman period and were found at the locality of Palkóvölgy. The settlement is first mentioned in writing in a document from 1225, when Benedek Epöli bought property here. Part of the property in the surroundings belonged to the royal court. In 1270, King Stephen V gave his property here to the Archbishop of Esztergom, in honour of his coronation. The Turks probably destroyed it in the first half of the 16th century, since a royal tax document from 1564 mentions it as a destroyed and uninhabited place. The village was resettled only in the 18th century. The Sándor family, who owned the village, settled German and Slovak families here. They cultivated cereals, especially rye, vines and reared livestock. Various mills operated in the village. Although the village was multi-ethnic in the past, a mainly Hungarian population lived there by about 1900. After the Second World War, some of the inhabitants found employment in nearby mines. For some time Epöl formed a single unit with neighbouring Bajna. Since 1989, it has again been an independent village with its own administration. The village already had a church in 1332. After being damaged in various ways, it disappeared at the beginning of the 18th century. The present Late Baroque Roman Catholic church was built in 1805.

The village of **GYERMELY** (1,150 inhabitants) is situated further south on the south-east side of the Gerecse range. People probably already lived in the territory of the village in the Stone Age. Signs of settlement in the form of various finds are also confirmed from the Celtic, Roman and Avar periods. The finds from the Roman period include some graves. The first written mention of the settlement dates from 1181. The name of the village was derived from the name of the local stream. The village originally belonged to the Bishopric of Veszprém. In 1529 it fell into Turkish hands, and was uninhabited until the beginning of the 17th century. After the end of Turkish domination, the first settlers were Hungarian members of the Reformed Church from neighbouring settlements, especially Zsámbék and Szomor. In the 18th century, the area belonged to Count József Esterházi and later also to the Sándor family. The new owners attempted to attract more Catholic families to the village. Quarrels between the Reformed and Catholic churches also affected Gyermely, and the problems were solved only by the reform measures of Joseph II. Almost 1000 inhabitants were recorded in the census of 1784 to 1787. In this period, the population lived on farming and on sale of timber, wine, fruit, cereals and cabbage. They used mainly the neighbouring markets at Esztergom, Dorog, Zsámbék and Tata. The Sándors remained the greatest landowners in the 19th century. At the end of the 19th century, Imre Osváth discovered a deposit of coal at the locality of Károly-hegy. However, this was no more important than the neighbouring deposits in the eastern part of the Gerecse range. In the 20th century, the majority of inhabitants left to work in the neighbouring industrial centres. However, some stayed to work in the well-known Gyermely pasta factory, which still produces successful products for the Hungarian market.

Gyermely originally had a 15th century Gothic Roman Catholic **church**. After its destruction in 1749, a new church was built in the course of the 18th century. The Reformed **church** was built in 1786. The subordinate village of **Gyarmatpuszta** has a **chapel** with a valuable interior from 1774. Its Baroque altar came from Venice. The legendary Móric Sándor was buried here with his horse Tatár in the crypt behind the chapel. The territory of the village also includes protected territory with a hunting castle, park and fish ponds, below the conifer covered Bagó-hegy hill (343 m). According to many who know the region, this is one of the most beautiful parts of the Gerecse range.

Nearby **SZOMOR** (1,000 inhabitants) also lies in the south- eastern part of the Gerecse range. Objects from the so-called Ludanic Culture of the Copper Age were found here. In the Roman period an important military road went through the area. An almost completely preserved, four-wheeled Roman carriage with bronze fittings and an inscribed Roman grave stone have been found in the subordinate village of Szomodorpuszta. The first written mention of the village dates from 1269 and gives the name Zumur. It was destroyed during the Turkish wars and re-settled in the 18th century. In this period it belonged to Gergely Pázmándy. He expelled members of the Reformed Church from the village and settled German Catholics here. Some Slovak families also lived here. In 1739 a plague epidemic broke out in the village. The population

Right: The Danube near Tát

lived mainly by cultivating vineyards and making wine. After the Second World War, the German families were deported. The dominant features of the village are the Late Baroque Roman Catholic **church** with finely carved pews and the cemetery **chapel** of the Kézdi-Vásárhelyi family from the end of the 18th century. A **statue of St. John Nepomuk** from the beginning of the 19th century stands behind the church. A **Calvary**, reconstructed in 1993, is situated on Kakukk-hegy hill above the village. There is a local **museum**, with a reconstructed blacksmith's forge among its exhibits.

TÁT (5,350) inhabitants is situated between the Danube and the north-eastern edge of the Gerecse range, 10 km from Esztergom, at the junction of roads from Komárom to Esztergom and Dorog. Various finds from the Bronze Age, the Roman period and the period of the House of Árpád have been discovered. Remains of the Roman road between Brigetio and Aquincum were found. A bronze coin of Trajan and a gold coin of Constantine were also found here. The village is first mentioned in a document from 1146,

when it was granted to Pannonhalma Abbey. In 1181, Béla III gave land in the area to crusaders at Esztergom, and it remained in their possession for a long time. The village was destroyed by the Turks, but not completely depopulated. Its most memorable day was 16th August 1685, when the troops of Charles of Lorraine defeated the Turks nearby. However, the village was completely destroyed in the war, and only resettled in the 18th century. Only a little more than 500 people lived in Tát at the end of the 18th century. They lived on cultivating cereals and making burnt bricks. In 1838 and 1876, the village was severely damaged by Danube floods. At the beginning of the 20th century, the population already exceeded a thousand people of Hungarian and German nationality. In the 1930s, car races were held here. The German families were deported to Germany after the Second World War. The village grew thanks to its position near large industrial facilities.

The most important cultural-historical and architectural monument of Tát is the Roman Catholic **Church of St. George** from 1747, built on the founda-

tions of the original Roman Catholic church from the 14th century. It was damaged by an earthquake in 1768, but later reconstructed. The **Chapel of the Holy Trinity** from the second half of the 19th century is also an interesting sacred monument. The **cross** in front of it dates from 1793. A Neo-Classical granary from 1846 is an important technical monument. The secular buildings of Tát include Eggenhoffer's **manor house** from 1908. One of the most beautiful restaurants with fish specialities (known as halászcsárda) on the Hungarian Danube is situated on the western edge of Tát by the Danube.

TOKOD (4,300 inhabitants) is situated further south in the north-east of the Gerecse range. It belongs to the Gete coal field in the eastern part of Gerecse. A Bronze Age hill-fort existed at the locality of Leshegy. A Roman military road went past the settlement, and there was a Roman fortress and settlement of Gardellaca. The foundations of the fortress survive. The first written mention of the set-

tlement dates from 1181. According to legend, it was named after a knight called Tokod. The subordinate village of Ebszöny was first mentioned in 1193. Both settlements were destroyed in 1543 during the siege of Esztergom by the Turks. In 1595 this territory came into the possession of the Archbishopric of Esztergom, but later both settlements were again destroyed in the final liberation struggle with the Turks. Christian troops won an important victory over the Turks between Tokod and Tát in 1685. Tokod was resettled in the course of the 18th century. The new inhabitants were mainly occupied in agriculture. Later, in the 19th century, they began to extract limestone and coal, and by the end of the century a glassworks was established, continuing an existing tradition. At the beginning of the 20th century, the population already surpassed 3,000. The population was three quarters Hungarian, with Germans and Slovaks making up the rest.

The most important tourist monument and attraction of Tokod is the reconstructed **foundations of the Roman fort** from the 4th century. The most interesting sacred buildings include the Baroque Roman Catholic **church** from 1786, built on the site of a former Romanesque church. The most valuable elements of the interior are the high altar, side altar and pulpit. The church also has a decorative chalice from 1700, originally from Bratislava. The cemetery **Chapel of the Holy Trinity** from the second half of the 19th century is also a valuable cultural monument. A house contains a **museum of folk crafts**, where it is possible to learn about local crafts. The valley between Tokod and Ebszönybánya contains **wine cellars**, a popular stop for the local population and visitors to the area.

The neighbouring community of **TOKODALTÁRÓ** (2,950 inhabitants) lies in the densely settled triangle Esztergom-Dorog-Tát in the eastern part of the County of Komárom-Esztergom, close to the right bank of the Danube. Until 1992 it was united with the neighbouring community of Tokod. The territory of the community was already settled in the Copper, Bronze and Iron ages. At the beginning of

Left: The church in Dág
Right: The rural house in Máriahalom

the Christian era, the Romans built a fort on the boundary between the present territories of Tokod and Tokodaltáró. Foundations of buildings, together with remnants of ovens and coins from the end of the 1st century and first half of the second century were found at the Erzsébet Mine. Together with the remains of the road from the fortress of Brigetio to the fortress of Aquincum, the finds are among the most important in the whole county. The Roman settlement was destroyed in the Migration Period, and the Avars settled here for a long time. The settlement was not important in the Middle Ages. The development of the settlement dates only from the beginning of the 19th century, in connection with development of coal mining. A smaller mining school was opened here in 1899. The mining past of the community is also symbolized by the miner's brass band, an essential part of all important social or cultural events here. The most important cultural monument in the area is the **ruins of the Roman fort**, surrounded by a stone wall, situated about 1 km south of the centre. It is a joint tourist attraction of the two neighbouring villages of Tokod and Tokodaltáró. The Reformed **church** dates from 1924. The abandoned **mines** in the area are industrial and technical monuments.

SÁRISÁP (2,850 inhabitants) is situated south of Tokod, on the eastern edge of the Gerecse range, in the south-eastern part of the County of Komárom-Esztergom. Various archaeologically valuable objects from the Copper and Bronze ages, the Celtic and Avar periods were found in the territory of the community. Traces of settlement in the form of fragments of pottery, goblets and grave stones from the Roman period were found in the Sápi-völgy valley. An 11th century bell was found in 1965. The first written mention of of the settlement dates from 1181, and gives the name Saphy. A document from 1389 gives the present name. The population fled after the fall of Esztergom Castle in 1543. It remained unoccupied throughout the period of Turkish domination. In the 18th century, it belonged to the Sándor family. Mihály Sándor settled some Slovak and Hungarian families from the County

of Nitra here. At the end of the 18th century, the village had more than 500 inhabitants. In 1833, coal mining began in the area. At the beginning of the 20th century, the population reached a level of more than 2,500, and the largest group were Slovaks (1,330). Mining remained the most important activity, although rearing of cattle and sheep was also developed. After the Second World War, a large part of the Slovak population was resettled at Handlová in Slovakia.

The most important architectural monument of the community is the Roman Catholic **Church of St. Michael**, built in the Baroque style by the Sándor family in 1766, on the site of a medieval church. The environs also contain a **warm karst spring** with a temperature of 17 ˚C. In the past the inhabitants used the water, which reached temperatures of up to 35 ˚C. The reduction of the quantity, quality and temperature of the water is a result of the long-lasting mining activity in the area of the eastern part of the Gerecse range-Gete.

The subordinate village of Annavölgy was administratively separated from Sárisáp in February 1997. **ANNAVÖLGY** (950 inhabitants) is situated close to Sárisáp in the valley of the Únyi-patak brook in the eastern part of the Gerecse range. The settlement originated on deposits of coal below the south-western slopes of Gete hill. It is a very young village, which shared the history of Sárisáp until 1997. Both settlements developed in connection with the spread of the extraction of coal in the area from the beginning of the 19th century. Today, their built up areas are almost completely merged.

The village of **DÁG** (950 inhabitants) is situated south-west of Sárisáp on the eastern edge of the Gerecse range, in the south-eastern part of the County of Komárom-Esztergom. Objects from the Bronze Age have been found in the territory of the village. Fragments of pottery from the Roman and Avar periods have been found at the subordinate settlement of Kiscsévpuszta, 2 km north-east of Dág. The first written mention of settlement in the area probably dates from 1181 according to one version. Dág is also mentioned in a Turkish tax register from the 17th century. However, at the end of that century there is no mention of the village, which had probably disappeared. The village was destroyed by the Turks and revived only in the 18th century. According to another version, a settlement named Dág did not exist in the Middle Ages. Settlement in the area was originally on the site of modern Kiscsévpuszta. The first written mention of the settlement of Csév (the original name of Kiscsévpuszta) dates from 1262. In the period before the Turkish invasion, various families had property here, as well as the Archbishopric of Esztergom and the Clarist nunnery on Margaret Island in Budapest. However, the most important settlement began in the 18th century, after the liberation of Hungary from the Turks. According to the census at the end of the 18th century, more than 400 inhabitants lived in the community. In this period it belonged to the Archbishop of Esztergom. Like the neighbouring communities, Dág was also influenced by coal mining in the 19th century. In this period, the Slovaks and Germans were the predominant ethnic groups in the community. Around 1900 almost 90% of the inhabitants were Slovak or German. After the Second World War, the ethnic structure of the community significantly changed. The majority of the German families were deported, and Dág was also influenced by the exchange of population between Hungary and Slovakia. The Slovaks were replaced by Hungarians from southern Slovakia. The dominant feature of the village is the Roman Catholic **church** built in 1826 in the Neo-Classical style. On the wall of the church is a **memorial tablet** to the inhabitants of the village who fell in the First World War.

MÁRIAHALOM (Kirwa, 650 inhabitants) is situated further south, but also in the eastern part of the Gerecse range, on the south-eastern edge of the County of Komárom-Esztergom. The area was already settled in the Bronze and Iron Ages, as is shown by finds in the form of fragments of objects in the surrounding loess and sandy sediments. Remains of a Roman camp were found at Békahegy (Frog hill) in the territory of the village. The first written record of settlement in the area dates from 1255. The settlement did not disappear even during the Turkish wars, but it was one of the smallest in the Gerecse area. In 1715, a long time after the defeat of the Turks, only a few, mostly Slovak families lived here. In 1785 and 1786, German Catholic families from Württemberg were resettled here. In the first half of the 19th century, almost 400 people lived here. It was still one of the smallest villages in the district. The inhabitants were concerned with cultivating vineyards, until they were destroyed by phyloxera. Then the farmers changed the vineyards into fruit orchards, mainly growing apples, pears and plums. The most important cultural-historical monuments of the village are the Roman Catholic church, built in 1821 to 1826 in the Baroque style, and two old houses on Széchényi utca with finely cut wooden balconies. Behind the village stands a chapel from 1934. The Török-kút (Turkish well), according to legend dug by Turkish soldiers, is also a well known feature.

The neighbouring village of **ÚNY** (650 inhabitants) is situated on the eastern side of the Gerecse range in the valley of the Únyi-patak brook. Various finds from the Copper and Iron Ages were found in the area. Foundations of houses from Roman and Árpád period houses were discovered. The first written record of the territory of the village dates from 1193, in connection with King Béla III. Various owners alternated in the village. It was

Right: The square in Dorog

completely depopulated in the period of the Turkish raids, and began to develop again in the 18th century, when the Miskey family owned it. In the course of the century, Úny was troubled by disputes between members of the Catholic and Reformed churches. The Catholics built a church here in 1732 and the Reformed in 1794. The local farmers were famous growers of plums, from which jam and plum brandy were produced. The Hungarian patriot Lajos Kossuth had property in the territory of the village. The agricultural character of the area changed only in the 20th century, when various inhabitants began to find work in nearby coal mines or not very distant Budapest (35 km). The most important cultural monument in the village is the Late Baroque Reformed **church** from 1794. The Roman Catholic **Church of St. Michael** stands on the foundations of a medieval church. Other note-worthy buildings include four **curias** (large houses) and the oldest, perhaps two hundred year old **house** in Deák F. utca. The cemetery contains some fine **grave stones** of some Esztergom nobles. In one of the houses, it is also possible to admire the collection of rocks and minerals of the collector László Varga. **Horse riding** has a tradition in the village. Races are organized every year at the end of August.

DOROG (13,000 inhabitants) is situated east of the Gerecse range, 7 km from Esztergom, and not far from the Danube in the Dorog basin, which was formerly the third most important brown coal basin in Hungary. The town's advantageous position in a valley between mountain ranges has meant that it has been on important trade and military routes since time immemorial. Goods were transported through here in Roman times, there was an important military road in the Middle Ages, and later it was an important stop for post coaches. Remains from every historical period have been found in its territory. Evidence of settlement in the Early Iron Age (remains of hearths, fragments of objects, pots and tools) were found at the locality of Hungáriahegy. Fragments of Copper Age pots were found at Homoki Szőlők. Pieces of burial urns have survived from the Bronze Age. The Romans and Longobards left various remains. There was probably a large settlement here in Roman times. Coins, medallions, pottery, remains of baths, parts of an aquaduct and milestones have been found.

The first written mention of medieval settlement dates from 1181 (according to another source from 1223). It is mentioned in the form *Dorogh* or *Durug* as the property of a chaplain of Esztergom. The name is derived from a Slavonic name or from the word *drug* (friend, colleague). According to another version, a man called Dorog was one of Attila's commanders. The present form Dorog has been used since the 18th century. In 1307, the magnate Matúš Čák of Trenčín forcibly took the property of the Archbishop of Esztergom. After his death, the property was returned to the archbishop. The original medieval settlement lay in the valley near the present town. It was depopulated during the period of Turkish domination, and resettled only at the end of the 17th century. The new settlers were mainly German and Hungarian families. However, in the

mid 18th century, documents mention only German inhabitants, who supported themselves mainly by cultivating vineyards and potatoes. Life in the settlement changed in the mid 19th century, with the beginning of coal mining. Rapid development occurred in the following decades. By 1930 the population reached 6,000. Dorog became the centre of a wider mining area. Industry, developing in the course of the 20th century, was established in connection with the coal mining. In 1970, Dorog was already a greater village, and from 1984 a town. With the present decline of mining and the associated industry, the town is attempting to change its economic basis.

Hősök tere square is the central and most beautiful feature of the town. The Baroque Roman Catholic **church** from 1775 is situated in this part of the town. Most of the notable features of Dorog are connected with the mining history of the town. Some surviving **shafts** and facilities for sorting coal are industrial monuments. The so-called miner's Roman

Catholic **church** was completed in 1931. Arrival of people to work in the mines produced a need for a Reformed **church**, completed in 1938. Since 1981, Dorog has been adorned with a **mining monument** by the sculptor Ferenc Árvai. Later the town had a **statue** of the creator of the monument erected. A **monument** in honour of the fallen in the First World War was erected in the town in 1928. The cultural historical monuments of the town also include the **Roman settlement** on Leányvár road on the slope of the Pilis range. It is often visited by tourists. The Neo-Classical **chapel** on Calvary from the first half of the 19th century is a valuable sacred monument. An **archaeological exhibition** has been installed in the house of culture. It includes finds from the territory of the town and its environs, for example, a Roman pottery kiln. On the eastern edge of the town is the Palatinus-tó lake, used by lovers of relaxation by water. For visitors to the town desiring recreation by water, there is also a swimming pool in summer.

Nearby **CSOLNOK** (Tscholnok, 3,400 inhabitants) is situated on the east side of

Left: Rural architecture

the Gerecse range, near the south-eastern edge of the town of Dorog. Various fragments of pottery and other objects from the Early Bronze Age. An extensive cemetery confirms the presence of the Avars. Pieces of pottery and horse harness were found in the Avar graves. According to finds of coins, Romans probably also lived here.

The village is first mentioned in 1232. A document from 1262 mentions the settlement, which lay close to Dág. In the 14th century, the Archbishop of Esztergom and religious orders had property here. Later, the settlement belonged to the Lordship of Esztergom Castle and the royal court. Other owners of the territory included the Clarist monastery on Margaret Island in Budapest. The Turks spared the village, but it was destroyed during the war of liberation. Normal life returned to the village at the beginning of the 18th century. After a cholera epidemic in 1738, some German families settled here. By the end of the 18th century, 170 mostly German and Slovak families lived here. At the beginning of the 19th century, coal mining started in the territory of Csolnok. Mining attracted many more people. The place grew, with its population exceeding 4,000 by the 1930s. In recent times, the population has declined as a result of the decline of mining. Csolnok still has a culturally active German minority, which uses the German name of the place.

The most important cultural historical monuments include the Roman Catholic **church**, completed in 1775 thanks to Count Antal Grassalkovich, and the **Holy Trinity Monument** from the 19th century. Other valuable buildings include the old school building and the **technical monuments** connected especially with mining. During the year Csolnok has an active social and cultural life. Various cultural events are organized here every year – music festivals, concerts of brass band music, June festivals, wine festivals and others.

LEÁNYVÁR (Leinwar, 1550 inhabitants) is situated on the eastern slopes of the Gerecse range, 6 km from Dorog and only 30 km from Budapest. Finds from the territory of the community show that it was settled in the Bronze Age, the Roman and Avar periods. The first written mention of the settlement dates from 1270 and uses the name Volmód. Another settlement – Aberth – is mentioned in 1320. It was founded by the administrators of the royal forests. It is thought that a monastery and castle stood on the site of the present settlement, but no remains of them have been found. The area was abandoned during the period of Turkish domination of Hungary. A new settlement was founded only in the second half of the 18th century, when the owners from the Sándor family invited German Catholic families to settle here. At the end of the 18th century 500 people lived here. They supported themselves mostly by cultivating vineyards. Their wine reached the tables of the inhabitants of Pressburg (Bratislava) and Győr. At the beginning of the 20th century, stone was quarried and lime was burnt. In spite of a partial deportation after the Second World War, the German speaking population still preserves its traditions and customs. Apart from the Hungarian name Leányvár, the German name Leinwar is used. A dominant feature and the most important architectural monument is the Neo-Classical Roman Catholic church from 1823 (according to other sources from 1806).

KESZTÖLC (Kestúc, 2,400 inhabitants) is situated in the western foothills of the Pilis Mountains, 6 km south-east of Dorog, on the north-eastern edge of the County of Komárom-Esztergom. Limestone and dolomite, moderately undulating karst landscape with small caves and karst springs prevail in the environs. The adjoining part of the Pilis Mountains is part of the Pilis Protected Area. The natural beauty and proximity to various towns including Budapest create good conditions for the development of tourist and recreation activities in Kesztölc and its immediate environs.

The territory of the community was already settled in the Stone Age, as smaller finds in the Sármánk cave show. Fragments of Copper Age pottery have been found, as has evidence of Celtic occupation. There was probably also a Roman settlement. Fragments of objects from the

Early Iron Age have been found at the subordinate village of Klasztrompuszta. The first written mention of the settlement dates from 1075, when it is recorded that King Gejza I gave part of the local fields and vineyards to Hronský Beňadik Abbey (now in Slovakia). A document of Andrew III from 1294 mentioned the village as a property of a monastery at Esztergom. Kesztölc also remained settled during the period of Turkish domination in Hungary. In 1722, the Archbishop of Esztergom began to move Slovaks to the village. At lower levels they grew cereals, while on the hillsides they cultivated vineyards and fruit orchards. In the 20th century, ever more people had to seek work in neighbouring towns and mines. The Second World War cruelly intervened in the history of the community. In December 1944, the Soviet army took 320 local inhabitants for forced labour in the Soviet Union. After the war, 180 Slovak families were resettled in Czechoslovakia. The remaining population of Slovak nationality has its own ethnic minority administration and uses the Slovak name of the community – Kestúc.

A Roman Catholic **Church of St. Clement** already existed here in the 14th century, and was probably built in the time of the House of Árpád. A new church in the Late Baroque style was completed in 1800. A Late Baroque **stone cross** depicting Jesus Christ and Mary dates from the same period. It is also necessary to seek the origin of the Baroque **statue of St. Orbán** in the 19th century. An 18th century **farm house** containing the local **museum** is an interesting building. There also some note-worthy old **cellars**. The community also includes the subordinate village of Klasztrompuszta, which was already an important place in the Middle Ages. A Gothic church and monastery was built here in the 13th century at the foot of the hills. A small settlement called Szent Kereszt (Holy Cross) developed around it. The settlement with the church and monastery was destroyed by Turkish troops in 1526. It did not regain its original importance, and so in later periods it

Right: A wine cellar in the Pilis Mts

was called *puszta*, which means "abandoned place". An overall picture of the past of the locality was gained in 1961, when the ruins of the monastery and adjoining buildings were studied in detail. The place together with the nearby **Legény-barlang** cave is attractive to visit.

Nearby **PILISCSÉV** (2,300 inhabitants) is situated in the western foothills of the Pilis Mountains, 10 km south-east of Dorog, on the north-eastern edge of the County of Komárom-Esztergom. Undulating karst landscape with smaller caves and karst springs prevail in the environs. The adjoining part of the Pilis Mountains is part of the Pilis Protected Area. The natural beauty and proximity to various towns including Budapest create good conditions for the development of tourist and recreation activities in Piliscsév and its immediate environs.

The territory of the present community was probably already settled in the Stone Age. Remains of a Roman watch tower surrounded by a system of ditches was found on Margaréta-domb hill. A paved road went along the valley below it, from the Danube to the fortress of Aquincum (in the area of modern Budapest), as is shown by the milestones discovered by historians since the 18th century. There was probably no more developed medieval settlement in the territory of the community. A settlement called Csév is mentioned in a document from 1262, but it lay 6 km to the west of the modern community of Piliscsév, in the area of the settlement of Kiscsévpuszta, in the present territory of Dág. Therefore, it cannot be regarded as the forerunner of modern Piliscsév. Piliscsév was founded under the supervision of the Archbishop of Esztergom, by settlement of Slovaks in the 18th century. It was named Nagy Csév (Great Csév) or Boldog Csév (Happy Csév). It grew quickly, and had 900 inhabitants at the time of the census at the end of the 18th century. The people supported themselves by growing cereals, mainly rye, cultivating vineyards, extracting timber, and burning lime and charcoal. In the first half of the 20th century, Slovak Catholic families predominated here. After the Second World War, some families were deported to Slo-

vakia in the framework of the post-war exchange of population. However, Slovak minority culture, customs and story telling still survive here.

A dominant feature of Piliscsév is the several times rebuilt or reconstructed Roman Catholic **church**, built in the period 1763 to 1780. The Baroque high altar and pulpit from the 18th century are noteworthy features of the interior. The font dates from the first half of the 19th century. Two statues - of **St. Vendel and St. Orbán**, placed on **Roman milestones**, discovered in the 19th century, are interesting monuments, situated on the road to Kesztölc.

PILISMARÓT (1,950 inhabitants) is situated by the Danube at the foot of the Visegrád range, a few kilometres from Esztergom. Its territory is one of the richest parts of the region for archaeological finds. Objects from the Stone Age were found in Miklós-deák völgy valley. Remains of Celtic and Avar cemeteries were uncovered at Basaharc. Most remains of historic settlement date from the Roman period. There was a camp at Kis-hegy in the time of Valentinian I, and the former

fortress of Ad Herculeum at the mouth of Malom-patak (Mill Brook).

The first written mention of the village dates from 1138, when it was a royal property. In 1260, Queen Maria gave a property called Marót to the Monastery of St. Andrew at Visegrád. Later it became the property of various religious orders, and remained in their hands until the 18th century. It was almost completely depopulated during the period of the Turkish threat. For example, in 1570 there were only 18 houses in the two settlements of Kismarót and Nagymarót. More rapid development began in the 18th century, with members of the Catholic, Lutheran and Reformed churches living along side each other. In 1787, the population was already more than a thousand. A medieval Reformed **church** survives at Pilismarót. It was originally Catholic and dedicated to St. Laurence. After the defeat of the Turks the Reformed Church used it, and definitively bought it in 1810. Other monuments include a Late Baroque **statue of St. John Nepomuk** from the beginning of the 19th century. The **Heckenast Curia**, built in 1860 in the romantic style is also

an interesting building. Statues by a local artist are exhibited in its cellars. Various interesting events are held at Pilismarót in summer – **music evenings,** the **St. Laurence day festival** and the **international motorists' meeting.** One of the most beautiful **natural beaches** on the Danube is situated at Pilismarót. In the 1930s, the locality was called the "Danube lido". The environs provide good possibilities for fishing, hunting, walking and shorter tours. The most interesting destinations for tourists are the valley towards Basaharc and Vaskapu (Iron Gate) hill above Esztergom. **Poplars** called Dobosi poplars are planted near Pilismarót. They grow in memory of the legendary hero of the anti-Turkish wars Mihály Dobozi and his wife. According to legend, they committed suicide while escaping from the Turks.

DÖMÖS (1,150 inhabitants) is situated on the right bank of the Danube at the beginning of the Visegrád gorge, below the the northern slope of Prédikálószék hill in the Visegrád range. It is 16 km east of Esztergom. A ferry joins the two banks of the Danube here. Dömös is an important, easily accessible tourist centre by the Danube. Its relative closeness to Budapest results in a lot of weekend visits throughout the year.

Various remains from early settlement, such as fragments of artifacts and bones, have been found here in the sediments deposited by the Danube. Most finds date from the Late Bronze Age. Fragments of pottery and worked building stones from the reign of Valentinian I, and

11 Avar graves have been found. In the Middle Ages, the community was a royal and ecclesiastical centre. King Béla I already regarded this place as his favourite seat. He died here in 1063.

At the beginning of the 12th century, Dömös became the seat of a provost. It successively belonged under the Bishopric of Veszprém and the Archbishop of Esztergom. In 1501, Pope Alexander VI assigned it to the Bishopric of Nitra. It was abandoned for a long time during the Turkish domination of Hungary. Settlement developed more rapidly in the 18th century. The census at the end of the 18th century showed a population of almost 800. They supported themselves by agriculture, fishing, extraction of timber and trade. They especially excelled in cultivating fruit and vines. Their most important products were red wine, raspberries, chestnuts and oak wood, which were sold not only in Esztergom, but also in more distant towns. At the beginning of the 20th century, almost 1,500 people, mostly Catholics, lived at Dömös. Most of the property belonged to the Archbishopric of Esztergom until 1945. After the First World War, Dömös became a recreation resort, where four restaurants and four pensions were established in a short time. It has retained this function until the present. Apart from tourists, many painters, who come to paint pictures in the beautiful surroundings, have found inspiration here.

The most important cultural monument of Dömös is the **ruins** of the former provostry church of St. Margaret, built in the Romanesque in 1107. The village already had a church in 1303. A new Baroque **church** was built on its ruins in 1743. Its tower was completed in 1824. A Neo-Classical **statue of St. John Nepomuk** from 1821 can be admired in the courtyard of a house in Kossuth Lajos utca. A **chapel** from 1845 is also an important monument. The local harbour is an interesting place, evoking times over a hundred years ago. The local government building contains a **gallery** (Dömösi galéria), established on the initiative of the local artist József Vertel. It holds exhibitions of works of painters and sculptors of

Left: The Danube near Dömös
Right: Visegrád

the area of the Danube Bend about four times a year. Some of the works of artists working directly in Dömös are included in a permanent exhibition. A **spring festival** is held on the last weekend in May. Theatrical performances are also sometimes held here. Dömös is relatively well equipped for tourism. Accommodation is available in pensions, a camp site and private homes.

Dömös is a starting point for walking and cycling tours in the Visegrád mountains and along the Danube. The hiking footpath from the village to **Dobogókö**, which is named after Ödön Téry the pioneer of hiking in Hungary. It is one of the oldest marked hiking paths in Hungary. Dobogókö is a small settlement and hill with a fine view on the boundary between the Pilis Mountains and Visegrád range. The settlement was built on the hill of the same name, at a height of 700 m above sea level. Only a hikers' hostel stood here at the beginning of the 20ᵗʰ century. Today it is surrounded by hotels and recreation cottages. The facilities are directed towards hiking. There is a bus service between Dobogókö and Bu-

dapest. Dobogókö is one of the most important and best known peaks in the whole of Hungary. On its summit, at a height of 700 m is a **rock**. According to a local legend, it is hollow and when knocked it produces a thundering noise. This is also the origin of the place name (*dobog* - beating, stamping, *kö* - rock). There is an outstanding panoramic view from the summit. The view of the Visegrád gorge on the Danube is captivating. In clear weather it is possible to see far into the western part of Hungary and the southern part of Slovakia, including the Štiavnické vrchy Mountains, Burda, Tribeč and Považský Inovec. When visibility is exceptionally good, the ridge of the Vysoké Tatry Mountains, 180 km away, can be seen. A hikers' cottage stands on the summit, with a **monument to Téry** nearby.

VISEGRÁD (1,650 inhabitants) lies on the right bank of the Danube below the steep slopes of the Visegrád range. It is one of the most important and most visited tourist places in Hungary. The village lies at the beginning of the Visegrád gorge on the Danube, of which there is a splen-

did view from the neighbouring peaks of the range.

Man has lived in the area since early times. The oldest finds were discovered at the mouth of the Csuk brook. Objects from the Iron Age were found in an old quarry. The Romans came here after the Celts, and built the first fortress called Pone Novata on Sibrik-domb hill, with a triangular plan. Pone Novata was one of the weakest points on the Limes Romanus, especially in winter, when the Quadi could attack across the frozen Danube. In the Migration Period, the Goths, Huns, Avars and Slavs passed through Visegrád, with the Slavs staying longest. The name of the place comes from them. In 973, the Magyar Prince Gejza moved his capital city from Fehérvár to Esztergom, as a result of which the importance of Visegrád increased, and it became the centre of a county. When Béla IV transferred his royal court from Esztergom to Buda in 1249, he started to build the castle of Visegrád for the forward de-

fence of his new capital city. A settlement grew up below the castle, and enjoyed a golden age during the reigns of Ladislav IV and Andrew III, when the town also included Maros (modern Nagymaros) on the other side of the Danube. The town revived again under the rule of the House of Anjou. King Charles Robert from the House of Anjou moved his court here, because Buda did not allow him to settle in the residence of the House of Árpád. In 1320 he was already able to celebrate his wedding to his third wife Elizabeth, in the palace. In 1323, he also placed the crown jewels in Visegrád Castle. In November 1335, a meeting between King Charles Robert, John of Luxembourg King of Bohemia and King Kazimír III the Great of Poland. The settlement and castle also developed during the reign of Matthias Corvinus. In 1473, he started construction of the royal palace, which can still be seen. After the death of Matthias Corvinus, Visegrád declined. In 1543, the garrison of the castle surrendered to the might of the Turkish army. It remained a centre under the Turks, although of much less importance. The army of Charles of Lorraine be-

Left: The castle walls
Right: The royal palace

sieged Visegrád in 1686. The Turks blew up the castle and burnt many houses. The remains of the castle were finally destroyed in 1703-1704 during the Kuruc uprising. German immigrants from Würtemberg settled in the destroyed settlement.

The activity of the local parish priest József Viktorin after 1869 ensured that Visegrád would not be completely forgotten. He collected subscriptions and constructed a path from the village to the upper castle (Fellegvár). Then a path was also constructed between the lower and upper castles. Viktorin published the almanach Concordia, Lipa and other Slovak books. He initiated in the National Assembly, restoration of the lower castle and investigation of the ruins of the upper castle. The archaeological excavations were directed by Imre Henszimann. The builders Frigyes Schulek, Kálmán Lux and later János Schulek participated in the restoration of the lower castle. From 1886 tourists came by boat on the Danube. Around 1900, people started coming for recreation, including important artists, who drew inspiration from the surroundings. The university teacher Dr. Tivadar Bakody began to build a new sanatorium here. In 1934, János Schulek discovered the first part of the remains of the original royal palace. Archaeological research has continued until today.

The most visited place at Visegrád is the Renaissance royal palace (királyi palota). Its excavated and restored parts are accessible through the courtyard of house no.27 on Fö utca, the main street of the village. The royal palace was built on different levels of a slope. It was divided into three parts – the **Matthias Palace** (Mátyás-palota), **Beatrix Palace** (Beatrix-palota) and the **chapel**. Construction of the palace was started by the Angevin kings – Charles Robert and Louis the Great. In the 15th century, the palace was improved by King Sigismund of the House of Luxembourg, and in the second half of the 15th century Matthias Corvinus had it reconstructed in the Renaissance style. According to historical records it had about 350 rooms. The best preserved or uncovered part is the Matthias Palace, with an impressive courtyard testifying to the wealth and glory of past ages. The

most effective part of the palace is the **arcaded courtyard** with an octagonal red marble fountain, from which wine is said to have flowed on ceremonial occasions. The coat of arms of Matthias Corvinus can be seen on both sides of the fountain. Another courtyard contains the so-called lion fountain. The ruins of the Beatrix Palace are still mostly buried, and archaeological work is continuing.

The **upper castle** (Fellegvár) is most easily accessible by the 6 km scenic route Panoráma út, which climbs from the centre of the village and then descends to **Solomon's Tower**. The route also passes the observation tower on Nagy Villám (378 m). The upper castle or citadel is triangular in plan. The lower courtyard is cut into rock. After the defeat of the Turks, the German settlers used stones from the abandoned castle to build their houses. The castle complex is entered by the **East Gate** (Keleti-kapu), the best preserved of the gates. It was built at the beginning of

the 15th century by King Sigismund. It was badly damaged in 1702 during the siege. However, it was repaired and is one of the oldest surviving monuments in Hungary. Inside the gate are remains of a so-called outer courtyard, now containing sellers of souvenirs and various attractions such as period photography, crossbow shooting and falconry. Wooden steps lead from the outer courtyard to the lower courtyard of the original triangular castle. In the centre of it is the **castle well**. Through the courtyard we reach the damaged **South Bastion** (Déli-bástya), close to which was a drawbridge. The residential **north wing of the castle** (Északi-palota) stands on the inner courtyard. The **castle tower** and **west wing** (Nyugati-palota) stands out among the preserved parts of the castle complex. It contains an **exhibition** on the history of the castle. The chapel, of which little survives, is one of the most damaged parts. Reconstruction work is continuing at the castle, with individual parts of the original complex being renewed. Thus, visitors can find a surprise every year, in the form of the uncovering of the fascinating history of Visegrád.

Left: The Solomon's tower
Right: The church in Pilisszentlászló

Construction of the **Lower Castle** (Alsóvár) began in the mid 13th century on the northern edge of the town. The 31 m high hexagonal **keep** with Romanesque windows has been reconstructed. It was built in the 13th century, and was one of the main elements of the defensive system. It is called **Solomon's tower**, although King Solomon was imprisoned here almost 200 years before the building of the tower. The tower contains the **Museum of King Matthias Corvinus**. Near it are gates, for the castle and the town. A **monument to Matthias Corvinus** stands at the junction of Fö utca and Salamon-torony utca. A **chapel** stands on the bank of the Danube, and a Roman Catholic parish **church** from 1782 stands on the main square.

PILISSZENTLÁSZLÓ (Senváclav, 900 inhabitants) at 381 metres above sea level is the highest village in the Visegrád range. It is situated south-east of Esztergom in the embrace of a ring of mountains extending towards the Visegrád gorge of the Danube, dominated by the peaks of Szent László-hegy, Bükkös-hegy and Kukac-hegy. It is a favourite summer resort, and a starting point for tours of the most beautiful parts of the range – Visegrád Castle, Rám-szakadék pothole, Prédikálószékek peak, Dobogókö and others. The closeness of Visegrád and Esztergom was advantageous for the development of art. The kings from the House of Árpád already knew the beauty of the place. They built a hunting lodge on the route from Visegrád to Buda. Andrew III gave property here to the Pauline (Pálos) order, which built a monastery here. The Papal legate Gentilis negotiated here with Matúš Čák, who did not want to recognize the Angevin Charles Robert as King of Hungary. Later kings including Matthias Corvinus also liked to visit the monastery. After the battle of Mohács, the Turks also destroyed Kékes, as Pilisszentlászló was called then. At the beginning of the 18th century, Slovaks settled here and gave the village its present name. They supported themselves mainly by forestry, quarrying

and rearing of horses. The village did not develop much in the 19th century, because it was too isolated from other towns and villages. In 1947, some of the Slovak inhabitants were resettled in Slovakia. In spite of this, the remaining Slovaks preserved their customs and language. Apart from the name Pilisszentlászló, the Slovak community in the village also uses the the Slovak name Senváclav. Among sacred monuments, a chapel and especially the Roman Catholic church from 1790 are of interest to visitors.

Pilisszentlászló is ever more concentrating on the development of tourism. The surrounding country has been declared a biosphere reservation under the supervision of UNESCO. The territory of the village has been made part of the **Danube-Ipoly National Park** (Duna-Ipoly Nemzeti park) The forests contain many hunted animals - deer, mouflon, fox, badger and wild boar. The surroundings of the village are popular for collecting mushrooms.

BIKE TOURS

Cycling abroad possesses a specific charm. Different cultures attract and one likes to drop in on the neighbours' and compare everything: people, towns and villages, and services. The Slovak-Hungarian-Austrian frontier area is one of the few corners of Europe where one can cross the territories of three countries, which used to form one monarchy until 1918, literally after a couple of kilometres. In spite of many common features cycling in the individual countries you will find certain differences we would like to point at.

The best infrastructure for cycling is undoubtedly in Austria. The network of quality and well-marked cycling tracks provides a comparatively safe ride separated from the road traffic. Perhaps the best known bike route in Central Europe is the Danube International Cycling Route, sections of which are also included in the ones offered here. Road network is of excellent quality but the traffic density experienced in the seat of bicycle is its negative side.

The infrastructure for cyclists in Hungary is improving. Although no network of bike tracks exists here, quality and marking reaches the Austrian level, and in many places or sections separated lanes for bikers were made. Road surface is comparatively good, though their width is not altogether adequate.

The lowest level of network and quality of separated cycling tracks is in Slovakia, although on the other side the number of cyklists is higher than, for example, in Hungary. Quality of road network is passable but as the roads are not consistently maintained because of lack of finances, there are problems with poor quality surface.

The common trait of all routes is that they are somehow connected with the second greatest river of Europe, the Danube. They lead either directly along its stream or they cross it also passing through the riparian landscape.

We have chosen twelve routes for wandering in the Slovak-Austrian-Hungarian frontier area. They are mostly circles. They often start in or pass through larger towns (Bratislava, Győr) or through frontier settlements with dense traffic. Consequently, vigilance is necessary and it is also convenient to enquire about the regime and status of the border crossings or the operation of ferries over the Danube if that is the case in advance for a particular route.

We are convinced that you will chose one of our routes and discover many interesting spots offered by this part of Central Europe.

Left: The cyclists on Hlavné námestie square in Bratislava

THE AUSTRIAN DANUBELAND

1. Around the Hainburg Mts.

Direction: Hainburg – Bad Deutsch Altenburg (3.5 km) – Prellenkirchen (9 km) – Berg (9 km) – Hainburg (10.5 km).
Length of the route: 32 km
Elevation difference: Mild ascents from 148 m above sea level to about 200 m above sea level.
Brief description: Little demanding route running mostly on the marked bike lanes.
Map: The detailed bike map of Bratislava-Podunajsko in scale 1:100 000 (sheet 7), edition of bike touring maps published by VKÚ, š. p., Harmanec.

Detailed description: The route starts on the main square in **Hainburg**. Cross the square and descending by one of the lanes you will reach the street advancing close to the Danube embankment towards the railway track. Turn left up the stream of the Danube. Then follow the green marked cycling route (Radweg) in the direction of Bad Deutsch Altenburg and Vienna. Pass under the railway track, pass by the railway station on your left and leave the town through a little forest. After about 1.5 km you pass under the bridge over the Danube, turn left and ascend to the crossroads of bike lanes. Turn right in the direction of **Bad Deutsch-Al-**

tenburg. Now you are passing by a quarry and it is practically the suburb of this little spa. Turning left you will arrive at its centre, where you have to ride carefully in order to respect the limited traffic regime. Arriving at the main road leading to **Petronell-Carnuntum** you have to observe the traffic signs for motor vehicles in the direction of Prellenkirchen. The road mildly ascends; it crosses the main road to Vienna and the railway track. A large quarry is on your right in front of you.

A less pleasant way to get to this point is to continue from Hainburg on the main road to Vienna. On the one side you will avoid several little ascents and orientation will be easier, but on the other you will be exposed to the risk of collision in dense traffic. We do not recommend this option to less experienced cyclists and families with children.

A kilometre beyond Bad Deutsch Altenburg a short detour turning left will bring you to the village of Hundsheim. Return then to the main road and continue around the pilot school about 3 km to **Prellenkirchen**. Cross the village in the direction of Edelstal and Berg. Mild ascent follows and the route continues in an undulated landscape along the vineyards and picturesque wine cellars 4 km to the adjacent village of **Edelstal**. At its lower end you pass by the bottling plant of the local mineral water Römerquelle on your right. Beyond the plant turn left onto an ascent in the direction of **Berg**, where you arrive after about 3 km through mildly undulating Hainburg hills. The vineyards and wine cellars also accompany you in this stretch. Bratislava and its quarter Petržalka are well visible on horizon from various points of this section of the route.

Descending through Berg you will arrive at the crossroads with the main road. Turn left in the direction of **Wolfsthal**. Now you advance about 3 km on a busy communication leading along the forested foothills of the Hainburg hills. At the crossroads with the main road Bratislava-Vienna cross the roundabout and you will get to the flood bank with the marked cyclist lane Bratislava-Vienna marked in German as Pressburg-Wien. Continue left. At the beginning of the village of Wolfsthal

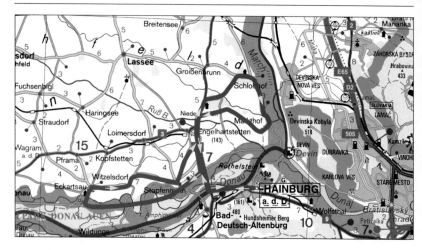

the cyclist lane interrupts and you cross the village on normal road. Watch for the green mark of the cyclist lane, which turns right in the centre of the village. A side alley and short descent will bring you to the Danube alluvial forest. The well-marked cyclist route to Hainburg (about 5.5 km from Wolfsthal) then continues through the fields along the railway and a mild ascent before Hainburg. It is an asphalt road with practically no traffic.

Part of the Little Carpathian Mts. and the Devín rock in Slovakia are visible on the opposite bank of the Danube. In front of you on the left side are the **Hainburg Mts.** and directly in front of you is the isolated massif of **Braunsberg** (346 m a.s.l.). Fit enough tourists can climb it starting in the suburb of Hainburg and following the sign Braunsberg. The elevation difference is about 170 m and its top offers an interesting view of the National Park of Donauauen, the Little Carpathians and the capital of Slovakia, Bratislava.

Alternative route from Wolfsthal to Hainburg is the shorter but much more frequented main road.

2. Visiting the castles of Marchfeld

Direction: Hainburg – Eckartsau (15.5 km) – Stopfenreuth (7 km) – Markthof (8.5 km) – Neiderweiden (7 km) – Hainburg (11 km).
Length of the route: 49 km
Elevation difference: The route runs in a flat terrain with the exception of a short ascent and descent near Schloßhof.
Brief description: The route leads to three important and picturesque castles of Marchfeld: Eckartsau, Schloßhof, and Niederweiden. As a part of route, about 13 km, leads on gravel unpaved roads, MTB or tracking bikes are advisable.
Map: The detailed bike map of Bratislava-Podunajsko in scale 1:100 000 (sheet 7), edition of bike touring maps published by VKÚ, š. p., Harmanec.

Detailed description: The route starts on the main square of **Hainburg** and continues on the Danube cycling route in the direction of Bad Deutsch Altenburg up to the bridge over the Danube the same as in the route *Around the Hainburg Mts.* When you reach the bridge ascend up to the level of the road, cross it carefully and continue on its right side turning left onto the bridge by the safely separated lane for cyclists and pedestrians. Cross the river and its branches and

Right: Niederweiden

after about 2 km turn in a sharp bent in the opposite direction downward (green mark Radweg, direction Vienna). Now you are in the National Park of **Donauauen**, so please observe the guidelines about movement in the protected area.

Pass onto the flood bank and continue to the right on the **Danube cycling route**. On the edge of the village of Stopfenreuth after about 2 km cross the normally empty seepage canal of the Danube, turn right beyond the bridge while following the signs in the direction of Vienna. The first about 5 km from the Hainburg bridge the road surface is of a good quality gravel which later changes to asphalt. Continue on the Danube flood bank. About 7 kilometres beyond the crossroads and the little bridge near Stopfenreuth get of the flood bank turning right (direction sign of Eckartsau) and leave the territory of the National Park of Donauauen. You are again on gravel road leading through alluvial forest and it brings you crossing the castle park to the castle of **Eckartsau**, visible among the trees on your left. After seeing it, continue about 300 m to the middle of the village and turn right in its square in the direction of Witzelsdorf. You are on a state road with denser traffic, continue about 4 km through Witzelsdorf up to Stopfenreuth where the road runs along the edge of the village.

In the right-turning curve of the main road turn left onto a field gravel road leading to the neighbouring village of Engelhartstetten visible in front of you. After about 2 km at the crossroads near a solitary locust tree and a cross turn right and you will arrive to the main road No. 49 Hainburg – Marchegg after about 300 m. Continue on it turning left. Pass by Engelhartstetten, the local waste water cleaning station and further by bridge over the Rußbach brook. Beyond the bridge and near the kilometre-stone 6.0

turn right onto a gravel field road. It will bring you first to the homestead of Niederweiden, which you pass from the left, then continue on a field road eastward. The gravel road has disagreeable rails in places so you should ride in its middle. A good orientation point is Devín Castle on the Slovak side of the frontier, which is visible on the horizon, and we should be coming closer to it at least optically. The massif of the Devínska Kobyla is right in front of you and the above mentioned Devín Castle is on the right side. North of Devínska Kobyla are the houses and chimneys in the urban district of Devínska Nová Ves. But all this is beyond the river **March**, which represents the frontier between Austria and Slovakia with no crossing in these parts. On the left side on an elevation **Schloßhof** Castle is visible. Turn left if you want to visit the castle. After seeing it continue around the castle area. At its end at the crossroads turn left in the direction of Niederweiden. A comparatively steep 3 km descent ends at the main road No. 49. Turn left in the direction of Hainburg. Immediately beyond the crossroads on the left is the last castle of this route, **Niederweiden**. After visiting continue on the main road about 8 km to the end of the bridge over the Danube near Hainburg. Descend in the opposite direction and return passing under the bridge to Hainburg (following the green mark of the Radweg).

THE SLOVAK DANUBELAND

3. The Route of Petržalka

Direction: Border crossing Berg – Pečniansky les wood – pass under the Bratislava bridges – The eastern edge of Petržalka – around the waste water cleansing station (ČOV) – on the dike to Čunovo.

Length of the route: 22 kilometres

Elevation gain: The route descends from 139 m to 130 m above sea level.

Brief description: The route follows almost the whole of the right bank section of the Danube on the territory of Slovakia, and follows its main stream with the exception of the first stretch. It is especially suitable for children as it leads on the dike except for a several hundred meter long stretch.

Map: The detailed bike map of Bratislava-Podunajsko in scale 1:100 000 (sheet 7), edition of bike touring maps published by VKÚ, š. p., Harmanec.

Left: The water sport area in Čunovo

Detailed description: The route starts on the Slovak side of the customs point **Petržalka-Berg**. The whole route is part of the **Danube bike route** leading from Passau in Germany, over Vienna in Austria and Bratislava ending in Budapest in Hungary. The first, about 700 m long section runs on a busy principal access road to the border crossing. Before the first crossroads with motorway turn left and proceed on the concrete pavement along the motorway, which is on your right. You are entering the **Pečniansky les forest**, one of the few remnants of the Danube alluvial forest. You are getting closer to the Danube. The parallel communication crosses the **Lafranconi bridge** further to the left side of the Danube (option to turn off to Mlynská dolina valley, Devín, the Little Carpathians and the housing estates in the western part of the city). However, before reaching the bridge you will take the sharp turn right under the bridge onto the dike which runs for another about 1.8 km in alluvial forest. Beyond the tall building of the **Incheba fair area** you will abandon the dike, pass onto Viedenská

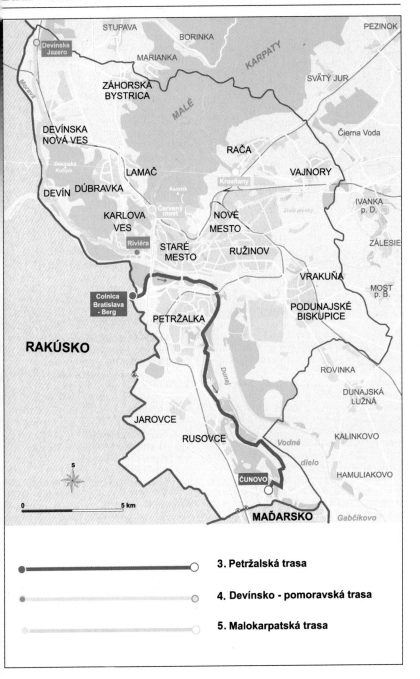

3. Petržalská trasa

4. Devínsko - pomoravská trasa

5. Malokarpatská trasa

cesta road (beware of traffic which is luckily not too dense here) and heading to the
left you will pass under the pylon of the
New Bridge. A little rest on a bench on the
embankment is the opportunity to get the
most beautiful and perhaps the most typical view of the dominant buildings of
Bratislava: Castle, the Parliament, St.
Martin's Minster and the hotels on
Rázusovo embankment on the opposite
bank of the river. Continue on Viedenská
cesta road on the right bank of the
Danube between the embankment on
your right and Sad Janka Kráľa park on
your right. After about 800 m you will
reach the crossroads, the fun-fair, and the
parking lot under the **Old Bridge.** Crossing the bridge to the opposite side of the
river is possible, but not recommendable
for the bike track coincides with that for
pedestrians. Next to the fan-fair turn left
to the river and continue under the bridge
on Klokočova street and the Danube dike
along the river. You are passing by the
open-air swimming pool Lido. The dike

Left: The Bratislava Castle
Right: The Danube

slightly turns to the right and follows the
sharp bend of the river below Bratislava.
After about a kilometre and half you will
pass under the last Bratislava bridge,
Prístavný most or the Port Bridge. Here
to you can cross the river and go to the
quarter of Prievoz or continue to the housing estates in the eastern part of the city.
The following section of the track, like the
preceding ones are easy for orientation.
Continue on the **Danube dike**. On the
right side is the area of the Economic University and the housing estate of Petržalka on your left are the floodplain forests.
The dike slightly turns to both sides. After
about 3.6 km you reach the south-eastern
edge of Petržalka near the gravel extraction plant and the waste water cleansing
station. Continue up to the village of
Rusovce (about 4 kilometres from the
waste water cleansing station). The
Danube on your left is constricted into the
Dam of Hrušovo, part of the Gabčíkovo
Dam. This part of the track is a real par-
adise for the bikers. In fine weather hundreds of bikers and roller-skaters of all
age categories frequent it. Mutual tolerance will make the trip pleasant for all. If
you want to get close to the main stream
of the Danube, turn left off the dike near
the snack stand before arriving at
Rusovce and go along the **Jarovské rameno branch** and further on the road directly along the Danube. You will come
back to the original route after about 4.5
kilometres. Another 6 kilometres will
bring you to the aim of the route in the village of **Čunovo**. You will get into the village by turning off the dike to the right.
Turn left at the crossroads and you will
arrive at the structure that dams the old
Danube channel with water sport area
(beware for the vehicles of the building
site and follow the road signs and warn-
ings!). The Danube branches at this spot
into the old channel (down the stream on
the right) and the feeding channel of the
Gabčíkovo Dam. This is also the place of
Bratislava's limit, which coincides with
the Slovak-Hungarian state frontier. You
can continue out of Bratislava to **Vojka**
(15 km) or to **Gabčíkovo** (20 km).

4. Devín and along the Morava

Direction: Karlova Ves – Devín – Devinska Nová Ves – Devínske Jazero.
Length of the route: 19 kilometres
Elevation gain: The route ascends from 136 m to 170 m above sea level.
Brief description: A comfortable trip. The first stretch is on the road and passing Devín it coincides with the instructive path through the Morava floodplain. This stretch is very suitable for the family trips. The whole route runs along asphalt roads.
Map: The detailed bike map of Bratislava-Podunajsko in scale 1:100 000 (sheet 7), edition of bike touring maps published by VKÚ, š. p., Harmanec.

Detailed description: The trip starts next to the **restaurant Riviéra**, on the crossroads on the southern or "lower" end of the Karlova Ves quarter. First you will pass by the **Sihoť water works** on your left and continue on Devínska cesta road between the foot of the Devínska Kobyla Mountain and the branch of the Danube. The first almost 1,000 metres up to the viaduct leading to the Dlhé diely housing estate are busy but there is no danger provided you are careful. The route carries on across gardens and along a quarry on the right side up to the **village of Devín**, 7.5 km away from Riviéra. On the crossroads at the beginning of the village continue right ahead on the Slovanské nábrežie embankment up to the rock of Devín castle. This is where **the instructive path in the floodplain of Morava** starts. The overall length of the instructive path is 21 kilometres and it has 16 information boards describing the natural and historical features of the surrounding landscape. The instructive path was made thanks to the initiative of the non-governmental conservationist organizations, their fans and enthusiasts. Practically the whole instructive path runs in the boundary belt along the Slovak-Austrian frontier, which was strictly guarded until 1989. Ironically, this politically motivated "protection" in fact prevented the damage to the precious riparian ecosystems. Then you continue up the stream of the Mora-va, which flows into the Danube precisely in this place. The route runs on the dike of the Morava. The foot of Devínska Kobyla Mt. is on our right the whole time before we arrive at Devínska Nová Ves. Soon the **Nature Reserve of Sandberg** emerges. On the left side on the opposite bank of the river is the village of Markthof in Austria. Further north the castle of Schlosshof is seen. This part of the route is comparatively busy with numerous bikers and pedestrians. If the Morava is too high some stretches of the route are unpassable. After about 3.5 km you will get to the southern edge of the village of **Devínska Nová Ves**. There are several ways how to get into the village. Before arriving at the little bridge over the **Stará mláka** brook (beyond the information board No. 5) the road divides in two. Both of them lead to **Devínske Jazero**, the aim of the tour. If you turn left and abandon the instructive path passing onto the asphalt road by the co-operative farm, you will pass under the railway track heading to Marchegg and continuing beside the railway track to Kúty, after 6 km you will

5. The Little Carpathian route

Direction: Patrónka (Červený most) – Železná studnička – Spariská – Krasňany.
Option: Spariská – Dolný Červený kríž – Rača.
Length of the route: 14 kilometres, option 16.5 kilometres
Elevation gain: The route ascends by 170 m or 230 m (from 180 m above sea level to 350 or to 410 m a.s.l. on optional route).
Brief description: A dissected route for ascents and steep descents requiring a certain experience and good physical condition. It runs in the valley of the Vydrica, which is the most comfortable access to the main ridge of the Little Carpathians.
Map: The detailed bike map of Bratislava-Podunajsko with a scale of 1:100 000 (sheet 7), edition of bike touring maps published by VKÚ, š. p., Harmanec.

Detailed description: The trip starts in front of the **Military Hospital** (Nemocnica Ministerstva obrany) by the public transport stop. Pass under the railway viaduct known as the **Červený most** bridge and continue in the valley of the Vydrica around **Partizánska lúka meadow** on a mildly ascending road. You will reach **Železná studnička** after about 2.3 km passing by the turn off to Kačin. Continue straight ahead in the valley of the Vydrica passing by Sneženka (the former lower station of the ski lift to Kamzík Mt.) and around the Rehabilitation Centre of the Heart Diseases for about 5.7 kilometres before arriving at the locality **U Slivu**, where you join the blue marked route. The valley of the Vydrica turns to the right here and again to the left after about 500 metres. Continue straight ahead following the blue mark, and leaving behind the valley of the Vydrica you arrive at **Spariská** (350 m a.s.l.) the highest point of the route ending in Krasňany (at the crossroads with the red-marked path turning left is the option of the route ending in Rača). Stick to the blue mark. After about 700 metres on flat terrain comes a steep descent (by 180 m over 2,500 m) passing through the forest and amidst vineyards ending in Pekná cesta road in **Krasňany**.

come back again to the instructive path immediately before the aim of the route. There are interesting remains of fortifications along this part of the track built here as part of the defence system of Czechoslovakia against the expected German invasion in the thirties. But a much more interesting alternative way of entering Devínska Nová Ves is the one, which continues along the instructive path. After about four kilometres pass under the railway track to Marchegg and stick to the river on your left. After 3.5 km you will reach a crossroads with a parking lot, the end of our route. One can continue turning left and after a 9 km ride arrive at **Vysoká pri Morave** across the Nature Reserve Dolný les reaching the end of the instructive path or by turning right reach the centre of the town of **Stupava**.

Left: The Little Carpathian forests

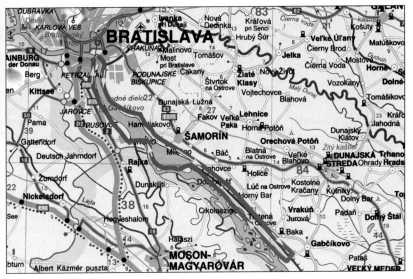

6. Around the Gabčíkovo Dam

Direction: Bratislava (Prístavný most or the Port Bridge) – Hamuliakovo (16 km) – Kyselica (12 km) – Gabčíkovo Dam (16 km) – Vojka, ferry (17 km) – Čunovo (16 km) – Bratislava-Petržalka (Port Bridge, 15 km).
Length of the route: 92 km
Elevation gain: The route descends compared to Bratislava by 16 m and ascends about the same 16 m on the return trip.
Brief description: Undemanding trip with minimum elevation difference. As it mostly avoids the public roads it is suitable for family trips. Contains some comparatively dull parts.
Map: The detailed bike map of Bratislava-Podunajsko with a scale of 1:100 000 (sheet 7), edition of bike touring maps published by VKÚ, š. p., Harmanec.

Detailed description: The route starts next to the bundle of access roads to **Prístavný most** bridge on the left bank of the Danube in Bratislava. The route partly coincides with the International **Danube Cycling Route**. This major route connects the towns along the river from Passau in Germany to Budapest in Hungary. It is marked in green on a rectangular board, which will help you to find your way in the first section of the route in the periphery of Bratislava. Following the route you are heading to the Malý Dunaj river. Passing the bridge over the Malý Dunaj, which is the greatest branch of the Danube in Slovak territory, turn left; pass by the port of Nový prístav and Lodenica (Dockyards). Then your are passing by the water sport area of the Inter sport club and continue on the asphalt flood bank of the Danube. After about 7 kilometres from the Inter boathouse you reach the upper end of the **Hrušov reservoir**, which is part of the Gabčíkovo water works. This route section from Hrušov to the Gabčíkovo Dam runs parallel to the flood bank on the outer side of what is called the seepage canal with bridges, which provide the only possibility to abandon the flood bank and turn off to the surrounding terrain. But they are rather distant from each other. About 5 kilometres beyond Hamuliakovo and near Čilistovo you are pass the town of Šamorín. This is the place for which a water recreation centre is planned. The Hrušov reservoir is becoming narrower and gradually tapers into a straight several metres wide feeding canal. It contains a substantial part of water of the Danube, which drives the turbines of the Gabčíkovo Dam.

While its height is the same, it is the terrain that drops with the dropping stream of the Danube. This solution was chosen to reach the minimum gradient of the feeding canal and the greatest possible elevation difference to obtain the best effect for driving the turbines in the Gabčíkovo cascade. This is how the height of the flood bank over the surrounding terrain reaches in places 17 metres. About 7 km beyond Čilistov you pass the community of **Kyselica**. Here you can use the ferry and visit the village of Vojka nad Dunajom on the opposite bank of the canal and return to Bratislava, which means shortening the route by about a third (34 km). The following 16 km to the cascade runs in rather monotonous landscape and on the top of the straight running flood bank. The biggest attraction of the **Gabčíkovo cascade** are undoubtedly the lock chambers, which enable the ships to overcome the elevation difference of more than 20 metres. You pass across the Dam to the opposite bank of the feeding canal and follow onto the bridge over the seepage canal. Turn left at the crossroads and after about 2 km the road will bring you to the original bed of the Danube, which is progressively decaying in the consequence of a constantly low discharge. Go back to the crossroads next to the Gabčíkovo cascade. If you are bored by the monotonous trip on the flood bank, you can continue in the direction of Vojka nad Dunajom on the old road running on

Right: The cyclists near the Danube

the edge of the Danube floodplain forest or you can chose the new road at the foot of the flood bank or you can go again on top of the flood bank of the feeding canal. The first two options are good in case of headwind, which is only too frequent in this place. Approximately 7 km from the crossroads next to the Gabčíkovo cascade you pass by (or through, depending on the chosen alternative) the village of Bodíky. You reach Vojka nad Dunajom after 9 km where there is a possibility to cross the canal by the ferry. About 5 km before you reach the village there are the lakes of Vojka, good for a refreshing bath. Continuing from Vojka you cross the neighbouring village of Dobrohošť and some 2 km beyond it you continue on a narrow strip of the dike and road. The old Danube channel is on your left side and the Hrušov reservoir is on you right. After this unusual 10 km long section you reach the structure, which divides the waters of the feeding canal and the original Danube bed near Čunovo. You cross the feeding structure and on your left is the area of water sports with artificial water slalom canal. At the crossroads before reaching the little bridge over the canal turn right (if you do not decide to visit the village of Čunovo) and continue on the flood bank for about 15 km before you return to the Port Bridge of Bratislava-Petržalka.

7. Small circle in the upper part of Žitný ostrov

Direction: Bratislava-Podunajské Biskupice – Dunajská Lužná (9 km) – Šamorín (10.5 km) – Tomášov (15 km) – Bratislava – Podunajské Biskupice (13 km).
Length of the route: 47.5 km
Elevation gain: The route runs in flat terrain 126-134 m above sea level.
Brief description: The route runs in the hinterland of Bratislava – Žitný ostrov. Its profile is not demanding, but there is busy traffic in some of its sections near Bratislava.
Map: The detailed bike map of Bratislava-Podunajsko with a scale of 1:100 000 (sheet 7), edition of bike touring maps published by VKÚ, š. p., Harmanec.

Detailed description: The route start is Bratislava, urban district of **Podunajské Biskupice**. Continue from Podunajské Biskupice eastward up to the crossroads Dunajská Lužná-Tomášov. Turn right at this crossroads in the direction of Dunajská Lužná. After about 2 km you cross the railway track near the artificial lake Nové Košariská, a popular bathing place of the inhabitants of the south-eastern part of Bratislava for its clean water though it lacks any services. Another 2 km ride will bring you to the centre of the big village of Dunajská Lužná and the crossroads with the busy 1ˢᵗ class road Bratislava-Komárno. Turn left and after several metres on the main road turn right in the direction of Kalinkovo and Hamuliakovo. The road is winding and on the right side it follows the protective dike of the Danube, which can also used be as a safer route on the section to **Hamuliakovo**. Fortunately, the state road is not to busy. Go through Kalinkovo and after 6 kilometres from Dunajská Lužná you will reach Hamuliakovo. From the crossroads you will continue in a sharp left bent on the state road another 4.5 km to Šamorín. If you did not arrive from Dunajská Lužná on the flood bank you can reach it from the above mentioned crossroads in the centre of Hamuliakovo by going on straight ahead. After about 300 metres you will pass the church and reach the bridge over the canal to the dike of the Gabčíkovo Dam. Cross the bridge in the direction of Šamorín and continue passing by farm buildings. The road turning left will bring you to the western edge of **Šamorín** where you join the state road coming from the left from Hamuliakovo. Continue in the same direction of the town. At the crossroads where the old main road turns left continue about 100 m to the bus station and the crossroads with the state road heading to Komárno.

If you want to see the centre of Šamorín follow the old main street that will bring you there after 500 metres. Crossing the main road to Komárno and continuing in the original direction on the opposite side of the street and later amidst vineyards and a locust grove you will arrive at Kvetoslavov four kilometres

away. At the end of the community turn left at the crossroads in the direction of Hviezdoslavov and **Štvrtok na Ostrove**. Several tens of metres beyond the crossroads you cross the railway track. Continue through Hviezdoslavov, pass by the left turn leading to Alžbetin dvor, cross the canal Tomášov-Lehnice and 6 km from Kvetoslavov you will arrive at Štvrtok na Ostrove and the crossroads with the 3ʳᵈ class road No. 572 Bratislava-Dunajská Streda. Go on turning left to the centre of the village (direction Bratislava). After about 500 m you will leave behind the main road and turn right in the direction of **Tomášov**, which is five kilometres away. On the edge of the community turn left onto the main road in the direction of Malinovo and Bratislava. In **Malinovo** after about 3.5 km from Tomášov you can see one of the romantic meanders of the Malý Dunaj river. Pass through Malinovo and by the manor house, pass by the right turn to Ivanka pri Dunaji. After 2 km you will get to the crossroads of the road No. 572 in the middle of the village of Most pri Bratislave. Continue through the village sticking to the original direction of Brati-

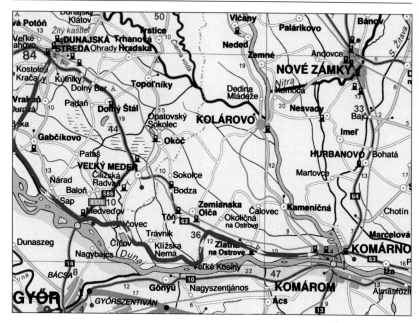

slava. The following stretch up to Bratislava is usually very busy, so concentrate on the ride. Similar situations are hard to avoid in the proximity of large cities. After about 2.5 km from the crossroads in Most you come to the next crossroads where you can turn left and arrive at the starting point of the route after 4 km or you can continue straight ahead in the direction of Nová Vrakuňa and further to a peripheral part of Bratislava – Ružinov, which is another 6 kilometres away.

8. The lower part of Žitný ostrov from Dunajská Streda to Komárno

Direction: Dunajská Streda – Gabčíkovo Dam (14.5 km) – Medveďov (14 km) – Zlatná na Ostrove (32 km) – Komárno (13 km).
Length of the route: 73.5 km
Elevation gain: The route runs in flat terrain 110-118 m above sea level.
Brief description: The route will take you from the principal town of Žitný ostrov, Dunajská Streda around the Gabčíkovo

Dam, along the middle part of the International Danube Cyclist Route to Komárno, an important port on the Danube.
Map: The detailed bike map of Bratislava-Podunajsko with a scale of 1:100 000 (sheet 7), edition of bike touring maps published by VKÚ, š. p., Harmanec.

Detailed description: The route starts at the crossroads in the centre of **Dunajská Streda**. You will start towards the south (direction of Gabčíkovo). Cross the railway by the over pass around the thermal swimming pool and after more than 1.5 km you will arrive at the crossroads with the by-passing road. Turn right in the direction of Bratislava and after about 500 m turn left to the road, which was originally used during the construction of the **Gabčíkovo Dam**. Continue on this road parallel to the rails also leading to the Gabčíkovo Dam, which you reach after about 12 km from the crossroads with the by-pass of Dunajská Streda. If you want to see the Dam, ascend to the wall of the Dam of the Gabčíkovo cascade.
Our route continues by turning left in front of the wall of the Dam and on the

flood bank of the wastewater canal. The short descent ends on the International Danube Cyclist Route. You will continue 7.5 km on the dike of the wastewater canal from Gabčíkovo Dam up to **Sap** (former Palkovičovo). In Sap you will ride down from the dike to the village and continue 6.5 km on a straight stretch of the state road along the floodplain forest to the bridge over the Danube to **Medveďov**. If you are riding a mountain bike, you can continue in Sap on the flood bank of the Danube practically as far as Komárno. This option is shorter (by about 10 kilometres) and relatively safer, but the gravel and loamy surface with spots of asphalt is not suitable for normal road bikes. In practice it means that the longer trip on state roads can be eventually more advantageous in terms of time as it allows higher speeds. In Medveďov you can also cross the bridge over the Danube and visit the interesting town of Győr in Hungary 14 km long ride on busy roads. The route to Komárno continues from Medveďov by a 4.5 km long winding stretch to **Kľúčovec**. Before entering the village you can take the turn around the farming buildings ascend the flood bank and have a look around the protected area of Dunajské Luhy with the nature reserve of Čičovské mŕtve rameno (The Dead Branch of Čičov). At the crossroads in Kľúčovec turn right in the direction of Zlatná na Ostrove and Komárno. After about 1.5 km from Kľúčovec you arrive at the crossroads to Veľký Meder (former Čalovo). If you turn left you will get to the popular thermal swimming pools of Veľký Meder. However, our route continues straight ahead to the village of **Čičov**. The whole about 20 km long section of the route between Medveďov and **Veľké Kosihy** is winding and full of bends. It may look strange in a completely flat landscape but the reason is that the road was formerly avoiding numerous branches of the Danube. At the crossroads beyond Čičov and at the beginning of the community Trávnik turn right in the direction of Kližská Nemá (3 km) and after 7 km you will arrive at Veľké Kosihy. The road turns perpendicularly to the north at the beginning of this long village and after 4.5 km it joins the main road No. 63 to Bratislava and

Komárno. Turn onto the road and continue in the direction of Zlatná and Komárno. The road is comparatively busy but wide enough with a lay-off lane and a smooth surface. As a matter of fact, it is one of the safest 1st class roads in Slovakia for bikers. Continue on this road by-passing **Zlatná na Ostrove** (7 km) and you will reach after another 9 km the edge of the town of Komárno. It is another 3 kilometres to the main crossroads near the town centre. Turn right in the direction of **Komárno** for the historical centre of the town and the border crossing to Hungary, but if you want to stay on the International Danube Cyclist Route, continue on the road No. 63 onto the bridge over the Váh river (in the direction of Štúrovo).

9. To the boat mills around Dunajská Streda

Direction: Dunajská Streda – the mill in Dunajský Kláštor (8 km) — the area of the boat mill in Jahodná (3 km) – boat mill in Tomášikovo (7.5 km) – Topoľníky (21.5 km).
Option A: Topoľníky – Ohrady (7 km) – Dunajská Streda (6.5 km).
Option B: Topoľníky – Veľký Meder (15.5 km) – Kľúčovec (9.5 km) – Padáň (17 km) – Dunajská Streda (11 km).
Length of the route: 53.5 km
Elevation gain: The route runs in flat terrain 111-118 m above sea level.
Brief description: The route offers a visit to reconstructed boat mills on the Malý Dunaj river and bathing in thermal swimming pool in Topoľníky.
Map: The detailed bike map of Bratislava-Podunajsko with a scale of 1:100 000

(sheet 7), edition of bike touring maps published by VKÚ, š. p., Harmanec.

Detailed description: The road starts at the crossroads in the centre of **Dunajská Streda** (the railway line No. 131). You are heading to Galanta on the road No. 507. Go through the village of Veľké Dvorníky and after 7 km you will reach **Dunajský Klátov**. Cross the little bridge over the Klátovský canal and after about 150 metres turn right around the agricultural area and ride another 700 metres to the boat mill. After seeing it go back to the main road, turn right and after several tens of metres cross the bridge over the **Klátovské rameno** branch (National Nature Reserve, one of the few natural streams on the Žitný ostrov). Continue for a while along the Klátovské rameno. About 800 metres beyond the bridge turn right at the crossroads in the direction of Horné Mýto. The road follows the left bank of the Malý Dunaj. Continue on it for about 800 metres and then turn left at the crossroads. The local road

will bring you to the group of cottages called Alba Regia. Cross the Malý Dunaj and the little bridge will bring you directly to the area of the boat mill **Jahodná**. You will get to the village bearing the same name after 1.5 km ride on the local road. Turn right at the crossroads next to the church and you will be again on the road No. 507. Continue 3.5 km to the contiguous village of **Tomášikovo**. Continue through the village around a park 1.5 km and near the petrol station turn to the left. After about 1.5 kilometres, now outside the village, turn left onto a field road and continue 700 metres to the boat mill on the Malý Dunaj river. Near the mill is an interesting natural phenomenon, a dune called **Tomášovský presyp**. Go back to the village by the same way and continue going back to Jahodná. At the lower end of Tomášikovo where the road divides into two turn left onto the local road, which leads to the homestead Pašienky after 4 km. The road can be soiled by mud. Better road is that from Pašienky to the place called Kráľov Brod-Slovenské Pole (4.5 km). Pass by the turn left to Kráľov Brod, con-

Left: The water mill near Jelka

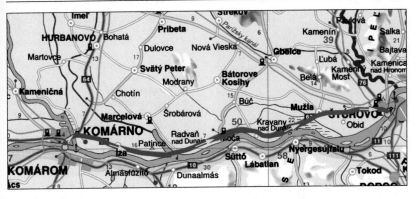

tinue straight ahead and after 3.5 km you reach the large village of **Trstice**. At the crossroads with the main road (No. 561) turn right and continue 7 km to **Topoľníky**. On the way you cross the bridge of the Malý Dunaj and immediately before arriving at Topoľníky you also cross the Klátovské rameno branch. In its right bank is the area of the thermal swimming pool of Topoľníky.

If you decided to return to Dunajská Streda turn right on crossroads at the upper end of the village (direction of Trhová Hradská, Dunajská Streda). Passing through Trhová Hradská and Ohrady you will arrive after 13.5 km at the centre of Dunajská Streda.

10. Along the Danube

Direction: Komárno – Patince (13 km) – Mužľa – (26 km) – Štúrovo (9 km).
Length of the route: 48 km
Elevation: The route descends from 110 m above sea level to 107 m.
Brief description: The route leads along the lower part of the Slovak section of the Danube on state roads and in flat terrain. It is a part of the International Danube Cyclist Route. Easy orientation.
Map: The detailed bike map of Podunajsko-Pohronie with a scale of 1:100 000 (sheet 8), edition of bike touring maps published by VKÚ, š. p., Harmanec.

Detailed description: The route starts at the centre of **Komárno** at the main crossroads. You are going eastward in the direction of Štúrovo by the road No. 63. Cross the bridge over the Váh river and after 700 m at the crossroads turn right in the direction of Štúrovo. After a 6 km ride you cross the village of Iža, then after 1.2 km you can turn left onto a field road leading to the nature reserve of Brokoľské slanisko with salt vegetation. The following village of **Patince** is 5 km away from Iža. If you want to go to the southernmost point of Slovakia (47^0 44' latitude north) you have to cross the Danube flood bank to reach the river bank and the locality called Čierny hon. Several villages on the route, for instance Iža and Patince, were almost completely destroyed by the disastrous flood in 1965 and it is the reason why you do not see old houses there. If the weather is fine we recommend turning left about 800 m from the edge of the village in the direction of Štúrovo and after several hundreds of metres you will arrive at the area of thermal swimming pools with hotels, restaurants and a camping site. Another attraction of the spot can be seen after 1.2 km from the turn to the swimming pools on the right. It is an old steam pumping station, a technical monument from 1897. Immediately beyond it you will cross the flood bank and after about 500 m you will reach the crossroads. Turn right to the village of Žitava. On the opposite bank of the Danube are the slopes of the Gerecse mountain range in Hungary. This part of Slovakia though is flat compared to the mountain ranges in the otherwise flat landscape of Hungary.

About 1 km beyond the village of Žitava you will arrive at **Radvaň na Dunaji**. The road runs for about 2 km close to the stream of the Danube. The landscape on the left side of the road gradually starts to undulate. Continue through the following village of **Moča**. About 4 km beyond the village you pass by the left turn to Búč and Bátorové Kosihy in the direction of a more dissected and higher part of the Danube lowland called the Pribetský les. On the right side of the Danube in Hungary and above the village of Süttő you can see travertine quarries; 2 km after the crossroads you pass by the village of **Kravany nad Dunajom** on your right and beyond it the road again draws closer to the Danube. A forest-steppe type of vegetation appears on the left side of the road. You are passing the National Nature Reserve of Čenkovská forest-steppe. Now you ride about 4 km through the forest, a pleasant change compared to the monotonous farming landscape. You will reach

Left: On the bank of the Danube

Mužla after a 2.5 km long mild ascent. Continue on the road No. 63 on an elevation above the stream of the Danube, which is now 3 km away south of our road. On the right side ahead you will notice the chimney of the paper mills of Štúrovo. However, the monumental dome of basilica in Esztergom on the Hungarian bank of the Danube with the silhouette of the Pilišské vrchy mountains in the background is a more interesting sight. Pass under the railway track and shortly after the road from Nové Zámky joins our route on the left. Continue around Štúrovo railway station (railway lines No. 130 and 152) and after a mild 2 km long descent you arrive at the centre of **Štúrovo**. The main street of the town ends on the bank of the Danube at the ferry port to Esztergom. Do not miss the wonderful view of Esztergom Cathedral with the remains of the road Maria Valeria Bridge. If you ride a mountain bike you can use the field road leading on top of the Danube flood bank. Immediately after crossing the bridge over the Váh in Komárno you will find yourself on the dike of the Váh and continue to the confluence of the Váh and Danube rivers. Stay on the dike until you reach Iža. Cross the village and you will briefly ride on the state road No. 63. After about one kilometre you can ascend the dike again and this will take you to the estuary of the Stará Žitava river. The following section up to Moča is again common with the above mentioned route option. You will get to the dike in the centre of Moča by turning right. Once on the dike you pass by Kravany nad Dunajom and continue up to Čenkovský les where you join the road No. 63 again. After about 2 km when the road starts to retire from the Danube channel, you enter the last section of the route running on the dike. Then you pass by Mužlianska sihoť, a shrubby and watterlogged area with a dead branch of the Danube on the right side. After about 6.5 km from the turn next to the Obidský kanál canal you abandon the dike and continue on a local asphalt road. You will cross several little bridges of the canal system to the village of Obid. At the end of the village and on the street heading to the road No. 63 turn right. At the next crossroads 1.3 km away you will enter the road leading from Obidská pustatina. Turn left, cross the rails leading to the paper mill and next to the railway station in Štúrovo enter the road No. 63. Continue to the right to arrive at the centre of Štúrovo.

11. Around Burda

Direction: Štúrovo − Kamenica nad Hronom (5 km) − Chľaba (7.5 km) − Leľa (7 km) − Štúrovo (11 km).
Length of the route: 30.5 km
Elevation: 94 (from 111 to 205 m above sea level).
Brief description: An interesting route leading in the gorge-like valleys of the Danube and Ipeľ rivers. The landscape is mountainous.
Map: The detailed bike map of Podunajsko-Pohronie with a scale of 1:100 000 (sheet 8), edition of bike touring maps published by VKÚ, š. p., Harmanec.

Detailed description: The route starts in the centre of **Štúrovo**. Start northward at the crossroads taking the road no. 564 in the direction of **Kamenica nad Hronom**, and Šahy. In front of you and on the right is the massive mountain range of Burda and our route runs around it. You will abandon the road No. 564 at the crossroads in the centre of the village and continue straight ahead in the direction of Chľaba. The road draws closer to the Danube on the foothills of the Burda. You will pass under the railway track and after about 4 km continue along the Danube, parallel to the railway track on your left. Now you have reached the beginning of the Vyšehradská brána Gate, an impressive section of the Danube. The Danube opens its way here through the mountain range of Burda on the Slovak side of the frontier and the Börzsöny and Visegrád Mts. on the Hungarian side. The Burda mountain range constitutes a part of the National Nature Reserve of the **Kováčovské kopce**, which is only another and seldom used name for the same mountain range. It is an extra valuable landscape above all for botanists, so

please observe the principles of correct conduct in the protected area. You will pass under the railway track again after a 4 km ride along the Danube channel, pass by the group of cottages of Burda and reach the village of **Chľaba** after another 5 km. The landscape slightly changes and the vineyards on the southern slopes enjoy here excellent climatic conditions. At the end of Chľaba on the south-eastern edge of Burda you come to the Ipeľ river, a gorge-like valley between the Burda mountain range on the left and the more bulky mountain range of **Börzsöny** on the right side in the direction of our route. You ride now on a forest road leading on the foothills of Burda about 6 km before you get to more open landscape outside the gorge. Then you come to a game-keeper's lodge followed by farm structures and continue by local asphalt road about 500 metres to the village of **Leľa** where you join the state road. You are ascending the road trough the village gaining about 80 m of elevation before you come to the section traversing the northern foothills of Burda arriving after 2 km at the village of **Bajtava**. Then comes Bajtavská brána Gate, a depression between the Ipeľská pahorkatina hill land in the north and the Burda in the south. In about the middle of Bajtava the road starts to descend. At the crossroads at the end of the village is again the road No 564 where you turn left in the direction of Štúrovo. You are slightly descending along the western foothills of the Burda mountains 3.5 km to Kamenica nad Hronom and there are only 5 km to get back to the centre of Štúrovo.

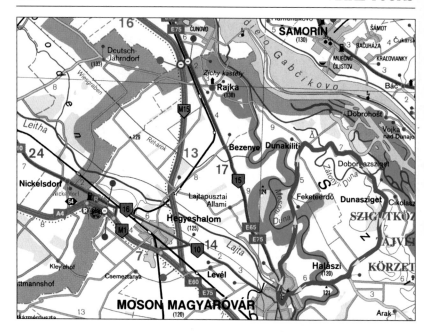

THE HUNGARIAN DANUBELAND

12. In the environs of Mosonmagyaróvár

Direction: Mosonmagyaróvár – Dunakiliti (10 km) – Halászi (15.5 km) – Mosonmagyaróvár (6 km).
Length of the route: 31.5 km
Elevation difference: The whole route runs in flat terrain.
Brief description: Undemanding trip on marked cycle lanes with the exception of the stretch between Dunasziget and Halászi.
Map: The detailed bike map of Bratislava-Podunajsko with a scale of 1:100 000 (sheet 7), edition of bike touring maps published by VKÚ, š. p., Harmanec.

Detailed description: The route starts in the middle of **Mosonmagyaróvár** on the square next to the church. Pass to the Lajta by an alley on the eastern end of the square, cross the bridge and continue

turning right onto the Cserháti utca street. At its end cross the branch of the Lajta and shortly beyond the bridge turn left in the direction Dunakiliti, Feketeerdő. The road leading to Feketeerdő, 5.5 km away first winds in the outskirts of Mosonmagyaróvár, then after 4 km you pass by the floodplain forest and cross the branch of the Danube. Having passed through Feketeerdő continue about 4 km to the centre of the village of **Dunakiliti** and again you pass by the floodplain forests and the stream of the Moson branch of the Danube. In the middle of the village on a T-shaped crossroads near the church continue on the main road, which turns sharply to the right in the direction of **Dunasziget** after a while. The road winds again, it runs trough a solitary homestead and the village of Dobor-gazsziget and crosses the Zátonyi-Duna branch twice. The road winds apparently without any logical reason, but it is so because in the past the roads followed routes safe from floods or they ran along the meandering branches of the rivers. In Dunasziget, 7 km away, continue on the main road and turn left in the middle of

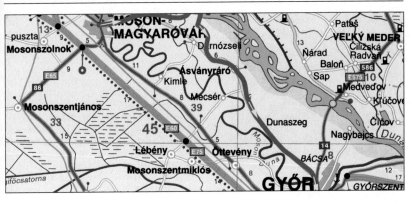

the village, while you cross one of the numerous branches of the Danube. At the crossroads after about 1.5 km continue to the right in the direction of **Halászi**, reaching it after 6 km. You will enter the main road at the edge of the village, turn right across the middle of the village. At the other end of the village cross the Moson branch of the Danube and you will arrive at the centre of Mosonmagyaróvár again after about 4.5 km.

13. From Mosonmagyaróvár across Szigetköz to Győr

Direction: Mosonmagyaróvár – Halászi (6 km) – Dunaremete (8.5 km) – Ásványráró (13.5 km) – Győr (20 km).
Length of the route: 48 km
Elevation difference: The whole route runs in flat terrain.
Brief description: Undemanding trip leads through the middle and lower parts of Szigetköz. Except for a short stretch it runs on marked cyclist tracks.
Map: The detailed bike map of Bratislava-Podunajsko with a scale of 1:100 000 (sheet 7), edition of bike touring maps published by VKÚ, š. p., Harmanec.

Detailed description: Starting in **Mosonmagyaróvár** you have to get to the crossroads in the direction of Dunakiliti, **Halászi** in the same way as described in the route in the environs of Mosonmagyaróvár. Continue straight ahead from the crossroads in the direction of Halászi,

which you will reach after 4.5 km beyond the bridge over the **Moson branch of the Danube**. Passing through the village you pass the turn left to Dunasziget. At the end of the village the road turns to the right, shortly after the bend, turn left off the main road and continue past a farm in the direction of **Püski** 5 km away. It is at the beginning of the village and near the church where you turn off the main road again turning left to the village of **Kisbodak** (1.5 km), which lies on the edge of the floodplain forests of the Danube. The route turns in the village and continues on the edge of the floodplain forest on top of the flood bank almost in the opposite direction towards the main road, which you reach about 2 km after passing through Kisbodak. Turn left on the main road and then after about 500 m you enter the village of **Dunaremete**. About 3 km from Dunaremete is the neighbouring village of Lipót with a thermal swimming pool and camping site, which lie on your left at the beginning of the village. In the middle of Lipót from crossroads near the church continue straight ahead by a sharp right turn in the direction of **Hédervár** 3 km away. Join the main road again in Hédervár at the crossroads near the church and continue straight in the direction of the village of **Ásványráró** 3.5 km away. The road passes by the southern edge of Ásványráró and then passes around the Moson branch of the Danube near the community of Zsejkepuszta. You will arrive at the village of **Dunaszeg** after another 4.5 km. Beyond

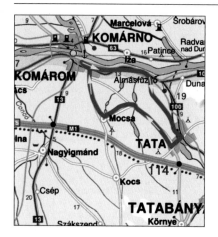

the village you pass by the Moson branch of the Danube on its right side to **Győrladamér**, and later through **Győrzámoly** and **Győrújfalu** (7 km) you reach the edge of Győr. Turn right here and continue along the Danube's branch through the suburbs (following the marking of the cyclist route) cross the Moson branch of the Danube arriving at the historic core of the town, which starts immediately beyond the bridge.

14. From Komárom to Tata

Direction: Komárom — Naszály (14 km) — Tata (10 km) — Mocsa (13 km) — Komárom (11 km).
Length of the route: 48 km
Elevation difference: The route runs on flat terrain, slightly undulating in places.
Brief description: Undemanding trip offering possibilities to visit the interesting and picturesque town of Tata. It leads on less frequented roads with the exception of the first stretch.
Map: The detailed bike map of Bratislava-Podunajsko with a scale of 1:100 000 (sheet 7), edition of bike touring maps published by VKÚ, š. p., Harmanec.

Detailed description: The route starts at the main crossroads in the centre of **Komárom** (arriving from Komárno). Start eastward (direction of Tata, Tatabánya, Budapest) on the main road

No. 10. The first about 10 km runs in the busy and scarcely interesting suburbs of Komárom and the neighbouring town of Szőny. The local refinery, which you pass by on your right after about 6 km is certainly not a tourist attraction either. The cyclist lanes, which are available on a great part of the route until reaching the crossroads in **Naszály**, represent perhaps a kind of compensation. You will reach Naszály after about 10 km. At the point where another complex of refineries start, this time on your left, turn right off the main road. You will reach the community of Almáspuszta after about 2 km. Naszály comes shortly after. Beyond it after 6 km and a short stretch along the vineyards on your right and a pond on your left you reach the outskirts of **Tata**. Arriving at the town on the Komáromi utca street turn left at the first crossroads onto Új utca street, which is skirting the town. After about 1 km turn right parallel to the canal draining the local lake Öreg-tó. This street will bring you after about 400 metres to the Öregvár castle, which is practically at the centre of the town. After seeing it you can return by the same way to the edge of the town where you come to a branching of the roads. The right branch leads to Naszály where you came from. Chose the left one in the direction of Szőny. After 6 km along the elevation called Grebics hegy on the left side you will reach a crossroads at the edge of a wood where you turn left in the direction of the village of **Mocsa**, 4.5 km away. At the crossroads in the middle of the village turn right in the direction of Szőny and Komárom. Now you gradually descend to the Danube and after about 8 km join the main road No. 10 between Komárom and Szőny. Turn left for the centre of Komárom, which is 3 km away.

15. A small circle around the Danube meander

Direction: Esztergom — Visegrád (25 km) — ferry to Nagymaros — Nagymaros — Szob (12 km) — ferry to the right side of the Danube — Esztergom (12 km).
Length of the route: 49 km (without the ferry)

Elevation difference: The route runs on a plain along the Danube with short and mild ascents in the suburbs of Esztergom and in Pilismarót. Undulated terrain in the territory of Slovakia.

Brief description: The route runs in one of the most interesting areas of Hungary in terms of history and landscape beauty. A certain disadvantage, though also a refreshment, can be the double trip by ferry over the Danube. The operation of ferries is limited or depends on the height of water table of the river. Enquire about the operation of ferries in advance.

Map: The detailed bike map of Podunajsko-Pohronie with a scale of 1:100 000 (sheet 7), edition of bike touring maps published by VKÚ, š. p., Harmanec.

Detailed description: The route starts in the middle of **Esztergom**. Leave the town in the direction of Pilismarót and Visegrád, road No. 11. Ascending past the **basilica** you will get out to the suburbs, later descend past the vineyards to the Danube. The road is comparatively busy. Pay attention to cyclist lanes, which can occasionally be used for safer ride. About 2 km beyond Esztergom you pass by the small village of Búbánatvölgy. The road leads along the foothills of the Visegrádi hegység Mts. on your right. After about 2 km the road retires from the Danube's stream and you will pass the turn leading to the ferry to Szob. A slight ascent leads to the village of **Pilismarót** and then after 2 km of descent you pass through **Dömös** again to the Danube. You are now coming to the most picturesque part of the Danube meander. The river creates a "meander in meander" here as its bed is narrowest here. It is squeezed between the protuberances of the **Visegrádi hegység** Mts. on the right side of the Danube and the Börzsöny Mts. on its opposite side. Continue close to the river on a road turning to the north-east to Visegrád (3 km). Im-

mediately before entering the town rehabilitation works with the aim of liquidating the unsuccessful construction of the Nagymaros Dam can be observed in the channel of the Danube. On the bank of the Danube in Visegrád by a turning to the centre of the village, you will find the ferry to Nagymaros on the other side of the river. You will ride again on the main road No. 12 for a while and then turn left in the direction of **Szob**, going back up the stream of the Danube. The road leads on the foothills of the Börzsöny Mts. between the railway track and the river almost up to Szob. Do not forget to look back to see the majestic panorama of Visegrád from this side of the rive. After about 5 km in wonderful landscape you will reach the village of **Zebegény**. Cyclist lanes are available in this stretch of the route. About 500 m beyond Zebegény the road passes under the railway track and the mountain range is now farther from the river. Two kilometres beyond Zebegény you enter Szob. Passing under the railway you arrive at the middle of the village and the access to the **ferry**, which will carry you to the other bank, is marked by boards. On the right side of the Danube you pass a row of trees to the main road Esztergom-Visegrád about 800 m away. Turn right at the crossroads for Esztergom and now you are on the same stretch of the route you started the trip with.

INDEX

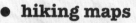